2008 BPM and Workflow Handbook

2008 BPM and Workflow Handbook

Methods, Concepts, Case Studies and Standards in Business Process Management and Workflow

Published in association with the
Workflow Management Coalition

Workflow Management Coalition

15 Years of Thought-Process Leadership

Edited by

Layna Fischer

Future Strategies Inc., Book Division

Lighthouse Point, Florida

2008 BPM and Workflow Handbook

ISBN-13: 978-0-9777527-6-8

ISBN-10: 0-9777527-6-3

10 09 08 8 9 10

Published by Future Strategies Inc., Book Division

2436 North Federal Highway #374
Lighthouse Point FL 33064 USA
954.782.3376 fax 954.782.6365
www.futstrat.com; books@futstrat.com

Cover design by Little Blacktop Studio, Florida

Publisher's Cataloging-in-Publication Data
Library of Congress Catalog Card No. 2008900155

2008 BPM and Workflow Handbook:
/Layna Fischer (editor)

p. cm.

Includes bibliographical references, appendices and index.

ISBN 978-0-9777527-6-8

1. Business Process Management. 2. Workflow Management.
3. Technological Innovation. 4. Information Technology. 5. Total Quality Management. 6. Organizational Change 7. Management Information Systems. 8. Office Practice Automation. 9. Business Process Technology. 10. Electronic Commerce. 11. Process Analysis

Fischer, Layna

TABLE OF CONTENTS

TABLE OF CONTENTS

SECTION 2—STANDARDS AND TECHNOLOGY

SECTION 3—DIRECTORIES AND APPENDICES

Foreword

Jon Pyke, WfMC Chair, United Kingdom

As I sit here at the beginning of January 2008 pondering what I might write by way of introduction to the new edition of the Workflow Management Coalition's yearbook, I am reminded of the renowned Roman God Janus from whence the word *January* evolved.

Janus was a mythological Roman God often associated with doorways and beginnings. His unique capability was that he was able to look into the future and the past at the same time. This is what we need to do now. We are at the doorway of some developments and changes that could have a profound affect on the way we do business, yet much of the technology and approaches we use are firmly rooted in the past.

The next generation entering the workforce is being dubbed "The Einstein Generation". They are the first generation of school and college-leavers that are totally *au fait* with the way the internet works; they are not interested in artificial splits between departments or technology silos—they expect to use the communications and services available to help them do the job they are employed to do. The problem is that much of what is available today is not so much Einstein as *Flintstone*. Business needs to open up, it needs to look towards services, and it needs to see itself the way the customers see it so that it can respond to the customers needs before the customer is aware the need exists.

But what does this have to do with the development of BPM and its associated standards and methodologies?

The relevance of the WfMC in 2008 and beyond:

Over the years there was distinct (and arguably artificial) split in the world of BPM and Workflow. This is a topic that has been covered in the WfMC and other publications frequently (some might say too frequently) in the past. The reason for mentioning it again here is quite simple—the split is healing itself. One of the major trends in 2007 was the consolidation of the system-centric and human-centric "solutions". We are seeing a new generation of BPM solutions emerge which might be called Total BPM or even BPM 2.0.

These products are designed to deliver concepts such as Model Driven Architectures, full and complete support for service-oriented architectures and total integration between the needs of the people and the integration of systems to support the people. We are reaching a stage where the business process is being put back where it belongs, in the hands of the business.

As BPM 2.0 emerges it will be seen more as a Business Operations Platform than as an IT solution. BPM will be at the heart of delivering business services, and these services will be, essentially, small reusable business processes that are readily available and easy to use and easy to understand—a common library of processes.

One particular BPM standard is playing a key role in helping this happen—XPDL.

Developed by the WfMC, XPDL's primary goal is to store and exchange the process diagrams, or specifically to allow one tool to model a process diagram, and another to read the diagram and edit, another to "run" the process model on an

XPDL-compliant BPM engine, and so on. The XPDL file can provide this design interchange because it offers a one-for-one representation of the original BPMN process diagram. It can be written and re-read to recover the original diagram.

For this reason, XPDL is described, not an executable programming language like BPEL, but specifically a process design format that literally represents the "drawing" of the process definition. To wit, it has 'XY' or vector coordinates, including lines and points that define process flows. This allows an XPDL to store a one-to-one representation of a BPMN process diagram. For this reason, XPDL is effectively the file format or "serialization" of BPMN, as well as any non-BPMN design method or process model which use in their underlying definition the XPDL meta-model.

There are some who believe that XPDL is a dead or irrelevant standard that has been overlooked by the major platform vendors. These comments are at best ill-informed and, at worst, uttered by those that don't really understand the dynamics at play—so it would be a foolish individual that uttered "XPDL is dead in the water".

To date there are over 50 major BPM and application vendors that support the XPDL standard these include IBM, Oracle, BEA, Fujitsu, Tibco and Global 360. In fact eight of the 11 top vendors listed in Gartner's 2006 BPMS Magic Quadrant 11 support XPDL.

Furthermore, because XPDL has been stable for such a long time, there has been a large uptake in the open source community. Unlike some standards, XPDL is made freely available without any licensing restrictions.

The next challenge we will face is that of interoperability. With the expected proliferation of process-based Business Services there will be an increasing need to make them fully interoperable right across the process network. To do that we will need a well defined interoperability standard—perhaps WF-XML could help...

But what of the Coalition back in 2007?

Very similar to 2006. We continued to make significant progress during the year. XPDL has continued to be a great success and the importance of this particular standard is now well understood. We ran more technical and business seminars throughout the world helping to drive awareness, understanding and adoption of XPDL. As a result, it has been cited as the most deployed BPM standard by a number of industry analysts, and continues to receive a growing amount of media attention. More seminars and webinars are planned for 2008, so keep an eye on www.wfmc.org for further announcements.

Once again, on behalf of everyone involved in the Coalition and those that work tirelessly behind the scenes, mostly in their own time, I sincerely thank you for continuing to support us. As I have said on many previous occasions, it never ceases to amaze me just how much can change and the progress that can be made in a 12-month period. Enjoy the book.

Jon Pyke, Chair WfMC
and Chief Strategy Officer, Cordys.

Workflow and BPM in 2008:
A New Business Value Imperative

Nathaniel Palmer, Transformation+Innovation, and the Workflow Management Coalition, United States

ABSTRACT

2008 has already proven to be year filled with uncertainty, due to macroeconomic trends and business cycle factors that are not likely to change any time soon. We are in an environment today where every investment requires a bullet-proof business and a clear path to immediate cost-cutting. Workflow and BPM have traditionally been favored at moments such as these, due in large part to the relatively low technology and resource investment required to realize significant gains in process efficiency, productivity, control, and business agility. Workflow first emerged in the early 1990s as part of the reengineering initiatives following the 1991 recession, saw its next wave begin in the 1999 as part of the '99-'00 business downtown, and once again in 2008 we are seeing the third wave of workflow and BPM interest and investments as a vehicle for combating economic uncertainty and growing business transaction costs. Yet although interest is widespread, the need to build a compelling business case is as important with BPM as with any other business investment. What we are seeing today is the new business value imperative; the need to demonstrate value growth and cost reductions with every current initiative, as well as a new opportunity to realize these through the strategic embrace of business process management.

INTRODUCTION

After nearly a decade of market research on what drives BPM implementations, the answer for what *prevents* them is consistently "lack of sponsorship" by upper management. Specifically, finding someone (an executive or a department) to pay for and champion it. Often departmental teams find the opportunity but not the resources to implement a BPM project, and are unable to win management support despite what may be to them an obvious need or potential benefit.

Gaining sponsorship is about building and presenting a credible business case. If sponsorship is lacking, it is almost always so because a cogent business case has not been developed. Goals and metrics are integral to every BPM initiative, and should be defined in the beginning stages of process definition. You cannot improve what you cannot measure, so clearly defined metrics and success criteria are essential to the business case and to the success of the overall BPM initiative. The business case must always include:

1. Validated and clearly understood project goals;
2. Clearly defined success criteria that are agreed to by all stakeholders;
3. Milestones that indicate 'how' and 'when' success will be measured;
4. A high-level outline that maps process metrics to corporate objectives.

Keeping metrics aligned to corporate objectives is key to understanding how to continually improve processes and resources to most effectively contribute to the organizations overall goals. This visibility is the foundation for continuous process improvement.

WHERE INVESTMENTS IN BPM WILL COME FROM IN 2008

At the end of 2007, we conducted a global cross-industry survey of approximately 500 organizations regarding their current and planned investments in Business Process Management and Enterprise Architecture initiatives. A summary of reported project maturity and investment plans is summarized below, categorized by industry sector.

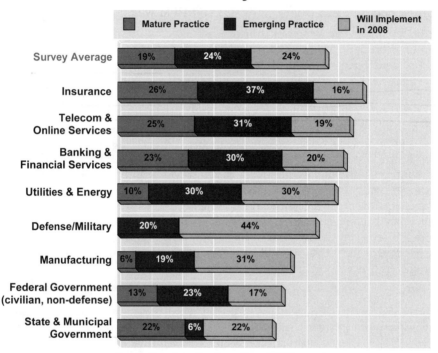

Source: Transformation+Innovation, 2008 Research

Among the results was the discovery that the traditional sectors investing BPM, notably *Insurance, Financial Services/Banking,* and Telecommunications, are among the least likely to invest in 2008. These sectors have mature or emerging workflow and BPM initiatives, and are more focused on realizing value from these existing investments than committing to new ones. In contrast, areas that have seen little to no investments in BPM historically are among the most likely to invest in 2008. These sectors include *Utilities and Energy,* Manufacturing, as well as *Military and Defense Agencies.*

Traditionally, agencies inside of the Pentagon have been early adopters of leading edge technologies such as Service-Oriented Architecture (SOA), but very slow to take advantage of business process investments. Their historic reluctance is clearly evident in the summary above, with no reported "Mature" deployments of BPM, yet nearly half (44 percent) of the respondents identifying with this sector expect to invest in 2008. This notable statistic is not an anomaly but represents a sea-change in the investment patterns in BPM. The trend it illustrates is one away from the transactional-oriented investments typical of Teleco, Financial Services, and Insurance, and towards the more human-intensive processes found in sectors such as defense industry, as well as middle and front office processes of service industries.

One of the factors driving demand for workflow and BPM in human-intensive process is the growing level of uncertainty in 2008, combined with growing or otherwise high human capital transactional costs. Specifically, it costs too much to hire new personnel, and in the face of business uncertainty firms are reluctant to bring new staff without optimal planning and performance management. Workflow and BPM today has evolved to a solution for personnel planning, for ensuring faster ramp-up of new staff, and for tackling the most difficult and dynamic processes that are impossible to complete automate, yet critical to manage.

The transactional process where workflow and BPM was first applied has largely been resolved. Although there will continue to be innovation in these areas, the really opportunities for organizations to build value is not in the lower tier where those processes are found, but by exposing those system capabilities as services, and connecting these to human-facing processes. The next focus for business improvement, and as a result the next wave of workflow and BPM investments, will be found in the optimization of human capital. Yet the challenge remains that in the face of the challenging economic environment of 2008 (circumstances likely to continue through 2009) even investments with as much potential for value creation as business process management still require a clearly understandable business case. What follows is an explanation of the steps required to create a compelling business case necessary to win sponsorship and business support for investments in workflow and BPM.

ASSESS WHERE YOU ARE BEFORE DECIDING WHERE YOU ARE GOING

The first step in building a business case for BPM is to establish a "current state" benchmark of the process or processes targeted for improvement. This is not intended to be a comprehensive re-engineering exercise, but rather an opportunity to better understand the process in question. Every process has its "cow paths" where practice has outlived the original design, and may or may not reflect how it should be performed in current context. Often this offers great opportunity for improvement. Yet overly scrutinizing this at the beginning can lead to a political battle or cause stakeholders to become defensive. So rather than getting entangled in politics, begin by simply documenting how things are done *today*, including specific steps and activities, the frequency with which they are performed, and the duration of individual activities—and be sure to note obvious bottlenecks, issues, or areas of improvement.

Next, start to identify the interdependencies and links between activities in terms of individual roles. Examine each individual's role in the process, asking "when do you...?" and "why do you...?" questions about process "steps." The goal is to build the context around process steps, so that a process can be defined and modeled as a set of interrelated but discrete activities, rather than simply a loosely defined sequence of actions. In addition, start to identify system dependencies in the process—what data is accessed when and by whom and in what system does it reside. Next focus on the "white space" between activities, specifically the precedents (what happens before) and dependents (what happens after) as well as the flow of information and how it changes from one activity to another. This is also an opportunity to identify bottlenecks, without directly implicating any specific roles or individuals. Do this by asking questions such as "What are you waiting on most often?" and "How could the process be improved without changing your job?"

PLAN TO WIN: DEFINE THE SUCCESS CRITERIA

As the stated in the famous mantra of Taylorism, "you can't improve what you can't measure." This has never been more true for BPM investments. Both the availability of rich performance metrics and the growing focus on measurable success mean that, for any successful BPM initiative in 2008, there must be clearly defined success criteria. Take the time to develop consensus on a common vocabulary and a standard set of terms for describing the process. This is not only necessary for the final implementation, but it is also critical to accurate validation of the process and to gaining buy-in from stakeholders and project sponsors. This should also include the establishment of specific goals and metrics for measuring project success.

The calculation and determination of a project's success should be based on milestones and measurable goals, not an arbitrary notion of completion. While the business case requires structure, it should also be fluid and adaptable. Business performance is dynamic and so should be the ruler used to measure it, particularly during the formative stages of the business case. This means that metrics should be both quantitative, such as time and cost variables, as well as qualitative, such as being easier to do business with, increasing visibility, or improving employee productivity. A business case should contain measurements that are tactical and quantitative as well as factors that are strategic and qualitative such as enabling 'round-trip BPM' so that business processes can be adapted in real-time by process owners.

CLEARLY ILLUSTRATE WHAT BENEFITS CAN BE EXPECTED

Once a process is captured in its current state and associated metrics are defined, it can be leveraged to model a more optimal future state. Improvements can be identified in part through process modeling and simulation alone but the greatest opportunities for improvement, however, will come from the successful deployment of a complete BPM suite—which will provide not only modeling and simulation, but also the automation, management, and analysis capabilities necessary to realize the full potential that true business process management has to offer.

Improvements can be made in both the human-centric and system-based activities associated with a process. Simulation can be applied to both types of activities. Because a change in one area might impact the results of another, the ability to model and simulate both system-facing and user-facing activities in the same solution offers substantial advantage over specialty tools that focus only on human-centric processes or only on system-to-system integration. A combined view allows for the discovery of process inefficiencies, design problems and potential application improvements across the entire process, all during the analysis stage when changes are the easiest and least costly to make. A word of caution, however, simulation introduces the risk of focusing on sizzle over substance. When presenting the business case it is better to avoid hyping animated simulation and instead focus on the quality of the data and the degree of "what-if" analysis supported.

Often getting a process automated and deployed even in its current state yields fast cost savings and productivity improvements. It is better to realize these savings early and then focus on analyzing real data captured by the BPM suite to simulate and apply process improvements. For this reason, many organizations opt to leave process simulation to the end of the implementation—a decision that has paid off in high return-on-investments and fast wins to justify additional process deployments.

DEVELOPING A RETURN ON INVESTMENT MODEL

ROI, in basic terms, is Profit divided by Investment. For the purpose of the business case, it is the total value anticipated to be returned from the BPM initiative minus the anticipated investment required (i.e., "net return") divided by the investment. For some firms Return on Equity (ROE) is of greater interest, as this captures the value realized from existing assets. For the purpose of the BPM business case, however, a new investment will be required and thus ROI is the more appropriate metric.

A positive ROI (i.e., when net value exceeds the cost of the investment) is any percent calculated as greater than zero (0 percent). Because returns and investments are made over a period of time rather than a single year (typically the business case is based on a three to five year horizon) the calculation of ROI needs to be made in terms of Net Present Value (NPV) or a discounted cash flow stream—although it is worth noting that actual cash flow is likely only a fraction of the value measured and you should expect the majority of the business case to be presented in terms of non-cash benefits.

Calculating NPV requires an understanding or estimation of the firm's cost of capital. The cost of capital is literally the cost of debt or equity required for obtaining funds and it is generally used as the minimum rate of return a firm requires for any single investment. In general it is the rate of return that is of most interest, since the BPM initiative alone is not likely to directly involve borrowing to pay for it. Organizations use the rate of the return as the hurdle rate for determining the lowest level of acceptable ROI. For some firms the Weighted Average Cost of Capital (WACC) or the average of debt and equity cost is a known and valuable factor and can be used as the driving factor. For firms where this information is unavailable, however, a conservative cost of capital can be estimated (3 percent is used in the examples which follow).

When building an ROI model, typically two scenarios are modeled—the first is labeled as "conservative" and includes minimal projections and easily verifiable data, and the second is labeled "aggressive" and outlines the potential for greater return factoring a wider range of potential benefits and incorporates more optimistic return forecasts. In both scenarios the cost basis is the same. The difference between the two is meant to illustrate the spread of reasonable expectations.

Avoid the trap of tiny numbers, such as saving 10 minutes a day across every employee's schedule. These are often the low-hanging fruit of process automation, and there is always the temptation to roll these up and present them as 1,000 of hours of labor savings. Yet these sorts of micro-productivity improvements are expected to be absorbed and are of no real measurable benefit. What would you do with an extra 10 minutes a day? Probably not much, as such a time savings would soon be consumed all the many distractions we face every day. Instead, base ROI calculations where time-savings impact real transaction overhead, such as verifiable labor savings or reduced workload with actual redeployment of resources.

CONCLUSION

Business Process Management (BPM) is not new—it is an established, proven discipline that combines a focus on process with an integrated set of specialized software tools to deliver real business results. Organizations around the world and across industries have proven the value that BPM can deliver greater efficiency, increased visibility, better control, enhanced operational agility, and measurable ROI showing payback in the first year of investment. This level of success is not an unrealistic expectation, but to do so requires clearly articulated plan from concept to execution.

Developing the business case for your first BPM initiative will be the most time-consuming and the most important because it will include the evaluation, selection, and justification of a BPM software suite to support the implementation. It will also serve as the first proof-point for BPM in your organization. The goal of the ROI model is to provide quantified assessment of the anticipated value-added through the BPM deployment, specifically to estimate both the cost and net benefit expected. A secondary goal is to frame expectations for the planning and design of the BPM deployment initiative, in particular as it relates to procurement of BPM software.

Follow the steps outlined here and the result will be a strong business case as well as a set of valuable metrics to monitor and measure results during the implementation. From that point on, you will have a repeatable approach, a solid technology foundation on which to build, and a set of benefits and benchmark ROI numbers to make justifying future BPM initiatives a breeze—putting you the fast path to realizing continuous process improvement and strategic business value from BPM.

Section 1

The Business Value of BPM

BPM, SOA and Web 2.0 Convergence: Business Transformation *or* Train Wreck

Linus Chow, WfMC Public Sector and Peter Bostrom, BEA Systems, USA

ABSTRACT

Government and commercial enterprises are driven to accelerate change while remaining agile enough to quickly adapt to evolving markets, policies, regulations, and business models. While the convergence and maturation of technologies and methodologies provide opportunities for agility and business transformation, this same convergence introduces new questions of risk surrounding security, inefficiencies, disruptions, and possible misalignment within the organization.

This paper will assess the benefits and risks of these solutions and how the solutions benefit executive initiatives such as Lean Six Sigma, portfolio management, and acquisition transformation, as well as mission-focused solutions in intelligence, defense and logistics. The focus will be on strategies for getting the most value with the least risk through the use of structured collaboration combined with tacit processes and agile BPM combined with SOA abstraction. Industry experts and case studies will provide the foundation for this analysis.

INTRODUCTION

BPM, SOA, and Web 2.0 currently are three of the hottest (and arguably the most hyped) technology strategies, with BPM and SOA a little more mature than Web 2.0. Enterprise adoption and convergence are fundamentally changing how IT and business (or mission) stakeholders work together. Because of the dynamic differences in use and perceptions of these different technologies both opportunities and threats impact both the strengths and weaknesses of organizations. We will be looking at real world implementation and how they moved forward while avoided pitfalls and present cases for moving forward with new ideas in taking advantage of these key trends in technology.

DEFINITION: WHAT ARE BPM, SOA, AND WEB 2.0?

Most IT and Business Executives are already aware in some form of BPM, SOA, and Web 2.0. Below is a quick summary of what these technologies are by our definition.

BPM is a strategy for managing and improving the performance of the business through continuous optimization of business processes in a closed-loop cycle of modeling, execution and measurement. In essence BPM is a combination of both a best practice methodology and an integrated technology solution. BPM was created from the business driven evolution and merging of different technology trends. It is easy to see that BPM solutions have evolved technology to run as the business. Many features, in whole or part, were combined to satisfy the BPM lifecycle. And this lifecycle is driven directly by organizational goals. This merging of technologies into a seamless Integrated Design Environment (IDE), provides the level of abstraction needed for both technology and business specialists to "talk" the same language. This is no insignificant feat, as this builds trust as well as agility throughout the organization.

SOA is an architectural approach that enables the creation of loosely-coupled, interoperable business services that can be easily shared within and between enterprises. The true value of an SOA is found in reuse and agility. While these attributes have been promised by various methodologies and technologies, what differentiates a Service-Oriented Architecture from other approaches is that it is uniquely geared to encourage reuse for generations of applications which will last not just years, but decades. Systems implemented today may live beyond the lifetimes of their original implementers in the form of virtualized enterprise applications managed as "black boxes" that are defined by their interfaces.

The phrase Web 2.0 is a trend in web design, development and can refer to a perceived second generation of web-based communities and hosted services—such as social-networking sites, wikis, and folksonomies—which aim to facilitate creativity, collaboration, and sharing between users. The term gained currency following the first O'Reilly Media Web 2.0 conference in 2004. Although the term suggests a new version of the World Wide Web, it does not refer to an update to any technical specifications, but to changes in the ways software developers and end-users use webs. According to Tim O'Reilly, "Web 2.0 is the business revolution in the computer industry caused by the move to the Internet as platform, and an attempt to understand the rules for success on that new platform."

Web 2.0 hints at an improved form of the World Wide Web. Technologies such as weblogs (blogs), social bookmarking, wikis, podcasts, RSS feeds (and other forms of many-to-many publishing), social software, and web application programming interfaces (APIs) provide enhancements over read-only websites.[3]

SUMMARY: SO WHAT DO BPM, SOA AND WEB 2.0 MEAN TO ME?

BPM and SOA have a history of clear benefits to the organization. Meanwhile, customers, industry and vendors are still formalizing the key value propositions of Web 2.0.

BPM and SOA

BPM	SOA
• Optimizes business processes	• Organizes IT infrastructure
• Demand for insight	• Demand for encapsulation
• Driven directly by business/agency goals	• Driven indirectly by business goals, translated to a need for IT agility and governance
• Does not require SOA but SOA greatly simplifies BPM implementations	• Provides a layer of control and governance for IT underneath BPM

Figure 1.2: BPM & SOA

BPM and SOA are both produced by the natural progress of business and IT striving to work together more efficiently and effectively. It is easy to note that these who technology solutions are complementary in nature (Figure 1.1).

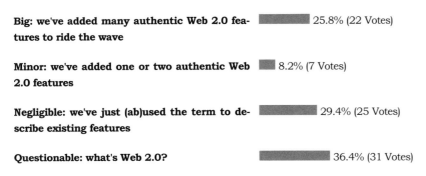

Big: we've added many authentic Web 2.0 fea- 25.8% (22 Votes)
tures to ride the wave

Minor: we've added one or two authentic Web 8.2% (7 Votes)
2.0 features

Negligible: we've just (ab)used the term to de- 29.4% (25 Votes)
scribe existing features

Questionable: what's Web 2.0? 36.4% (31 Votes)

Total Votes: 85 *Source: Web Survey BEA 2007*

Figure 1.2: What's the impact of "Web 2.0" on your development projects?

Video over the web	54%
Wikis	49
Blogs	48
RSS (Really Simple Syndication)	47
Podcasts	39
Social networking (e.g., *tagging, social bookmarks, community sites such as delicious, LinkedIn, Technorati*)	33
Expertise location and sharing	21
Mashups	13
Virtual worlds (e.g., Second Life)	12
Instant mobile updates (e.g., Twitter)	11
None of the above	11

Source: CIO Insight, August 2007

Figure 1.3: CIOs: Which of the following Web applications do you use personally?

From Figure 1.2 and 1.3 it can be seen that Web 2.0 technologies are just beginning to be adopted, yet CIO's are already adopting it personally. Social Computing and Web 2.0 have contributed important new designs for online collaborative work, information sharing, and workplaces, adding to the prior work on Information Workplaces (IW)[4].

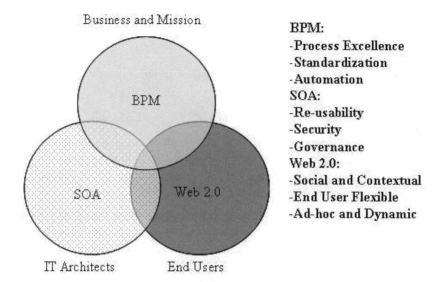

Business and Mission

BPM

SOA   Web 2.0

IT Architects   End Users

BPM:
-Process Excellence
-Standardization
-Automation
SOA:
-Re-usability
-Security
-Governance
Web 2.0:
-Social and Contextual
-End User Flexible
-Ad-hoc and Dynamic

Figure 1.4

From a highly simplified view BPM, SOA, and Web 2.0 intersection provides many challenges. Firstly, different stakeholders normally are the chief sponsors or stakeholders. Secondly, the primary value propositions of these technologies require political, cultural as well as technological compromises.

Obviously, this simplistic view does not capture all the challenges and opportunities inherent in the convergence of these strategies (both methodologies and technologies). Just as enterprises were getting used to combining BPM and SOA, now they have to adjust to Web 2.0 as well.

IMPLEMENTING: HOW ENTERPRISES ARE OVERCOMING THE CHALLENGES OF CONVERGENCE.

We have the unique opportunity to learn from some of the thought leaders currently implementing BPM, SOA, and Web 2.0 technologies. Rob Jett, Chief Information Officer of Red Buffalo, focuses on the organizational challenges he has dealt with as a trusted advisor to the US defense community and Federal Government. Meanwhile, Kevin M. Brown, Associate and Eric Yuan Program Manager, Booz Allen Hamilton; discuss their decision driven approach in implementing these technologies for the US Military. Finally, Robert H. Hodges, Chief SOA Architect, Lockheed Martin Company, encapsulates the challenges inherent in bringing these technologies together.

Case Study #1: Overcoming Organizational Challenges

Rob Jett PMP, CIO of Red Buffalo

Very early in our professional experiences we are taught some of the core values we later appreciate in our professional lives as the building blocks to our success. One of those building blocks from junior years talks about how to create solutions for business. The core saying goes like this "To provide solutions you must understand the business as if it was your own before you can make a difference."

What that meant was that to provide solution, it's not just about technology. One can look at the transformation of business in a similar light. With-out and understanding of where the business is as well as where it needs to go to be successful there could be a TRAIN WRECK out there looking for its next business victim.

A key to success is for all audiences involved in the transformation understand their roles and some of common issues that arise when *transformation* occurs. The organization will be an ever-transforming entity as long as there are variables in the business that need change to maintain or grow the business. The change is usually driven by a goal adjustment at highest level based on a need to adapt to a new situation. That situation could be a market trend, a core mission objective change, a stakeholder desire and even just normal growth patterns. The following chart introduces an organizational, technology and cultural look at how all of these business characteristics can exist together.

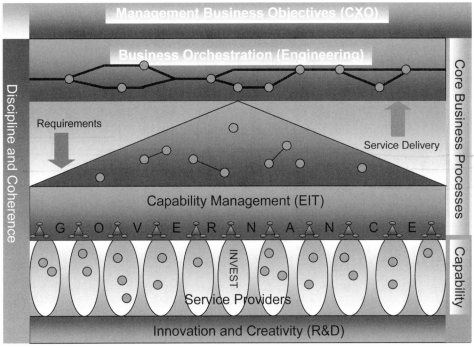

One of the first key concepts to transformation is that you can't break the parts of your business that are working and in some cases paying the bills while introducing new solutions. With that said, it is important to remember that *discipline* and *coherence* have to be maintained in the day-to-day business while not depreciating your *innovation* and *creativity*. Therein lays the one of the main challenges to transforming any business.

DEFINITION OF TERMS

Management Business Objective—A set of one or more linked business or policy goals, normally within the context of an organizational structure.

Business Orchestration—A set of one or more linked procedures or activities which collectively realize a business objective or policy goal, normally within the context of an organizational structure defining functional roles and relationships.

Capability Management—An area of a business entity that is responsible for the services or capabilities a business uses. The entity is responsible for the end services being offered to business consumers. This element governs approved active services, monitors the maturity and life cycle of active and new services waiting to be offered. The entity also manages the availability and failover of services.

CXO—The CXO consists of the Chief Executive Offices of a business. These offices are responsible and accountable for the business strategy, mission and transformation as it relates to the goals and objectives of the business. These offices are also responsible for the policy and cultural values of the business.

EIT—The EIT consists of the Enterprise Information Technology group or division of a business. This group includes systems level design, development and support organizations within a business. These groups would normally report to the Chief Executive Office for technology or operations depending on your business structure

R&D—The R&D consists of the Research and Development group or division of a business. This group is responsible for the Innovation and Creativity components of the business. This group would normally have tight bonds with the EIT and CXO groups. This group would also have extensive multi-industry networks to include: schools for higher education, industry related partners and suppliers.

Process Definition —The representation of a business process in a form which supports automated manipulation, such as modeling, or enactment by a workflow management system. The process definition consists of a network of activities and their relationships, criteria to indicate the start and termination of the process, and information about the individual activities, such as participants, associated IT applications and data, etc.

Business Process Management—The practice of developing, running, performance measuring, and simulating Business Processes to effect the continued improvement of those processes. Business Process Management is concerned with the lifecycle of the Process Definition.

THREE DIFFERENT AUDIENCES

Normally in a business there are at least three distinct cultural audiences. The first group is the life's blood of the organization, the End Users. The End Users are the people who use the Information systems every day to complete business essential tasks or work. It is important to understand at this point in most cases End Users are not interested in the technologies used or the next new thing. They are often the most challenged group during times of transformation. They understand very well the responsibility they have in the organization and are not looking for change unless something is severely broken. They will even find ways around broken processes and systems to still get the job done. It is important to understand that users sometimes feel the new systems actually lose functionality they require in the name of transformation.

An example from our Federal Government activities: Business Analysts were primarily using the keyboard as their interface to the systems. They knew the series of key strokes required to do almost any task they needed in the system. The new system was all about the mouse and how to minimize the number of mouse clicks. The key stroke methods were not included in the new system so the older users' performance was hindered. While the new users liked the mouse orientation because that was easier for them, they lost their senior mentors on the step-by-step process. We found this by capturing their process as a candidate for automation. The senior user community was still not happy with their situation on the new system and asked us to include both methods.

It is very important to also understand the communication requirements for this group during transformation activities. The next group is the Enterprise Information Technology (EIT) group. For this audience example this group also includes the engineering and R&D groups. This group normally has an almost completely self-reliant internal culture that is sometimes hard to understand. The Enterprise Information Technology group also understands the tasks they are responsible for and in most cases are happy to maintain the business systems while designing and developing new ones. Because this group bridges the gap between End Users and the CXO group, good leadership, clear roles and responsibilities, and again a clear communication strategy are all key to having the groups propagate the vision and business objectives into their solutions. "They need to understand the business and technology to develop the proper solutions".

The last cultural audience is the Chief Executive Officers (CXO) group. This group drives the cultural and has the responsibility for the business at the same time. This balance is very delicate. To transform the business the CXO group has the hardest job. They have to first create a vision that can be shared throughout the organization. Strategic planning along with a shared vision provides long and short term business goals and objectives. The CXO group has to maintain everything in the current operating business structure to include the health and status of its people, and manage the change associated with the transformation to a new business structure.

SAME SITUATION DIFFERENT DAY

Transformation is hard no matter how big or small an organization is, but there are a few common challenges to watch for that this paper will touch on. The first, of which, is the importance of communications and the communication strategy during times of change. Communication issues can affect any project and organization. Clear communication to all as to their respective roles and CXO level expectations in the transformation activities are an important part. The communications strategy should include clear roles and responsibilities as well as the high level vision and derivative short and long term goals and objectives for the groups involved in the transformation execution.

The next issue is a larger issue that plants itself throughout the organization and is related to communications as well. The business as a unit understands that it needs to change or transform to grow and survive. Each one of the three audiences addresses the change in a different way. The end users of the system find ways to work more efficiently and sometimes just plain work more to produce more business-related product. The CXO and related management groups develop new strategies, policies and plans for the next grouping of transformational activities. The EIT group puts more time into maintaining the system and looks for ways to make the current system even better.

Once this cultural shift happens it is hard to bring transformational activities back in line with the over all Vision and Management Objectives. If this cultural shift and its associated activities are not managed correctly the business begins to take on risk that affects the current business and the transformational activities. Some of the risks are people-related. Turnover may rise as more people feel the stress of the change from their cultural perspective. The three groups have new risks related to cutting communications to focus on trying to manage the new challenges thus creating an "us and them" separation in the business. The business also takes on new technically-related risks, such as building new applications in the same mold as the current system. One of the potential causes for this type of activity is limited funding. When faced with limited funding it is important to keep the long term vision in mind and plan for iterative development instead of fixing the easier bumps in the road and sacrificing the vision or master plan.

These are sometimes referred to as stove-pipe or one-off solutions. These types of solutions can create re-work and additional cost to the business. Removing the question of the end user for a second, the CXO group and related managers know that there are Business Objectives directly tied to the overall vision that need to be met and the EIT group is doing everything they can to fix the problems before they arise. A fundamental alignment is needed. What does the business need in order for the alignment to occur? The groups need to align around the shared vision, related business objectives and core business processes and procedures that are vital to the success of the new Management Business Objectives. These processes and procedures as well as an inventory of current services and capabilities available and in development can be the common bond between all three groups in the transformation of the business.

BPM TO THE RESCUE

Since the business process is now a focus how does the process come to life and create a service based architecture that not only maintains the current business practices but allows for agile change or transformation? Business Process Management (BPM) is the answer.

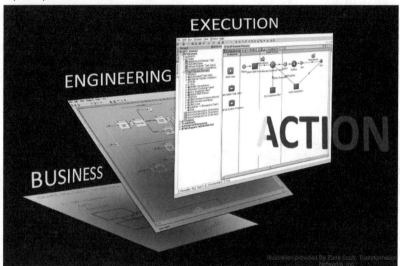

The chart above captures a numbers of high level steps required to realign transformational activities. This BPM approach understands that the transformation is based on a top-down understanding of the business and its new vision and related goals and objectives, while maintaining that the end user work is the life blood of the organization. The top-down understanding drives the scope and priority of requirements for the bottom up process capture and modeling. The BPM approach provides a common picture of the system as it is to be built. The beauty of this approach is that the people who truly understand the business build the picture of what is needed. Core processes are captured through facilitated sessions, modeled and simulated to allow for a robust to-be process. The models are shared and enhanced based on now visible automation opportunities. All groups should be able to see their new work roles and how the system will help them, thus providing buy-in and a clear understanding of the road ahead. This picture or model also helps to guide what service inventory artifacts are required from the existing services inventory and where the business needs to invest in new capabilities. A byproduct of the visible model is now the business can also see where investment is no longer needed or where the business process is in need of repair.

The core business models become the basis for more formal use case and requirements activities. Requirements can be derived directly from the models providing requirements traceability and the probability clearer priority weighting of the requirements. The models will also identify pain points for the end users and now visible Return On Investment (ROI) areas. Iterative development techniques can be used to tackle prioritized pain points and (ROI) areas to provide bite size chucks value. The models and the BPM approach also allow the EIT and CXO groups to see where iterative development concepts can be used. Being able to now see where your biggest returns are is a significant aid in the planning and development process. Also, by iterating the development effort the business can shorten the development cycles and better steer the overall activities against objectives and overall vision.

Most BPM tools provide an Integrated Development Environment (IDE) which enables the CXO and EIT groups to work together in one tool using a common set of models. Some BPM tools even provide a very good level of integration capability right out of the box, such as Introspection of back-end services. The introspection and included code libraries make development easier by providing syntactical examples and a standards-based platform for developers to work from. BPM tools also allow for the monitoring of Key Performance Measures of the business in real or near real time with out too much development effort. In some cases the CXO group would have tools to answer even the "What if" questions based on data captured from the live processes or simulations.

By bringing all groups together, iterating development cycles, providing standards-based development and working from the common picture, BPM tools will help to create a smooth transformation to the new business vision for success

Identify Services Inventory

Equally important is the inventory of current systems. Now that the models have laid the plan for transformation the first question that should be asked is; can the business transform with the services already in the services inventory and what is needed in order to complete the service points and bring our Business Orchestration layer to life? It is also important that during this stage that single points of failure in the process related service areas are identified. The organization will be able to see the areas where investment is required to complete and maintain the new transformed system. The services inventory and its related governance together with the BPM and its core business processes are the basis for any Service Oriented Architecture.

ACTION NOT WORDS

Now that the business flows have been captured, everyone is on the same page, and the services or capabilities have been identified, the processes can be brought to life with the BPM tool suite that allows not only for the business process automation, but also allows for ease of enterprise integration with back-end services. Executable models can be built and deployed over many servers spanning many geographic areas that allow the business to grow and transform no matter its size. It is also never too late to think about the metrics you need from the system. What business questions do you need to answer at which level? How will the answers be presented so that all level may take the correct action quickly based on real data? Even though transformation is hard for all businesses, the use of proper technologies like BPM will help businesses avoid the train wrecks.

Case Study #2: Decision Driven SOA-Enabled Logistics

Kevin M. Brown, Associate and Eric Yuan Program Manager, Booz Allen Hamilton

In the military a typical situation repeats itself daily; a Commander is instructed to prepare for a combat mission to take place the next day. The Commander immediately turns to his planning staff to describe the mission and go over the details of the plan. Inevitably, he asks the same question each time, "What is the status of our equipment? Will we be able to provide the firepower and support needed to protect our soldiers?"

These questions are well-known in the military; routine status requests trained and rehearsed for by every member of the Commander's Team. Each member knows their part well and is equipped with the latest communication and computer equipment to assist in the decision-making process. The team knows the importance of providing timely and accurate unit status reports. They provide the commanders with critical information needed to make immediate decisions on combat operations. Currently, the military is attempting to help the commanders with unit status information by providing several different global data bases to manage information such as, property book information, maintenance status reports and parts ordering/tracking information. Unfortunately the data stored in those systems is often days or weeks old and not readily accessible by commanders or warfighters in the tactical environment. Additionally, systems at the edge of the battlefield are often providing information in the form of lengthy spreadsheet-type reports, which must then be manually converted to a format that leaders can understand and use to make decisions.

As a result, and despite the fact that very powerful computer systems and massive databases are made available to the military, field combat leaders may still have to rely on a large number of staff to manually solve a very standard problem every day. Often the commander's staff is forced to find the real status of their equipment the old fashioned way—by making phone calls, sending emails and consolidating notes onto slides. The data collected, however timely, may also be error-prone due to misunderstandings, tired soldiers or any number of reasons, which may have dire consequences in real combat situations.

The challenge now is to find a way to integrate the disparate data sources and incorporate them with the proven real-time processes the combat staff uses to determine unit readiness status. This challenge requires overcoming both technological hurdles as well as business process hurdles:

The technological hurdles include challenges with data integration, non-standard access, lack of enterprise-level Business Process Management (BPM) tools and the lack of a SOA-enabled infrastructure. Individually, each of these hurdles could be addressed with individual vendor solutions. However, it is the orchestration of these components together which provides the warfighter with a complete decision-making capability.

Just as important and some would argue even more important, are the business processes used to make combat decisions. The business process hurdles are steeped in tradition and rigidly followed to ensure career progression. This is because the Combat Commanders staff officers are staking their careers and the lives of many soldiers on their reports to the Commander. Staff officers will not take process change lightly, because the business process and Standard Operating Procedures (SOPs) they use to answer the Commander's questions are proven through validation in combat. An outside consultant or vendor will be hard pressed to change this culture and its processes to fit the tools or solution they are selling.

To overcome these technological and process hurdles for this military client, Booz Allen Hamilton, a global consulting firm, utilized a new approach to solve the problem: a decision-driven design approach.

The decision-driven design approach helps determine the technical solution set used for this problem. Based on the above use case, it was clear that an SOA would be required to integrate the various disparate data sources. An SOA is an architectural paradigm through which monolithic, stove-piped systems (and the data within them) are transformed and exposed as a set of loosely-coupled web services. The SOA also enables greater data accessibility from the various databases when creating the unit status reports. To accomplish this data gathering quickly, industry open standards are used as well as Best-of-Breed vendor tools. This, in itself, is not new. The key to this decision-driven approach, as explained by Kevin M. Brown, the project manager, is to use the decision maker's information needs to drive SOA and web service development. By focusing on the decision to be made (in this case, determine equipment readiness status) rather than blindly exposing existing data sets, the resulting web services are more mission-oriented and directly support the warfighter's needs.

The decision-driven approach to web service development is just one component of the story; the integration of the data to the business process is also necessary for success. The business process used for determining the unit status reports follows very strict military protocols, doctrines and regulations which are similar in complexity to business rules in commercial industries. Modeling that process in a BPM tool is not a trivial activity, however, the result is worth the effort since the web services can then be orchestrated and managed through the BPM tools. This enables automated enforcement of the governance and controls on the use of property information, parts status and vehicle maintenance status, all of which are mission-critical information whose timeliness and accuracy will determine the future careers and lives of soldiers.

Booz Allen's decision-driven approach focuses specifically on how the data will be used in decision making. By utilizing a well-defined methodology to collect the metadata used for making the decision, such as the data format (PDF, word files, slides, spreadsheets, etc.), frequency of use and distribution methods, targeted web service interfaces are identified which support the creation of automatically generated status reports. This significantly improves operational efficiency of the system and drastically reduces bandwidth requirements.

To support the rapid execution of the BPM process, Booz Allen helped the client set up a set of SOA infrastructure services using open standards and commercial off the shelf (COTS) tools, such as BEA's AquaLogic ESB, an Enterprise Service Management (ESM) product from AmberPoint, and the Microsoft Office SharePoint Server (MOSS). These foundational services enable easy reuse of existing information systems/data sources, process orchestration, security and provide user-defined interface capabilities to allow decision-specific data reporting and manipulation. The integrated architecture is shown in Figure 2.

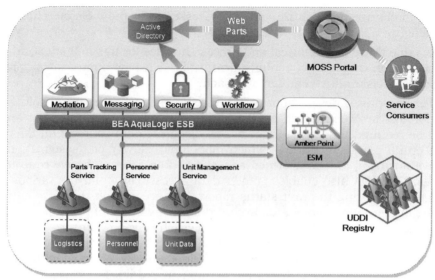

Figure 2: Illustrative Architecture

Mr. Eric Yuan, Booz Allen's program manager for this effort, explained that while the initial design of the system is driven by a typical use case for one particular military organization, many other use cases are quite similar and often can utilize the same architecture. As a result, the decision-driven approach allows a repeatable process for streamlining other future decision making needs. More importantly, should new decisions need to be made using similar data; the SOA enabled web services will be available for rapid consumption. This is a key tenet of information sharing and network-centric warfare for today's military.

Booz Allen's innovative solutions brought some significant benefits to the client. First, the immediate value added to the commanders' staff by enabling them to rapidly collect existing data and easily update it based on real-time field reports. Second, risk is reduced as more staff officers are able to view the data to double check accuracy, as well as to update the authoritative databases. The resulting reports are accessible via a collaboration portal allowing each unit to review the reports. Finally, the ability to personally configure the data for presenting the reports is a key aspect of the solution set and an aspect that ensures the users will adopt and leverage this new information capability.

In conclusion, the integration of SOA, BPM and the decision driven approach has enabled the military to address a significant, yet typical challenge, in data gathering and data sharing. The decision-focused development of the web services is not a radical new technology but rather a new way to view our complex world. Too often the focus is on massive enterprise level problems and the opportunity is missed to solve small, difficult problems, ending up with repeatable, reliable and scalable solutions.

Case Study #3: Challenges bringing BPM, SOA, and Web 2.0 together

Robert H. Hodges, Chief SOA Architect; Lockheed Martin Company

A SOA-based workflow approach facilitates cooperation among agencies that need to share tasks in working together. Using SOA workflows to enable networked data sharing and analysis tools could lead to greater levels of meaningful cooperation among defense and civilian government organizations where information sharing is a critical-need capability. Lockheed Martin recently experimented with using a SOA approach to analyzing intelligence and surveillance data, and making it available to multiple users in real time. The experiment demonstrated how two distinctly different government organizations could work together to respond to a possible missile threat.

For the experiment, data sharing was made possible in a number of ways through the technical capabilities of the service architecture test bed. Standard operating tasks required for repetitive analysis were programmed into the Business Process Management (BPM) system. The enterprise service bus in concert with Web 2.0 and Social Computing (such as Aqualogic Pages and Aqualogic Interaction products) allowed operators to access and extract needed information from many sources. Operators obtained data from several simulated sensors and web services from the test bed network. Operators were able to build personalized operational pictures either through workflow driven tasks or through direct intervention with the system. Workflows were preprogrammed in Business Process Execution Language (BPEL) or XML Process Definition Language (XPDL) to drive user interactive tasks or to automate machine tasks. The workflows took advantage of the previous states to set variables that made it easier to work with the data, and share operator views of it.

During the course of creating the workflows, domain experts adept at running real live operations centers were used to define processes on easel paper using colored markers. When the processes were exposed to the workflow engineer, the experts were able to quickly learn a few basic BPM subtleties then proceed to assist with converting processes into BPM workflows. As a result, the engineer completed the workflows and played them back to the experts for evaluation. The experts were able to see just how their operational concepts flowed, or in some cases, did not flow with the test bed scenario. After tweaking the workflow using the BPM development tool, the engineer tested the workflow in the test bed. The workflow engine is depicted in the figure below.

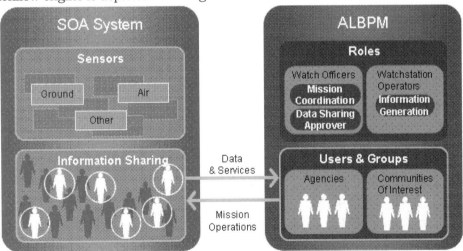

One special feature of the test bed was the ability for the operator to download new web services and web applications onto operator watchstations. This allowed the operators, using Web 2.0 technologies such as social computing, RSS feeds, mashups, open source software, blogs and many more to drive home particular analyses and to adapt to ever changing mission timelines. In some cases, the newly added services were "workflowed" into the operational tasks for inclusion during the next scenario run. In one case, the operator who developed the workflow with the engineer fell ill and had to replaced at the last minute by a rookie operator for the scenario run. Had the first operator built up workflows for his particular watchstation activities, the replacement operator could have performed at or near the expected level of the first operator. As it was, the rookie operator had to be re-trained thus delaying the scenario run. The vision is to someday have dynamic adjustment of the workflows based on newly added Web 2.0 technologies during the scenario run.

Initial results are mixed. There is obvious benefit to using BPM but there are still considerable engineering skills required to translate expert input into viable BPEL and XPDL that couples with the SOA system. In addition, use of the workflows by other systems in a heterogeneous environment is difficult at best. As an agnostic system integrator, Lockheed Martin envisions a day when workflows (or portions of workflows) can be shared as easily as data in wikis, blogs, and mashups are today.

While the benefits of using the SOA BPM technology may be apparent to many, an appeal made even stronger by use of adaptable, purchasable commercial software, much work on re-thinking and testing operational tasks to share government information is being addressed. To avoid the train wreck of the ever expanding Web 2.0 technologies that are not properly "workflowed," BPM developers will need to more tightly couple their product to services while allowing experts to create the workflows in real time. There is much to consider in the debate over how much of the operations should be committed to BPM versus solely human driven or a combination of both. Clearly, agility in complex systems must be balanced with controlled collaboration in order to operate in mission critical environments. Today, it can be said BPM is about better collaboration around workflows in a mission setting. Agility of operations especially given the asymmetric view of modern warfare is eased through workflows. There is promise for the future SOA systems.

FUTURE TRENDS: WHAT NEXT?

It's hard to have a crystal ball when business and new technologies are in question. But, as more enterprises successfully implement these convergent technologies, industry experts and analysts predict trends in convergence and new ways these technologies will impact the way we do business. John Wylie, BPM Specialist, covers how BPMS are evolving to handle the dynamic future of business, adding collaborative elements to normally structured processes. Finally, Keith Sink discusses how new real-time Event Servers are pushing BPM and workflows to the "edge."

Case Study #4: Collaborative BPM – Convergence of Technologies to Enable the Knowledge Worker;

John Wylie, BPM Specialist BEA Systems

Organizations are realizing the need to leverage BPMS in new area's previously thought to be too complex to automate, human-centric non transactional workflows. The benefits of BPMS are far too compelling for organizations to not ask the question; how can we leverage BPM technology to further help our knowledge workers to be more productive in the work that they perform that is not transactional?

We are finding through our BPM implementations that not all of the work that our employees are performing fits into a process that can be modeled, automated and repeated. We don't have to look very far to understand that up to 80 percent of the activity we engage in to complete our tasks does not fit into a repeatable process. The nature of the interactions our knowledge workers are performing are more complex than what can be identified, modeled and repeated across process instances and other knowledge workers. We rely upon our knowledge workers to use their judgment and insight rather than strictly adhering to a documented procedure.

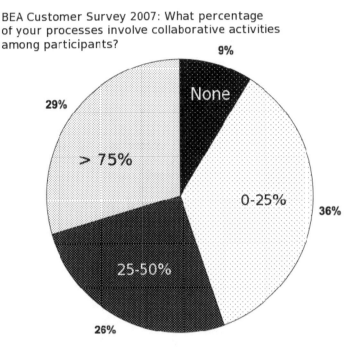

BEA Customer Survey 2007: What percentage of your processes involve collaborative activities among participants?

Organizations have tried to help the knowledge workers through implementing myriad knowledge management- and collaboration-based solutions, to only find out that these systems are not widely adopted due to their lack of scope, ease of use or applicability to the specific needs of the knowledge workers. A new approach to enabling knowledge working is emerging; one that provides knowledge workers with easier access to information, improved communications and greater collaboration technologies. BPM is at the center of this new approach.

As we have discussed in this chapter, BPM does a great job at providing the right information at the right time in the process to help both systems and humans be more productive. What we have found is that within each task within a workflow or process, there exist mini-workflows; what is the individual doing to be able to get their tasks done? If the information the individual needs to complete their task can be captured and included in the workflow work item, then BPM alone is a perfect technology to help drive efficiency. Many times we see a different requirement; the information that people need to complete their tasks isn't readily available for the BPMS to capture from other systems, documents, or data sources. This need in the market has driven BPMS vendors to further innovate to provide the same benefits of BPMS (greater efficiency, agility and control) to the areas of non-traditional workflow.

As McKinsey noted in 2006:[1]:

> "Some of [software spending] growth will come from continued automation of transactions (which continue to make up 44 percent of labor activity in the United States)... [however, other software spending will need to] empower 'tacit interactions' the judgment-based, highly collaborative interactions that account for more than 40 percent of workforce activity today... but have not yet had substantial software investment support."

While the focus of the majority of BPM implementations will remain focused on supporting transactional business processes, BPM products are also starting to play a supporting role for enabling manual, knowledge worker processes which are largely done today through email, documents and spreadsheets into a more robust collaborative knowledge worker environments.

BEA customer survey 2007: Which collaborative human activities are most important to business processes you are managing or plan to manage?

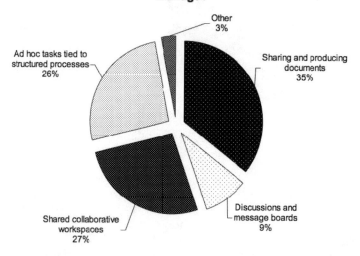

These highly dynamic and collaborative situations require that BPM play a new role; one of facilitator of delivering the right technologies to the knowledge worker to enable the end user with the ability to create their own environment to facilitate the collaborations within the process.

Civilian and Commercial Example: Claims Management

Claims management is a classic transactional workflow, the process starts with a request or submission of a claim which is processed through to completion, many times this process is completed as a straight through process; meaning that the process can be completed by routing information provide in the claim through a system-to-system workflow and does not require any work by humans. Many times exceptions are created which require that humans be involved to apply their subject matter expertise and knowledge to the instance of the process in order to complete the processing of the claim; an area for which many organizations are implementing BPMS in order to facilitate the management of the transactional

---

[1] "Software 2006 Industry Report", McKinsey & Company and Sand Hill Group, 2006

process. In many cases this type of process requires subject matter expertise, additional information that may not exist within the "workflow" and the ingenuity of our knowledge workers in order to complete each task and the process. We have found that it is this type of process where people "step out" of the technology to gain information in order for them to complete their tasks.

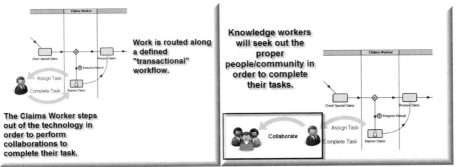

From the perspective of a computer program, or a modeled process, the work people do is easily completed. Here, we see the system assigning a task to an individual user, with the expectation that the user will complete the task to advance the program or the process forward.

We are finding that reality tells a different version of events here. In order to accomplish this type of knowledge-based task, often the individual must engage other people within the business, and work together to achieve the best outcome or share information with one another to derive the best solution to complete the task.

Sometimes we can immediately identify those people; other times we need to discover them. Discovering the right people in a timely manner, in the context of what our needs are, saves the knowledge worker time and makes them more efficient.

Effective collaboration is often fed by information we've created and are managing within the business and by external sources. So in order to complete this assigned task, we must discover the appropriate key pieces of information that will inform our decision and the eventual outcome.

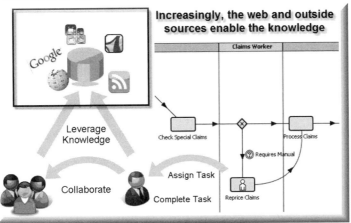

The requirement for this knowledge has increased the number of people that are now involved in a completely unscripted and undefined chain of events. This lack of definition of the process begins to slow down the activity completion.

In addition to discovering information that already exists and people that may aid our decision-making, we often create new information, using a variety of tools and resources at our disposal, both within and outside our company. These tools are often completely out-of-hand, and not coordinated in the context of what we're working on, or even more troublesome, many of our knowledge workers may not have access to them.

Managing complex interactions, unstructured activities, and coordinating that in the context of business processes, is a real shift and one that is becoming more and more critical to the way that organizations can further impact their performance. The best means of facilitating these capabilities falls on the shoulders of BPMS. BPMS is the orchestration engine that provides the knowledge worker with pre-defined templates of capabilities comprised of Portal, Collaboration, Web 2.0, and Service Oriented Architecture services and technologies to create a Collaborate environment to complete their complex tasks.

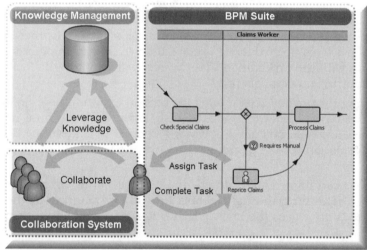

The evolution of BPMS is putting the user at the center of each experience, providing the foundation for dynamic applications that bring the right tools and information in the context of each instance of a process.

These dynamic applications or collaborative workflow capabilities helps to address the collaboration issues at the heart of our knowledge workers needs and the needs of the business at large. Collaborative BPM is going to create significant new productivity gains for modern businesses and better enable organizations with the ability to execute their mission. As capital and information were synonymous to the 20th century, collaborative interaction will be one of the most important assets to manage to gain the efficiency, agility and control in order for organizations to properly execute their specific mission.

Case Study #5: BPM on the Edge – Real-time BPM for US DoD

Keith Sink, Principal Systems Engineer, BEA Systems

As Programs find new and innovative ways to support mission systems for the US Department of Defense (DoD), Services Oriented Architecture (SOA) is firmly anchored as the centerpiece for enterprise architectures. Current Joint Programs reflect the relative impact of SOA technologies by focusing on the collaboration and sharing of data among families of systems supporting the warfighter. Examples of this concept are readily available. The Net-Centric Enterprise Services (NCES) program is driving the deployment and adoption of a common services infrastructure improving the efficacy of mission components running within the service "fabric." The Net-Enabled Command Capability (NECC) program extends the notion of common service infrastructure to provide decision support to the Command and Control (C2) family of systems. Each of these programs heavily relies on the concepts and methodologies of SOA to be effective.

Either through a subscription process or automated integration points, events flowing within the service fabric are typically processed individually and propagated through robust messaging infrastructures. While SOA provides the design and runtime structure for building and leveraging these event interfaces, new and interesting capabilities can be achieved when the event streams themselves are treated like actors in the consumption of the data. The recognition of patterns within independent and varying event streams is known as Complex Event Processing (CEP). CEP engines have capabilities to interact with SOA using common readily available standard protocols via robust frameworks.

Working in concert with SOA, CEP technologies can be integrated to form a new super-charged form of Event Driven Architecture (EDA). Applying this architectural approach to challenging DoD use-cases is the concept that will be explored in this whitepaper.

Background

It is widely known that Services Oriented Architecture represents a paradigm shift in enterprise application infrastructure. This paradigm shift manifests itself within enterprise systems as faster time-to-market for new capabilities at a reduced cost. These factors are propelled by the fundamental constructs of SOA, which support distributed deployment and reusability.

From these fundamentals, SOA provides the pallet that enables enterprise architects and business/mission analysts to support a number of new types of applications. From collaboration environments exposed through hybrid application portals to loosely coupled integrated back-end systems controlled by business management workflow platforms, new capabilities are emerging every day. Distributed deployments and operational awareness within the underlying platforms help tie it all together within a robust management infrastructure, which drives the return on investment.

Within this SOA philosophy, the enterprise application becomes the sum that is greater than the application parts. However, upon closer inspection, the underlying resources supporting the SOA largely revolve around the classical notion of the IT data center. The underlying platform persist data to transactional data stores and application components run within application server containers. Its the management views, remote-ability, and protocol standardization that provide the catalyst to propel SOA as *de-facto* reference architecture for enterprise systems. In today's IT infrastructure, you can readily find high-volume applications that provide remote-able interaction in the form of subscriptions, notifications, alerts, and long-running business transactions. In increasing numbers, the interfaces to these applications are based on the SOA methodology.

Upon further inspection, the aggregation of the individual data events used to formulate end-user mission decisions is sophisticated over first generation IT applications, but, from a high level, resemble classic brute-force data capture, with more robust and optimized implementations. So, the determination of patterns and trends is based largely on an optimized implementation that provides the answers faster with triggers firing within the back-end systems. For example, an event sink may register a subscription to an event, and will be notified via a back-end pub/sub messaging infrastructure. This approach is highly effective, but there is data loss from the point that the event occurs and the point that the triggering mechanism is fired. Conceptually, the data loss is the context in which the event itself is firing. It would be more effective if the streaming data as a whole were an active participant in the processing of the individual events.

The next generation end-user requirements are beginning to move the design requirements for applications to recognize the events that drive the mission application as an entity unto itself. CEP rules engines provide the container to aggregate over high-volume event streams and identify patterns and act upon them in real-time. Complex events can range in contextual meaning from logistical delay based on geographical conditions to intelligence data points that reflect a broader threat. Rules are applied over the flow of events as opposed to a query following persistence to a relational data store. Through the use of lightweight adapter frameworks, implementation is made to integrate with complex physical sources and standardized for event processing query languages.

With a small strategic footprint and adaptation frameworks, CEP engines can be plugged into edge systems to add new extended capabilities to back-end systems. As a result, CEP technology is a first class actor within SOA based systems.

THE NEXUS OF BPM COLLABORATION AND EDA WITHIN DoD SYSTEMS

The discipline of Business Process Management provides the backbone for coordinating human interaction with automated back-end systems. The template-based process supports long-running transactions. From the SOA Reference Architecture, Enterprise Service Bus can be used to leverage back-end assets in new and extended capability use-cases. Plugging in service-enabled applications, exposed through an enterprise service bus, BPM systems can consume and invoke services as an orchestration layer than is not tightly coupled with the supporting resources. The value to the enterprise cannot be understated, as tight coupling often has broad implications to release cycles, operational readiness, and maintenance costs.

From a user interface perspective, enterprise portals are an effective way to manage back-end assets and coordinate activities that rely on humans within this environment. Using the combination of BPM and service enabled messaging based systems, the coordination and collaboration of different forces can be achieved very effectively. The key to future capabilities is to drive proactive action over reactive, as well as, enabling the data flowing within the system itself to recognize patterns before a human resource need get involved. Often the struggle in this type of scenario revolves around the sheer volume of events flowing through the network.

Sensor data is a perfect example of high-volume event streams. Sensor data has state implications in terms of readiness, demographic information, and operational context. However, the volume of data is often at odds with the traditional notion of IT management techniques. This is further exacerbated in high-volume mission critical use-cases which require low latency and deterministic performance.

Now, consider the notion of processing the streams through a system that can support temporal queries to recognize patterns as the events flow through the system. Under this approach, the coordination of sensor data, intelligence data, and logistics can be triggered in real-time. Moving the processing of the event streams closer to the edge, BPM and SOA concepts can be extended to these use-cases without the overhead of classic processing within IT data centers.

For example, Atomic Biological and Chemical warfare events can be triggered with integrated streams of intelligence, weather, and logistics information to trigger the coordination of humans in the process proactively. Using the constructs of SOA, the consuming events can be translated sooner into highly coordinated and traceable downstream results. The rules driving the force projection can be infused in the system in a generic fashion, which drives the ability for the event structure and the back-end system to vary independently, improving maintainability and operational readiness.

The following high-level interaction diagram illustrates the interface capabilities for CEP technology to consume and operate on event streams with reach back into the SOA enterprise. With this approach, events have more context and event consumers can take more relevant action quicker.

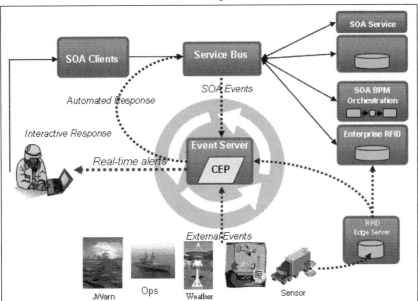

Figure 5 – Event Driven Infrastructure interacts with SOA Infrastructure at the aggregate level of the streaming data itself

The advancement and availability of robust event-driven platforms provides a unique opportunity for architects within Mission-Critical DoD systems to associate high-volume temporal data with traditional operational IT system to the edge.

Services Oriented Architecture provides the network to drive and expose the interfaces to operational C2 systems, and the emerging CEP based systems can provide the decision support and triggering mechanisms.

With the powerful combination of Services Oriented Architecture and Event Driven Architecture, new capabilities will support the warfighter with lower latency and less overhead in real-time. These emerging platforms supporting EDA, with highly productive design-time and runtime frameworks, serve to provide the connectivity of the physical event oriented networks with the rest of the application ecosystem. In a dynamic world, this will serve to extend the benefits of SOA to proactive real-time use-cases for the DoD going forward.

CONCLUSION:

As Enterprises strive for greater efficiencies and effectiveness, technologies are created or adapted to fill the needs of these organizations. This dynamic convergence provides both opportunities as well as threats to these organizations. BPM, SOA, and Web 2.0 are on the front lines in the war for business transformation. There will be battles lost and won as stakeholders from end-users, IT, business, vendors, and analyst move enterprises to become real-time mission-focused without losing control. We have seen how some thought leaders that are successfully implementing these technologies are currently dealing with the challenges as well as taking advantage of the opportunities.

END NOTES AND REFERENCES:

1. Tim O'Reilly (2005-09-30). What Is Web 2.0. O'Reilly Network. Retrieved on 2006-08-06.

2. Tim O'Reilly (2006-12-10). Web 2.0 Compact Definition: Trying Again. Retrieved on 2007-01-20.

3. Web 2.0; Wikipedia, http://en.wikipedia.org/wiki/Web_2.0

4. http://www.cioinsight.com/article2/0%2C1540%2C2174694%2C00.asp

5. http://www.informationweek.com/software/showArticle.jhtml?articleID= 201201627

6. John R. Rymer and Connie Moore, "The Dynamic Business Applications Imperative", September 24, 2007

7. Kevin M. Brown, Associate and Eric Yuan Program Manager; Booz Allen Hamilton; brown_kevin_m@bah.com, yuan_eric@bah.com

8. Company; Robert.h.hodges@lmco.com; http://www.lockheedmartin.com/innovation/about.html

9. Keith Sink, Principal Systems Engineer, BEA Government Solutions

10. Another View: The Federal SOA Watershed Do you have what you want or do you want what you have? - Jeff Simpson BEA Systems http://www.gcn.com/online/vol1_no1/42609-1.html

11. Need to Share Doctrine – Jeff Simpson's blog http://fed-soa.blogspot.com/

12. NCES Program Website – http://www.disa.mil/nces/index.html

13. NECC Program Website – http://www.disa.mil/necc/overview.html

14. Wikipedia – Event Driven Architecture at http://en.wikipedia.org/wiki/Event_Driven_Architecture

15. Orchestration for GCCS-J using ALBPM – presentation from Lit Jones and Mike Beauregard Northrop Grumman Mission Systems

16. Robert H. Hodges, Chief SOA Architect, Lockheed Martin

17. Rob Jett, Chief Information officer Redbuffalo, Inc., rjett@red-buffalo.com, www.red-buffalo.com

Building a Scalable and Sustainable BPM Center of Excellence

Clay Richardson, WfMC Public Sector, USA
David Atwood, Bermuda Government, Bermuda

INTRODUCTION

Gartner predicts that by 2008, over 30 percent of the Global 2000 will implement BPM Centers of Excellence to support the rapid growth and adoption of enterprise-wide BPM initiatives[1]. Much of this growth will be fueled by public and private sector organizations embracing BPM as the most effective approach to improving organizational efficiency, collaboration, and competitive advantage.

In most organizations, the BPM Center of Excellence (BPM CoE) serves as the program office for coordinating, prioritizing, and implementing mission-critical BPM projects across the enterprise. In addition, the BPM CoE provides basic governance guidelines for analyzing, implementing, and improving internal business processes.

The need for establishing a centralized BPM program office grew out of political conflicts that were encountered as processes were automated across various departmental and system boundaries. As organizations began to roll out numerous enterprise-wide BPM solutions, they found it effective to consolidate key roles, best practices, and toolsets into a single BPM CoE.

In order to establish successful BPM CoEs, organizations must strive to achieve three major goals:

Sustainability—BPM CoEs must put in place the organizational structures to sustain the cross-department collaboration and momentum for BPM to continue beyond the initial projects, when enthusiasm and commitment are naturally strong.

Scalability—Many organizations have ambitious goals for BPM initiatives and are looking to implement and maintain several BPM projects in parallel. This means creating a CoE framework that can scale to meet their respective visions for BPM.

Collaborative Implementation Methodology—BPM is a new discipline that requires IT and business departments to collaborate and partner in new ways. Organizations must upgrade their implementation methodology to provide a platform for effective collaboration and rapid execution of BPM solutions.

The first generation of BPM CoEs emphasized the need for governance and basic guidelines on how departments should work together to deliver BPM solutions. However, the next generation of BPM CoEs must focus on establishing best practices, skills, and methodologies that are both scalable and sustainable over the long-term.

SUSTAINABILITY: MAINTAINING AND DRIVING MOMENTUM FOR BPM

While BPM introduced new ways of doing business, it also produced many turf wars and political battles. The first generation of BPM CoEs was established to referee many of these internal turf battles. In most cases, BPM CoEs primarily served as cross-departmental "committees" designed to help prioritize, sponsor, and establish basic standards for implementing BPM projects. In addition, many initial BPM CoEs focused on increasing knowledge, awareness, and adoption of BPM within the organization.

Initial Centers of Excellence emphasized establishing governance models that could be enforced across the enterprise. These governance models provided rules and guidelines for prioritizing which BPM projects should be implemented. In many cases, this meant establishing and documenting criteria for evaluating potential BPM projects. Additionally, these initial governance models focused on defining project roles and responsibilities required for BPM projects.

The Next Generation of BPM CoEs

As companies began implementing enterprise-wide BPM, many found that the basic governance components outlined above were insufficient for maintaining momentum and buy-in across the enterprise. In most cases, traditional approaches to establishing BPM CoEs were met with cultural resistance, with many departments viewing the CoE as an additional layer of complexity and governance that could potentially slow down progress and innovation.

Successful BPM Centers of Excellence must begin to address cultural factors within the organization that could hamper enterprise-wide adoption. In this regard, the most important aspect of setting up a BPM Center of Excellence is deciding whether it will act as a "Central Authority" or a "Shared Service" in motivating the enterprise to adopt BPM. Ultimately, this decision will drive the underlying governance model that will need to be established to support the enterprise.

Organization Type	ROI
BPM Center of Excellence	107%
BP Team	26%
No BPM CoE or BP Team	18%
All Respondents	44%

Figure 1: The Next Generation of BPM CoEs Will Drive Greater ROI for Organizations[2]

The "Central Authority" Approach

The first wave of BPM Centers of Excellence emphasized a "Central Authority" model, forcing the rest of the organization to conform and adhere to established guidelines for improving business process or suffer the consequences. While this approach ensured that all BPM projects were implemented and managed in the same way, it also increased the potential that people would see BPM as a negative influence on the organization.

The "Central Authority" approach works best for organizations where strong executive sponsorship has already been established and the organization has embraced BPM as a strategic discipline across the enterprise. This approach is not concerned with driving BPM adoption throughout the enterprise, because it has already been mandated from the "top down."

In some cases, this authoritarian approach might drive line of business managers to explore using other tools or disciplines to improve processes, instead of having to conform to the dictated rules and guidelines forced upon them.

The "Shared Service" Approach

Many organizations have found it more effective to use a "Shared Service" approach that provides basic guidelines, best practices, and knowledge sharing for implementing enterprise-wide BPM. While the "Shared Service" approach typically starts out with a small group of enthusiastic sponsors and key stakeholders, it represents a more sustainable approach that can scale out over time as BPM successes are achieved and adoption spreads throughout the enterprise.

This approach is common within organizations where BPM has not been mandated across the enterprise; or in cases where a small set of pilot projects will be implemented to assess the overall impact of BPM to the organization. If the BPM Center of Excellence is established using the "Shared Service" approach, it is often set up as a support office for helping lines of business with process improvement projects. In some cases, organizations have opted not to even use the term "BPM Center of Excellence" in order to minimize the perception of the "BPM Center of Excellence" as an overarching or overbearing authoritarian entity. For example, some organizations refer to their BPM CoE as the "Better Process Group" or "Process Support Team" to avoid potentially negative perceptions.

Establishing the Ground Rules

After deciding whether to establish a "Central Authority" or "Shared Service" model, organizations should create a basic charter that documents the purpose of the BPM Center of Excellence and its primary goals. Many BPM Centers of Excellence failed simply because they did not define a purpose and key goals. Additionally, the charter should define the basic roles and skill sets that will make up the BPM Center of Excellence.

Of course, a separate "BPM Governance" or "BPM Guidelines" document should be created to begin documenting key governance parameters and guidelines. This includes criteria for prioritizing and selecting process projects, funding considerations, standards, and best practices.

SCALABILITY: ORGANIZING THE BPM CoE FOR GROWTH

Many public and private sector companies have set ambitious goals for implementing numerous enterprise-wide BPM projects simultaneously. These organizations are beginning to view BPM as the key ingredient to improving operational efficiency and competitive advantage.

In order to scale to meet the internal demand for BPM, public and private sector organizations must extend the scope of their BPM CoE to better address *prioritization*, **code management**, and *staffing requirements*. These three factors directly impact the ability of an organization to scale its BPM initiative to support internal requests for BPM solutions.

Improving Process Prioritization

Most BPM CoEs have adopted the "Impact vs. Complexity" model for prioritizing and weighting potential process improvement projects. Using this approach, organizations are able to assess the potential return-on-investment and risks associated with each process improvement project that has been identified. While this approach is simple and elegant, it typically only evaluates the complexities and risks of end-to-end processes within a company.

In many cases, once an end-to-end process is broken down into smaller components, it yields an even richer set of potential initial projects and wins that can be built upon over time. Some organizations refer to this as the "Lego" approach, allowing them to implement low-risk, high-ROI sub-processes first, and then add on new processes over time.

For example, your initial process prioritization matrix might have included your mission-critical "Order to Cash" process. Within the initial matrix, this process might have been categorized as "High Impact," "High Complexity." Typically, these are the types of processes you want to avoid doing first. However, if this is a mission-critical process, it might be difficult politically to avoid doing it first. If this is the case, then consider breaking the "Order to Cash" process down into its sub-components. Once you have the sub-components, use the "Complexity vs. Impact" matrix again to plot each of these sub components. Using this approach, you can quickly see which parts of the process could be implemented immediately and then built onto at later stages.

Code Management and Reuse

One of the dirty little secrets of BPM that most project managers quickly find out is that 60-70 percent of the level of effort on BPM projects is spent on actually developing the underlying solution. Of course, by leveraging BPM Suites, these project managers also are able to deliver solutions in one-half to one-third of the time associated with traditional development projects.

This ability to get things done faster often introduces an unexpected dilemma for organizations: "How do we execute parallel BPM projects without project teams stepping on each other's toes (from a development perspective)?" Most IT managers and project managers are just now beginning to grapple with the fact that shorter delivery cycles often increase the complexity of managing various solution components under development.

Many organizations have resolved this code management challenge by synchronizing Service-Oriented Architecture (SOA) initiatives with their BPM CoE. In many ways, SOA is a natural extension of BPM and vice-versa. Instead of development teams building overlapping components that might introduce conflict these teams are able to develop individual reusable components that can be maintained by a single component repository. As these components are updated, potential compatibility issues can be easily identified and resolved prior to deployment.

> "There are a number of legacy systems in Bermuda Government which have a need for process functionality to support cross-functional workflow. Leveraging our company's consulting resources in conjunction with the Government's BPM tools we are beginning to add needed and reusable process and application services to extend the lifespan of key Government systems."
> Dr. Kevin Mayall, President, AG Research (Bermuda) Ltd.

Overcoming BPM Staffing Challenges

The primary factor limiting the growth of most organizations' BPM initiatives is the lack of internal resources skilled on BPM analysis and development. In a recent report, Gartner indicated that organizations would continue to experience difficulty staffing and retaining BPM talent through 2010[1].

Part of the challenge of staffing BPM projects is that it is difficult to find individuals with the right mix of analysis and technical skill that is required by most BPM projects. However, in order to reap the true benefits of BPM, organizations must find creative ways to mentor and train key personnel to become proficient in analyzing and implementing BPM solutions.

Many organizations are now beginning to embed seasoned external BPM consultants and contractors with their internal BPM team. The embedded model allows team members to be mentored by individuals that have implemented numerous BPM solutions, gaining invaluable best-practices and insights that could not be gleaned from traditional training. Through mentoring and coaching, organizations can quickly ramp up teams of analysts and developers on BPM in six to twelve months.

Additionally, some organizations are exploring the concept of a "co-opetition" model to expand the base of consultants and internal staff that can support enterprise-wide BPM. For example, with its BPM Center of Excellence, the Government of Bermuda invited local vendors to learn best practices and development from its lead BPM vendor.

Using this approach, the Government has been able to increase its pool of BPM resources to include numerous solution providers from across the island. In addition, this approach allows the island to introduce increased competition for implementing BPM solutions, thereby keeping costs at a reasonable level.

METHODOLOGY: FINDING THE BEST FIT

Combining BPM and Agile Development

As a discipline and a technology, business process management provides a platform for business and technical teams to collaborate more effectively and to rapidly deliver process improvements to the enterprise. However, absent a well-defined and standardized implementation methodology, business process management often devolves into two silos operating independently along the fault lines of business and technical.

When selecting a BPM implementation methodology, organizations should choose an approach that:

- Is led by the business owners and business stakeholders;
- Supports rapid solution development and provides a continual feedback loop between business and development teams;
- Supports the ability to capture functionality in a syntax that is understandable to the business;
- Balances the need for requirements documentation against the need to move quickly.

An examination of the various traditional methodologies uncovers that the standard "waterfall" approach is not ideally suited to BPM implementations. Waterfall's emphasis on drawn-out phases of analysis, design, development, and testing increases the likelihood that process requirements will shift before a final solution is released. In addition, the waterfall approach does not provide a continual feedback loop between the business and development teams throughout the development cycle.

By contrast, "agile" methodologies have evolved to support collaborative and rapid development requirements of BPM implementations. Agile development consists of several development and management principles that allow projects to be completed in short time boxes, called iterations. Typical characteristics of agile projects include:

- Early and continuous delivery of usable components;
- Usable deliverables that measure progress;
- Ability to accept changing requirements even late in the project;
- Short delivery cycles;

- Sound, flexible design/architecture.

Most organizations seeking to implement BPM should standardize on an agile methodology that provides sufficient tools for capturing high-level requirements, estimating development time, and fostering collaboration between the business and technical teams. Given these considerations, Scrum, Feature-Driven Development (FDD), and eXtreme Programming (XP) agile methodologies are best suited for implementing process-driven solutions.

	Strengths	Weaknesses
XP	• Most widely known and adopted approach • Business ownership of feature priority, developer ownership of estimates • "Pair Programming" increases knowledge transfer	• Documentation primarily through verbal communication • Difficult to accommodate architectural or design concerns
Scrum	• Solution definition led by self-directed development teams • Priorities based on business value	• Terminology and practices oriented towards technical teams • Little business control over managing and prioritizing features – difficult to scope
FDD	• Solution definition and features owned by the business • All aspects of project tracked by feature – improved control, management, and scoping • Scales well to large teams or projects	• Full implementation requires model-driven approach • Takes time to adjust to "feature" modeling

Figure 2: Identify Which Agile Methodology Best Fits Your BPM Environment

Measure Twice, Cut Once

The key to improving BPM delivery is accurately scoping and estimating the level of effort. Successful BPM Centers of Excellence are beginning to determine and document key drivers that impact overall scope and level of effort for BPM projects. The following are examples of key components or drivers that have a direct impact on overall project scope and level of effort:

- **User Interface Complexity**—In many ways, user interface requirements have the greatest impact on process-related projects. Much of process development and design is about creating an improved "user experience" that simplifies data capture and submission for the user community. If requirements dictate a highly customized user interface that leverages little out-of-the-box functionality, then the project will require custom development using a J2EE or .NET framework, thus, driving up the time required for development. However, if the user interface requirements are simple and require little customization, then out-of-the-box functionality can be leveraged to design processes and forms for capturing user input.
- **Data Management and Synchronization**—Processes that are data intensive typically require a more customized interface to simplify data entry. For example, a process that captures hundreds of records from a user for routing might require a custom user interface in order to implement functionality that improves database performance. Less data intensive processes can leverage out-of-the-box forms and worklist capabilities provided by BPM tools.
- **Application Integration**—Most processes have some form of application integration with backend or legacy systems. To accomplish this integration, in most cases interfaces will need to be developed and integrated into the

process. This usually requires an additional layer of testing to ensure that the integration is functioning properly. The greater the number of integrations, the greater the complexity of the project. A positive note here is that once an integration for a particular application is developed it can be reused within across the enterprise.

- **Number of Activities and Business Rules**—Although the number of activities and business rules can have a major impact on the level of effort, this component usually has less impact than other drivers. The process itself is typically easy to design regardless of the number of activities. An average process contains 10-15 activities which can be modeled out in relatively short order.

CASE STUDY: BERMUDA GOVERNMENT'S "BETTER PROCESS GROUP"

History of the Bermuda Government's BPM Initiative

Bermuda Government's BPM effort first took shape through an enterprise-wide BPM initiative called the "Forms & Transaction Engine" (TXE) project. The primary objective of the TXE project was to automate Government forms and to enable on-line self-service to businesses and citizens across the island.

After identifying an initial list of potential self-service transactions, Government prioritized and ranked these processes based on overall process complexity and impact. Self-service transactions were then organized into three broad categories: 1.) simple on-line forms, 2.) transactions that referenced target systems for validation, and 3.) cross departmental transactions which were more "horizontal" in nature and would facilitate real service transformation.

Once these processes were prioritized, Government quickly realized that it needed to acquire a BPM Suites platform to rapidly deliver self-service solutions to constituents. Bermuda Government ultimately acquired the BEA AquaLogic BPM platform and considered a full scale attack or "D-day approach" to implementing the TXE project. The approach would focus on automating numerous simple online forms first, followed by the more complex transactions.

However, the "D-Day" approach was modified to be a more focused "Special Operations" approach, where the emphasis would be on low hanging fruit and on applications which had strong departmental support and promised real service transformation.

The Cultural Appetite for BPM

One of the challenges in implementing a BPM program in Government is addressing the lack of understanding or appreciation for the benefits of a BPM approach to service transformation. There are generally two drivers for technology enabled change in Government. One is more political or external in nature and is concerned with putting citizens and business "online not inline." The second is more internal and departmentally driven. It is concerned with progressing operational efficiencies as well as online services. When prioritizing change management projects, the issue of "service" will often carry stronger weight than that of "efficiency." Additionally, minimizing speed to deployment is always another critical selection criterion.

But, process improvement by its very nature involves a rigorous analysis of existing procedures. Typically this is a time consuming activity involving detailed process reviews with key stakeholders. Therefore, there is likely to be a natural resistance to implementation of a BPM program in a Government organization and that resistance needs to be countered by an effective means of quantifying and communicating the benefits of a BPM approach based around real deployed examples. Secondly, the delivery cycle of BPM projects should be shorter than traditional development without compromising the rigorous evaluation and improvement of existing processes.

With the demand for fast delivery cycles and a general lack of awareness of the benefits of BPM, the question could be asked as to what were the drivers for the purchase and deployment of the Bermuda Government's TXE solution. One of these was the availability of capital funding. In 2004 when the TXE was acquired, Government was under-spending its IT capital budget. This left room for taking on technology solutions that might be considered more experimental or developmental in nature. Additionally, the department of E-Governments stated mission calls for improving of processes in Government.

> "The focus of IT planning therefore needs to be on the underlying business processes and objectives of the organization, rather than on the technology itself Identifying and improving the interactions that form the foundation of any government process is essential for an E-government initiative to realize its full potential."[3]

Initiating the Solution

A key challenge for the TXE project was internal and on-island staffing. Although there was a commitment to acquire the technology there were limited operating funds for the business analysis resources needed to design and develop candidate processes. A response tactic has been to encourage the vendor community to learn and adopt the tool and provide services to develop subsequent TXE applications. This called for a "co-opetition" model where Project Performance Corporation would actively transfer skills to other solution providers and bring them up to speed in the use of the BPM methodology and toolset.

The first project selected for development was the annual e-manpower survey which is managed by the Statistics Department and collects manpower survey data from the island's employers. The survey is in effect a computer printout of staff sent to each employer for review and revision and then resubmitted to Government. The data is keyed into the Manpower survey system which was developed in the 1980s and runs on the Government's AS400. Two of the key aims of the project were (1) eliminate the need for temporary additional data entry resources to key in the survey returns by providing an online capability for employers to key in their own revisions and (2) leverage the investment in the existing AS400 application and data bases.

Managing BPM projects

The introduction of BPM projects into the mix of IT initiatives has highlighted some governance issues which hold both benefits and challenges for BPM projects moving forward. These concern budget and selection of resources to develop BPM solutions.

IT projects in the Bermuda Government are reviewed and approved by an intra-departmental IT Secretariat, and are subsequently managed using a federated governance approach. While the server infrastructure is centralized in the Governments data center using either the Government's IBM I-series platform or the Government's VMWare environment for Intel-based solutions, the selection of software solutions is driven by the user departments through the Government's tendering process.

The TXE initiative has created the potential for realizing significant benefits in terms of providing a common solution platform where all BPM applications could share the same server, systems, and applications framework. This reduces time to delivery as infrastructure setup has often been one of the primary obstacles in deploying applications. Software - and to some extent, the systems and server infrastructure - deployment issues need not be tackled continually for every new self-service solution.

The TXE has also triggered a return to a more centralized budgeting approach, at least for BPM projects. In fact, there is now a shift towards adopting an IT budget strategy that provides for federated departmental budgets for large scale change initiatives but maintains two centralized budgets one for minor development projects and the other for BPM initiatives.

> "The Government's approach in leveraging its consulting relationships and providing its process technology to those partners is an effective method for providing resources on BPM projects."
> Reno Fiedler, President, Financial Geographics International

This does result in some advantages in managing the pool of capital funds. For example, it is easier to manage and leverage centralized budgets versus decentralized budgets. In addition, departments are not left with the problem of finding funding for their BPM initiatives. One of the risks though, is that the TXE can be used as means of advancing online applications that are not necessarily true BPM projects and could possibly be addressed more effectively by other technology solutions. Moreover, because the budgeting problem for BPM projects has been taken away from departments, the TXE could be used as a means of progressing initiatives which are based more on whimsy than practical need.

To counter these and other issues it is important to develop a clear set of criteria for BPM projects. The following criteria have being established to help identify which projects could and could not benefit from BPM.

Number of Process Steps—If an initiative is really a BPM project then it should have at least five key steps involved in the process. If there are less than five steps, then the initiative likely can be better met by the development of an online database.

Ownership—Without a strong commitment from the user department a BPM project will flounder or at least its time lines will be significantly extended. That's because the drive from the project will have to come from the solution provider rather than the users which is not a good recipe for successful implementation. If a situation exists where there is a limited readiness from the client department but it's not politically expedient to avoid the project, it's then advisable to do the initial requirements and limit the scope to a prototype and first release product. This can be enhanced later in step with the department's overall priorities.

Inter-departmental Deployment—Ideally BPM should be used to create horizontality in the organization and should be leveraged to developing and deploying cross-departmental processes. However, if similar ownership issues arise with a particular stakeholder department, it would better to adopt a strategy of reduced scope and future phasing of subsequent releases until ownership issues have been addressed.

Level of Complexity—BPM projects come in one of two flavors: (1) smaller process initiatives within a single department, or (2) larger initiatives involving two or more departments and incorporating several legacy applications into the solution. A larger project will require significantly more (and probably external) development resources whereas smaller projects can be developed and deployed using minimal internal technical resource. User interface (UI) requirements should also be carefully considered. Complex UI requirements can often drive up cost.

Post implementation Reviews

As noted earlier, BPM projects need to show a demonstrable improvement in the business environment and so it is a good practice to conduct post implementation reviews of projects, quantify the improvements made and document lessons learned for future initiatives. The BPM software used by the Bermuda Government has a "Business Activity Monitor" component which measures and forecasts volumes and costs. This capability can reduce the level of resource needed for post implementation reviews, thus increasing the likelihood of conducting them.

Resourcing BPM projects

The appetite for BPM in the Government and the resulting challenges in finding business analyst resources has called for creative methods in resourcing projects. E-Government did not want to depend on its primary vendor to resource its projects over a long period of time so it has taken steps to create an alternative resource method.

To encourage a more process-oriented culture in the organization and as a "seed bed" for potential resources, the department of E-Government creates a center of Excellence called the Better Process Group or BPG. The BPG is made up of a "coalition of the willing" of business professionals from a number of Government departments; these are not business analysts per se, but civil servants with a leaning or interest in "process." Representatives from the local vendor community are also involved and will act as a resource backbone for future BPM projects. In some cases the vendor can add process functionality to projects they already support. The BPG acts as a think tank for reviewing and improving processes and as a steering committee for BPM projects. E-Government has organized several BPM training sessions for the BPG. The intent is, that at the very least, these officers will promote the BPM message to the rest of Government.

In conclusion, the formation of the BPG and E-Governments BPM strategy in general is essentially taking the "carrot approach" to an enterprise BPM implementation. Currently, Departmental Directors are not held accountable for progressing service horizontality but for the delivery of their specific program objectives. Therefore it is felt that this is a realistic and pragmatic path to an enterprise adoption of BPM.

WORKS CITED

1. Hill, J. (2006). Predicts 2007: Internal Skills Are Inadequate for BPM. Stamford: Gartner.
2. Palmer, N. (2007). Survey of Business Process Initiatives. BP Trends.
3. Bermuda E-Government Report. March 2002

Disclaimer: The views expressed in the paper are those of the authors and do not necessarily reflect the views of the Bermuda Government.

Making Intelligence Actionable: Business Process Management and Business Intelligence

Patrick Morrissey, Savvion, United States

ABSTRACT

Business Process Management picks up where Business Intelligence leaves off—by making intelligence *actionable*.

INTRODUCTION

For more than 15 years, Business Intelligence (BI) has lived at the intersection of people and data with the noble goal of making people and organizations smarter. The vision of turning data into intelligence has become a reality for many corporations and groups. Numerous studies suggest that BI projects deliver measurable ROI. The premise behind the growth of the tools and the BI category is simple: Information is good.

But, for many organizations, the ability of individuals, teams and departments to apply the "intelligence" they've gathered from BI into an actionable plan or process isn't possible. The information companies get from BI projects isn't matched to the underlying processes that inform how people work. So, the processes aren't repeatable, measurable, or captured in any enterprise systems.

Most organizations using BI solutions don't see sustainable, repeatable business improvement for three key reasons:

- Most functional business line owners don't know the details of their daily business processes.
- BI metrics and analytics aren't made actionable.
- Existing applications and systems that track process don't map to the way people work.

Despite these challenges, companies pour millions of dollars into analytics, reporting, infrastructure, and systems every year and don't see full return on their investments. Many common escalation issues and exceptions to common business rules are handled as one-offs, in a combination of manual work, e-mail, and meetings. BI awareness doesn't turn into action, much less repeatable improvement. The opportunity is to turn that information into action. This is where Business Process Management (BPM) picks up and BI leaves off—by making intelligence actionable.

Many organizational issues are really process issues. The "as-is" process of "how things are done" isn't well-understood, documented, or audited by functional departments and leaders. The process of doing something as simple as approving, booking, and shipping a sales order isn't well-understood, nor consistent across teams and organizations.

Compounding the problem are:
- The complexity of legacy systems
- Regulatory requirements
- Mergers and acquisition job rotations

- Evolving business and product strategy
- Varied processes due to language and culture differences.

BPM enables work processes that are captured in people's heads and as shared experiences to be recognized, defined, and translated into automated processes. This simplifies and expedites workflow across an organization and on the global stage.

Forrester Research and IDC are both doing research on the intersections and convergence of BI and BPM. IDC has coined the term Intelligent Process Automation (IPA) to help explain the convergence and complementary nature of the BPM and BI markets. Both research organizations are commenting on the need to make BI actionable and process improvement repeatable.

The leading BI vendors have recently expanded their product portfolios to move out of IT departments and directly address the needs of business operators. The goal is to help companies manage the complexity of the business and process of improving performance. Balanced Scorecards and Total Quality Management (TQM) remain buzzwords. While the industry has consolidated into a handful of leading players—Business Objects, Cognos, SAS and Hyperion foremost among them—their product portfolios have expanded with a myriad of dashboard, scorecards, custom and packaged analytics.

The marketing message for business audiences is simple: Manage your most important metrics consistently across all departments and functional areas to drive improved financial performance. The message for IT is almost equally as simple: Manage your entire applications systems infrastructure and data warehouse with centralized administration, data cleansing, data integration and metadata management to provide complete intelligence for the enterprise. All these things should mean enterprise improvement. Unfortunately, just having information is useless unless you can apply it in a constructive way to productive ends. In essence, BI provides information, but doesn't provide the decision makers with the tools needed to gain benefit, or create action, on the processes that yield inefficiencies.

PEOPLE OR PROCESS?

Many companies can't articulate the way they work today. Corporate leaders know, for example, that they have too much margin exposure, that returns management is a problem and that new product introduction is key to success over the next several quarters. Yet those same leaders can't clearly articulate the order management process, don't have confidence that everyone on the team is executing against the same metrics, and know it's still taking them too long to get sales orders approved, inventory shipped and sales people paid. Wasn't BI going to solve these problems?

If you can't manage what you can't measure, then the first step to business performance is process articulation. The first step in a performance management strategy should be to bring business and IT owners and contributors to the table to share in a common definition of the current process. This may be a new product introduction, expense management or quote to cash. Almost without exception, any process can be improved and many can be automated. BPM provides the catalyst required to take the information gathered from BI and create actionable processes for improvement.

All the data and analytics in the world are worthless if no one understands how they inform the process of how people work. The core value proposition of BPM is the ability to articulate, simulate, and optimize this informed knowledge of how people work and integrate it into the enterprise.

When organizational improvement starts from a focus on people, it increases the likelihood that analytics can be applied to decision points that drive measurable, repeatable improvement. BPM provides a prescription for analytics and progressive, measurable improvement. It also helps configure information and context to accommodate the way people work, increasing repeatability of the process.

PROCESS: MAKING IMPROVEMENT ACTIONABLE

Once the process is defined and optimized, it's critical that it become actionable. This is where the intersection of BI and BPM is best illustrated. BI and analytics platforms with Business Activity Monitoring (BAM) are great for helping identify a problem—often in near real-time. However, they often fail when it comes to helping the user actually do anything about the problem.

For the IT side of the house, a BPM platform allows system-to-system, system-to-human interactions and human-to-human exchanges to be captured in a repeatable, manageable way as a complete solution. BPM allows execution on business activities without production system or code changes or human intervention. In addition, these solutions can be supported with minimal IT involvement while working with existing legacy infrastructure and systems. BPM often fills in the gap where existing anchor applications leave off when business conditions change and people have problems.

For business line owners and management, BPM makes metrics actionable, often without requiring direct human interactions. It lets business owners drive process improvement while providing the flexibility for the process to reflect the way people and teams actually work. It enables process improvement without big bang costs or large IT integration projects. Often, initial process projects can be deployed in 30 to 90 days. The result is a strategic approach to process that starts with rapid modeling and iteration followed by a fast roll-out, enabling measurable results. Using BPM, organizations can begin improving top-line and bottom-line metrics in the same quarter they're rolled out.

AVOID UNNATURAL ACTS WITH EXISTING APPLICATIONS

The reality for many organizations is that process improvement is stalled by the legacy of past failed projects and a lack of concrete requirements from business owners. IT budgets are often constrained and IT departments naturally default to existing infrastructure and systems for new projects when possible. The hard truth is that existing systems don't match the way people work and every system that ever reached the capital expenditure committee has some form of workflow. With multiple projects, teams, applications, geographies and workflow tools, process improvement can turn into chaos. The result: workflow gone wild.

The outcome is that organizations attempt to respond to people-driven process issues by attempting to perform unnatural acts with existing applications. While BI has helped fill some of the information gap for people, it hasn't truly unlocked the promise of putting data in the hands of people where it can become actionable. In addition, complex middleware and application infrastructure may conspire to make the problem worse. Add the buzz about SOA, the requirements around compliance, and business owners' insistence on "real-time" everything, and process projects and problems become hugely complex and costly. In this scenario, the likely outcome is highly taxed IT systems and people who aren't equipped to truly solve the underlying problem.

BPM provides the ability to capture users and system requirements to optimize how people work. It's more than just workflow or a Visio diagram. In BPM, the same process model that's defined, iterated, and optimized becomes the application specification to deploy in an enterprise environment. The model becomes the common language to meet user requirements for automating and improving processes and the IT specification for system connections, business rules, and data architecture.

Process management tools also become a highly customizable platform to enable the continued, rapid roll-out of process applications while maintaining common security, administration, flexibility and control.

When considering investments in BI, don't just think about the ability to consistently monitor metrics and reports; instead, think about intelligence as content and context for how people and organizations work. The ability to unlock the power of intelligence is usually directly connected to the organization's ability to define their current processes, optimize and improve those processes and make them actionable.

BPM becomes the engine to drive the performance-driven organization to the next level. It should be considered a strategic part of a business improvement strategy and IT architecture. More importantly, process should be considered key to competitive advantage, something you can't get from BI alone. Process makes your BI strategy actionable.

CONCLUSION

Business

- BI provides information, but doesn't provide the decision makers with the tools needed to gain benefit, or create action, on processes that yield inefficiencies.
- The first step to business performance is process articulation—any process can be improved and many can be automated.
- BPM lets companies articulate, simulate, and optimize the knowledge of how people work and integrate it into the enterprise, making intelligence actionable.

Technology

- Existing systems often don't match the way people actually work. A BPM platform lets system-to-system, system-to-human interactions and human-to-human exchanges be captured in a repeatable, manageable way as a complete solution.
- BPM begins with a process model that becomes the common language to meet user requirements for automating and improving processes and the supporting IT specifications.
- Many initial BPM projects can be deployed in 30 to 90 days.

Applying Decision Management to Make Processes Smarter, Simpler and More Agile[1]

James Taylor and Neil Raden,
Smart (Enough) Systems LLC, United States

ABSTRACT

Identifying, automating and managing the decisions within a process are critical next steps for greater efficiency and effectiveness in organizations today. The focus of automation to date has been on efficiency gains from streamlined workflow, automated integration of information systems and managed worklists. Many largely automated processes remain over-reliant on human intervention at critical junctures. Others are burdened with legacy code or complex processes to handle decision making and are unnecessarily resistant to change as a result. Smarter, simpler and more agile processes are needed.

INTRODUCTION

When organizations work on process automation and process management, they often focus on efficiency gains. They streamline workflow so that tasks are linked more directly and so that integration of existing systems is automated. They eliminate duplicate entry and rework, reduce handoffs and improve utilization through better work management. What they often fail to do is make significant strides toward true straight-through processing because they remain dependent on human interactions to move transactions along. Using business process management technology to improve the situation often results in overly complex processes that are difficult to change, especially if the process is a long running one.

The primary reason for manual intervention in a process is decision making—when a decision is required the process waits for a person to make the decision. While many organizations invest much time and energy in improving one-off, high impact decisions, they often neglect the decisions that drive the day to day operations of their business. These operational decisions are abdicated to programmers or left to front-line staff with no strategic control or management understanding. Many of these decisions are not even recognized as such and are hidden in processes or systems.

Organizations must identify the operational decisions that are hidden in their processes if they are to move to the next level of process automation. Only by automating and managing the decisions within a process is it possible to deliver greater efficiency and effectiveness of processing. Decision automation can eliminate manual reviews for faster throughput. It allows decision making approaches to change independent of process changes. It puts business users in control of the logic in their processes. All of this contributes to the creation of precise, consistent and agile operations. Furthermore, decision points represent the ideal

---

[1] All quotes are from the authors' book "Smart (Enough) Systems", Prentice Hall 2007, unless otherwise noted.

place within a process to add analytic insight, increasingly a source of competitive advantage for companies as they try to use their data more effectively.

The limitations of a purely process-centric approach can be addressed by identifying and managing decisions, especially certain kinds of decisions, and there are some practicalities involved in creating linked processes and decisions to drive a business.

THE LIMITATIONS OF A PROCESS-CENTRIC APPROACH

The adoption of business process management and workflow technologies is often driven by a desire for greater efficiency. Organizations find themselves burdened with inefficient processes that require multiple systems to be used by various groups of employees. Data must often be re-entered from one system to another and completion of a step in one system has no linkage with the next step in a different system. The power of a business process management system (BPMS) to integrate these systems and coordinate these steps eliminates waste and improves throughput.

The risk that a process automation project will simply automate inefficient processes has been extensively covered in the literature. Even if a "to-be" process is the one automated, however, a process-centric approach tends to assume that only two basic components must be coordinated—existing systems and tasks performed by people. The problem with this is twofold.

- Firstly, many existing systems are extremely "dumb"—they store data, manage it and regurgitate it on command. They have little or no ability to learn from the data they collect and no knowledge of the rules and regulations that constrain how the business operates. These "legacy" systems have been built to support the largely stable business of the past rather than to cope with the dynamic business environment in which organizations now operate. These "dumb" systems tend to wait rather than act—wait for some human to come along and push a button, select a menu option, approve a work item. If organizations are to introduce any kind of intelligence into their processes, then, they have to assign a human to provide it. This brings us to the second problem.

- The assumption that the intelligence in processes can be provided by humans has a number of critical challenges. As the speed at which businesses must respond increases it becomes increasingly unreasonable to rely on humans in the process. Not only do humans take too long to respond in transactions measured in milliseconds, they may not be available when a decision is required (after hours, for instance, or while they are in a meeting), leading to long delays. The irresistible trend towards self-service compounds this by creating more situations in which there is no-one (besides the customer) to make a decision anyway. Finally, in an era of dynamic pricing and terabytes of relevant data, it is not clear that a human is capable of the best decision anyway, even if it were possible to wait for one to make a decision.

If an organization decides, or is forced, to inject intelligence into processes, then a process-centric approach runs a risk that its "process hammer" will make everything look like a nail. An organization **can** use a BPMS to define the steps in a decision and try to manage the decision like it is part of a process. However, this leads to overly complex processes with dozens or even hundreds of steps and branches tied into the process to automate a business decision. Furthermore, changing these decisions is now tied inextricably into the process definition, forcing updates in the process for any change in the rules governing the decision. This forced synchronization drains business value from the effort. The definers of the process steps and the decision logic are different groups and synchronizing their work is not simple.

In Smart (Enough) Systems we summarize the risks from a purely process-centric approach:

> A BPMS doesn't manage business rules or decisions properly. It manages process orchestration and process flow design, but not rules or policies. A BPMS does have some support for rules, but usually only as part of the definition of orchestration or composition. As a result, business rules and the decisions they automate are an afterthought.

> Without explicit management, business rules are reburied in the new process, which makes the process complex. Routing rules aren't business rules; decision centered business rules are about the organization's underlying behavior, not its processes.

> Inconsistency in business rules is likely. This inconsistency is a problem, particularly if you need several kinds of BPMSs, and embedding policy rules in each BPMS means duplicating them and failing to manage them as an asset. Ensuring enterprise consistency in processes is hard unless you manage the decisions in them separately.

> Problems with consistency and rule management can cause trouble when regulators ask you to explain how you picked a particular branch in your process. Being able to explain just the process is not enough. Noncompliance caused by faulty business rules is likely, leading to fines.

> Although you can add process analytics to a process, you can improve the process only manually. Someone must examine and redesign the process. If you have automated decision points and manage them, you can use analytics to improve a process by adding analytic models to aid automated decision making.

> Personalizing transactions for customers is hard unless you make transaction-centered decisions in the process. You probably don't want to create a personalized process for each customer, but personalizing the decisions you make about customers as they run through a standard process might be just as effective.

> You might not get the business agility you're looking for. Although some problems require a change in process definition, others do not. Especially in a core process that doesn't change much, agile management of decisions could matter more.

The solution is to consider the business decisions within these processes as "first class" objects to be managed—to adopt an approach known as "enterprise decision management".

ENTERPRISE DECISION MANAGEMENT

Enterprise Decision Management (EDM), or Business Decision Management as it is sometimes known, is an approach for automating and improving high-volume operational decisions. Focusing on *operational decisions*, it develops *decision ser-*

vices using *business rules* to automate those decisions, adds analytic insight to these services using *predictive analytics* and allows for the ongoing improvement of decision-making through *adaptive control and optimization.*

The five concepts identified in italics in the definition above and shown in the figure below underlie the approach. Decision Services provide a standard architectural concept to handle decision automation, business rules are the backbone of decision automation while predictive analytics ensure that corporate data is put to work in automated decision making. Finally adaptive control and related optimization techniques ensure that the inherent uncertainties involved in decision making can be managed and that decisions can be improved over time.

Operational Decisions

EDM improves processes by externalizing the operational decisions that control them. These decisions are not the big, high-value decisions beloved of management consultants and CEOs. These decisions are those required to make day to day operations run effectively. They ensure that customers are treated consistently, that the right price is offered, that policies are applied correctly and consistently, that the most effective offer is made. While the value of each individual decision is small, the cumulative effect is very largely thanks to the huge numbers of these decisions in all but the smallest organizations.

Decision Services

> A **decision service** can be defined as a self-contained, callable component with a view of all conditions and actions that need to be considered to make an operational business decision. More simply, it's a component or service that answers a business question for other services.

Best practices for business process management include using a service-oriented architecture to underpin the process definitions. Services expose the legacy applications to be integrated into the process and ensure that new components are built in a reusable way. The most effective way to introduce the automation and management of decisions into a process management environment is to create Decision Services. A decision service is typically a stateless service invoked at a point in time where the decision is made and synchronously returning an answer. A decision service makes no change to the organization's state—it does not update the core systems of an organization. It just makes decisions. This separation of concerns is very helpful when managing the decision over time as any system or process can call the decision service to get an answer without having to worry about side effects. This allows a decision to be reused across all the processes that need it and there are often many.

Business Rules

business rules can be considered statements of the actions you should take when certain business conditions are true.

Business rules are the core building block of decisions and of decision services. Business rules are atomic, in that each is a single statement that can be reused and managed separately, and declarative in that the order of execution of business rules is not determined when they are written but is determined by the state of the business and of the information about the business at the time they are executed. For example:

If Customer has at least 5 orders and Customer's LastOrderDate is less than 90 days and Customer's Order's Value.Total is more than $10,000 then set Customer's Status to "Gold"

If Patient's DrugList contains "Drug1" and Patient's DrugList contains "Drug2" then set DrugConflict to True and add "Drug 1 and Drug2 can interact in patients with high blood pressure" to DrugConflictReasons and set DrugConflictLevel to "Warning"

If thisPart is of type "Fuel Tank" and thisPart's Position is less than 10cm from anyPart of type "Battery" then move(thisPart)

While these examples seem straightforward to code in almost any environment, the use of business rules to encode them has a number of advantages: the syntax used is typically clearer to a non-programmer; the rules (and decisions) can easily be reused in multiple processes and systems; no sequence is implied in the rules making them easier to edit independently and without unintended consequences. Business rules also lend themselves to graphical representations such as decision trees and decision tables.

The use of business rules in decision management should not be confused with the use of business rules in the definition and management of a process. Business rules, being declarative and atomic, are often used to manage routing and other workflow-related issues. This is a perfectly good use of rules but it is not the same as decision management and should not be confused with it.

The most effective way to manage business rules for EDM is to use a Business Rules Management System or BRMS. A BRMS is a complete system for authoring, managing, maintaining and deploying the business rules of an organization. There is a flourishing market for these products and a number of well established vendors.

Predictive Analytics

Descriptive analytics use various techniques to improve understanding of the data, such as clustering, grouping, or segmenting information into useful categories.

Predictive analytic models are designed to make predictions about a specific customer, product, or transaction, such as the likelihood of a transaction being fraudulent, a customer accepting an offer, or a delivery being late.

One of the most powerful features of EDM and the inclusion of decision services in automated processes is the ability to bring analytics into play. When people make decisions they increasingly rely on reports, dashboards, and visualizations of large volumes of data, OLAP cubes and more. When a decision is automated, new ways are required to bring to bear the insight afforded by an organization's data. Our decision services cannot read reports or use Excel, however. Here the tools and techniques of data mining and predictive analytics come into play.

Data mining can investigate data about customers and products, stores and delivery routes. The trends and characteristics derived using these techniques can be represented as business rules about how best to handle the next customer or the next delivery. Going beyond data mining and into more advanced predictive analytics, predictions can be made about how customers, prospects or products might behave in the future. New rules can be written to take advantage of these predictions, such as customer treatment rules for those customers predicted to be retention risks or to become more profitable in the future.

While Business Intelligence/Performance Management platforms often have data mining and predictive features, the use of predictive analytics in EDM will typically require a specialist workbench. Such data mining or analytic workbenches are aimed mostly at statistically-aware users, although some are focused on business users. These workbenches handle the complex math involved in analyzing the data and developing a valid model from it.

Decision services allow these insights to be applied not just to broad statements or corporate strategies, but deep down into the day-to-day operations of your business processes.

Adaptive Control and Optimization

While you have control of many of the forces that drive a particular process or system change, the things that affect a decision are often out of your control. The "best" decision at any given moment might be constrained by company policies and external regulations, determined in part by the behavior of competitors and influenced always by how the customers impacted by the decision respond and how that response changes over time.

This means that a decision must constantly be challenged to see if the situation that led to it being automated a certain way remains valid. Using an adaptive control infrastructure, one that allows multiple approaches or strategies to be compared, is by far the most effective way to do this. Multiple approaches, typically one "best" called the champion and several other candidates called challengers, are available when executing a decision service. The service picks a small number of transactions and randomly assigns them to each challenger. The process using the decision service is responsible for keeping track of which approach was used and for ensuring that results can be compared. Performance management tools are then used to compare the results of the challengers to the champion approach. Poorly performing challengers are replaced with new approaches while one that outperforms the champion is considered for promotion to be the new champion going forward.

This approach both protects against unforeseen or unexpected changes in the environment, it also allows for constant improvement. Even this approach is still judgmental, however, as someone has to design the new approaches. Adopting optimization technology to come up with the new challengers can be event more effective but requires a deeper and more mathematically precise understanding of how the decision works.

While it is common to find adaptive control infrastructure in pre-packaged EDM applications, these are typically built specifically for the decision being automated. Thus a credit line management system will have adaptive control for new credit offers built in. For new or custom applications, organizations will need to build their own infrastructure. A combination of a BRMS and standard performance management capabilities is usually best.

PRACTICAL CONSIDERATIONS

Organizations pondering EDM should bear in mind some practical considerations. Not all organizations are ready for EDM, some new technology is likely to be required and there will likely be some impact on the organization as a whole.

Readiness

There are a number of ways in which organizational readiness can be an issue when adopting the techniques and technologies discussed in this paper. Part of the value added by EDM comes from being able to derive usable insight from your data. At some level, therefore, organizations must be ready to use this data (have some idea of its quality, cleanliness, degree of integration and so on) and have a basic understanding of what analytics tell them about this data. Even organizations with a good understanding of their data will need to consider their analytic sophistication. Predictive analytics and data mining are typically considered the more complex as well as the more valuable uses of data. While the return on investment can be very great, there are new skills and approaches to learn.

EDM also changes the balance of power between business and IT groups and forces (or enables, depending on your perspective) much more business and IT collaboration than is common in most organizations. Organizations with a history of cooperation between business and IT organizations will find this easier than those with more challenging relationships. A lack of such collaboration may well be one of the driving forces for adopting EDM, however, so the issue is mostly one of assessing the degree of investment needed to bring the organizations together sufficiently.

Finally, like all projects, adopting EDM requires executive sponsorship. Because the focus of EDM is on the decisions in **operational** processes, this requires an executive team that has a focus on operations. The executives must regard operational excellence as important. They must also "walk the walk" when it comes to running the business "by the numbers" and be committed to the effective implementation of business strategy at every level. Surprisingly some executives consider themselves above worrying about day-to-day operations. Organizations with this orientation should probably not attempt broad adoption of EDM, and might want to think about some executive changes also.

Technology adoption

Most organizations do not have all the technology they need to successfully adopt EDM. It is true that most BPMS solutions contain both business rules and analytics. However, in almost all cases, the rules capability of the BPMS is focused on the handling of workflow and process-centric rules not the automation of real business decisions. Some BPMS solutions have partnerships with Business Rules Management System (BRMS) vendors to address this need.

Similarly the analytics most BPMS vendors discuss are often reports and graphs, not true analytic models. While reporting and dashboards are important in understanding the dynamics of a process and enable some improvements of the process over time, this is not the same as embedding analytic models into the process. To adopt EDM, organizations will need to upgrade their analytics skills to include those of data mining and building executable analytic models. More often than not this involves adopting additional data mining or analytic workbenches.

Organizational change

Adopting EDM will change the processes that run an organization's operations. It will change how many of those processes run "hands-free," how many staff are needed to manage and execute those processes, what it means to perform certain roles, and how executives influence the behavior of their business going forward. The power of EDM to affect this kind of change is part of its value but, like any transformative approach, its impact must be managed.

EDM can change not only processes and systems, it can also have a very real impact on the jobs people do. A knowledge worker may go from reviewing many applications, for instance, to focusing on exceptions and business growth while a system handles most applications. A call center representative may have to change her or his behavior in the face of improved and more detailed advice from an automated system. Organizations with a history of resisting change will need to plan for more of a transition than those who have done better in this regard.

CONCLUSIONS AND SUMMARY

Taking a purely process-centric approach to automation can result in less complete automation and more complex processes than necessary. Organizations attempting to automate their business processes and achieve both straight-through processing and true business agility will need to do more. The diagram below shows what is required. Decisions previously taken by people, or not made at all, are replaced by embedded, automated decisions. Decisions previously hidden in process definitions or legacy code are exposed and managed thoughtfully. Processes that used to wait for a person to be available and then rely on that person's judgment are replaced with fully automated processes that take advantage of compliant, accurate, automated decisions. This automation in turn frees up the people involved in the process to spend their time making new decisions—decisions that improve customer service, handle corner-cases more effectively or have the potential to grow the business.

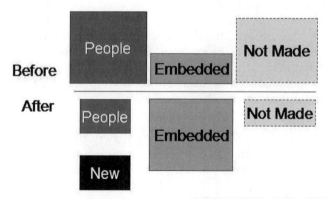

Larger boxes represent more decisions, by volume

Identifying the high-volume, operational decisions that are part of an organization's day-to-day business processes and then applying enterprise decision management or EDM to automate, manage and improve those decisions will make the processes smarter, simpler and more agile.

Business Process Architecture and Business Transformation

Chris Lawrence, Old Mutual South Africa, South Africa

INTRODUCTION

Logical process architecture and change methodology are two sides of the same coin. Organizations who know this and know what to do with it will beat the competition. This is why BPM is so crucial. But architecture and methodology sound academic and expensive, so people in organizations are often reluctant to think about them long enough to see the coin.

This paper takes, as its point of departure, a proven business process metamodel which has been elaborated from a number of perspectives elsewhere.[1, 2, 3, 4, 5] The metamodel sees process as an architectural entity derived from data and rules rather than an empirical fact or democratic artifact. It can support selection, design and configuration of IT systems, and therefore also the evaluation of IT systems in the service of business processes.

Systems shape work and how people see and think about work. Internal and external support teams employ cognitive models shaped by the systems their careers and incomes depend on. Systems and system ownership have so shaped organizational design and politics that even 'logical' architecture and delivery methodologies often only have meaning in terms of systems which happen to be in place.

From a process perspective business IT history was back to front. Recordkeeping first, with process (workflow) a later add-on. This was understandable as history but less forgivable in its unexamined, protectionist result: back-to-front legacy thinking, translating the profound tautology 'process-centric = customer-centric' into a complex overhead of duplication and falsehood. Meanwhile Lean and Six Sigma stay aloof and go for soft targets. But this won't do for 'BPM', and it won't beat the competition. A new generation of business analysts must not take everything vendors and consultants throw at them, but must understand a business as a set of interacting processes; understand a process as an architectural entity derived from data and rules; and only then evaluate the solution space.

---

[1] Lawrence, C. P. (2005a). *Make work make sense: An introduction to business process architecture.* Cape Town, South Africa: Future Managers (Pty) Ltd. (http://www.makeworkmakesense.com)

[2] Lawrence, C. P. (2005b). *Integrated function and workflow.* In Layna Fischer (Ed.), *Workflow handbook 2005.* Lighthouse Point, Florida: Future Strategies Inc, in association with the Workflow Management Coalition.

[3] Lawrence, C. P. (2007a). *Business process architecture and the Workflow Reference Model.* In Layna Fischer (Ed.), *BPM & Workflow handbook 2007.* Lighthouse Point, Florida: Future Strategies Inc, in association with the Workflow Management Coalition.

[4] Lawrence, C. P. (2007b). *Architecture-driven business transformation.* In Pallab Saha (Ed.), *Handbook of enterprise systems architecture in practice.* Hershey, Pennsylvania: Idea Group Inc.

[5] Lawrence, C. P. (2007c). *Business process integration in a knowledge-intensive service industry.* In Wing Lam & Venky Shankararaman (Ed.), *Enterprise architecture and integration: Methods, implementation, and technologies.* Hershey, Pennsylvania: Idea Group Inc.

AN ELEPHANT IN CONTEXT

Business process architecture, or rather the need for it, is like the elephant in the room. We know it's there but we don't know what to say about it. Why is this? One reason is the IT investment mantra: *reuse, then buy, then build*. From a corporate IT customer's perspective anything that smacks of *build*—design included—is immediately on the back foot. Product selection meanwhile enjoys the happy end of the continuum, particularly if product promises to make legacy reusable.

There are good reasons for *reuse, buy, build*. But it can discourage analytical thinking about business architecture and critical thinking about the alignment between technology and business. If *reuse* is top prize, then arguments that what you have is OK will be rewarded. If *buy* gets silver, then discovering that what is for sale is OK will also be popular.

This is not to imply that legacy and proprietary technologies are always bad. That would be absurd. The intention is in any case not to critique legacy or proprietary technologies *per se*, but expose assumptions they might encourage or reinforce.

A word on context. Much of the discussion will involve generalizations, but a generalization is not a universal truth. The context is not necessarily all business processes. It is that large subset describable as rule-based administration: financial services, local and central government, purchase ordering, contracting, HR management etc etc. It is a huge domain—the potential market for BPM systems in fact.

A BRIEF HISTORY

Economic trends affecting business IT over time are summed up as in *Figure 1*.

It is no surprise that systems first focused on record-keeping: products, orders, payments, contracts, applications, agents, customers; and then transactions—event records changing the status of these 'master' records. A business process was something people did around (and in interaction with) systems, occasionally fast-tracked by bursts of automation inside or in between the systems themselves.

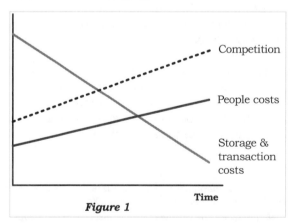

Figure 1

Then workflow made at least some parts of some offices paperless. A 'workflow' is kind of the same thing as a business process and kind of not. Workflow starts when it starts, which might be after the 'end-to-end process' begins. It controls sequences of interaction and distributes work between and within teams. But important subsets of the business rules coded as either data or program logic inside administration systems have process implications. These rules must be duplicated in or somehow accessible to workflow if workflow is to be coherent and comprehensive. Hence the debate about what is a product rule, what is a process rule, what is a compliance rule; and where does process logic belong—as if this was a question about the world like 'where do fish belong?'.

IT has archaeological strata, but IT systems are not natural kinds. Administration systems are rarely process-architected to any extent—the concept of 'business process' is rarely implemented inside them. Even their 'long-running transactions' reflect few of the ifs, buts and maybes of a real end-to-end process. Workflow systems on the other hand typically come from vendors who need their products to be generic like email and spreadsheets. Workflow fits outside or alongside administration systems because it primarily supports, controls, organizes and empowers the human users of those systems. Ergo the business process is something people do around administration systems.

But this is a false paradigm, created by IT history. Before exposing it though we must bring our history more up to date.

PROCESSES AND SERVICES

Service-oriented architecture (SOA) is the 21st-Century panacea, the redemption of legacy and proprietary technology. What we have is OK or can be made OK by componentizing it. What we can buy is OK as long as its services are exposed. 'Services' is business-speak. We have all we need—or do we?

A business needs services, needs to offer services to customers, suppliers and partners. How does a business process relate to a service? Is a process a service or a type of service? Is a process a set of services? Is a service a set of processes? Do we need processes if we have services? We need workflow, because we need people's work to be organized, distributed and controlled: is workflow a service, or a set of services?

We have a metamuddle. We want a number of things to be true, and true together.

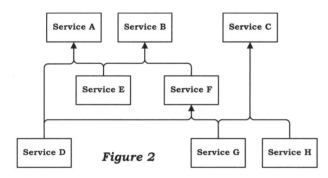

Figure 2

We want componentized services, and we want them modular and hierarchical. In *Figure 2* service B is made from services E and F, while F is made from D and G.

We want end-to-end business processes; and relationships between processes and services. In *Figure 3* process BP1 uses services A, F and H, and BP2 uses B and H.

But we also want 'business services', where an organizational entity can provide services to other entities, and perhaps receive revenue for supplying them: see *Figure 4*.

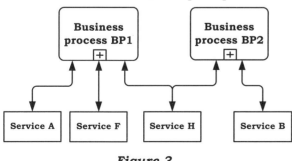

Figure 3

How do business services BS1-BS5 in *Figure 4* relate to processes BP1 and BP2 in *Figure 3*? Are they the same thing? Or are BS1-BS5 in *Figure 4* the same thing as services A, B, C etc in *Figure 2*?

The vision seems to be of organizational entities controlling portfolios of services and offering them to internal and external customers. They are modular and composable—sets of services assembled into composite services as in *Figure 2*. But does this work all the way down, so the service portfolio of division D1 in *Figure 4* could include (say) services B, E and H in *Figure 2*, and division D2's could include services A, C, D, F and G?

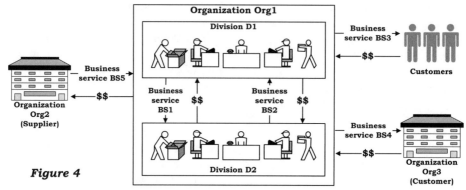

Figure 4

Questions like these need choices rather than answers. At a business-architectural level an organization must choose its 'primitives', its 'axioms'. Otherwise those accountable for technology architecture will not have clear guidelines to follow or share.

In particular, if the definitions of, and relationships between, *service* and *business process* are left undefined the result could be a conceptual free-for-all eating up both real cost and opportunity cost. This kind of thinking is not trivial. It is after

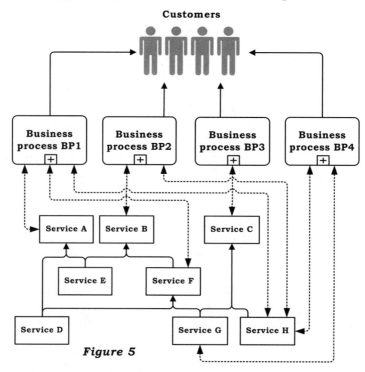

Figure 5

all what underpins debate about how BPM and SOA can or should work together to deliver business value.

Three models will now be contrasted. It is not that one is right and the others wrong. Nor are they the only models. But they show the kind of choice organizations need to make at logical architectural level. They may not all hold true for the same place at the same time. Remember also the context: rule-based administration in financial services, government, ordering, contracting etc.

Figure 5 is a model where the reference point is the business process. Processes BP1-BP4 call on one or more componentized services A-H, some of which will be composite. Processes BP1-BP4 and services A-H are physically and explicitly implemented: physical solution constructs control and coordinate services A-H within processes BP1-BP4. Business services do not feature, unless they are the same as business processes.

Figure 6 is a variant of *Figure 5* where business services do feature, but as 'bun-

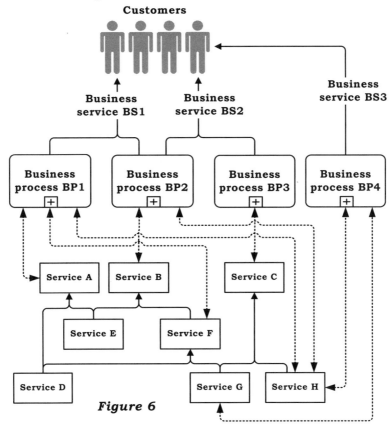

Figure 6

dles' of one or more business processes. Business services BS1-BS3 may or may not be physically and explicitly implemented.

Figure 7 is a service-based model, where componentized services A-H are assembled into business services BS1-BS3. Business processes do not feature unless they are the same thing as business services. Componentized services are physically and explicitly implemented, while business services may or may not be.

If business service BS1 is physically and explicitly implemented, solution constructs control and coordinate services A, B, F and H as BS1. If BS1 is not physically and explicitly implemented, then operational procedures may instead ensure that when business service BS1 is provided, services A, B, F and H are called upon.

A FALSE PARADIGM

Business systems deliver functionality, which is specified by users and business analysts and designed and built by developers. Users interact with systems as they do their work. A series of interactions with one or more systems (plus related off-line activities and/or relevant automation) is a business process. If workflow organizes, distributes, delivers or automates the work, then it is a workflow-supported business process.

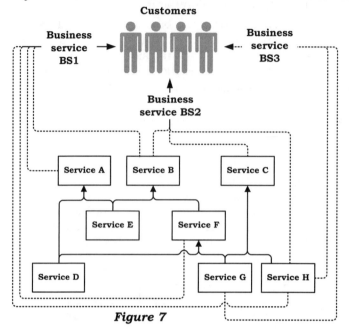

Figure 7

The paragraph above may be true as history but a business process management (BPM) initiative based on it may not succeed as well as it could.

It assumes a business process is nothing but an empirical fact: person X does Activity1; person Y does Activity2 using system S1; person Z does Activity3; and so on. The same paradigm generates optimized processes by getting X, Y and Z in a room with other stakeholders and experts to map and debate until leaner, tighter, 'to-be' models emerge, complete with lists of system changes to make everyone's lives easier.

The problem is the 'nothing but'. It ignores the elephant, perhaps because it is a supplier-centric paradigm. An organizational entity, say division D1 in *Figure 4*, is responsible for a set of functions, employs a number of people and uses and invests in one or more systems. It will be rewarded on how efficiently and effectively it carries out its functions. Its IT investment will be geared to optimizing its functions. It may have close relationships with internal or external IT suppliers, who will be rewarded on how efficiently and effectively they maintain, develop and support the systems D1 depends on. Anything likely to extend the functionality and deployment of those systems will be in the IT suppliers' interest, as careers and incomes depend on it. This is a world where 'business analysts' specialize in system S1 or system S2 or 'workflow'; where it would be incomprehensible to see a business process other than in terms of the systems which happen to be implemented; a world as in *Figure 8*.

It is a world where system boundaries influence organogram. But local ownership of systems and devolved IT funding also entrench system boundaries. Key to extending the functionality and deployment of systems is the successful promotion of the design patterns the systems are based on. The more they are promoted, the better the fit, as if system and business context were made for each other. Eventually the patterns become the cognitive models the support teams think and communicate with. Workflow team D3.5 sees the business context in terms of workflow system S5; team D3.2 supporting product P1 sees the business context in terms of system S2. All well and good unless S2 axioms and S5 axioms conflict with each other, and until S2 and S5 need to integrate. Then if they do clash, shared self-interest will bring a negotiated truce. So what if this means duplication? Both teams get work.

A good example is the business process itself. For workflow team D3.5 the business process is a set of queues plus allowable pathways. For support team D3.2 the business process is a series of screens in system S2, along with automated processing when a long-running transaction reaches specific statuses. As psychologist Abraham Maslow would say: *It is tempting, if the only tool you have is a hammer, to treat everything as if it were a nail.*[6]

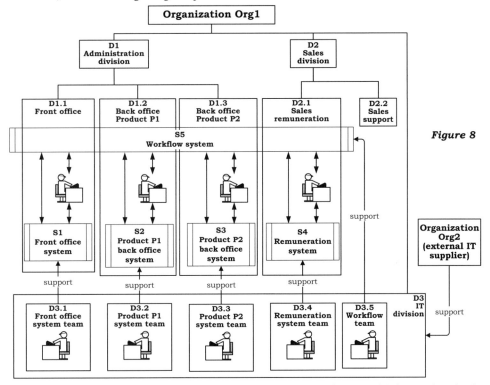

Figure 8

It is in the interest of both teams to see two separate things which need to be kept in step, as the alternative is for the business process to be only in S2 or only in S5. Either decision throws a different baby out with the bathwater, as the real issue is that neither system treats process very well because the original designers had a flawed process paradigm or no process paradigm at all. Which in turn would mean the teams' cognitive models are flawed—an inconvenient truth. In the (rather sexist) words of novelist Upton Sinclair: *It is difficult to get a man to understand something if his salary depends on his not understanding it.*[7]

---

[6] Maslow, A. (1966). *The psychology of science: A reconnaissance.* New York: Harper, 1966.

[7] Sinclair, U.B. (1935). *I, candidate for Governor: And how I got licked.* New York: Farrar & Rinehart.

BUSINESS PROCESS ARCHITECTURE AS A METHODOLOGY

The intention is not to demolish all other models to leave just one standing. Instead the benefits of a particular model will be offered as a way of navigating through choices and providing clear methodology and architecture guidelines.

The model is based on the premise that the business process comes first. The business process is not what people do as they interact with systems; nor what systems do between user interactions; nor a combination of the two—except in the case of a process-architected solution where the physical model corresponds exactly to the logical process model.

The model has been described in detail elsewhere: see INTRODUCTION for references, and in particular www.makeworkmakesense.com. So the focus here will be on the implications of employing it within a development and transformation initiative.

We start with organization Org1 in *Figure 8* and a project scope covering one or more end-to-end processes spanning front office D1.1 and the two back offices D1.2 and D1.3. The sales remuneration department D2.1 may also be affected. An early question will be on project resourcing. Should it be the front-office team D3.1 as processes start in the front office? Or workflow team D3.5 as all processes involve workflow? Or product support teams D3.2 and D3.3 as systems S2 and S3 handle most of the process detail, so those teams hold and control most of the relevant knowledge?

We need only ask questions like these to see what possible answers imply. Let's assume Org1 is bold enough to set up a new team D3.6 including members from at least teams D3.1-3 and D3.5. An immediate risk is that a large and powerful group of people left behind in teams D3.1-3 and D3.5, along with client colleagues in departments D1.1-3 and supplier colleagues in Org2, may want to see team D3.6's process project fail. They will not say that of course. More likely they will rubbish the process team's methodology.

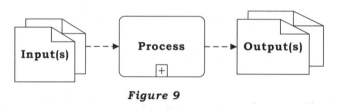

Figure 9

The methodology starts by qualifying a familiar generic model: *Figure 9*. In the case of a business process there is advantage in identifying a specific input (the **request**) and a specific output (the **outcome**). The model in *Figure 10* has three immediate benefits:

(i) It is customer-centric: the request is typically from a customer; the outcome typically for the customer.

(ii) The request and outcome are linked: the request is for the outcome; the outcome is typically the thing requested.

(iii) The request can be understood as a data entity belonging to the organization's logical data model, therefore with foreign keys to other business entities.

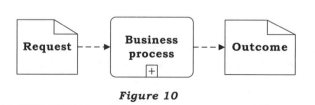

Figure 10

The link (ii) between request and outcome borders on identity—certainly close enough to draw a key architectural implication: the request entity initiates the process and changes status as it passes through the process, until the last status change of all, representing the outcome.

The next steps bring in business rules. A **process** is a sequence of status changes from request to outcome, and the status changes are governed by rules. The rules applicable to all request entities of the relevant type (eg all orders, for a purchase order process) split the process into **subprocesses**, as in *Figure 11*.

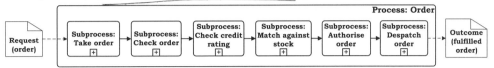

Figure 11

Subprocesses are typically sequential, but could be in parallel if that is what the rules specify. For example **Subprocess: Check credit rating** could run parallel to **Subprocess: Match against stock**. The BPMN notation in *Figure 11* is ultimately just another way of saying:

First take the order.

Then check the order.

Then check the customer's credit rating.

...etc.

The third and final level is **task**. A subprocess consists of one or more tasks plus the routing between them. Where subprocess-level routing applies to all request entities for the process, task-level routing differs for different request entities—because the attributes of the request instances will have different values. The task structure of the process must accommodate every possible request instance. A request instance will typically pass through every subprocess, but only through the tasks it needs to pass through.

A task is either automatic (all data available; the next status change achieved by applying rules mechanically); or manual (human interaction needed, eg because data is missing, authorization is required, or a decision must be made).

Figure 12 shows a simple task structure for the first two subprocesses—allowing manual data capture, automated validation, and correction of validation errors. *Figure 13* applies the same design principles to show a rather more complex structure for the third subprocess.

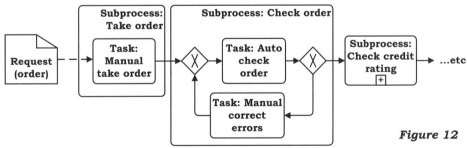

Figure 12

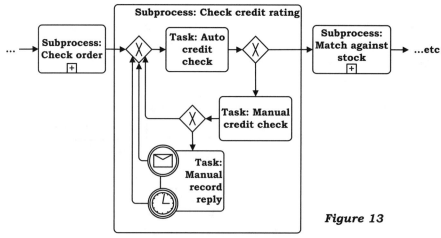

Figure 13

It is important to see the model free from existing systems. This is not to throw everything out and start from scratch, but to have a basis for evaluation and a target to aim at.

The model is at request entity instance level—the individual order. If implemented it would provide complete control over each instance, regardless of attribute values. This is true by definition, as the task structure is designed to handle every possible combination of values. The task structure of **Subprocess: Check order** in *Figure 12* only allows well-formed orders to progress further. The task structure of **Subprocess: Check credit rating** in *Figure 13* automatically passes orders already satisfying the organization's credit rules to **Subprocess: Match against stock**, and routes all others to a manual task where an authorized user applies discretion and/or communicates with the customer (for eg advance payment or a bank reference justifying increase in credit limit).

Each subprocess (except perhaps the first if the request entity can only be captured manually) will typically have a controlling automatic task representing the 'straight-through processing' (STP) route. STP is at subprocess level: an error-free order would pass straight through **Task: Auto check order** in *Figure 12* but might need manual credit authorization in **Task: Manual credit check** in *Figure 13*. It might then pass straight through **Task: Auto match against stock** (not illustrated) because the ordered goods are in stock, and so on.

Relating this now to existing systems we could envisage a 'purchase order system' providing, say, a screen to capture orders (the main part of **Task: Manual take order** in *Figure 12*), but where the only data validation (**Task: Auto check order** and **Task: Manual correct errors** in *Figure 12*) is within the capture screen itself. This might mean an incomplete order cannot be captured—following the garbage-in-garbage-out (GIGO) design principle. There might also be a workflow system presenting scanned orders to users for data capture, but the order which is the controlling entity in workflow is a physically different data record from the order captured in the order system. It must be different in the example just given because it exists in workflow but has not yet been accepted by the order system. It may also be a different entity logically—in workflow it may be a document (image) whereas in the order system it is a data set including foreign keys to customer, product etc.

More generally, a workflow system would focus on user interactions: in our model, **Task: Manual take order**; possibly **Task: Manual correct errors**; **Task:**

Manual credit check; **Task: Manual record reply**; etc. *Figure 14* shows an example queue structure.

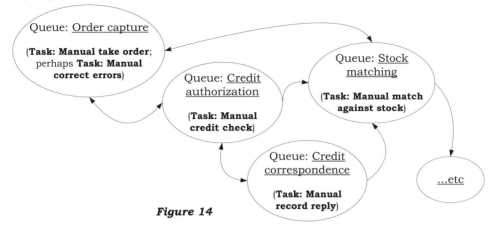

Figure 14

Meanwhile the likely home for the data and rules featuring in **Task: Auto check order**, **Task: Auto credit check**, **Task: Auto match against stock** etc would be the purchase order system itself. So must we have two processes implemented or reflected, one in each system? How do they keep in step? Is one always in control, and if so, which one?

These issues arise not from 'poor design', but from IT history following IT economics: record-keeping first, then generic workflow. Now that storage and transaction costs have dropped to make integrated, instance-level process support economically viable (and competitively vital) we have two obstacles. One is 'how to get there from here': the recalcitrant legacy architectures we must navigate. The more insidious obstacle is legacy thinking—assuming the reasons system boundaries and system design are as they are must hold true for all time.

The model depicted in *Figure 10* to *Figure 13* may also not hold true for all time, but it is a far more effective response to current IT economics and competitive pressures. It can be implemented given appropriate BPM and SOA architectures. The cost and difficulty of 'getting there from here' are constraints on logistics and phased delivery, not reasons for rejecting it.

Relating this now to the componentized services of *Figure 5* brings us to the overall schematic of *Figure 15*. The final step should now be obvious: task is the fundamental unit of a business process, so componentized services link to tasks. We thus have a framework for logical and physical architecture and delivery methodology, which suits process-based transformation projects and avoids both supplier-centric legacy thinking and the kind of empirical, anti-architectural pragmatism which too often drives Lean-type process re-engineering.

These last two are related. It is tempting to assume that, because business processes are generally poorly implemented in IT systems, business processes must be 'something else', something people do with systems, or the bits in between system functionality. That 'something else' is a popular target of Lean-type transformations which pride themselves on not getting bogged down in IT development backlogs.

There is nothing wrong with Lean *engineering*. Process architecture is Lean by design. The problem is empirically based *re*-engineering initiatives which see a process as a *de facto* sequence of improvable activities, but which lack the analytical tools and/or appetite to cut through layers of technology.

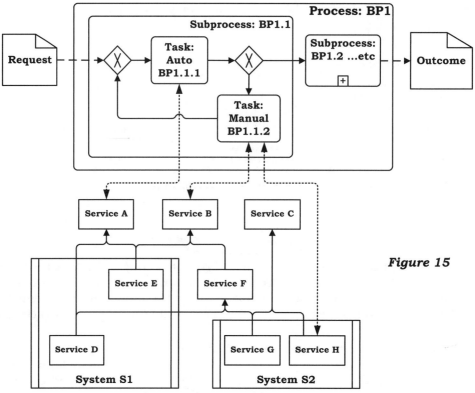

Figure 15

Seeing or not seeing a logical process model is like seeing or not seeing a logical data model. In a forest it is breathtaking how close you can be to an elephant before you realize it's there.

EXAMPLES

We shall now apply the metamodel to real-life examples to draw out a few methodology implications.

Request

If we focus on the customer request as the initiating entity then the format the request is in should be secondary. An order could be captured by the customer on a web page, posted or faxed as a form or a letter, telephoned to a call centre, or received by email. The process should cater for all of these. There will be format-specific rules, but also generic rules regardless of format. There should not be one project to develop a 'web-based order process' resourced by a 'web team' and another 'back-office order process' project resourced by a different team.

Figure 16 shows an example process design for a context where orders and other incoming requests can be received by a variety of channels.

Organization Org1 in *Figure 8* could be a financial services company, where (say) P1 is a loan product and P2 is an investment product. Org1 may not have a purchase order process as such but a range of other processes initiated by different request types: loan application, loan redemption, investment application, investment payout, change of address etc. Again each process would be the same regardless of format or channel, but no doubt with format- or channel-specific rules. So a truly process-based Org1 should not have a 'web team' developing a 'web-based loan system'.

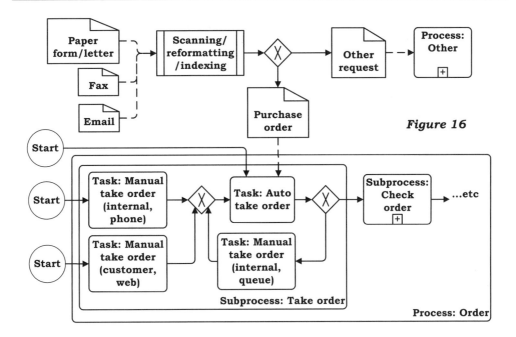

Figure 16

Data and Rules

Empirical observation is often key to re-engineering initiatives, whether to understand and measure a process or to identify improvement opportunities. The metamodel provides a framework for structuring the results and, more fundamentally, a program for what to observe—so as to understand the data and identify the rules.

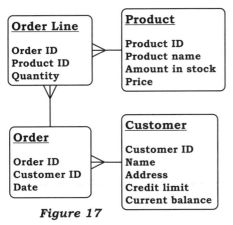

Figure 17

In the order process the request is the purchase order. *Figure 17* shows a straightforward logical data model.

An order could be for many products. In the draft process design of *Figure 11*, when the order gets to **Subprocess: Match against stock**, some items could be in stock but others not. We need a rule: can we despatch part orders? We will assume yes, but only if the part order value exceeds a certain parameter.

Our draft design must change to something more like *Figure 18*. Here one instance of **Process: Order** creates an instance of **Process: Fulfillment** for each part order which can be authorized and despatched. **Subprocess: Complete order** terminates **Process: Order** when all part orders have completed.

The process implications of part orders may call into question the logic and position of **Subprocess: Check credit rating**. In both *Figure 11* and *Figure 18* the assumption is that the value of the whole order is checked against the customer's credit limit and current balance. But the value of the first part order could be within the credit limit, so maybe the rules should apply at part order level—which would mean a more sophisticated task structure factoring the credit checking rules into **Subprocess: Match against stock**?

CONCLUSION: DESIGN FIRST

Examples like these show a draft logical process design and draft logical data design being used to tease out and clarify business rules. It is hard to overstate the significance of this for a process project. This is the elephant in the room. The process metamodel both allows and requires logical design to start early, in order to identify requirements. We do not 'define process requirements' and then pass them to a development team for 'process design'. This is fatal, as business users and business analysts typically define requirements in terms of systems they are familiar with. Logical design needs to be done by someone who understands data analysis and process architecture. That someone could be called a process analyst or process designer or process architect or process modeler or business analyst or business architect or business modeler. What is crucial is that he or she must understand how process components (request entity, rule, process, subprocess, task) fit together at a logical level in order to engineer a customer-centric process solution which works within the logical data model. A business transformation initiative which has a significant process component will be less successful than it could be if it does not acknowledge this and does not factor it into its project and engagement design.

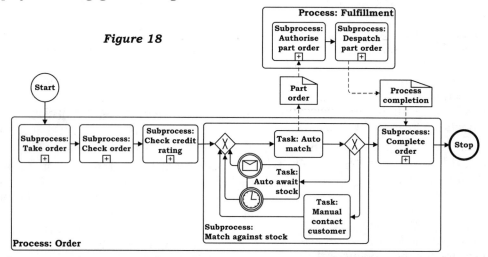

Figure 18

This approach is very different from familiar systems projects, and both 'business' and 'technology' people can find it a struggle—particularly if it questions structures of power and influence. (It can be difficult to get a man or woman with a hammer to understand that everything isn't a nail.) It calls for a holistic engagement and delivery model and holistic data and process design skills. But it works. It avoids massive duplication and it *delivers* because it opens people's eyes to the elephant.

Keeping it Simple in the Complex World of BPM

Amit Rajaram, HSBC Group, India

ADVICE FOR THE NEW BPM USER

Too many vendors, too little value; this feeling of frustration frequently sums up the attitude for many organizations that jumped onto the BPM bandwagon with the aim of transforming their businesses. I have been through the experience of implementing a BPM solution a few times and learned several valuable lessons along the way. For the benefit of other IT users I am happy to share the knowledge gained. Essentially this paper is a how-to approach for those looking at implementing BPM for the first time.

Senior management of many enterprise companies bought into the hype surrounding BPM, only to find that the path to the Promised Land—greater business control over business systems, predictive analysis, and enhanced customer experience—is not as smooth as expected. Issues from lack of standardization, difficulty in integrating with existing process modeling systems and immature products that don't scale, to small and expensive development communities and organizations failing to understand and adapt to the paradigm shift that BPM mandates—have resulted in several stalled, or even worse, cancelled projects; while many organizations have ended up using expensive BPM suites simply to automate workflows or replace existing workflow applications, without really drawing the benefits of BPM—linking up disparate people and processes, metrics-based performance monitoring, delegating control to the business and the rest of the benefits we hear so much about.

Given the large number of vendors in the market, and the fact that BPM has moved from hype to mainstream (most market analysts agree on at least $5 billion being spent on licenses alone by 2011), there is an anticipated market consolidation around the corner, so confusion is inevitable in the IT user community. While some vendors are preparing themselves for the imminent M&A activity by shoring up their bottom lines (data from Gartner & Forrester in Figure 1 show several of the leading players in the BPM segment are small or mid-size companies ripe for the picking). In such a scenario, demystifying the implementation of BPM products (and reducing customer dependency on high-priced services) often takes a back seat to increasing sales quickly and dramatically by trying to create a one-size-fits-all product, which unfortunately may end up being clunky, unstable and difficult to use.

Therefore, it is up to the enterprise organizations and their service-providing partners to demystify BPM for themselves. *This is in fact, not that difficult to achieve.* The over-riding and consistent theme for initial BPM success is to **keep it simple**.

Business Sponsorship is Key

The key is to start small with the big picture always in mind. Keep it simple until the people and processes involved in the BPM program have gained experience and maturity. In order to get the most out of BPM, the process of building your business systems has to change. The way these systems are developed will change, and so will the way in which they are used. You will need the support of the people in your organization who are capable of propagating and sometimes enforcing these changes, in order to be successful. Too often, regional business entities are used to doing things in their own silo-ed ways. BPM brings to the table the ability for businesses to provide a commonality across all their regional business units, providing a common user experience for users anywhere in the world—a philosophy that is spreading quite rapidly in today's global village. This means the end of 'regional' business process and reveals the need for people to stop doing 'their own thing' and to abide by the 'global' business process. This is quite often a major stumbling block—business users rarely like to change the way they work (they're certainly not going to do so just because their IT departments ask them to), and therefore, this will only work if the BPM siren is being sounded by senior management within the business. If the program is the brainchild of the business, then you're in luck. If it happens to be an IT-driven initiative, ensure that you are able to sell it to the business first, before embarking on building an ambitious BPM program, as you will need the business with you every step of the way. It needs to be a COO, not CIO, driven initiative, or at least one which is strongly supported by the COO.

From an IT perspective, the key areas of a successful BPM-based program (and the ones that need most focus while starting up) are:

1. The Business Case
2. Product Selection
3. Building BPM Delivery Capability
4. Iterative Development Methodologies Across Functions—the Paradigm Shift
5. Management Information(MI) and Business Intelligence (BI) for Continuous Process Improvement(CPI)

MAKING THE BUSINESS CASE

Obviously, your projects should be fully funded before embarking on the real work of building the systems. Many BPM projects falter at this, the first hurdle itself, as the business case does not fully detail all the benefits that BPM accrues, and given the higher than average costs of developing a BPM system, the project costs seem unjustified. Quantifying some of the benefits in terms of dollars is not always easy—you would definitely need a partner from the business in order to put a dollar value to some of them.

Increased Productivity

Automation, one of the keystones of BPM—will provide the basis for increased operational productivity. The story does not end here though. The plan to maximize the gains from this increase in productivity needs to be thought through completely, and this is where the participation from the business unit comes in. The simple answer is that increased productivity increases throughput. However, there could be deeper implications; you might be able to release some senior staff to more value-added tasks like cross-selling, up-selling products within other lines of business or to start a new set of products or services altogether. Or, to train junior staff thus further reducing the cost of doing business. This is the promise that BPM brings the ability to turn your business on a dime—provided there is always someone looking at the bigger picture.

Enhanced User Experience

Most BPM systems allow the deployment of 'versioned' processes which means that the application can support multiple versions of an automated process at the same time. A single application can be deployed to multiple regions with the system determining at runtime which region a user is from, and applying that version of the process. This allows for the creation and deployment of a unified, global process (while still allowing for regional variations for purposes of compliance etc.) and a consistent user experience for global users. This also allows for easier data sharing across regions giving your customers reason to stay loyal even if they shift countries. Ensure you have quantified this in your Return on Investment (ROI) calculations.

Increased Project Success Probability

According to the Standish Group[1], 'project waste' in the US alone has come down from 56 percent of the total spent in 1994 to 22 percent in 2004. While this is good news, the truth is that even today millions of dollars are being spent in cost over-runs, or even worse, failed projects. As described in more detail later in the chapter, BPM brings with it a paradigm shift in building business systems, which resolves many of the issues that cause such projects to fail, by bringing together various stakeholders into a single team, offering a way out of the traditional waterfall model and by facilitating a more agile, iterative way of development. Admittedly, this benefit is rather intangible, and hard to put a dollar amount to, but this benefit must be included into any real ROI calculation and might necessitate bringing in a professional company that focuses on Business Value such as Total Cost of Ownership (TCO), ROI etc., if you do not have in-house expertise.

Increased Business Agility

This one is the most obvious, as it is the premise on which most vendors start their sales pitch, yet sometimes this doesn't make it to the business case because IT teams are unable to provide a comparative estimate on the costs involved in 'implementing change' to an existing business process. The best source for help on this one would be from the product vendors themselves who have this data with them based on experience with other customers.

Once you have included these items into your ROI calculations, your Business Case will definitely look more appealing and the probability of getting your funding would have increased manifold. Now, the real work of building your system starts, and while IT might have been involved to some extent in creating the business case, this is where we really start to roll up our sleeves and get to work. A good place to start is selecting the right product.

PRODUCT SELECTION

The number of Software Vendors with BPM products in the market today are legion; the Gartner[2] Magic Quadrant for BPMS' and the Forrester Wave[3] give you about 25-30 to choose from, with other market researchers adding to this tally. For an enterprise organization about to join the BPM bandwagon, the process of selecting the right product can be rather overwhelming.

How do you choose from a plethora of feature-rich, nicely-engineered (in some cases, over-engineered) products, given that there really aren't too many differentiating factors between them. If you do your due diligence and interview even five or six of these vendors, you will find that their Unique Selling Propositions aren't maybe all that unique. Caveat Emptor.

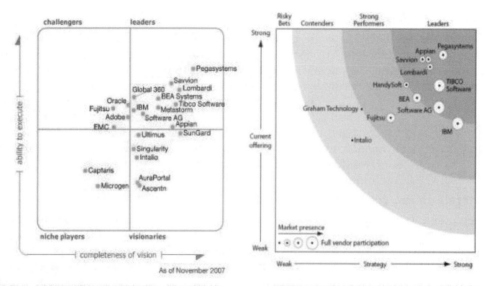

Fig. 1. 2007 Gartner Magic Quadrant for BPMSs   2007 Forrester Wave for Human-Centric BPM

Step 1—Understanding Your Requirements

The best place to start is to understand your requirements completely with a long term view and to reconcile yourself to the fact that you might need more than one product in your stable. There are many categories into which BPM systems can be divided, but in line with our strategy of keeping things simple, I suggest that you view them as falling under one of the following two categories—

1. **Document-centric products**—If your processes are driven by the documents attached to each case, which need to be edited or manipulated, and decision points are calculated solely by the data contained in these documents, then you need a product that combines Workflow Automation with Document Management. The leaders in this segment typically come from a Document Management System ancestry and offer the complete suite of operations required for indexing, storing and retrieving documents of all types, and basic workflow functionality. These processes are typically quite static, and do not use complex business rules.

   Example processes—Case creation and logging based on incoming paper documents (Insurance Claims, Loan Originations).

2. **Process-centric products**—If your business processes are focused more on business rules and on processing the information and making automatic calculations based on available data(documents are few and their contents do not change) then you need a product that is capable of accurately modeling, implementing and monitoring complex business processes, while allowing the creation of complex, multi-level decisioning rules. Most products in this line come with strong business rules capabilities which will be a mandatory requirement. If your business processes are likely to change frequently, look for a product that allows you to empower your business users to make changes to business rules (if changing an interest rate for 9 percent to 10 percent requires opening up a Java class then you can safely strike the product off your list; there are much more evolved products available).

   Example processes—Payments and related reconciliations, Card Disputes Management.

The question then is; what about processes that are both document-centric and are driven by complex rules and/or are likely to change often? Well, the ideal situation would be to accept the 'horses for courses' dictum and use two systems; one for managing documents and another for processes. However, despite the claims of industry standardization by the vendors, integrating these two isn't always easy. Maintenance of the system going forward (imagine having to upgrade one of the two systems and then finding that the newer version of one isn't compatible with the older version of the other) might also prove difficult. If this is your first project in the BPM program, and you are looking for a quick win, stay away from the two-system approach if at all possible. This would mean getting the business to compromise on either the level of document manipulation (they might have to live without annotations) or fewer business rules (and a less dynamic process) but in return they would get a simpler product, easier to build and maintain and a quicker return on their investments. This is a decision that should be made in conjunction with the business. The good news is that most business processes quite clearly fall into one of the two categories described above.

Step 2—Identifying Your Integration Needs

All BPM based systems will need to draw data at some point from external applications. More complex systems will also need to update data to such systems, and in many cases this is key to achieving maximum automation and eventually Straight Through Processing. Given this, you should be looking for products that provide the capability to integrate with all the systems needed (take a holistic, organization wide approach here, not just focused on the current project). Most common integration requirements are:

- Support for Industry-standard Messaging formats and protocols
- Connectivity to external relational databases
- Support for Web Services (connecting to externally published web services and also the ability to expose internal functions as services)
- Ability to send and receive email/fax from within the business process
- Ability to background print to remote print centers.

Highly-evolved products will offer built-in adapters that conform to industry standards for most integrations, and this should be the preferred option. Avoid products that require the use of additional middleware products, as this unnecessarily introduces an additional layer and more potential points of failure—remember, keep it simple. You should also look to avoid using proprietary vendor standards for any integration as this would lock you in to the vendor (who might or might not be around a year from now).

Step 3—Evaluate Ease of Development & Maintenance

By now, you should hopefully be down to just a handful of eligible contenders, and should be ready to put them to the final test; how easy is it to build and maintain the system, from both a business and IT perspective.

The Business Perspective

The true promise of BPM—Continuous Process Improvement—can only be delivered if the ownership of the system can be transferred to the business. To make this happen, the products should offer the following features—

Must Haves:
- Ability to delegate rules to the business
- Rules should be built in languages/formats that business users can work with

- Ability to constantly monitor the state of the business system, identify bottlenecks and take remedial action in real-time
- Comprehensive recording and reporting of Management Information
- Ability to run multiple versions of the process simultaneously

Nice To Haves: (in the early days of BPM adoption, the user community will probably not have the requisite expertise to perform these tasks anyway, so as long as your vendors have these in their product roadmap for the next couple of years, you can consider them eligible)

- Process Simulation—ability to run what-if scenarios to analyze the impact of process changes
- Integrated Modeling & Process Mapping—Ability to modify processes in real-time

The IT Perspective

The IT-specific criteria for selecting a product should not be much different from those of any other IT initiatives. BPM being less mature a field than most IT disciplines, the following criteria should also be carefully considered:

- **Adoption of industry standards**—This gives you the ability to switch vendors if you have to, without having to completely throw away what you already have. Be warned—standards in the BPM world are still being formulated and are far from being universally accepted—so they are not as 'standard' as one would expect.
- **Large development community**—Ensure that the expertise required to develop, deploy and maintain applications is available outside of the product vendor. Several BPM vendors are either too young to have spawned a development community, or in a misguided attempt to sell their own services, have not done enough to grow one. In too many cases, lack of sufficient development resource (in both, quantity and quality) has caused BPM projects to flounder.
- **Efficient and Responsive Support Organization**—BPM Products are relatively new to the market and most vendors plan multiple releases each year. In this mad rush to include every new feature and claim compliance with every new buzzword, the quality of the product suffers. Add to this the fact that in most cases, the development community is also fairly immature, and you quickly realize how important your vendor's support organization is. Ensure the vendor can provide 24/7 support in all regions in which you operate. References from other customers also help in making a decision.

Once you have whittled down your list of eligible candidates based on the criteria defined above, and apply the standard rules of cost, platform acceptability, existing vendor relationships etc., you should be able to have reached a decision on which product(s) is right for your organization, and can now embark on the adventure that is building your BPM system(s).

THE BPM SYSTEM DEVELOPMENT LIFECYCLE—PREPARE FOR THE PARADIGM SHIFT

The Waterfall Dries Up

Without a doubt, BPM requires a paradigm shift from the traditional way of developing software applications. As mentioned earlier in this paper, a large number of software projects fail, and billions of dollars are wasted in these efforts. Industry experts are unanimous in their verdict that we owe this to a failure in the traditional The Waterfall approach towards project development, wherein, someone within the business user group prepares a Functional Requirements Specification, which is handed over to IT, and then the business re-appear within the life-cycle several months later at the User Acceptance Testing phase. By this time, requirements have changed (or were poorly documented/understood in the first place) and the project has run out of time and money to do anything about it. These tales are well documented elsewhere (the 2005 IEEE Spectrum article on Why Software Fails[4] makes interesting reading), and the important point is that BPM accords us the opportunity to get around these weaknesses of the Waterfall model. If done right, BPM based systems can really provide us with—

- Shorter Development Cycles
- Fewer defects (and nasty surprises) at UAT
- Significantly more agile applications

In order to reap these benefits though, the organization has to be prepared to change. The first thing that needs to change is the team structure.

Building Cross-function Project Teams

BPM blurs the traditional line between the Business and IT, and the team composition needs to reflect this. In order to enable the BPM team to succeed, you need to ensure that all required skills are covered within the team. In the world of BPM, these would be:

- Business Operations Expertise
- Business Analysis
- IT Development

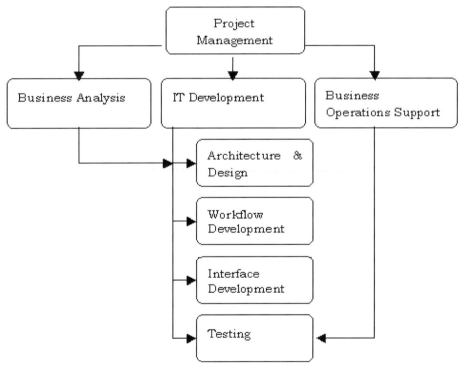

Fig. 2. BPM Delivery Team Structure

Team Structure That Promotes Re-use—The Holy Grail

Reuse has always been a popular amongst the IT community. Well, at least talking about re-use has been popular, actual re-use has probably been only partially successful. Reuse is possible at many levels—process reuse, IT artifact reuse etc. BPM makes reuse a little bit easier—simply because all stakeholders are involved right from the inception of the project and are available to identify opportunities for re-use within their sphere of influence, early enough to build or design the component in a manner suitable for reuse. This is probably the biggest advantage of lowering the wall between IT and the Business. Apart from making it easier, it is also much needed since this would reduce the cost and time required to build expensive BPM systems.

Process Reuse—The Business Analyst/Business Process Champion should identify opportunities to reuse parts (or even the whole) business process. E.g. Account Opening; a large part of this process will be common across the organization and across the globe. Identify and design the process in a manner such that most of the process can be reused, and only mandatory regional variances need to be rebuilt. This can also be used as a vehicle to identify and propagate organizational change, as it incentivizes regions to subscribe to the global process, since one is already available.

IT Component Reuse—The IT Architect/Designer should identify opportunities to design modularized or componentized functions. Ideal candidates are interfaces (hence it makes sense to have a team dedicated to interface development), which should typically be build-once, use-anywhere modules with key properties parameterized. E.g. Authentication and security modules, Document Composition and Remote Printing function etc.

Once the teams have been educated on how to maximize reuse, and the reuse philosophy becomes *de rigueur*, it will become easier to compose applications and orchestrate processes and services throughout the organization. This then has a direct and very positive bearing on the cost associated with building BPM-based applications.

Getting your first couple of BPM projects right isn't enough. Enterprises should look to develop the capacity to accelerate the program in a repeatable manner, learn from previous mistakes and failures and (once a critical mass of expertise has been achieved) to evangelize the use of BPM by delivering more and bigger projects, simultaneously. In order to grow this capacity in an organic matter (undoubtedly the best—not to mention, cheapest—way), the team structure should be planned in a manner that makes it readily scalable. Given that BPM is still relatively nascent, a lot of attention needs to be paid to specific and targeted training programs within each stream. Process Modeling, IT Application Performance Monitoring and Infrastructure Sizing are key areas which vary considerably depending on the selected BPMS product, and expertise needs to be built in these areas. As with anything else, ultimately, it is the people who will make or break the BPM program, and organizations need to devote sufficient resources toward building a team that has the capacity and authority to bring about the change that BPM promises.

Implementation Methodology

While implementing a BPM project, you should follow an iterative development approach in order to maximize the benefits offered by BPM. *Start small*; identify a key initiative within the business which is susceptible to being decomposed into multiple smaller processes. Implement a solution for the most likely candidate among these and then incrementally build on top of this by adding new processes/workflows, automating the integrations with external systems, implementing enhanced MI and reporting and finally the ability to delegate control of the process to the business. Each one of these items can be delivere' iterations. In this way, you will achieve the following:

- Multiple and quick application releases—potentially quicker t.. requirements to become obsolete
- More successful applications—with the business being involved at e. stage, potential issues are identified early, thereby easier to rectify
- Within a year (or 4-6 releases)—you will have implemented a fully auto-mated business process, with high degrees of Straight Through Processing, and greater monitoring and control by the business

In order to achieve quick wins while simultaneously preparing the ground for more significant transformations, use the following formula:

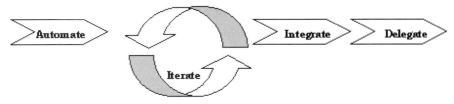

Fig. 3. BPM Project Implementation Cycle

BPM Project Implementation Cycle

1. **Automate** Manual Steps in the Process
2. **Iterate** through the Automated process, adding more processes, en-hancing the UI, adding more reporting/MI or adding additional busi-ness rules with each iteration. I would recommend each iteration take no longer than 20 elapsed days.
3. **Integrate**—Build in the integration with external systems, which is they key to achieving Straight Through Processing.
4. **Delegate**—The final step; passing on control of the business process and its execution to the business. Identifying key business rules and process control points, and then building them in such a way that they can be easily maintained by the business users, is the only way to achieve Continuous Process Improvement.

While iterating, remember to define clear milestones that validate the assump-tions of ROI, increased efficiency, enhanced user experience etc. that formed the basis of your business case. If the desired outcomes are not being achieved, fix those problems first, before proceeding to the next iteration.

Designing Your First BPM Application

The best guide to use while formulating the design and architecture for your ini-tial BPM applications is the WfMC's Workflow Reference Model[5] which while sev-eral years old, is still relevant and a good place to start. The Reference Model de-fines the components of a BPM-based application, as combination of the Work-flow Engine and five interfaces. For a detailed description of the Model, the WfMC website is the best place, and I will restrict myself to basic descriptions of each interface, and in order to keep things simple, what you need to consider and what you don't.

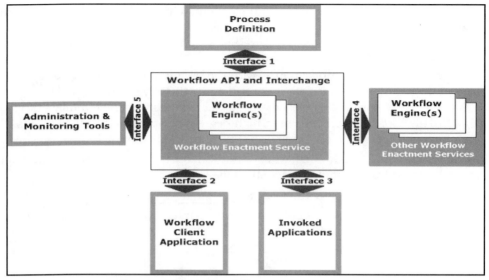

Fig. 4—WfMC Workflow Reference Model

Components of the Workflow Reference Model

- **Workflow Enactment Services**—This is part of your BPMS product. It refers to the core workflow engine and the services built around it that facilitate the functioning of the Workflow Automation piece.
- **Interface 1**—This is the interface between the Process engine and the Process Definition Tool. Most BPMSs have their own internal flowcharting tool which is used to define the targeted process. However, enterprises have always had their own favorite ways of mapping their processes, and most vendors claim that their product is capable of importing any process in a standard (viz., XPDL) format and translating it into a form that their Process Engine can use. This is what XPDL was designed for, essentially to provide a standard representation of the process model or the "picture" of the process. Accordingly, XPDL provides a round-trip development process between compliant design and execution environments. The caveat remains, however, that in order for an XPDL model to execute, it needs to be transformed into another format such as Java or BPEL, and this is not always a one-click process. Depending on the BPMS in question, and whether or not it interprets XPDL directly, this may require further programming to make the process executable. For a good understanding of where the industry is at with regards to adoption of modeling standards, Nathaniel Palmer's "Understanding the BPMN-XPDL-BPEL Value Chain[6]" is an excellent read.
- **Interface 2**—With most of the current BPMSs, the client application is part of the Suite. However, if your organization mandates its own UI Framework ensure that the BPMS you select can actually work with external UI's—in some cases this is not possible or too costly to implement.
- **Interface 3**—This refers to the interface(s) with external applications. These interfaces will provide the foundation for Straight Through Processing. While designing these interfaces, ideally, they should be invoked as exposed services, using robust protocols like Web Services or MQ etc. Avoid direct invocations using vendor-specific protocols. In situations where SOAP or MQ based interfaces are not possible, rather than at-

tempting anything fancy, try to use simple text feeds to import/export data from/to external applications. This would probably impede Straight Through Processing, but that is a lesser evil and full STP could be taken on at a later stage.

- **Interface 4**—Integration with other Workflow/BPM suites. Do not attempt this at home. In fact, do not attempt even under adult supervision. You should try to avoid having to split a process across two or more different vendors. Existing standards for connecting one BPM product to another (Wf-XML and ASAP) are not well supported in most products today. If you really must integrate a legacy process or a process from a different organizational unit, plan carefully; you may need to implement a custom adapter for one or both ends of the protocol.
- **Interface 5**—This refers to the interface with systems responsible for monitoring the state of the system, and is probably the most key of all the interfaces, at least with regard to achieving the goal of Continuous Process Improvement and is described in greater detail below.

MONITORING AND REPORTING—KEY TO CONTINUOUS PROCESS IMPROVEMENT

Monitoring the performance of the people and the state of your processes is of paramount importance to the business, and one of the primary reasons for investing in BPM (if you need to know why, simply read Derek Miers' "Too Much BP, Not Enough of the M[7]").

There are two aspects to monitoring the state of your BPM systems:

Business Activity Monitoring

The simplest way to do this is by leveraging the standard reports that come with your BPMS (every BPMS today has these) these will give you the performance metrics of different teams, identify queue load and average time to complete for a process etc. These reports can be available either offline (say at the end of the day) or online (thereby allowing supervisors to take corrective action, always assuming you've designed your system to be able to delegate this control to the business users). Hence, the BPMS product selected needs to provide a standard set of out-of-the-box reports, which satisfies most of the reporting needs.

Predictive Analytics and Business Intelligence

This refers to the provision of historical, current and predictive views of the business, by extracting data from the business application at different points-in-time into a data mart and then using a slew of OLAP techniques to slice and dice the data to provide the requisite information. The objective of this is to improve decision making. This should be treated as independent from your BPM not because it is not part of the holistic BPM landscape, but simply because BI is not the core competency of any BPM system. While many BPMSs offer BI capabilities, these are mostly difficult to use, and do not offer the full range of BI capabilities. The recommended approach is to export the data from your BPM system into the world of BI experts for BI functions, and then use the data coming out of them to make decisions that will improve your BPM system.

CONCLUSION

The BPM industry has some way to go before becoming 'standard.' Standard protocols for interoperability are not sufficiently supported in most BPMS products today. Visionary vendors will realize the opportunity that lies before them, and the concomitant risk that unless they get their act together, this opportunity will disappear. Then, as the market consolidates, it will become easier and cheaper to bring in the BPM revolution.

Does this mean that enterprises should wait till this happens to start improving their processes, and making them more efficient, cheaper and more agile? Certainly not. By following a few basic steps, it is not that difficult to put in place a program that creates a vendor-proof, yet simple and repeatable methodology for delivering the BPM promise.

- Start small—don't go for a big-bang approach. Identify candidate processes suitable for a transformation based on BPM.
- Prepare for a paradigm shift in the way business systems are built.
- Invest sufficient time in selecting and understanding your BPM product(s)
- Automate + Iterate + Integrate + Delegate = Transform
- Do not be sidetracked by vendor-generated hype on seamless integration with Process Modeling or Business Intelligence tools. At this point, this is unnecessary and troublesome. It is easier to use external tools.
- Focus on enhancing your in-house delivery capacity for BPM projects, by creating an adaptive, scalable organization structure.

In following these steps, within the short space of 12-18 months, you would have developed significant capacity to deliver BPM projects, and by the time the BPM landscape stabilizes and standardizes, the organization will be perfectly placed to accelerate the BPM revolution, and reap the benefits that come with it.

REFERENCES

1. The CHAOS Report, 1994—The Standish Group (www.standishgroup.com)
2. Magic Quadrant for Business Process Management Suites, 2007—www.gartner.com
3. The Forrester Wave: Human-Centric BPM for Java Platforms, Q3 2007—http://www.forrester.com/Research/Document/Excerpt/0,7211,38886,00.html
4. IEEE Spectrum—Why Software Fails—www.spectrum.ieee.org/sep05/1685
5. Workflow Reference Model—www.wfmc.org/standards/referencemodel.htm
6. Palmer, Nathaniel—"Understanding the BPMN-XPDL-BPEL Value Chain"—http://wfmc.org/documents/palmer.BIJ.nov-dec06.pdf
7. Miers, Derek—"BPM—Too Much BP, Not Enough of the M"—http://www.futstrat.com/books/downloads/Miers_too_%20much_BP.pdf also published in 2005 Workflow Handbook by Future Strategies Inc. www.futstrat.com

SOA: Simple Step-By-Step

Alfredo Cisterna and Federico Silva, PECTRA Technology, Inc., United States

ABSTRACT

When a company envisions a business start-up or plans the implementation of a new application, it devises which would be the best route to attain the goal; obviously the most cost-effective possible way and keeping potential risks to a minimum.

A significant number of corporations world-over are currently analyzing the costs and benefits of a possible migration of their IT structures toward a Service-Oriented Architecture (SOA). Why? Because, in an environment of constant technological innovation, the need to keep pace often prevails against any logical reasons. And we must be honest here: The belief that "the mere fact of acquiring technology will produce wonderful results" is misleading. However, the main factor that materializes the advantages and benefits that should lead a company to decide to adopt SOA is the profitable use of all technology resources currently existing. Not only in-house resources, but also those coming from outside the organization; all of them, packed as services.

Organizations seek higher profitability in every business they run. With this purpose they execute plans that result in greater savings through lower operating costs. And organizations seek growth as well, not only in revenues, but also in market share, by furthering productivity and looking for ways to become more efficient in order to remain competitive. We all know that the key to success in a global economy lies in the ability to perfectly integrate efficient and profitable value chains that are organized and automated in well-designed business processes. SOA allows standardization and integration. Also, reuse. But most important, higher speed, control, and, consequently, greater agility, strengthening two key aspects: governance and alignment. To *innovate*. To be always one step ahead.

Experience shows that nothing in IT happens overnight. Let alone establish a new way of doing things. Therefore, in order to provide our readers with a view on how to implement a Service-Oriented Architecture, we would like to share what we believe is the best way to follow the best practices that successful companies implement, in an easy, simple, and concrete manner by means of a gradual approach, defining the risks that can be decisive in the future of an organization.

A GRADUAL APPROACH

Let us discuss the concept of "gradual approach" in detail. As we make our way along new ground, we must move on gradually, step by step. In this way, we lower the risks and increase our confidence. This slow progress, we believe, is critical when it comes to the implementation of a Service-Oriented Architecture (SOA).

We'd like to share what we learned in designing a simple work methodology, both iterative and incremental, to ensure the execution of the entire process is standardized and limited to four steps, whenever a new implementation is required.

These steps, which facilitate and simplify the migration, are the following:

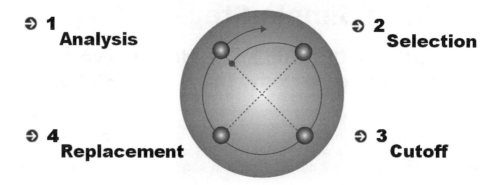

1 Analysis
2 Selection
4 Replacement
3 Cutoff

In a real life scenario, we may need only one or several iterations to deal with a given situation depending on the circumstances, as required by the complexity of the selection to be replaced. In all cases, however, the steps remain the same.

Step by Step

We will now discuss each one of these steps in detail:

Analysis

To initiate a gradual migration of systems to a Service-Oriented Architecture, we must first analyze our current business processes in depth. In this regard, it is essential to understand that Business Process Management System (BPMS) technologies as well as SOA models coexist bound by a very close relationship. Although these are separate concepts, they complement each other naturally, thus providing businesses with more responsiveness, increased flexibility, and a significant reduction of technological infrastructure costs.

In implementing an SOA, the use of tools which make up BPM systems is a crucial requirement. For instance, in order to monitor processes and thus identify tasks or sequences of tasks which are less efficient in our organization, performance measuring tools known as Business Activity Monitoring (BAM) are ideal.

Once the least efficient tasks in our organization have been detected, the next step is to identify what they do and why they operate in this way. In other words, we must gain an in-depth knowledge of the activity to be improved as a prior step to know how to improve it. From a general viewpoint, it is vital to define clearly the business goals of the organization from the very onset. There is no other way to ensure an adequate selection of activities to be replaced and the success of the migration project. To fully understand this explanation, we will illustrate the framework using the following real life case.

Our company recently undertook an SOA implementation on behalf of a global organization. The scenario included:

- An intensive number of transactions.
- The need to streamline the procurement process (critical for its business).
- Emphasis on risk management.

Something was fundamentally wrong with their BPM process. The initial diagnosis, following a thorough analysis of processes, revealed that the information shown in authorization activities (an integral part of many processes) by the BPM did not match actual values. The straightforward reason for this mismatch was that at the time the authorizations were to be granted, the officer responsible for these authorizations was not always at his desk. And although authorizations were granted using other methods (usually by phone), the actions recorded in the BPM were not genuine, and the information shown was not realistic; therefore, the BAM indicators were not genuine. This point is significant because if there is no feedback, it is impossible to refine the strategy and decide upon the matter, bearing in mind that adequate management and monitoring of processes are key elements to create an Ongoing Improvement environment in the organization (efficient and reliable management based on process metrics and management and quality indicators).

Selection

Once processes have been analyzed, the next step in the migration process is the selection of activities or sequences of activities to be replaced, usually those which are deemed less efficient in the organization. We must bear in mind that this is a key step in the migration process and, therefore, it must be extremely thorough and objective.

The functionality to be replaced may be present in several processes. Therefore, we suggest implementing a reutilization design. This design results in shorter time frames and, more important, lower development and implementation costs.

We also developed a set of questions used to determine if the decision to migrate to a SOA model is the best course of action. These questions include:

1. What would happen if this activity or set of less efficient activities in our organization was replaced by a service?
2. How would the business react to the implementation of this service?
3. Which option is best: replacing it by an activity, by a set of activities, by part of a process or by a full process?

The answers to these questions help us in our reasoning and, therefore, in reaching the best decision. At the same time, it will facilitate the description of inlet and outlet interfaces, in order to understand how our SOA section will operate in the process. Subsequently, we will describe the message that needs to be developed to turn the selected tasks into services to be used, i.e., to draft the service contract. For the case above, these were the answers to the set of questions submitted to the client:

1. The sequence of activities would not be affected. Moreover, the possibilities for integration would increase.
2. This implementation would not affect our business, as only a functional part of the process is involved.
3. Out of all business processes, only the "authorization" activity would be replaced.

The bottom line is that the analysis provided a clear identification of the activity to be selected.

Cutoff

Once all parts of the process to be migrated have been analyzed and selected, we cut off the section to be replaced. The new service will complete the same task, but in a simpler and more efficient way, reusing the capabilities of existing systems (both in-house and third-party). Implementation always involves drafting a contract which defines the method and the information issued and received by the service.

Replacement

Following the cutoff, we reach the last step of the process: replacement. To do this, we "plug" the section of the process to the SOA connector. Thus, the service may continue working with its known and defined interface, as published and managed by the SOA solution. This degree of autonomy provides enterprises with an unparalleled degree of flexibility and the possibility to change or add services as many times as needed.

IN-HOUSE OR THIRD PARTY SERVICES

When implementing SOA, two options are available:
- Developing an in-house service.
- Using a third-party service.

In-house development

The development of an in-house service is required when circumstances point to the need of a presentation service, such as mobile services, occasionally connected clients and smart clients, among others.

Using a third-party service

The option to use a service developed and managed by an external supplier is useful when the service provided is not an integral part of the main corporate business, for example, information based on weather reports.

GOVERNANCE

It is essential to bear in mind that these implementations must be undertaken under a service control and management scheme. Implementing SOA is not a project but a process which requires step-by-step monitoring and control to avoid undesired disruptions, as evidenced by the final outcome of the case provided earlier.

Final outcome

The company mentioned in the case optimized the authorization process and limited it to four steps. This was achieved through the implementation of a SOA architecture which merged the process into a presentation service based on mobile devices. This new functionality did not require any programming tasks; it was just established by adding a service layer.

In this way, managers may now grant authorizations using their mobile phones, immediately following intervention in the process. No Internet connection or phone calls are needed and, in addition, both the approval and the details of the authorization are recorded in the system. Accordingly, the information shown in the BAM tools is 100 percent reliable and accurately reflects the status of the process.

This functionality not only provided a high degree of flexibility to the company and its resources, but it resulted in increased speed and accuracy by putting an end to the not-available-at-desk syndrome, which affects daily management efficiency. The organization leveraged the flexibility it acquired for decision making with a view to foster operations dynamism and synchronization, by providing access to processes at any time, from any mobile device (including mobile phones, PDAs, and smartphones).

This was the first step taken by the organization toward a gradual implementation in the direction of a SOA, thus solving issues with a high impact on its business and achieving a flexible process which provides reliable information.

All this is accomplished in four simple steps: analysis, selection, cutoff, and replacement.

Implementing Your First BPM Project: Tips and Pitfalls Case Study

Karl Djemal, Citi, United States

ABSTRACT

Doing your first BPM project may not be easy. There is a lot to learn. Understanding what BPM really means to an organization can be a huge challenge and then you need to familiarize yourself with the products that you will use and apply them correctly.

This paper will describe a real-life example in which I participated. I will describe the problem we were looking to solve and the process that we went through to find the product to support our requirements. I will then describe the steps that we had to take to get our development up and running, some tips and possible pitfalls to be aware of and how we used Agile Development to help us achieve our delivery.

INTRODUCTION

Back in mid-2005, Equities Technology had delivered a number of projects over the course of the previous few years, to help support a number of key initiatives for the Global Equities Middle Office Department. This resulted in new systems (along with existing ones) that our users had to learn and use in order to carry out their daily duties.

The business vision was rapidly moving on which it needed to be if it was to continue to support new initiatives. Along with ever-increasing market volumes, it became a challenge for our organization.

Both the business and technology partner well together, but some of our efforts have taken time to deliver. We needed to find a way not only to improve our time to market, but to make it easier for the business to do their job. Our Equities Middle Office put together their requirements that would help us move on to that next stage and the resultant product is known as the 'Integrated Desktop.'

THE CHALLENGES OUR USERS FACED

The Equities Middle Office has automated much of their business process. For many of our clients we are able to achieve Straight Through Processing (STP) without a user needing to actually get involved and perform a piece of work. But occasionally things break, requiring someone to investigate and fix. For some of our clients we need to have processes in place that require someone to manually perform various tasks. The challenges our users are faced with include:

- Working with more than one system, each with there own user interface (UI) and separate login procedure.
- Some of these UIs have work pushed out to them, while others require you to search for (pull) work.
- It can be difficult for a user to know which piece of work to look at next so that clients' Service Level Agreements (SLA) are not breached or market deadlines missed.

- Being able to escalate work to your supervisor or route work for someone else to action.
- Appreciating any dependencies there could be between different pieces of work.
- Maintaining reference/static data.
- Being able to view work in a way that is appropriate to your role. For example as a supervisor I might be interested in seeing a high-level summary of the work that is being carried out by my Middle Office Sales-assistants.
- Being able to see any potential bottlenecks in the business process.
- Changes to the business process can be difficult as everything tended to be viewed from a systems point of view.

THE KEY REQUIREMENTS FOR THE INTEGRATED DESKTOP

From these challenges some of the key requirements for this effort became apparent.

- Depending on the role of a user, present a single view of all work that they need to action, regardless of where it is in the business process or which system they need to access.
- The work should be presented to the user in priority order based on factors such as Client SLA, Market Regulations and the Type of Work
- Allow the user to directly access the underlying system in order to action the work.
- The user should only need to login once (into the Integrated Desktop) without having to re-login to all the other applications they need to use.
- Depending on your role, provide different 'high-level summaries' of the work, with the ability to drill down into lower level detail.
- Being able to pass the work on to other users or have it escalated.
- Provide Business Activity Monitoring (BAM) so that our business can react early and take the appropriate action should bottlenecks in the business process occur.

Addressing these key areas will allow our business to make more efficient use of their resources, reducing the number of errors and hence risk and provide an even better service to our clients.

FINDING THE SOLUTION

We had produced a formal Business Requirements Document (BRD). Our next steps were to consider what solutions were out there in the market that could satisfy those requirements.

A team was initially formed that consisted of Global Senior Business and Technology heads, Local Regional heads and a Business Analyst, Business Users and Technical Architect (yours truly).

At first we started by just having an initial look at what was out there and inviting companies in for demonstrations. This gave us a feel for the variety of possible solutions which covered three different views:

1. BPM Products
2. Consultancy companies that could build solutions
3. Off-the-shelf solutions

We then produced a Request for Proposal (RFP) and invited around 10 organizations covering these three different views to submit their response. The RFP not only covered our Business Requirements, but also specified some of our technical requirements for today and the future based on the potential of increasing volumes.

The real challenge started when the responses came back. There was a lot to read! To help us we also developed a scoring system. We took our main requirements and broke them down into sub-requirements, with these being graded 1-5 to indicate how well a response from an organization catered for this need. The sub-requirements were also weighted within the requirement to get an overall score for that requirement. Finally the requirements themselves were also weighted against each other.

The requirements covered not only business related issues such as Organization of Work, Client SLAs and Presentation of work, but also technical items such as Performance and Stability, Reliability, Supportability (from the organization), Security and Audit, Integration tools and Technology supported.

From the initial 10 responses, we then asked five of the companies to formally present their proposal to the team, which then allowed us to follow up with the final two—both providing BPM Products/Tools.

We decided to conduct a Proof of Concept with one of the vendors. To do this, we took a real business flow that could demonstrate the vendor's products ability to satisfy a number of our key requirements. A team from the vendor came on to our site and worked very closely with the business users, business analyst and technical architect to develop the solution. During this five-day period we actually ran this as a mini Agile project and included a demo to the business heads and users at the end.

During this whole process we also worked very closely with other groups within our company who were also looking for a vendor solution for their BPM effort. We were therefore able to share our finding and views with each other. Our Global Architecture and Engineering Group were also engaged and were able to take the product through a number of tests before the final decision was made.

I should also add that I wrote the proposal to build the solution in-house, but I'm afraid that I was unsuccessful with my bid.

INTRODUCING AGILE DEVELOPMENT

I had been looking at alternative development methods to the 'waterfall' approach. I had read a number of books and articles on Agile Development and had even tried a few of the practices on some of the projects I had led. Therefore, when we were at a point where the next step in the project was to produce the Functional Specification as per our waterfall method, I put forward the proposal to run this as an Agile project.

WHY AGILE?

Some of the biggest issues with the waterfall approach are:

- Users typically don't see the system that is being developed until very late in the project lifecycle—typically when a lot of the code has already been written. Now this may not be a problem if the project is not very long, but normally waterfall is used for projects that aren't exactly small. Allowing a user to see what it is they are getting early on in the development provides opportunity for feedback.

- It expects us to understand all the requirements up front. This isn't as easy as it might sound. People can have ideas and vision, but isn't it sometimes better to look at the detail perhaps when we have developed some of the key functionality? Why put in so much effort defining how a particular requirement is going to work when it could be months or even years before it gets implemented? And if your business goals and objectives change, some of these requirements may never see the light of day.

- It is a very documentation-heavy process—business requirements, functional specifications, technical design—to name but a few. Taking on board the previous point could mean we have a large amount of paperwork that needs to be reviewed, which adds to the time before anything is delivered. Another common problem is then keeping that documentation up to date.

- It doesn't handle changes in requirements very well. I've certainly seen users asking for changes, but because we were fairly well into the project lifecycle, we have to turn around and say that it's too late to incorporate this or if we do, then the project will be severely delayed.

- Typically such projects are 'Big Bang' delivery, which could be high risk to the business. With so much functionality being delivered there is an increased likelihood of problems.

OVERVIEW OF THE AGILE PROCESS

With these above concerns and many others, this is where Agile can help. Agile is an approach for developing software in incremental deliverables. The approach that we adopted is based on an Agile process known as 'Scrum." Here is a quick overview:

1. A 'Product Backlog' is maintained by a 'Product Owner' and contains a prioritized list of features that the customer wants. Items can get added and taken away at any time.
2. The 'Team' (responsible for delivering features for the product) sits down with the Product Owner and members of the business users to discuss which features on the Product Backlog they should try and deliver in the next iteration of work (Sprint). This meeting, called the Sprint Planning Meeting, allows the team to hear verbally details of the requirements for the features and to ask any questions. It also allows them to estimate the size of the work required to implement the features and hence determine whether they can deliver them in the up and coming Sprint, which is 30 days long.
3. Items that the team will do in the Sprint are placed on a Sprint Backlog. These features are then broken down into underlying tasks that the team will need to carry out, which are also estimated.
4. Team members then pick tasks to work on. They also update the estimates on tasks they work on to show progress—which can be plotted graphically on what is called a Sprint Burndown Chart. This chart shows how much work is left to do as each day of the Sprint lapses.
5. Every day the team have a standup meeting (Daily Scrum) which lasts no more that 15 minutes. Each member of the team takes it in turn to report on what they have been working on since the previous Daily Scrum, what they will be working on next before the next Daily Scrum and whether there are any impediments that are actually stopping them from delivering their tasks. These standup meeting are used to

provide a daily verbal update on progress and therefore anyone with an interest can attend.

6. At the end of the Sprint, the team demonstrate the delivered features (Sprint Review Meeting), ideally allowing the users to actually try out these new features for themselves. This provides further opportunity for feedback from them.

7. The team also holds a Sprint Retrospective Meeting with the Product Owner to discuss how the Sprint went, highlighting things that have gone well, along with the lessons learnt and how to improve going forward.

8. Then the whole process is repeated again, by having the next Sprint Planning Meeting to pick out the next set of features to deliver.

9. The decision as to when to release a set of delivered features is always decided during the Sprint Planning Meeting. Therefore we could have a number of features delivered over more than one sprint before they are finally release into production.

The main advantages of working in this way are to overcome some of the problems with waterfall. Users are now able to see what is being delivered more frequently. By reviewing with them we get the feedback that allows change, but more importantly we deliver what they real want. We are better able to handle changes in business priorities, while still achieving and delivering into production.

GETTING STARTED—FIRST THINGS FIRST

One of the first things that we did was to actually get some training. We worked with the vendor and came up with a five-day training course that was run in-house and tailored to suit our needs. Both members of the business and technology teams attended. We all felt that this was extremely important if we were to have a working relationship where a common notation would be used to design business processes and form a key component for building our BPM solutions.

It was also recognized that while the training was extremely valuable, engaging the services of people who have previous experience with the vendor product would also help contribute to our success. This (at the time) wasn't as easy as it sounds as there were not a huge number of consultants with prior experience of the product outside the vendor itself. It may also be the case even today as maturity of BPM products is still growing.

SETTING UP OUR ENVIRONMENT

Setting up the development environment wasn't an easy task and involved quite a lot of effort. We had to set up Databases, Messaging Middleware and Application Servers to host the BPM Engine and Portal, and, of course, this was an additional learning curve for the development team. There may also be other technology products that we may need to consider going forward such as a Rules Engine.

This exercise of setting up development environments also needed to be repeated for our Integration, QA and Production (including Disaster Recovery). As there were a number of groups within our organization also looking to implement BPM solutions using the same vendor product, a shared-technology services team was created. They provide all the different types of environments that are needed from development through to production, along with the tools and products to help support this infrastructure. This group also helps in providing a source of subject matter expertise to other developers. The development team used Agile to help plan and set up the environment.

TESTING FRAMEWORK

As part of setting up our initial development environment we also started to think about testing. The developers were familiar with writing unit tests for their code, but now we had to also think about how we test business process models that we were working with. One of our consultants had experience of this before and had developed a framework that wrapped around the vendor products API. By using this we were able to write tests that would simulate processing by our business process as we were building it. The testing framework also allowed us to make assertions to validate that the correct paths were being taken within the process.

For example, we would create a test Order object and have this delivered to the process. Properties on this Order would be set such that an error should be detected by the process and hence create a piece of work assigned to the correct role, with the appropriate priority. We could then assert into the process that this work had indeed been created by using the testing framework to check that we had arrived at a particular 'interactive' activity—a notation used to indicate an activity requiring human intervention.

Other tools that we used to help us with our testing were to use Mock Objects. These are objects that are used to simulate the behavior of a real object in a controlled way. By using Mock Objects it is easier to unit test our work without having to do full-blown integration testing. As an example, one of the factors used to decide the priority of work within our process is the Clients SLA. These SLAs are held in a database, however there is some complex logic used to pick the appropriate SLA, implemented by another system. We therefore used a Mock Object to simulate the return of an SLA.

TESTING THE USER INTERFACE

While we were able to use the vendor products API and a framework around this to write tests to verify our business process, this didn't test the user interface (UI). For this we were able to engage our Quality Assurance (QA) to help. This team had the skills to use another well-known product that can be used to test UIs. They also put together the test scripts to help with integration and regression testing.

CONTINUOUS INTEGRATION AND THE BUILD PROCESS

Another practice that we use, that is very closely associated with some of the best practices on the engineering side of Agile development, is Continuous Integration. This is a practice whereby developers make small, frequent changes to the implementation of the business process. These changes are unit-tested and then committed back into the source control repository.

We also setup a very simple automated process that would run every hour and rebuild the application, picking up all the latest changes that had been checked into the source control system and then publish and deploy this into our integration environment and run the entire suite of tests against it. As the underlying code to implement the business process models was in Java, we were able to use the JUnit framework to help run all our tests, including those that I described above for testing our business process. Test result pages were generated in HTML format so that the team could view the results and fix anything that we might have broken.

We used Ant to help with this process, by creating scripts that would do the build, publish and deploy and execute the tests.

AGILE AND DOCUMENTATION

Agile prefers to replace much of the formal documentation process with more communication between users and developers and writing tests, which in themselves are a form of documentation for the requirements of the features being implemented. I've known some people to misinterpret the Agile view on documentation to meaning that we don't write any at all. In my mind what Agile is actually stating is to do things that add value. Therefore if writing some documentation will, for example, add value to a conversation with a user, then it clearly makes sense to do so.

With BPM and the designing of the business process we are able to use a graphical notation such that the business, business analysts and developers are able to come closer together in communicating their requirements. This was something supported by the vendor product. The developers are then able to take these business process designs and implement that code required to execute these processes.

It is also possible to add further descriptive documentation to the design and HTML pages can also be generated.

This way of working not only helps remove concerns people may have about the lack of documentation, but also allows BPM and Agile to really complement each other by generating only what truly adds value.

ADDING TO YOUR BUSINESS PROCESS

One difficult we have found, is when developers are adding to the business process diagrams, in particular, when they are working on the same process. When we do this with, say Java code, and developers run into conflicts when checking their code back into the source control system, it can be fairly simple (providing they are continuous integrating their code) to resolve these issues and this process can be further helped by tools such as Eclipse.

However, when we run into conflicts with processes, it can be difficult to try and merge the underlying XML format that is stored to represent the diagrammatic form. There are no tools that allow you to compare the process diagrams (and the underlying code that has been implemented) and merge them.

Therefore to overcome this problem, when we need to add to the process, we look to do a 'standalone' version of the change first. In some cases, depending on the nature of the change, we even found that we could demonstrate the change to our users and get their feedback—something that Agile strongly favors. Finally once the change was completed, then we would integrate this back into the main process and check this back into our source control system.

Another pitfall that became apparent was that we were using a number of activities on our processes and hence implementing underlying code, when writing actual classes was a better solution. By writing these classes, performance can also be improved as well as ending up with less cluttered business process diagrams. However, it can make it harder for the users to follow certain aspects of the business process if these end up being encapsulated within classes.

The above two issues present some interesting dilemmas. On the one hand we wanted to be able to support a working practice that would allow a business analyst to continue to add to our business processes as more features are introduced. On the other we potentially have issues when more than one person is working on the same set of processes. Then once in the hands of a developer, the processes are refined to suit a 'better' IT solution, removing or merging activities and adding modeling logic that on first impressions could be confusing to a business user.

By using Agile we overcome these issues as it encourages us to make smaller and more frequent changes to our processes. It brings everyone more closely together so that we are always communicating and gaining feedback as our models evolve.

GETTING IT UP AND RUNNING

The business processes that you design and the code that has been implemented need to be turned into a running system. The steps involved to publishing and deploying this into the BPM Engine and Portal running inside Application Servers can be quite involved. The Application Server hosts an EJB (Enterprise Java Beans) container. So while we never actually write any EJBs, the end results are that EJBs are generated. Therefore, we found that knowledge of EJB customization and configuration is required if we are to get the best possible production implementation (yet another learning curve). As this process is quite involved, prepare to automate this as much as possible—Ant scripts can once again help.

HANDLING CHANGE - REFACTOR

As we learned from our earlier implementations and using Agile to get feedback we have found that we have had to 'refactor' our business process designs. Refactoring is a term that has found it way into the engineering practices of Agile development and involves 'cleaning up code' to improve its design and readability, which in turn helps maintain it going forward. Not only is this a practice we used on classes and code that we wrote, but is also something that we used on the business process diagrams.

For example, as our processes began to evolve we could see that different sub-processes contained a collection of activities that were identical. Here we would encapsulate these into a single sub-process and have the other processes call this.

We have also made some large refactoring changes once we started to see our processes getting quite complicated and becoming difficult to maintain. The clues were typically seeing a growing number of conditional connections (transitions) leaving activities and going of in all kinds of directions.

Having a collection of tests to run before and after such changes becomes very important, but do be prepared to have to modify some of these tests.

CONCLUSION AND SUMMARY

Hopefully this paper has given you a flavor of potentially how big a task it can be to get BPM projects up and running. Figuring out what you are looking for to address not only your current needs, but also future needs provides some interesting challenges. Then once you have found the products and tools to help you on your way, you have to invest in training those developers to acquire new skills. Responding to changes in the business and time-to-market without impacting quality and service to our clients while maintaining operational efficiencies are critical. Where BPM can help support this and technology is required to achieve this, the close partnership between the business and IT is vital. We found that adopting Agile Development practices allows for small, frequent changes, improved communication and feedback, with quick turnaround times that will help meet these challenges and goals.

Engagement Transforms Processes, Inside and Outside the Enterprise

Raja Hammoud, Adobe Systems Incorporated, United States

ABSTRACT

As more and more businesses are discovering, even small improvements in streamlining and managing business processes can have disproportionately large impacts on the efficiency and competitiveness of a company. Smart approaches to Business Process Management (BPM) thus affect a company's bottom line and can deliver excellent returns.

Many process automation projects, however, fail to deliver the anticipated ROI results due to the inability to drive customers, partners, and employees to engage with these processes and adopt them. This typically stems from the fact that such projects put the sole focus on automating the overall process flow, without giving sufficient attention to all the activities process participants perform in order to complete a process task assigned to them.

Organizations quickly started realizing that just moving data to the right people did not ensure that processes got done more quickly with higher quality. People abandon processes if they cannot easily interact with them, or if they do not readily bring all the contextual information a person needs to rapidly make a decision.

INTRODUCTION

Ensuring that employees, partners, and customers can effectively engage with a process at every stage is critical to gaining the promised benefits of BPM.

According to a March 2007 survey by The Economist Intelligence Unit, 37 percent of executives believe they lose between 25 percent and 75 percent of their sales every year because their customers are not sufficiently engaged. Also, according to a September 2006 survey by eGov Monitor, 55 percent of European citizens who have used e-government services report a positive experience; "nevertheless, a considerable proportion (33 percent) of users experience at least one significant obstacle when using or trying to use online government services." Thus organizations must continue to support two channels of communication with stakeholders: the lower-cost digital environment and the high-cost, high-touch environment for those who refuse to, or cannot successfully, use more automated services.

Excerpts from the Economist Intelligence Unit survey highlight just how important engaged customers are:

- 79 percent of executives stated that engaged customers recommended products and services to others;
- 64 percent said engaged customers were frequent purchasers; and
- 61 percent of executives believed engaged customers provided frequent feedback on products and services.

The challenge for organizations is designing new processes that encourage engagement by people inside and outside an enterprise. Once processes are deployed, it is also critical to know how well they are performing to gauge in real-time the necessary actions to keep processes on track. By leveraging Business Activity Monitoring (BAM) as part of BPM technology, managers are creating personalized views of process analytics and can fine-tune implementations over the years.

This chapter focuses on how two companies are transforming their internal business processes (Dickinson Financial) and external-facing processes (GES Exposition Services) to increase user engagement and ultimately reduce costs, accelerate processes, improve the quality of services, and increase their competitive advantage.

CLOSING THE INTERNAL ENGAGEMENT GAP

While the world is getting increasingly more digitized, many of today's business processes still heavily rely on paper and manual routing. Until recently, for example, Dickinson Financial used paper forms to initiate and process customer service requests for new accounts, loans, account changes, and stop payments. These forms typically had to be routed manually to Dickinson Financial's central office for processing.

For instance, if a customer applied for a debit card, staff completed the paper form and sent it to headquarters for processing. Considering transit time, checking forms for errors, and manual approval processes, it could take up to three weeks for a customer to receive a debit card—and with customers demanding better, faster services, this delay was a competitive liability.

Dickinson saw room to improve various tasks within these processes. For instance, bank branches often had different versions of forms on file, increasing the likelihood that staff would complete and submit outdated versions of request forms. The result: more delays and higher everyday administrative costs.

To enhance services and streamline administration, Dickinson integrated dynamic digital documents as part of automated systems aimed at controlling the processing of forms for account changes, account openings, and other activities. The system blends Portable Document Format (PDF) forms, a Web 2.0 development environment, and process management capabilities to deliver rich user interfaces that speed delivery, completion, and processing of business forms.

Dickinson automated its first few processes, including its debit card process. By replacing manual, paper processes for ordering debit cards with an automated process, the company accelerated card approval and delivery to customers by 300 percent, thus reducing the total elapsed time for delivery from 15 days to five. Much of that efficiency gain is due to Dickinson Financial's new ability to automate the process, digitally route tasks instead of relying on paper routing, eliminate inaccurate and time-consuming rekeying of data, and engage process participants through easy-to-use dynamic interfaces that perform automatic lookups and validations.

Dickinson enforces consistency by making sure forms are only available as platform- and application-independent PDF files through the company's intranet, so staff always gets the latest versions, and no time is wasted due to staff submitting out-of-date forms. Staff only needs to enter a few details about existing customers or requested services, and backend systems will instantly pre-populate the appropriate forms with data on hand.

For Dickinson, the benefits of better engaging staff and then subsequently with customers are real. Employees are happy to use the new forms because they appreciate the fact that they can do their jobs faster, more easily, and more accurately. Customers are pleased as well. Forms are now almost always error-free, and customers do not have to restart a process because of incorrect data entry or illegible handwriting. Instead, they can get the services they requested, faster than ever.

Looking ahead, Dickinson's goal is to speed its processes by automating more than 300 form-based processes and providing users access to those forms via the corporate intranet or Internet. Meanwhile, IT is looking at capturing form data instantly from intelligent forms into backend systems, eliminating inaccurate and time-consuming rekeying of data altogether.

By mid-2008, the company plans to integrate digital signature pads into branches, so customers can electronically sign and complete transactions in real-time. With digital signature capabilities, banking branches can automatically route completed loan and other forms to all departments for processing. Digital signature capture should extend automation—and slash response time—for a host of vital bank services, including loan applications and account open requests. And faster closure should help Dickinson attract even more customers and get them into the system before other banks catch their attention.

REALIZING THE FULL POWER OF BPM WITH ENGAGEMENT

Most BPM projects over the years focused on the process flow to get information to the right people at the right time. Unfortunately, very little focus and attention were given to what a process participant does once he or she gets a work request, such as a new account enrollment form.

Organizations quickly realized that just moving documents or data to the right people does not ensure the process gets done quickly with high quality. People abandon the process if they cannot easily interact with it, or if it does not bring them all the contextual information they need to make a decision using an intuitive interface.

Steps to Success

For each process, an organization has to plan how it will engage users, connect all participants inside and outside a firewall, and automate the capture and processing of information across diverse groups and disparate systems.

Engage

People have to experience an easier way of doing things—faster, more effective, and more reliable—than the old, or they will not make the switch. Employees will continue to use outdated processes and subtly—or not-so-subtly—undermine new ones. Customers will turn to call centers or competitors, if the new processes are too complicated for them to complete with confidence. Partners will give up on the "proper channels" and just phone the contacts they have worked with in the past.

Rich and dynamic user interfaces help engage process participants. Technologies and environments built on open standards and integrated process management capabilities help ensure higher rates of user adoption and compliance with new processes, welcoming users with intuitive, easy-to-understand choices.

For instance, a familiar-looking form can help an uncertain customer feel confident enough to begin, and can then reveal its capabilities as needed. For example, some solutions today provide a way to engage customers with a *form guide*, a wizard-like approach that steps users through transactions, making sure they see only the information they need at a particular step in the process, to avoid overwhelming them with options. Form guides provide form developers options for reaching out to stakeholders with guidance, graphics, animations, calculations, and database lookups within the forms.

Automate

Automation is the great enforcer for any process strategy: it follows the rules with an unswerving accuracy that no employee can match, helping ensure that all business transactions and interactions comply with best practices and the highest standards of service. Businesses benefit from that consistency when form submissions are also automated and completed forms move automatically to the next step in a process, without a customer or employee having to know what that next step is.

Integrate

Typically large backend applications still deliver the goods and services. So while it is important that processes are engaging, it is also critical that they are built around industry standards, thereby providing greater assurance they will integrate seamlessly with middleware and enterprise systems, as well as support future services.

CLOSING THE EXTERNAL ENGAGEMENT GAP

For GES Exposition Services, a leading provider of services to tradeshow exhibitors, several key processes depend on customers completing forms quickly and accurately. Traditionally, GES compiled customized service kit order forms (SKOF) for exhibitors to complete to request and pay for services. Exhibitors had to fill out multiple lengthy forms, repeating much of the same information each time. Customers disliked the approach and mistakes were inevitable as people filled out long forms by hand.

Recognizing an opportunity to improve its tradeshow support services, GES decided to automate the process that exhibitors go through when completing and submitting requests. GES built an automated process called IntelliKit—a digital kit of dynamic forms that exhibitors worldwide can complete using free, readily accessible client software—to request services. In contrast to the paper forms, the digital documents are easy for exhibitors to navigate and can be completed in a fraction of the time.

Behind the scenes, process management solutions orchestrate several essential services for GES, such as importing and exporting XML data into forms and backend applications, as well as helping generate and decode barcodes to speed processing of forms submitted on paper. IntelliKit interfaces with Show Services, the main GES operational system for provisioning expositions, to submit exhibitor order data in XML.

The combination of internal process enhancements, intuitive electronic forms, barcode generation, and automated document generation is helping GES to realize long-term benefits such as cost savings by reducing paper use, improved efficiency in processing service kit order forms, and automated order entry using barcode scanning. IntelliKit also supports GES in standardizing products and pricing across the organization, and transforming the internal processes associated with generating and assembling long exhibitor packets. The results have been impressive, with administration savings of over $400,000 annually.

Equally important, the company's customers are engaging easily with the new system. They like the forms' resemblance to the once-familiar paper forms and appreciate even more the forms' new capabilities, which include auto completion of name and contact information and immediate notification when an answer does not match a range of answers for a given field. Not only are customers wholeheartedly adopting the new processes, they are also reporting increased satisfaction and ease in accessing services, which is expected to lead to growth in sales.

RIAs Extend the Power and Reach of Processes

Both GES and Dickinson Financial offered their users intuitive and readily accessible PDF forms in online and offline modes to better engage them in automated processes. Rich Internet applications (RIAs) based on Web 2.0 technologies offer another very powerful means for increasing engagement with staff, customers, citizens and partners.

To better engage people, organizations need web applications that provide a desktop application-style experience, where people can fill in information and have the application respond immediately to their choices. Users want to be able to get to the application wherever, whenever they are, and they have become accustomed to simple, intuitive interfaces. RIAs address these requirements, offering a valuable channel for capturing and processing information from people inside and outside an organization.

Well-designed RIAs welcome people with highly graphical, easy-to-navigate interfaces that connect to multiple backend systems and present functionality to users in intuitive ways. Even the technology-shy can easily access and provide information to the most complex of backend systems, without knowing anything about how many systems are involved in their requests.

Often, however, in regulated industries, there is a need to comply with well-defined forms that may be too long and intimidating for users. A dynamic transition from RIAs to forms offers organizations the ability to satisfy both requirement for keeping process participants engaged through an intuitive RIA-based application, and complying with a predefined form by generating it on the fly with all data captured through the RIA interface.

Conclusion and Summary

Organizations now have more options available than ever to engage staff, partners, and customers with interactive applications, real-time data capture, and dynamic and secure processes. There is no reason why multi-stage, cross-organizational processes like "bank account opening" or "manufacturing document review" should continue to be a challenge for organizations.

Today's technologies enable both customers and users inside an enterprise to create, deliver, and collaborate on a range of business content. Built-in document policies that limit who can review documents and how they move inside and outside an organization offer much-needed control, which is especially important when people engaged in processes cannot or do not understand the proper steps. At the same time, e-forms and e-signatures can add up to dramatic reductions in cycle and approval times, transforming the speed of an organization and the nature of the customer experience.

The benefits are too significant for organizations to ignore. Today's best tools have already been proven in hundreds of real-world implementations, as organizations have replaced manual processes with automated ones that connect internal and external teams.

Organizations should aim to deploy BPM solutions that integrate seamlessly with existing systems and bring together engaging RIA front ends with pervasive presentation technologies. In this way, they can leverage a broad set of capabilities to engage employees, customers, and partners with tools that quickly improve business processes. An organization that hesitates may soon find that these BPM technologies are already at work elsewhere, cutting costs and enhancing services for competitors.

Spotlight

Human-Centric BPM and Workflow

Automation vs. Facilitation

BPMN defines the look of a process, but not how to draw it.

Keith D Swenson, Fujitsu Computer Systems, United States

Keith D Swenson, Fujitsu Computer Systems, United States

INTRODUCTION

Business Process Modeling Notation (BPMN) is a graphical notation standard broadly adopted across BPM vendor products. BPMN defines the way that a process "looks." Some people think that his means that a given process is modeled the same way in all such products, but this is not true. Some people jump to the conclusion that a process drawn a given way will execute the same on all process engines that support BPMN, but this is also not true. The purpose of this article is to give a concrete example of a process that will be drawn different ways depending upon assumptions about the target of the diagram.

There is a strong desire for a *lingua-franca* for BPM—a single consistent language for describing a business process, which would work in all situations for all purposes. As organizations expend more and more resources to define processes to run their business, a *lingua-franca* would preserve their investment and allow reuse of process models across a variety of situations. Many people have hoped that BPMN would be that single common language for a process.

This article dispels the myth that BPMN defines a single way to draw a process. This is not what BPMN was defined to be, and there are good reasons why it cannot be as such. BPMN is a notation and not a language. The distinction between these is sometimes elusive. BPMN was designed to be methodology agnostic, so that it can be used in both business situations as well as technical situations, and this design goal is probably the reason for its success. This article will explore in some depth two different methods for designing processes, both of which use BPMN, aimed at two different audiences, and for implementation on two different process platforms.

This article will help everyone gain an appreciation that these differences in modeling are not flaws due to arbitrary differences in approach, but necessary differences due to the many different aspects of process modeling. Two approaches are compared. One is a data-centric methodology that focuses on how bytes are passed from one system to another. The other is a human-centric methodology that focuses on the activities that people do. It should not come as a surprise that a model of what people do will look different than a model of what data is passed between computer systems, even though the process is the same.

This article will cover:
- Setting the Stage—Brief overview of BPM standards and popular assumptions about their use as well as a few myths that need busting.
- Defining the Human Activity—how this differs from an activity in a Business Process Execution Language (BPEL) process and why this matters
- A Method for Defining Human Processes—an approach that focuses on activities of people and how they interact, instead of focusing on how data flows through the system

- The Email Voting Process for BPEL—diagrams from the process as it is presented in the BPMN specification
- The Email Voting Process for Humans—how BPMN can be used to define a human process that is the same process as the one in the BPMN spec, but looks completely different
- Discussion and Conclusion

In the end we will see that a diagram of a human process focuses on the human activities, and that this is useful for training people, as well as explaining where they are in the process. This diagram can be drawn using the BPMN standard, but it does not look the same as a diagram drawn for a BPEL. The surprising conclusion is that the exact same process is drawn more than one way using BPMN. Again, this should not be surprising because BPMN is not a complete language, but only a dictionary of notations that can be used in a diagram. As such, it still provides a huge benefit because a reader of the diagram can recognize things and know that the meaning is consistent.

SETTING THE STAGE

At the dawn of 2008 we find a wide variety of standards that are relevant for BPM. Three of them stand out as part of the BPMN-XPDL-BPEL value chain:

- Business Process Modeling Notation (BPMN) is widely accepted in the 1.0 release from the Object Management Group (OMG), and there is a 1.1 version being privately circulated to address limitations in 1.0 as well as plans for a 2.0 version, which is still in the far future.
- XML Process Definition Language (XPDL) is a widely implemented file format for exchanging process definitions between various process tools. The 2.0 release is two years old. A 2.1 version is ready for public review and will probably be ratified before this article is published.
- Business Process Execution Language (BPEL) is a widely discussed language for implementing web service choreography. The market has generally become aware of the limitations of the format: it focuses on exchange of data between servers, which is fine if that is what you are doing, but it misses the largest part of what most people view as being business-related. There are planned extensions to add human activities, subprocesses, and other missing features to this language.

The holy grail of BPM is a way to define a business process once and be able to deploy and run that process on any BPM server. The benefit of this is obvious: organizations spend tremendous resources on defining their processes, and they would like to be able to store and exchange them in a format that preserves their investment over time. In 2002, BPEL was introduced as a new standard for process engines. Unfortunately, most people did not realize that the intent of BPEL was simply to be able to write programs to send and receive XML data—something better known as Web Service Orchestration. Media hype around BPEL led the public to believe that this could be a common language for all business process needs. BPEL has largely failed to live up to the marketing hype for two reasons. First it is unable to represent human activities directly. The effect of this will be made clear later in this article. The second reason is that since every vendor has to resort to proprietary extensions to do all but the most basic things, the resulting BPEL output is not really portable between vendors. For these and other reasons, most vendors have stepped away from the language for human BPM uses, while it retains its position as a web service orchestration language.

It then seemed that the only hope for a common language would be BPMN, the modeling notation. Almost all vendors have endorsed BPMN and there are no large competitors. The theory was that if all vendors could support BPMN semantics consistently, we would finally have a way to draw the process once and run it everywhere. However BPMN does not fully define the semantics behind the elements as they are composed together; it was never intended to do this. The designers of BPMN knew that there were many ways to model a business process, and that the success of BPMN would lie in its ability to be used with multiple different process modeling methodologies.

Different approaches to the same problem can yield a different drawing—while still conforming to BPMN—because the approach to drawing a diagram makes implicit assumptions about the capabilities that can be used in that diagram. We will demonstrate that our two different approaches, two different methodologies, and two different sets of assumptions, will get two very different results.

The "Automator" Approach

"Human Process Automator" is a term I use for someone who is taking a manual business process and is attempting to replace humans with computer systems. Many tedious and routine business tasks could be automated by software, freeing up people up to focus on more creative tasks. The ultimate goal is to completely automate the process and remove all manual labor from it.

An Automator focuses on the inputs and outputs of human activity, and writes software to produce the same outputs automatically. BPEL is a language that is strongly oriented to support the needs of an automator in service oriented architecture (SOA). BPEL offers powerful capabilities to send data, receive data, and to transform data. BPEL's native support of XML allows it to work independent of the specific hardware and software platforms it communicates with.

An activity within BPEL is an activity that the computer performs. That activity might be to send information to a person. A later activity might be to collect the response from that person. This naturally can be used to implement a business process, or any other communication-oriented activity, but the BPEL itself is about sending and receiving bytes.

Much of the work on BPMN has been focused on how to make diagrams that can be converted to BPEL. The examples in the BPMN specification are of this flavor, and in some cases even provide the desired BPEL result of the conversion.

The "Facilitator" Approach

"Human Process Facilitator" is a term for someone who diagrams a business process that uses people to do things that cannot be automated. People make decisions based on criteria that are not formally defined. For example, which print advertisement should be used for this month's ad campaign? Or who is the best person to fill this open position? These activities will never be automated. The facilitator is not trying to replace the people in the process, but rather to facilitate people working together.

Since it is people who must perform the tasks, the facilitator needs a process diagram that describes what the people do, not what the computer does. This process diagram is composed of human activities, and a human activity is fundamentally different from a computer activity in a number of ways. People need reminders and ways to prioritize their tasks. People need to have the data presented in a human readable way. The characteristics of a human activity are expanded in the next section.

Process design patterns also differ for human processes. People do not like to be prodded a number of times in quick succession for the same case, so it is best to group everything that a person needs to do at one time into a single activity instead of creating series of small tasks as you might do for a computer.

A BPM system for human facilitation has built-in capabilities specifically designed to support typical human interaction patterns. If a facilitator did not make use of these capabilities, the resulting process diagrams would be many times more complex because they would have to include all the details of fairly standard interaction patterns. Such increase in complexity would make the diagram less useful for explaining to people what needs to be done.

A person trying to facilitate human business processes has very different goals from someone trying to automate a human process. Both approaches are valid, and different forms of BPM have evolved to handle these different goals. We should not assume that one technology will meet the needs of both, even though there is overlap. The approach detailed in the BPMN specification represents the automator approach. The facilitator approach is further defined below. We use this approach to create a facilitator-oriented process and then compare the results to the sample process using the BPMN specification.

DEFINITION OF A HUMAN ACTIVITY

Before we talk about a method for facilitating human processes, we need to be clear about what a human activity is. Clearly it is work done by a human. It is not work that is done by a computer on behalf of a user. In order to focus on the human activity, we need to consider those things that facilitate the work as part of the task itself.

Before anyone will perform a task, that person certainly must be informed that the task needs to be done, given the details of the particular case, and have a way to communicate the results of the activity. These are part of any human activity. When modeling human activity, we focus on the work to be done: decide the menu for dinner, wash the dishes, feed the dog, or write a blog entry. Naturally, for a group of people to coordinate these tasks, there must be communication among them, *but a facilitator does not model the communications.* If I want my son to wash the car, clearly I have to tell him that I want him to wash the car, but I don't write that as a separate task on my task list. Instead, it is part of getting the car washed.

It is no surprise that systems designed for facilitating human activities allow you to model the work that is to be done at every step in a process, without being buried in the details of how you will tell that person to do the work, or how the results are collected. Such systems often include customizable ways that each user can decide how they wish to be informed: some users prefer email, others like to receive an SMS message on their phone, etc. A facilitator focuses on the task to be done (e.g. review this document) and lets the system take care of how that user is informed about the task. Similarly, the facilitator knows that an activity may be concluded with a decision (e.g. to either "accept" or "reject" the document), and that may effect the path that the process takes, but does not want to be concerned at the high level with how the system collected that response.

In order to allow a process diagram to be drawn that describes human activity, we assume that the following capabilities are inherently part of a human activity step:

(a) inform that the task needs to be done	This is known as "notification" to the user. Different people have differing requirements on how this notification must be accomplished. In many cases email will be sufficient. Some people have Blackberries and are informed quickly about such notifications. Sometimes SMS or IM is preferable. Some systems use phone paging. Email-based notification is not perfect because the lifespan of the email is different from the task itself: an emergency task may be resolved in a few minutes, but the email will last until the user deletes it. There is a usually mechanism called a WorkList that the user can check at any point in time to see what tasks remain.
(b) give the details of the particular case	This is the presentation of the information. There is usually a "form" involved, but the term does not to denote a particular technology, but rather any technology that can take information and display it for the user to view and manipulate. There are many options from a Visual Basic or Java programmed UI, to Xforms, to PSP web pages, to any number of options.
(c) have a way to record the results of the activity	There must be a way to indicate that a task is completed. The thing about human activities is that the completion of an activity can be compared to the "declaration" speech act. A declaration is a speech act that in the performance of it, changes the state of a group or organization. Announcing that a document is "approved" or "rejected" is a speech act that is relevant to many people involved in the process. It is quite common that the conclusion of a human activity is also a decision, that is, that the activity can be concluded more than one way and the process should continue on a different route depending on how this activity was concluded.
(d) have a deadline date for an activity	Because people do not work on one thing exclusively until completion and often have many tasks in progress simultaneously, a deadline is a way to make sure that tasks are not dropped too long. Any task might need a deadline.
(e) provide reminders of the activity	Reminders help in the managing of many tasks, since one task might easily get lost among a number of others. A reminder might be used as a warning that the deadline is approaching.

A process built out of human activities is dramatically less complex than one that uses more primitive activities. One might say that human activities hide a lot of detail. If your goal is to present the actions that people do, then the detail about how that person is notified that something is to be done is not important. Similarly, if you include all the details of how everyone is notified about every activity, then the entire diagram is likely to be too complex to be readable.

general notification definitions

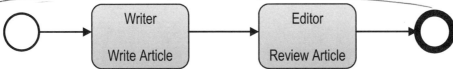

Process diagram for Human Facilitation

The effect of complexity on readability can best be demonstrated with the above extremely simple example of a human process: two human activities that represent a writer writing an article for a reputable publication, and an editor who must review that article to make a decision on whether the article is suitable for publication or not. This is a real process that when used in a real organization provides real value. A facilitator would draw it as you see above.

At the low level, a lot more is going on. If you model all the data that has to be exchanged between systems in order for these people to perform this, you would typically include all of this detail:

- send an email to a writer offering the chance to write an article
- receive an email from the writer agreeing to the task (presumably you ignore any later email message to this effect)
- send email to the editorial team informing them that the task has been accepted
- put the task on a task list that the writer can browse
- send an email (to writer and associates) prompting for the actual writing
  - send reminder email to writer
  - send escalation email to associates if it gets late
- receive the email message back with the document in it
- remove from writer's task list
- determine who should be the editor of this kind of article
- put the task on a task list that the editor can browse
- some editors also want an email message prompting them
  - send reminder email to editor
  - send escalation email to wider group of people if it gets late
- receive the email message back with the publication decision in it
  - OR receive an email saying to reallocate to a different person, loop back a couple steps.
- remove from editor's task list

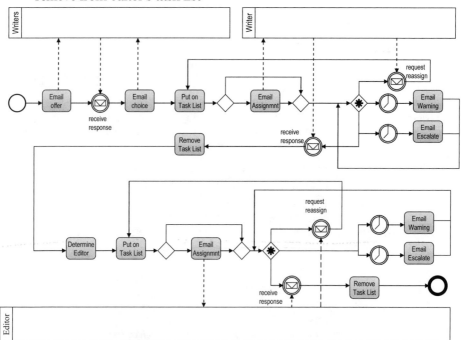

Process Diagram for System Automation

In a real human facilitation system, there would be a lot more flexibility than this, but this should be enough to show how complexity affects readability. BPEL is a language that is oriented toward this level of detail: the sending and receiving of bytes. A diagram that is drawn in order to implement the above process using BPEL, might look something like the following diagram.

The system programmer would welcome this diagram of the entire detail of exactly what chunks of information are sent at what time. But for the writers and editors, it is much harder to tell exactly what it is that the people are expected to do in the process. In fact this model never actually shows what the people are doing. It shows only what the systems are doing. This is a little like describing the work of an organization in terms of the telephone calls that people make. While you might be able to take a record of all the calls made, and deduce the work of an organization, the records of the calls are not a direct representation of the work. This is, again, fundamentally a tradeoff. If you are a facilitator, and want to model and facilitate human activity, then you want to make a diagram that shows human activities. If you are automating that work by transmitting information around the system using BPEL, then a lower level representation is appropriate.

A METHOD FOR DESIGNING HUMAN PROCESSES

So keep in mind that a human activity is a description of actual human work to be done, and that each activity is assumed to have (a) notification, (b) information, (c) conclusion, (d) deadline, and (e) reminders built in. The following 9-step method can be used to create a process for human facilitation.

Step 1: Identify Human Work

Start by enumerating the tasks that must be done by people. Ignore for the moment the paper form, the data on the form, or how that form is passed around. Those who expect this to be a programming exercise may be tripped up by this because of the tendency to focus on the artifacts that help people coordinate their work. We need at this point to look at work itself. These are tasks that depend upon a human skill to do.

There are three reasons why an activity might *not* be able to be automated:

- In some cases there are decisions to be made that cannot be automated and must be made by a person. For example, the determination of whether an article is fit for publication is a task that depends upon recent current events, suitability of the writing style, and the editorial preferences of a particular publication. Another example, the decision about which candidate is the best fit for an open position, is a task that depends upon the personalities of the candidate and the team they would join, as well as an assessment of skills and ability to perform the job. These decisions must be performed by a person because the most relevant attributes may not be able to be expressed in a quantitative way, like political correctness or personality. The rules behind what constitutes acceptable quantities are tacit and are not consciously known by the people who evaluate such rules. But indeed there are people who are very good at making such decisions. This is work that will never be automated.
- The second category is of tasks that might one day be automated, but to do so would require additional prep work that has not been done. For example, you might need someone to enter figures from a financial report that is received either on paper or in an electronic format that is not easily consumable. For the time being, it is simply less expensive to pay someone to do this than it is to pay a programmer to write the code that automatically converts the information. Eventually, these will be automated.
- The third category consists of physical tasks that must be done outside an information system. For example, driving a forklift to load goods from a truck into a place in a warehouse. Or to perform maintenance on a piece of equipment. It might be possible in the far future to automate these tasks

with robots, but there are significant barriers to automation due to the physicality of the task. For the time being, we must treat these as human work.

These human tasks are made explicit so that people with the right skills can be identified, or so that people can be trained to do those tasks. Everyone involved in the process needs to know what they do—not just those performing the task—so that everyone gains an understanding of how the tasks they do fit in with what the others are doing. The human tasks need to be described in a way that the people themselves will understand using the specific vocabulary that the people in that organization use. There will normally need to be additional documentation associated that contains detailed information that is useful for training or skills identification.

Avoid including activities that do not involve humans. For example, running a query on a database is something that might be needed at some point in order to support a human task. At this point in the process, you simply assume that the right information is available. There is a later step that defines what information must be available, and a final step that defines how that information is retrieved, but those should be defined at the right point, which is much later in the method.

Step 2: Determine Activity Conclusions

Human tasks can be concluded in more than one way. For example, the decision of whether to accept or reject an article for publication will be concluded in two ways: "accept" or "reject." The conclusion of an activity is an explicit part of the activity itself. In many situations, there may be a third conclusion to this example activity, which is something that means more or less, "I am not qualified to make this decision." That is a possible way that an activity might be concluded. Some activities will have acceptable time limits, and may be concluded simply by the passing of time. Each conclusion is given a name.

Conclusions are important communication events. When you model a human process, you are modeling things that need to be communicated to the people involved in the process. Take for example the process of writing a book where many people are involved in various roles, such as writer, reviewer, editor, etc. The writer will at some point declare that the book (a particular draft) is ready for review. While this concludes one phase of writing, more importantly it tells others that they may start their activities of reviewing and editing the current copy. The conclusion of a human activity is most often a speech act known as a "declaration," a statement that in the act of uttering it changes the state of a group of people. Declarations often redefine what many people are expected to be doing. Therefore in a modeled human process the completion of one activity redefines what other people in the process are expected to do.

A conclusion should be considered a distinct conclusion only if it matters to the group. Take for example a task "Answer Question." You might think of the answer to the question, as being the conclusion of the activity, and there are one (or more) answers to every possible question that might be placed. Clearly it is nonsense to consider every possible answer as a possible conclusion of the activity. Conclusions are grouped into sets that affect the flow of the process further on. To be specific, if the flow of the process does not depend at all on whether the task is completed or not, then it is sufficient to say that there is only one conclusion: "done." The president is given the choice to "sign" or "veto" a piece of legislation, and the process continues in different directions depending upon how this task is concluded. However, there is a time limit, and if Congress adjourns before the bill is signed, then this situation is called a "pocket veto." A "pocket veto" is considered to be completely identical to a "veto" as far as the process is concerned, so we would not need a separate conclusion for the pocket veto: the timeout rule would simply be another way to conclude the activity as a normal "veto."

Step 3: Put the Tasks in Order

The work and conclusions should be identified without getting overly involved in the sequence of activities. In many cases it is clear that a particular task needs to be done before or after another related task. There will also be branches, and certain tasks that are done only on certain conditions. This is where a diagramming tool becomes useful, but only if it can describe activities at the human level. If one activity must be completed before another, and that other activity can start as soon as the first is completed, then an arrow is drawn between them.

If an activity can be concluded in more than one way, and if each conclusion would cause the process to proceed in a different direction, then there can be an arrow coming out of that activity for each possible conclusion. Clearly, if the point of an activity is to "accept" or "reject" an article for publication, the process that continues after that point will be very different. Because this decision is the very point of the activity, the process becomes easier to read if there is a direct connection between the activity and the direction that the process goes. Some engines cannot represent this in this way, and instead save the conclusion into a variable which is then tested at a following branch gateway. This is an accepted and common practice, but because the branch is removed from the human task, it is harder to see the direct causal link.

The result is a network diagram of the human activities that must be performed properly set in a process that indicates the conditions and order of the activities.

Step 4: Determine Performers

After the tasks and order are identified, one needs to determine who should do the tasks. This is highly dependent upon a particular organization. It also changes from case to case. In some cases, there will be a pool of people who would be qualified to do the task, and anyone from that pool might be picked. What must be determined at this point is what set of rules will be used to determine who should do a particular job. It might be that a person with a particular skill is needed, and if a directory exists that lists all the people with that skill, then the rule is to find those people and pick one. More often the requirement will be that a particular person is chosen because of their responsibility in a particular part of the organization. For example, there may be a person designated to handle requests from a particular customer. Or there may be a person who is designated as handling all the purchase requests for a particular department.

Unfortunately such a rule cannot be specified without specific consideration of the organization that will be using the process. Each organization will have unique organizing principles, some of which are based on historical precedence. Even across a single organization, the rules to determine who does a particular activity may not be consistent. Any organization that grew by mergers of other organizations will have some "special" parts of the organization that are not like other parts. There also needs to be consideration about the specific representation of the organization in an organizational directory. If skills are not tracked, then that cannot be used to determine the person to perform the activity.

There generally will need to be an expression of some sort that can be evaluated in the context of the organizational structure that resolves the assignee of a particular task. This expression will usually make use of pre-existing groups and/or job titles in the organizational directory. It may require new groups or job titles. There may need to be multiple levels of groups, that is, groups that include groups. In some cases it may not be possible to determine *a priori* who will be performing a particular task. In some cases the assignee expression will narrow it down to a group of people, but immediate circumstances (who is available) may determine the final assignee. It might be necessary for the users to self-select for a particular job. There may need to be case-by-case adjustments, since it is not possible to know everything in advance.

Step 5: Determine the Information in the Process Context

Here you specify a schema or a set of schemas that carry the information context within which all the activities take place. If the process is for a customer to open a bank account, then there is specific information that needs to be carried for that process, such as the customer name, address, and references to other accounts or credit history. The context schema needs to be a superset of all information needed for every activity. For example, if there is an activity to assess the property value of a house, then clearly the details about the home address, prior sales information, and various reports about the locale are necessary to perform this activity. If one activity produces a result which is necessary in a later activity, such as the assessed value of a house, then there must be a variable that will hold that information between activities. By considering the information requirements of every activity in the process, you can compile a complete context schema required by the process.

The information content will be modeled differently by different implementation engines. For some there is a single schema for the context that is shared by all activities (effectively a union of all schemas required by the individual activities). Others have a collection of schemas that are transformed back and forth through the process. Either way, the idea at this point is to identify the information requirements of the entire process.

Step 6: Define Access to Information at Each Activity

At some points in the process, certain parts (variables) within the shared context can be read and updated. At other points information can be read, but not updated. There are also points in the process where information is completely hidden because it is either not yet specified at that point in the process, or not relevant to that particular activity.

Step 7: Determine Timeouts

An activity may have a requirement to be performed in a particular time period. What happens when that time period is exceeded? Does the process continue without the activity being completed, or does the process "fail" and go down a different path. There may be reminders that are additional notifications to the user that the task has not yet been completed. There may also be escalation to other people or management if the task is nearing the deadline without being completed. At this point for each activity, all time-dependent behaviors should be considered. Some tasks may have no time dependency at all, and may be allowed to remain uncompleted indefinitely.

We know that time equals money; so it is worth considering at this point the cost of every activity, as well as the cost to the organization of either delaying the activity, or not performing that activity. If you are simulating the execution of the process, these costs entered into the model can be accumulated across a simulation run in order to guide the further design of the process.

Step 8: Design the Presentation of the Information

This puts a face on the context information, mapping the schema to a visual presentation. This presentation might be specific to a given activity, or might be the same presentation over the entire process.

Humans don't read XML directly. Instead, the information has to be displayed in a way that is meaningful to the user. To be effective, the display should be organized for ease of use. Some of the information may be keys or links to other information, and the display should provide an easy way to access those external sources of information.

Technology to present the information is often described as "forms" in the BPM community, but you should keep in mind that any technology that can take data and generate a user interface can be used. The choice will depend on many factors outside the BPM system. Some organizations will choose Visual Basic or Java Swing because they have programmers experienced in these areas. Some might choose PHP or other web techniques. They might have powerful forms software designed specifically for this purpose. The process definition method should not get bogged down at this point in the specific requirements of the technology to be used. Instead, this step should focus on the look and feel of the displayed information.

Step 9: Integrate with Information Services

This is where the information needed in a process can be picked up from various sources and sent to various destinations. I use the term "service" in the generic sense of an SOA. This might be through web service calls or any other means to access other service types. The point simply is that there is a human activity that needs a particular piece of information, and so this is where you specify how that information will be retrieved for that human user.

It is this step where you finally consider how data is sent and received between computers. Many process designers start by considering how data is transferred through the system, and it leads them to a communications-centric view of the work. It can lead to activities that are optimized for computer communications, instead of being optimized for human work. Since human costs far outweigh computing resource costs in most business processes, it is important to start with the human tasks, and then work down to the integration tasks.

To access information from a web service, some of the process context information will need to be transformed appropriately into that XML that is needed as input to a web service. The resulting XML may need to be similarly transformed to be put back into the process context. For example, in an account application, the process may need to access a "credit rating" service to retrieve the applicant's credit rating for consideration in the application process.

Services are used not only for retrieval of information, but also for how the results of the human tasks will be sent out to destinations outside of the people directly involved in the process. For example, if the decision is made to approve a loan of a particular amount to a customer, then there are various parties that may need to be informed about this decision (e.g. by email) and there would also be calls to services to actually set up the account and initiate the sending of a contract to the parties involved.

There it is; nine steps that lead to a model of a human process. Not a complete methodology by any means, but still useful. The steps are repeated iteratively, with reviews at various points. Usually after each step there is some segment of the organization that is interested in reviewing the progress. It is also true that later steps will turn up details that were left out of earlier steps, and so there is some iteration through the method multiple times. A good system will allow simplistic execution of the process before you are complete, so that you can try out the process along the way. After Step 3 (Put the Tasks in Order), you should be able to run simulations of the process in order to gain confidence on the correctness of the process. After the process is implemented and deployed, you can collect statistics on how well it is running and cycle back through these to improve the process. We call it "Business Process Management" because you are never completely finished designing the process. This method is repeated as long as the process can be improved, and there are always new ideas on how to improve the process or to respond to external changes.

EMAIL VOTING PROCESS—AUTOMATOR APPROACH

In order to show how a human facilitation process would look different from a BPEL-oriented process, we need an example process that is done both ways. The BPMN 1.0 specification includes such a sample process. It is known as the Email Voting process. Bruce Silver, arguably the most respected analyst in the BPM field, has suggested that this be used as an example process to test interoperability between different process diagramming tools. One point in favor of this is that it is fairly well fleshed out and documented. Also, it is a real process that would be reasonable to use in real life.

The version in the specification was drawn explicitly to be converted to BPEL for implementation, so the process is designed around things that can be done in BPEL. As BPEL is a language for automating processes, the form of the process in the specification is an excellent example of an automator oriented diagram.

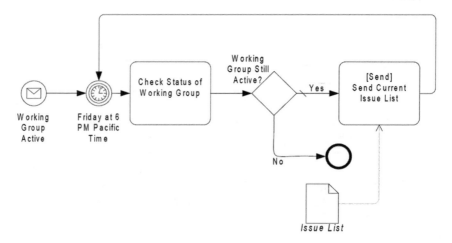

The Starter Process

Space restrictions prevent us including everything, so please refer to the BPMN specification itself for a complete description of the process. The process diagrams are included here as a more convenient reminder of the processes:

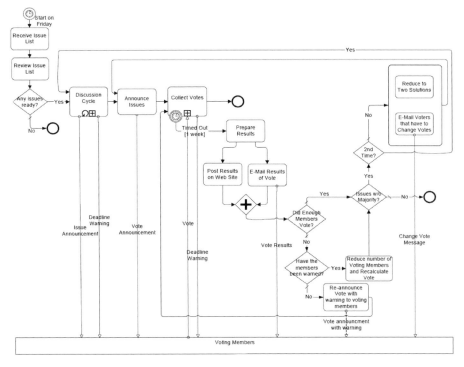

Top Level process, there are two subprocesses

EMAIL VOTING PROCESS—FACILITATOR APPROACH

As I set out to implement this process, it struck me how dramatically different the process would be drawn if you had an implementation engine that supported human activities directly.

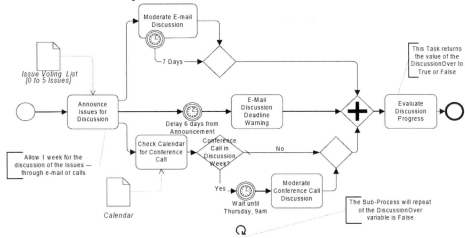

First Subprocess

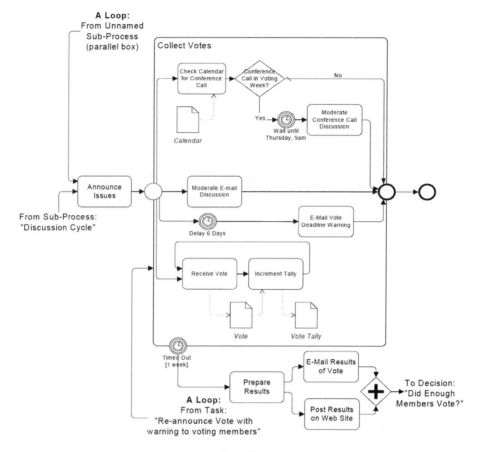

Second Subprocess

Many of the things that are broken out into separate activities would be combined into a single activity. Even at the basic level, the model would be different because you would be modeling the human activities instead of the flow of data back and forth.

The first step is to get a list of the actual human activities that appear in the process. To do this we fly up to the 40,000 foot level and look down, ignoring as much as possible the details that came into the process due to the need to execute it in BPEL. We start with the activities that have to be done by people, because they require human intelligence and really cannot be automated.

Activity 1: choose the issues for this week	The scenario assumes that there is an open ended list of possible issues that are being continually added to. It is not possible to talk about all issues every week, so someone must pick the most important issues. It is not possible to automate the determination of what the most "important" issues are, so this task of picking 1 to 5 issues for discussion and voting this week must be done by a person. There may not be enough issues this week, or it may be a holiday week, or any number of other possible reasons not to discuss issues this week, so the issue manager must choose whether there are "Issues" or "No Issues" this week.

Activity 2: discuss issues	There is a period of time within which people are allowed to discuss the issue, and that means having access to the issue descriptions, access to comments that others have made, and the ability to make comments on the issues. This is performed simultaneously by a large number of committee members.
Activity 3: determine if discussion is over	The issue list manager is asked in this process to take a look at the results of the current discussion, and decide whether the discussion needs to continue or not. Since this is a decision that is not automatable, we have to have the issue manager do it. There are two choices: "Continue the Discussion" or "Finish the Discussion."
Activity 4: vote on the resolutions to the issues	Mainly just recording the results of the activity. In this step, we can make use of a parallel activity called a "Voting Node" to allow everyone to be informed about the vote and to collect their responses in a convenient way.
Activity 5: remedy voting	This is a human activity in the case that voting "fails." Voting can fail when not enough people vote. The original BPEL-oriented process had a number of steps, most automated, to handle this situation. When considering the human tasks, an analysis of the process leads to the conclusion that a large number of the possible paths can be automated, but a few of the paths require a person to address the situation by either reducing the required number of voters or reducing the number of options being voted on. The key here is that in those situations a human must be brought in. What is important is that the person be notified that the voting has not worked and be given a couple of options to remedy the situation. So for the purpose of modeling the human process and for making the decision of how to proceed, I have collapsed this to a single activity node for a person to perform. The automated aspects are ignored at this point.

Then we have human activities that are necessary because the technology is somewhat limited, and not completely automated, and so there are some tasks which people do manage and maintain the systems

Activity 6: moderate the online discussion	Unfortunately, the discussion is not completely self-moderating, so someone must have special access to delete spam or inappropriate messages, and to help keep the discussion going.
Activity 7: hold or attend conference call	The discussion is not completely an online discussion. Conference calls are used to help people come to a common understanding of the issues and resolutions. Someone needs to set up the conference call and moderate it while it is happening.

These seven activities account for everything that is done by people in the process. There are only two roles in this process. The issue manager is the person managing the issue process. This could be multiple people, but only one of them would act at a time. The other role is the committee, which is everyone involved in discussing and voting on issues. The committee members are responsible for discussing issues and voting, while the issue manager is responsible for all other activities in the process.

The email voting process actually consists of two processes: a single starter process that loops and starts an instance of the actual issue voting process every week. The issue voting process then has two subprocesses. Because we have only seven human activities, I decided to keep it simpler and not use the subprocesses, and to do everything in the two main processes. If you wanted to, however, you could use subprocesses to group things differently.

In doing the analysis, I became aware of a strange behavior of the original process as written. You could very easily be in the position of being asked to run multiple conference calls at the same time. Remember that the issue handling process is started every week, which drops into a subprocess for decision handling and another for voting. Each of those subprocesses has logic for determining if there will be a conference call during that time period, and to trigger an activity for handling the conference call. The discussion subprocess may loop, potentially for multiple weeks. It is possible that you will have multiple instances running at a time, and if this is the case, each instance will prompt for a conference call. The issue manager might manually avoid having multiple instances running at the same time, by deciding not to discuss anything in the new process instance as it is started, but this rather begs the whole question of why there is the possibility of multiple issue resolution processes in the first place; why not simply have the single starter process do all the work?

Finally I settled on the idea that issues are grouped, and it makes sense to have the possibility of multiple issue groups being discussed and/or voted at the same time. The conference call on the other hand is scheduled every Thursday, and takes place regardless of the number of issue groups currently and therefore should be associated with the single starter process, and not the instances of the issue voting process.

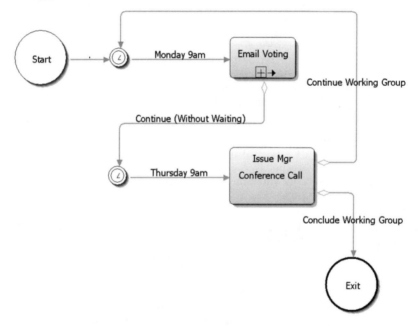

Email Voting Starter Process

There is a single instance of this process, which loops every week. There are timer delay nodes that cause things to happen at specified times. At 9:00 a.m. Monday morning, an instance of the issue list process is started. This is done with an "asynchronous" subprocess node; this is a node that starts a subprocess, but continues without waiting for that process to finish. The ability to start a subprocess and not wait for it is commonly available on human process engines, and is a standard part of the XPDL file format. This is one clear area where the capabilities of the engine will certainly affect how you draw the process. If you think about it, the purpose of this starter process is to create instances every week of the email voting process, but because in BPEL there is no operation for expressing this, the original process would "send the issue list" and the "receipt of the issue list" would cause the creation of the process.

This is quite strange when you consider that the issue list itself is probably on a server that is already accessible by everyone, and does not need actually to be "sent" anywhere! The sending and receiving of the issue list is an artifact created just to get around the problem that BPEL does not have an operation to create a subprocess! This is also partially because BPEL is not modeling the work that people do, but only modeling the sending and receiving of data. Of course, it is possible to model the whole world in terms of sending and receiving bytes, but it is far clearer and easier to read a process diagram with a node that creates the subprocess directly.

Then, on Thursday at 9:00 a.m. there is an activity to hold a conference call. This is assigned to the issue manager. I embellished the process a little bit to also give that manager a choice of whether to conclude the working group or not. The original process had a branch node that checked something to see if the working group was still active, but then someone would have had to have taken some action somewhere to indicate that the working group was completed. Drawing it this way ties both the human indication that the working group is finished together with the completion of the process. Every week, the conference call task will be concluded with the choice "Continue Working Group," which requires no effort beyond simply saying that the conference call is done. But, when the time comes that the working group is no longer active and there is no need to ever have another conference call or another issue vote, then simply choosing "Conclude Working Group" provides an easy way to complete the process without using the administrator's console.

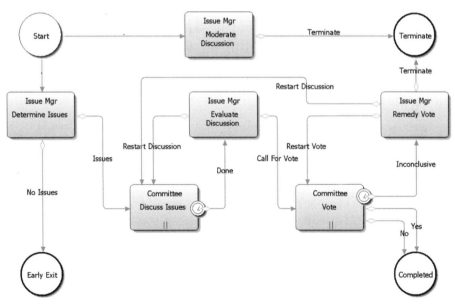

The Issue Email Voting Process

This process starts two activities from the start. "Moderate Discussion" is designed to remain active the entire time the process is running. Most of the time the process will be in the Discuss Issues step or the Vote step, so really this step allows a place where the issue manager can moderate both discussion and voting. I embellished it a little to add a "Terminate" option that would shut down the process before discussion or voting was finished.

The main process is the lower five activities. First the issue manager decides the issues to be discussed. Second, the issues are discussed by the committee. Then the issue manager decides if the issues have been discussed enough and completes that by either "Restart Discussion" or "Call for Vote." If it is the latter, the committee is asked to vote. If the vote is not conclusive, then the issue manager must Remedy Vote, where he will be able to reduce the number of voters or the number of resolutions to vote on, and choose either to Terminate the process, go back to Discussion, or go back to Vote.

How does the "Vote" work? Here we cheat a little bit by using a capability of the engine that presents the vote options to a number of people simultaneously. It gives the options of "Yes" and "No" to all committee members. People choose one, and the process engine tallies the results. On the outbound arrows, you can specify how many votes, or what percentage of the votes, are necessary to consider an option successful or not. As soon as the success criterion is met, the voting activity is concluded. There is also a built-in timeout so that if a vote is not concluded in a period of time, then the activity can be concluded down a third arrow which leads to the Remedy Vote activity. I know this seems like cheating to pull something like this out of the hat, but I did not make up this process. Voting steps are relatively common in the workplace, and this is a real node type available in a number of process engines designed for human facilitation. The voting node is a clear example of how a BPMN drawing is dependent upon the underlying technology.

How are people notified about what to discuss? How are they told what to vote on? When you assign a human activity to a person or group of people, that activity automatically includes a notification mechanism that tells them what they are to do, and includes information about the specific case. Simply assigning the "Discussion" node to the Committee means that everyone in the committee is automatically told what it is they are to discuss at the time that the discussion is to start. Simply assigning the vote node to the Committee means that they will be notified what the voting options are at the time they are to vote, and their votes are automatically collected and tallied.

What about the nodes to send reminders? Again, this does not need to be explicitly modeled because every human activity automatically includes (a) notification, (b) information, (c) conclusion, (d) deadline, and (e) reminders. We just set up the discussion activity to have a reminder after six days. Similarly on the voting node, we have a reminder after six days. That reminder on the voting node can be considered a "warning" since if the vote has been concluded, then the reminder will not be set. The BPEL-oriented process had to stop the voting, and then go back and restart the voting after the warning, but that is not necessary when the voting node can send reminders without stopping. Even the nodes for the issue manager can have warnings and reminders if the issue manager goes for a time without taking care of the task.

What is this human process good for? By showing the process, you see what everyone is expected to do. At each step in the process, a person is told that something must be accomplished, and given a set of choices. The diagram is oriented around what it is that people do, not what bytes are sent and received. As such, it is useful for explaining what will happen next in the process depending upon which choices are made. This is useful for training people, and it is useful to display the current running status of the process instance to people. But some will point out that it is not complete; it does not contain a representation of all the automated actions. This is true, but no process map is entirely complete. For example, the complete list of process variables is not displayed in either version of the process diagram.

DISCUSSION AND CONCLUSION

This article has demonstrated that using two different methodologies to define a single given process has produced two very different process diagrams. Neither diagram is more correct than the other, but the diagrams are useful for different things. Both diagrams use BPMN. The key point is:

> *The way that you model a given process in BPMN depends upon the methodology you use, and the assumptions you make about the technology that will support the process.*

There exists a strong desire for a *lingua-franca* of business processes. It would be great to be able to draw a diagram of a process on any drawing tool, and then execute it in any process engine. It would be great if BPMN could provide this, but it cannot, and indeed should not. BPMN does not define the full semantics of the process, and was designed to be used in more than one methodology.

> *A given BPMN diagram can execute only on a process engine that corresponds to the assumptions that are built into the diagram.*

"What good then is BPMN?" some will ask. BPMN is appropriately named as a notation, and it provides exactly that. BPMN provides a dictionary of symbols with associated meaning. To the extent that different vendors use the symbols for the same meanings, there is great value in this. The one who benefits is the business person who takes the time to learn the basic symbols in order to be able to read the process diagrams.

There is an analogy that one can use in the symbols of geographic maps. A set of symbols has evolved over time with clear meanings on maps: a school, a church, or an airport. The reader who understands those symbols is in a better position to interpret the map. Because most people have learned the associations between the symbols and meanings, maps are easier to read in direct proportion to the extent that a producer of a map sticks to the standard symbols. A map that makes use of proprietary symbols would benefit neither the producer nor the readers. So standard symbols are a benefit, but that is not to say that all maps are the same and have the same meaning. You might make a map to get someone from point A to point B, but that map will look very different depending upon whether the person is walking, riding a subway, or taking an airplane. There is no question that a walking map of a city looks completely different from a subway map of the same city. The map incorporates implicit assumptions about the people who will use the map. And while you might make an infinitely detailed universal map of all modes of transport, you will find that that map will be far less useful than the mode-specific maps.

It is the same with BPM. The business process diagram embeds implicit assumptions about the audience and about the capabilities of the process engine it will be running on. We have seen specifically that the approach of the process "automator" will lead to a process that focuses on how information is exchanged between systems, and result in a process that describes this. If your goal is to convert the process to BPEL in order to run it, then that process will tend to be designed in that way. We also have seen how a "facilitator" approach will focus on what the people do, and less on what the computers do, and result in an entirely different diagram. Again, if you can assume an engine that supports human activities directly with powerful concepts like "voting activities," then you are freed from most of the tedious details and can focus more on what the people are doing.

I should mention briefly here that there is a move to make BPEL more suitable for processes that facilitate human work by extending the specification to include a new human activity and by defining standard worklist services which can be invoked through standard BPEL means. This work is still very preliminary at the time of writing this, so it is impossible to say where it will lead. If the BPEL standards group was to add complete support for human activities as described above, it would be improper to categorize BPEL as an automation-only language, and we must also assume in that case that BPEL would be useful for facilitation diagrams. This would make BPEL far more useful, but would not change the message of this article. It would still be the case that a diagram drawn for use by humans which focuses on human tasks, would look different from a diagram drawn for use by a system programmer which shows all the data exchange.

In this article I contrast two methodologies, but I don't mean to imply that there are only two. There is, presumably, any number of such. BPMN should be used whenever it makes sense to be used to give common meaning to such diagrams. It should be further expected that BPMN will grow over time to become more suitable for more different situations. While many vendors have implemented BPMN, they almost always include proprietary extensions suitable to their particular approach. It is a benefit to all of us for common meanings not yet specified by BPMN, to be included into the standard in the future.

Though BPMN is not a universal language for describing business processes, it is still a great notation standard and is as relevant as ever.

METHOD FOR DESIGNING HUMAN PROCESSES (SUMMARY)

Step 1: Identify Human Work
Step 2: Determine Activity Conclusions
Step 3: Put the Tasks in Order
Step 4: Determine Performers
Step 5: Determine the Information in the Process Context
Step 6: Define Access to Information at Each Activity
Step 7: Determine Timeouts
Step 8: Design the Presentation of the Information.
Step 9: Integrate with Information Services

MyBPM: Social Networking for Business Process Management

Dr. Setrag Khoshafian, Pegasystems Inc., USA

INTRODUCTION

Social Networking is booming on the Internet via sites such as MySpace and, more recently, Facebook and YouTube. Demographically, the users of these sites tend to be a younger generation—especially the 17-25 age group.[1] The number of members and visitors to these sites is in the tens of millions. Social networking is exhibiting double- and, sometimes triple-, digit participant growth. The popularity and the frequency of visits to personalized social networking sites is any marketer's envy. This has not gone unnoticed by businesses.

The ease of set-up, ad-hoc exchanges, and the freedom of the experience through posting and commenting on text, photos, and video is creating a new web phenomenon—often characterized as Web 2.0. There are several definitions for Web 2.0. The "2.0" indicates the second generation of the World Wide Web. The first generation of the Web focused on relatively static websites and web presence. The new generation of the web provides a much richer experience and, more importantly, focuses on communities. There is not one single tool that captures the essence of networking on the Web, but wikis and blogs are perhaps the most popular social networking applications. Blogs allow the author to share ideas or comments on specific issues, while wikis provide a mechanism for collaborative authoring. And there are other applications, including discussion threads, surveys / voting, instant messaging (IM), shared whiteboards, shared bulletin boards and collaborative editing.[2] So Web 2.0 is about connecting people, inventing communities, and encouraging collaborative development on the Web. Web 2.0 permeates every aspect of human-computer interaction. However, as we shall see, the greatest benefit of Web 2.0 will be realized through the BPM Suite context of collaboration within the enterprise, between trading partners, and across the Internet.

The combination of rich Internet interaction with personalization and networking is proving to be extremely effective. The Web is, in fact, becoming the new *social* computing network. Publishing on the Web and having a "Web" site is now augmented and sometimes replaced with publishing on social networks. New editorial paradigms such as blogs are replacing traditional editorial articles.[3] You are what you blog. Technological advances combined with social networking are spurring sometimes unexpected innovation in social computing. For instance, virtual worlds such as Second Life are becoming a rich milieu of social interaction. These worlds are an extension of popular 3D video game models over the Web. Businesses have taken notice of this new medium and are starting to present their products and services in virtual worlds. Just as we had to have a web

---

[1] Interestingly, more recently, the fastest growing demography is the 25+ group.

[2] In fact, sharing documents with editing through check-in/checkout and even workflow are collaborative tools – and important ones at that. Here we are focusing on the more recent Internet-based social networking tools (Web 2.0).

[3] About 120,000 new blogs are created each day

presence towards the end of the 20th century, we now have to have a presence on social networks, and even in virtual worlds.

In fact, Web 2.0 reflects the fast-paced, focused, result-oriented, brief, frequently updated, personalized, and customized socio-technical trends of the 21st century. The penetration of social networking in schools and universities throughout the world is phenomenal. IM, blogs, wikis, discussions, and commenting on media—sometimes with extreme openness—are the norm. This means a new generation of entrepreneurs will be entering the job market, expecting the same type of openness, exchange, and rich experience that they were accustomed to while at college. They will continue the social networking via the popular portals, but, inevitably, social networking will be brought to the workplace and accepted as the cultural norm. As noted above, this represents the second generation of the web. Thomas Friedman called it "the Steroids" of the flattened world, and he is right on the mark![4]

SOCIAL NETWORKING IN THE ENTERPRISE

So what about the current trends in adopting social networking in business? Professor Andrew McAfee of the Harvard Business School provides an excellent definition of Enterprise 2.0 as "the emerging use of Web 2.0 technologies like blogs and wikis (both perfect examples of network IT) within the Intranet."[5] He goes on to elaborate on the Web 2.0 social networking phenomenon of Enterprise 2.0.

There are conflicting messages and studies on the adoption of Web 2.0 within enterprises. Initially, some enterprises and IT departments saw social networking as a distraction from productive work. The resistance to Web 2.0 tools within the enterprise reminds me of the reservations some managers had when e-mail was introduced in the workplace a couple of decades ago. E-mail had a flattening effect. Suddenly, the higher-level executives were accessible and only an e-mail away from any of the employees, even those several levels below in the organizational hierarchy. There were even incidents where e-mail was "uninstalled" due to management fears or security concerns. But e-mail survived and flourished. It became an essential tool for networking, communication, marketing and conducting business.

It is interesting to note that a considerable portion of e-mail traffic today is *spam*. The ubiquitous e-mail has opened other undesirable doors, and this is the price one has to pay for any tool or platform that encourages openness. We need e-mail, and we cannot function effectively without it. The same will happen and is happening with Web 2.0 tools. It is relatively easy, for instance, to abuse IM within the enterprise or create blogs and wikis with questionable quality or value. Nevertheless, IM and other social networking tools are becoming essential in the enterprise. These tools are appearing as key components in enterprise portals. Every enterprise has an Intranet portal, and increasingly these portals are utilizing social networking aspects within the organization. Portals are becoming the milieu where employees can interact via discussion threads, express their opinions in blogs, and collaborate on creating wikis pertinent to the business. The enterprise is encouraging and stimulating communication, as well as innovation, via social networking within the firewall.

---

[4] http://www.thomaslfriedman.com/worldisflat.htm

[5]

http://blog.hbs.edu/faculty/amcafee/index.php/faculty_amcafee_v3/the_three_trends_underlying_enterprise_20

But what about business process management applications? BPM suites represent the fastest-growing discipline in enterprise software. In 2006, the segment showed more than 25 percent growth. This trend is expected to continue over the next five years. Enterprise applications are increasingly becoming BPM applications (vs. point solutions or ad-hoc applications developed in-house). So what is the synergy between the ever popular social networking tools and the most popular enterprise software paradigm: BPM? This is what we will focus on for the rest of this article.

BPM AND SOCIAL NETWORKING

Before we delve into social networking for BPM, it is important to briefly clarify exactly what we mean by a BPM Suite. The various dimensions and features of BPM Suites are illustrated below: human workflow, service integration, business rules, solution templates or frameworks, and business activity monitoring. BPM Suites also support collaboration, which is where BPM and social networking intersect. Collaboration is an essential feature in a BPM Suite. As we shall see, there are different dimensions of collaboration in social networking, especially within a BPM context.

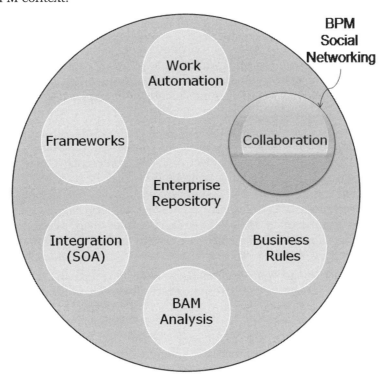

SYNCHRONOUS AND ASYNCHRONOUS NETWORKING

In Groupware and Work Group computing, you have two dimensions for collaboration: Time and Place. For Time, you have *Same Time (Synchronous)* or *Different Times (Asynchronous)*. For space, you have *Same Place* or *Different Places.* These two dimensions create four quadrants as illustrated here:

	Same Place	Different Places
Synchronous Networking and Collaboration (same time)	• Computer-enabled Meeting Rooms • Virtual Meeting Rooms • (e.g. Second Life)	• Chat and/or Instant Messaging • Electronic Meetings: Videoconferencing, Web Meetings • Shared White boards • Shared Applications
Asynchronous Networking and Collaboration	• Walls (e.g. on Facebooks) • Discussion Threads • Virtual Rooms • Kiosks • Electronic Bulletin Boards • Blogs and Wikis	• E-Mail • Workflow • Task Lists • Collaborative Document Authoring • Shared Calendaring • Surveys and Voting

There are a number of popular synchronous communication and collaboration tools that are becoming essential within enterprises. At the low-end, enterprises are deploying IM tools for immediate ad-hoc communication. IM is less disruptive than, say, a phone call. You can communicate while interacting with multiple applications. And IM is ad-hoc: You can check if the party or parties are on-line or available to chat[6].

The more semi-formal approach, especially within enterprises, is to schedule a synchronous meeting such as an electronic live conference meeting that potentially involves voice, presentations, whiteboards, and even video. These meetings are now leveraging more advanced synchronous collaboration tools. Web conferencing and meeting platforms such as Live Meeting and WebEx are examples of sophisticated collaboration tools. These and similar tools allow you to share a presentation, an application, or a desktop. Some tools allow you to synchronously author shared documents or other artifacts.

Synchronous—or the temporal dimension—is quite clear: you are either collaborating at the same time, or you are not. Place, however, is more nebulous. Place can mean a "physical place" with a geographical location, or a "virtual place." It could also mean the same collaborative application that is used by all the participants. You could consider, for instance, a live meeting application a virtual place or you could alternatively consider two different personalizations of the live meeting interface as different places. Typically collaborating in different places involves different tools. Thus a Facebook Wall is more of a same place than, say, collaborating on a document with different tools. In first generation groupware, the "same place" was typically a computer assisted meeting room that was equipped with monitors and shared screens. It required physical attendance. Today, we can use various tools or even utilize computer assisted equipment (e.g. computer enabled white boards) in conjunction with electronic meetings or conferencing for

---

[6] The concept of electronic synchronous chat is more than 30 years old. I used to do chat on mainframes and minicomputers while at college in the early 1980s! It was on text terminals, but the concept was the same.

geographically remote participants. More recently, with the emergence of virtual worlds such as Second Life, we can have exchanges and collaboration within a virtual world—including same "virtual" place meetings. For BPM, we will primarily focus on the temporal (synchronous or asynchronous) dimension.

COLLABORATION DIMENSIONS FOR BPM

The BPM continuous improvement lifecycle involves modeling process applications, deploying the application, executing, and analyzing process performance. Monitoring, analysis and optimizations are used to realize continuous performance improvements. The following illustrates the three phases in BPM.

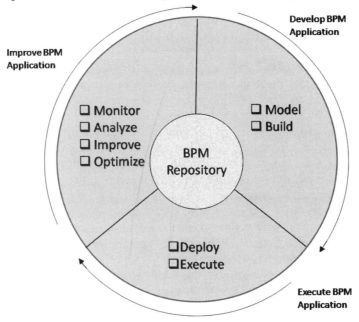

These three phases can be summarized as follows:

- *Model Driven Development:* The business use cases and requirements are directly captured in business process and business rule models. There are other models, such as information, integration, collaboration, and user interface. Modern BPM Suites include a complete set of process design constructs that are organized in multi-dimensional repositories.
- *Deployment and Execution:* Within a single unified BPM Suite, the models are deployed for execution. A process model that is deployed can be instantiated to assign tasks to participants, invoke external applications, or execute straight-through processing through business rules.
- *Business Performance:* The activation of process models during execution creates process instances. Each process instance will have its own copy of the process data—stored in relational databases. Business activity monitoring interfaces then allow managers to view and control the performance of their processes. Continuous improvement methodologies such as Lean or Six Sigma can be used to introduce change or improvements to the

processes. The changes are then deployed and the improvement cycle continuous.[7]

How about the "society" of the BPM social network within an extended enterprise? There are at least three categories of BPM societies.

- *BPM Projects Within The Enterprise*: This is perhaps the most obvious application area for social networking. When building, executing, or analyzing the performance of BPM applications, you can have social interactions between the different participants of each phase. In fact, for mid-sized and large organizations, the BPM project can span across internal value chains or across lines of businesses or functions. For instance, a sales process or a customer service process is specific to a functional unit or department. Manufacturing a product, on the other hand, crosses multiple business units: marketing, engineering, sales, and distribution. The fundamental difference is the reporting structure. A process within a function or unit has participants in the process all reporting to the same manager. Processes across functional units or departments imply a matrix organization. Collaboration and social networking between functional units is more challenging than collaboration within a unit.

- *BPM Across Trading-Partner Value Chain*: Enterprises typically interact and exchange with suppliers and consumers. The supply/value chain of processes spans multiple organizations. This is similar to processes that cross departmental boundaries, but now at a larger inter-enterprise level. So this next level of BPM collaboration can potentially involve enterprise participant roles across a supply chain. Here, business-to-business communities can engage in social networking, and the extended enterprise process spans the partner ecosystem.

- *BPM Communities*: Then you have the BPM "community" at large. These communities could network on BPM standards, best practices, methodologies, and templates. There are several ad-hoc discussion and research communities on BPM, as well as BPM bloggers. However, the greater value is achieved when the community is focused on a particular vertical domain (e.g. manufacturing, telecommunication, financial services, insurance, healthcare, transportation, education, government, and others).

BPM CONTEXT

Social networking is typically ad hoc. However, almost everything in an organization takes place in the context of a process. A business is an aggregation of policies and procedures. A process involves both policies and procedures. This does not mean, however, that all the procedures or policies are modeled and automated. Most are not. Nevertheless, it is essential to remember that each collaboration—whether for innovating, developing, marketing, selling, analyzing performance, negotiating, procuring, building partnerships, or handling customer requests—is to support a business policy or procedure: in other words, a "business process."

There is a powerful synergy between BPM Suites and social networking:

---

[7] There are many phases and aspects of business performance management with BPM Suites. For a more detailed discussion, see "Active Business Process Intelligence" by the author: http://www.alignjournal.com/index.cfm?section=article&aid=477

Business processes provide the context of collaboration, and social net-working supports and augments the various phases of the BPM continuous improvement lifecycle.

Without the BPM context, it will be difficult to establish the relationships between the collaboration and the "process." On the other hand, BPM tasks in innovating, modeling, executing, or optimizing processes can leverage synchronous or asynchronous collaboration.

The following illustrates the entire taxonomy of BPM communities and their activities in BPM applications:

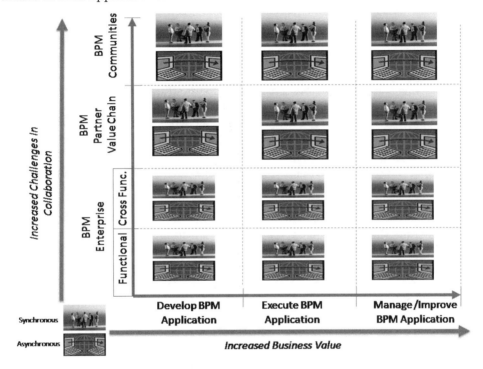

As you go to the right on the X-axis, collaboration provides added business value. For instance, discovering opportunities to improve BPM applications through collaborative innovation could provide tremendous business value in either increased revenue or reduced process execution costs.

As you go up the Y-axis, you will have increased challenges in collaboration. It is much easier to collaborate within an enterprise and even then, easier within a functional unit than cross functionally. In the upper right hand corner, you have core BPM and, perhaps more importantly, vertical communities to come up with the best practices and improvement strategies for continuous change and automation through BPM suites.

EXAMPLES

Any of the social networking tools can be used in conjunction with processes. Here are several collaboration examples of the BPM taxonomy:

- *Blogs and Wikis for Complex Compliance Applications:* One of the most difficult and costly projects both within Finance and IT is regulatory compliance. Control objectives are often complex. For example, Control OBjectives for Information and related Technology (COBIT) has an extensive list of controls, organized in a hierarchy of control objectives. COBIT controls are organized in various domains such as "Plan and Organize," "Acquire and Implement," "Deliver and Support" and "Monitor and Evaluate." BPM automation can capture all the control objectives as well as procedural flows of compliance and keep them under the close scrutiny of real-time activity monitoring. Examples of automated processes include risk assessment management, control test automation, exception management, changing management, and escalation management. However, compliance controls could be difficult to interpret. Furthermore, they get updated periodically. So collaborative social networking tools could be used to explain and discuss the general best practices for compliance. For instance, Wikipedia has an entry for COBIT and COSO.[8] However, the BPM solutions for compliance could have their own application and deployment-specific discussion threads, blogs, and wikis—explaining and discussing the specific flows, rules, screens, methodologies, optimizations, and practices that automate the compliance processes and rules. These wikis and blogs could reference the public wikis and blogs. However, they will be specific to the process automation solutions that manage financial or IT compliance within an enterprise.

- *Synchronous Collaboration within Process Execution:* As an example, consider a process for contract negotiations. At some point within the process, you would like to have an electronic meeting and, potentially, end with a vote—all in the context of a process instance. The invitation to the meeting, the acceptances, the recorded meeting session, as well as the artifacts (in this case the contract) all pertains to the process instance. So in this example you have:
    - *Scheduling Collaboration Session:* This could be accomplished in the context of a process flow. As with most BPM activities, the participant or scheduler can be a human participant. Alternatively, a rule within the application can determine if a collaboration session is needed. Here, the integration of the BPM engine is with the calendaring server.
    - *Synchronous Collaboration Session:* The session itself could be conducted within the context of a BPM application. The simplest way to view this is a step or activity within the process. Thus you have process activities that schedule the meeting, send notices, reserve the meeting on calendars, send invitations, and then a process step that holds the synchronous meeting—using an electronic meeting tool.
    - *The Session:* The session itself could be recorded and become a part of the process instance. This is important. In addition to process data such as the contract date, the type of the contract, the customer, the negotiator, and attachments containing the documentation, you will also be able to store and access the recorded session itself—as part of the process instance data.
- *Discussion threads, surveys, and blogs when building a BPM application:* One of the most important aspects of BPM context is the association of collaboration with process application. For example, in a procurement application, there are several BPM Suite elements:

---

[8] http://en.wikipedia.org/wiki/COBIT and http://en.wikipedia.org/wiki/COSO

- The flows involving the management, finance, and procurement office.
- The business rules that decide the number of approvals that are needed based on the amount, urgency, or type of the item(s) being procured.
- The suppliers and supply chain for procurement: from the distribution warehouse, to the shipment, to the procurer receiving the merchandise.

Various departments are involved in procurement: the requester's department, the finance department, the procurer, and, depending upon the type of procurement, the suppliers. Thus you can have discussions on the various activities of the flows. Surveys can decide the service level that is required for each category or type of item being procured. Employees in an organization can submit procurement requests through activating the procurement process (or creating a procurement process instance). In large organizations—especially with more complex procurement processes—a collaborative wiki for procurement could be created to help explain and hyperlink the applications explanations to various rules, flows, items, and suppliers.

CONCLUSION AND SUMMARY

This paper discussed emerging trends in social networking, especially the BPM context of collaboration. We provided several practical examples of the collaborative BPM taxonomy. This taxonomy had two dimensions: the continuous improvement lifecycle and BPM communities. Web 2.0 tools such as blogs and wikis capture the essence of social networking. While sites such as MySpace and Facebook are ever popular with the younger generation, businesses have started using these social networking concepts, techniques, and tools to promote their products, solutions, and services. Businesses are aggregations of policies and procedures. Business Process Management Suites model, automate, and execute the business policies and procedures. There is, therefore, a powerful synergy between BPM and social networking. Social networking and collaboration can be organized along both time (synchronous vs. asynchronous) and place dimensions. BPM continuous improvement has different phases: model development, execution, and performance monitoring. The BPM user community spans functional units, cross departmental value chains, trading partners, and general BPM communities. Each cell of the BPM taxonomy can leverage synchronous or asynchronous social networking. So while business processes provide the context of the collaboration, social networking supports and augments the various activities of the BPM applications' continuous improvement lifecycle.

Human Services: Integrating User Interfaces into a Service-Oriented Architecture

Jeffrey Ricker, Jeffrey Ricker LLC, United States

ABSTRACT

As unfashionable as it may be to point out, there are still a great number of critical processes in today's businesses that are not automated. How do we create a complete enterprise service-oriented architecture when many of the services still require human interaction or even human execution? Human services are a pattern for connecting user interfaces into a Service-oriented Architecture (SOA). This pattern consists of six major components that interact through a process of five major sequences. Human services are dependent upon Asynchronous Service Access Protocol (ASAP), a web services protocol that overcomes the "instant gratification" barrier. Through the use of human services, we are able to connect non-automated business processes into our overall SOA, which provides the means for rapid implementation and the pathway to future automation.

CHALLENGE

Service-oriented architecture provides a breakthrough in enterprise and trans-enterprise integration. SOA has so far been focused on application-to-application integration and, as such, has lacked a certain human element. As efforts such as business process orchestration and the enterprise service bus (ESB) expand, implementers are facing the question: what if there is no application on the other side to which to connect to?

As unfashionable as it may be to point out, there are still a great number of critical processes in today's businesses that are not automated. How do we create a complete enterprise service-oriented architecture when many of the services still require human interaction or even human execution? Must we automate every service before achieving results? Is SOA an all-or-nothing proposition like so many failed technology efforts of our past? If so, SOA becomes a burden more than a boon.

What we need is a simple, standard means of integrating into an SOA those business processes that still require human interaction, approval or execution. I call this means *human services*. We must be able to treat human services just like other services so that they are interchangeable with other services. To the business process, web services and human services should look and act the same way. The interchangeability enables us to combine manual processes with applications. It also allows us to replace the manual processes with applications in the future with no disruption to the business process.

Human services must not dictate a particular user interface implementation. To be successful we cannot insist that human services user interfaces must be HTML, Java, .NET, Flex or any other single technology. Human services should be able to integrate most any Internet-friendly client technology.

How are human services different from existing business process orchestration? Current business process orchestration efforts, most notably Business Process

Execution Language (BPEL), do not address human interaction, let alone user interfaces. Placing humans into an automated business process raises all kinds of messy issues such as:

- Assignment of tasks to individuals
- Sign-on and verification of individuals
- Notification to individuals that they have a task
- User interfaces for entering the data

These messy issues are why workflow and process flow have remained in different realms.

Am I just describing workflow by another name? I can answer that "yes and no." Yes, human services achieve much if not all of the objectives of workflow. However, human services are different from the workflow reference model published by the Workflow Management Coalition (WfMC). The WfMC developed its reference model as a client-server architecture. It pre-dates SOA. Human services most closely equate with WfMC Interface 2 and 3 which was last updated in July 1998.

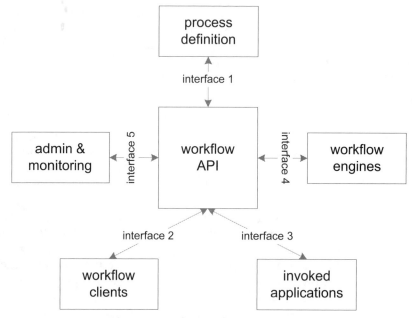

Figure 1 WfMC reference model

The objective of human services is to enable arbitrary user interfaces to plug into an SOA. To that end, it must address the messy human things of workflow, but the resulting architecture is as different from the WfMC workflow reference model as client-server architecture is from SOA.

OVERVIEW

Human services comprise six major components:

1. ASAP factory service
2. ASAP instance service
3. Assignment service
4. Work list service
5. Notification client
6. Data entry client

The execution of a human service has five major sequences:

1. Instantiation
2. Assignment
3. Retrieval
4. Data entry
5. Completion

The overall relationship between these components and sequences is shown in Figure 2. We will discuss each of these major components and major sequences in order.

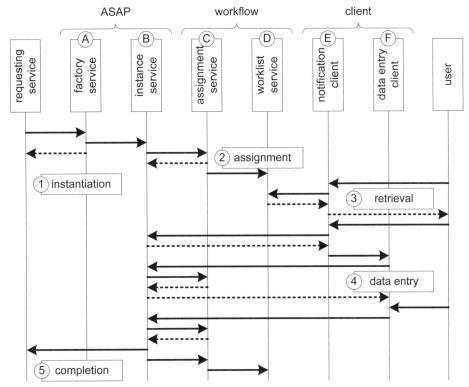

Figure 2 Overall patterns of human services

ASAP COMPONENTS

Asynchronous Service Access Protocol (ASAP) makes human services feasible. ASAP is designed to overcome the instant gratification barrier of Hypertext Transport Protocol (HTTP). Normal web services must respond within 60 seconds, or the HTTP connection times out. Many services, such as data mining and chained services, require more than 60 seconds to generate a response. Each service in a chain may individually take less than 60 seconds, but when the services are chained together they exceed the time limit. Most certainly, anything involving a human decision will take more than 60 seconds, as anyone who has stood in line at a coffee shop can attest.

ASAP allows a service to respond to a request, "Where would you like me to send the result when I am done?" There are three types of endpoints to an ASAP service: a factory service, an instance service and an observer service. The requestor sends a request to a factory service. The factory service responds with the URI of the instance service. If the requestor implements the observer endpoint type (otherwise known as an interface in object oriented parlance), then it can add itself as an observer to the instance service to receive notification of any change of state, most notably completion. When the instance service is complete, it sends the results to the observer service. If the requestor cannot implement the observer endpoint type, then the requestor can continually poll the instance service for its state.

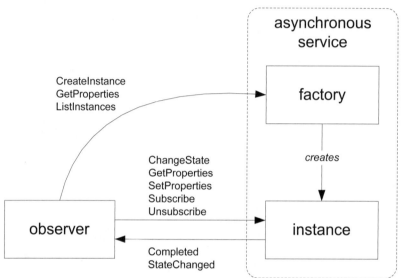

Figure 3 The ASAP endpoint types

A human service is an ASAP service. As such, a human service has as its first two components a factory service and an instance service. What make it *human* are the other four components.

WORKFLOW COMPONENTS

An instance service requests an assignment of the task to an individual from an assignment service. The assignment service can be very simple and assign all instances of a particular factory service to a single individual, or it can be complex and balance the assignment of tasks across a pool of individuals. To the instance service, there is no difference. The instance service submits its URI to a well known assignment service and the assignment service acknowledges the request. By well-known, I mean that the association between the instance service and the assignment service is specified either in the code of the instance service or in the instance service deployment environment. Note that the assignment service implements the ASAP observer endpoint so that it receives notification of the completion.

The assignment service notifies a work list service of its assignment decision with the URI of the instance service. The implementation of the work list service can be very simple or very complicated, depending on the needs of the deployment, but the interface itself is very simple.

The assignment service and work list service form a decoupling of the user interface from the service. This decoupling even enables multiple user interfaces to be used for the same human service.

CLIENT COMPONENTS

The last two components of the human service comprise the user interface. The notification client is any user interface that notifies the human user that he or she has a task to complete. For instance, the notification client could be a POP email application, an XMPP instant messaging client or a Java portlet. The human service does not care so long as the notification client can communicate with the work list service endpoint.

The notification client has only the URI of the instance service. It is up to us how we build the connection between the notification client and the data entry client. We may have the notification and data entry inside a Java-based web portal, or we may have it as a simple LAMP application, or maybe we build it all as an Eclipse Rich Client Platform. In fact, we could build all three implementations for the same task if we so desired.

The data entry client is really where the rubber meets the road. It is the objective of human services for us to integrate this user interface into the SOA. Some readers might be frustrated by how openly I have defined the user interface implementation. The point is that the user interface is now decoupled from the service. Using the human service pattern we can put any user interface into a SOA so long as it conforms with the basic endpoints specifications.

INSTANTIATION SEQUENCE

We have discussed the six major components of a human service. Now we will describe the process by which these components interact in five major sequences.

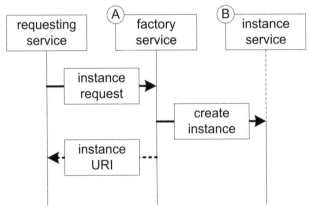

Figure 4 Instantiation sequence

The instantiation sequence is pure ASAP. The requesting service sends a request to the factory service. The factory service creates an instance service and responds to the requesting service with the URI of the instance. If the requesting service implements the observer endpoint type, then it would add itself as an observer to the instance service. Refer to the ASAP specification for more details on the instantiation sequence.

ASSIGNMENT SEQUENCE

In the assignment sequence, the instance service sends an assignment request to the assignment service. The correlation between the instance service and assignment service is completely arbitrary. That is to say, the implementer decides what assignment service the instance service calls. It may be hard coded in the instance service or perhaps determined by the Instance service container.

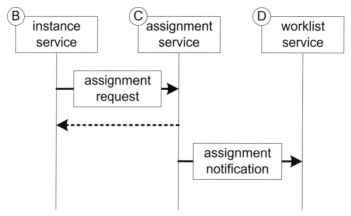

Figure 5 Assignment sequence

The assignment service acknowledges the request and sends an assignment notification to the appropriate work list service. The assignment service contains the internal logic for which work list service to assign the instance service. The assignment service can be as complex or simple as the implementer needs.

The instance service does not need any knowledge of the work list service. The assignment is nothing more than a URI.

RETRIEVAL SEQUENCE

The human user learns what tasks he must complete through the retrieval sequence. The user connects to his notification client which in turn connects to the work list service to retrieve the list of instance service URIs. The interaction between the notification client and the work list service is a simple SOAP exchange. The protocol and user interface technology between the user and the notification client, however, can be anything and is completely independent of the human service pattern.

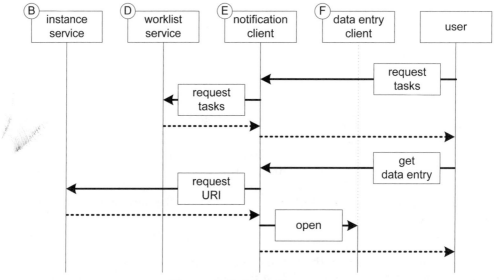

Figure 6 Retrieval sequence

The user requests a particular item on his work list. The notification client fetches the list of data entry URIs, picks the most appropriate one and forwards it to the user.

DATA ENTRY SEQUENCE

The next sequence is data entry. Using only an instance service URI from the notification client, the user should be able to open a data entry client. The specific means of translating a data entry URI into the appropriate data entry client is completely up to the implementation of the user interface. For example, an AJAX application will execute this important sequence completely different than a Visual Basic application.

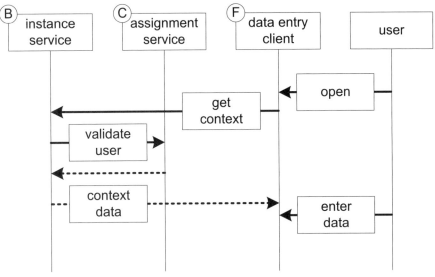

Figure 7 Data entry sequence

The data entry client sends the request for the context data to the instance service. The request from the client includes credentials of identification. It may be a simple user name login or it may be a public key exchange. The actual validation is up to the implementation. The critical point, however, is that the instance service does not handle the validation itself. Instance service asks the assignment service to validate the credentials of the user. If the assignment service approves the credentials, then the instance service sends the initial data to the data entry client.

COMPLETION SEQUENCE

When the user has completed entering the data, the data entry client submits the result data to the instance service. Note that with ASAP and human services, the context data and the result data are XML. That XML could easily be a Service Data Object (SDO).

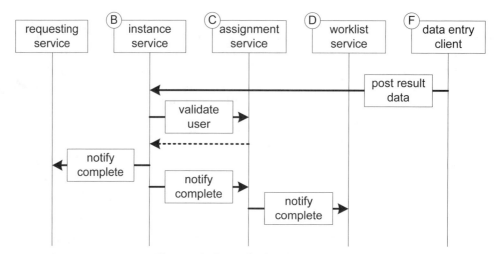

Figure 8 Completion sequence

The instance service once again validates the user with the assignment service. If approved, the instance service notifies all of its observers that the service is complete. In ASAP, such a notification includes the result data, which in our case would be the data created by the data entry client. The requesting service and the assignment service should be observers to the instance service. The very last sequence is for the assignment service to notify the work list service to remove the URI from its lists of tasks.

CONCLUSION

Human services are a pattern for connecting user interfaces into a SOA. This pattern consists of six major components that interact through a process of five major sequences. Human services are dependent upon ASAP, a web services protocol that overcomes the "instant gratification" barrier.

The objective is to enable developers to integrate into SOA any Internet-friendly user interface technology, such as Java, HTML, .NET or Flex. The drawings have shown the SOA on the left and the user interface on the right. As we move from left to right the specification of human services had become more and more generalized. As we get closer to the SOA, there are specific interfaces. As we get closer to the user interface, decisions are left up to the implementer. In between is a set of simple services that decouple the specified from the improvised.

Through the use of human services, we are able to connect non-automated business processes into our overall SOA. With human services, we can implement SOA now with the business processes that we have now. At the same time, human services enable the pathway to future automation. We can gradually replace manual processes with automated ones without disrupting the business process. With human services, SOA does not have to be "all or nothing." That could mean the difference between success and failure for SOA.

Impact of Organizational Changes on Running Processes: a Challenge for Achieving Business Agility

Salvatore Latronico, Gianpiero Bongallino and Francesco Battista, openwork, Italy

INTRODUCTION

Examining differences between *Human-to-Human* processes and *System-to-System* processes, one clear fact stands out: *System-to-System* processes are very often synchronous and usually last for a very short time while *Human-to-Human* processes usually last for much longer time and so are heavily subject to time changes.

In this paper we will analyze most relevant cases of *Human-to-Human* processes changes, from common ones related to organizational structure changes to most complex ones related to process rule and topology changes and related impacts on process instances already-running, with reference to standards (BPEL4People and WS-Human Task).

DEFINITION OF TERMS

It's useful to point out some definitions in order to better understand subjects we will face: we will mainly refer to well-known and still valid definitions from Workflow Management Coalition.

Organizational structure

The representation of organizational entities and their relationships: it may also incorporate a variety of attributes associated with the entities, such as skills or role. Such a model may be realised in a directory or other form of database[1].

Business process

A set of one or more linked activities which collectively realize a business objective or policy goal, normally within the context of an organizational structure defining functional roles and relationships[1].

Process model

A formalized view of a business process, represented as a coordinated (parallel and/or serial) set of process activities that are connected in order to achieve a common goal[1].

Process instance

The representation of a single enactment of a process including its associated data. Each instance represents a separate thread of execution of the process[1].

Activity

A description of a piece of work that forms one logical step within a process. An activity may be a manual activity, which does not support computer automation, or a workflow (automated) activity. A workflow activity requires human and/or machine resources(s) to support process execution; where human resource is required an activity is allocated to a workflow participant[1]. Synonymous of human activity is task[3]. The types of activities are: Process, Sub-Process, and Task[8].

Activity Instance

The representation of an activity within a (single) enactment of a process, i.e. within a process instance[1].

Participant

A resource which performs the work represented by a workflow activity instance. This work is normally manifested as one or more work items assigned to the workflow participant via the work list[1].

WHAT ORGANIZATIONAL CHANGES INVOLVE

During the lifetime of a long running business process, changes may occur. As a consequence, it is needed to manually modify the process model and/or process instances and is desirable that process instance automatically adapts to organizational changes. The ability of adapting a business process to changes is a key factor for the success of a BPM project and can be achieved mixing technology solutions and good practices in business process modeling.

Modeling a business process substantially requires the definition of process topology (logic and temporal relationships among activities), participants and other attributes for each human activity.

For long duration processes, we can expect:
- "participants" changes due to temporary or permanent organizational structure changes
- process topology and attributes changes

Temporary organizational structure changes happen for example when a person is sick or on vacation: another person has to undertake the role of the absent colleague in order to take charge of, execute and complete activities assigned to him/her. This type of change may be managed using *substitution* and is not a real change to the organizational structure, i.e. it doesn't modify organizational elements (organizational units, roles and persons) and relationships among them.

Organizational structure changes are *permanent* when they imply deleting, moving, creating an organizational element. For example assigning a person to a new role or splitting Research & Development Area into Research Area and Development Area could be permanent organizational structure changes. These changes often happen in complex organizations such as Financial Companies or Hospitals where managers and operators are daily moved from an organizational unit to another or undertake different roles in the short run.

Process topology and attributes changes impact process diagram and/or attributes of the process and/or its activities. Those changes are required to satisfy new or resolve old business requirements not properly mapped during process analysis and reengineering. These changes may require not only process model changes, but also currently running process instances changes, in order to let them correctly get to completion.

ORGANIZATIONAL STRUCTURE CHANGES

In order to analyze the impact of organizational changes on process model and running instances, let's examine, for example, how BPEL4People[2] and strictly related WS-Human Task[3] manage activity's participants lifecycle.

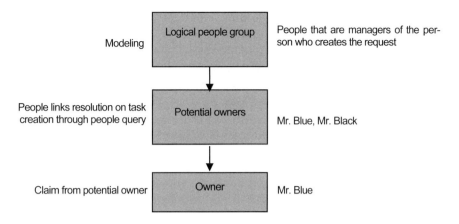

Figure 1 Participants lifecycle according to WS-Human Task

Suppose that we map a business process where a vacation request must be approved executing and completing a "Vacation approval" activity and that a vacation request is created (i.e. one process instance is triggered) from a person belonging to the Marketing Area.

1. During process modeling, we define activity participants as one logical people group bound to a *people query:* persons that are managers of the person who triggered the process instance. Note that the above definition is relative to the context in which the activity will be instantiated (the person creating the request is different from one process instance to another) so we can say that we define *relative participants*.

2. During process execution, when the process flow gets to "Vacation approval" activity, *people query* is evaluated to retrieve the actual persons the task has to be assigned to. *People query* returns a list of persons called potential owners. People are now not relative any more, but applied to the context of the specific process instance and refer only to the organizational structure. We can then say that *people query* returns *absolute participants*. In this example absolute participants are Mr. Black and Mr. Blue.

3. Mr. Blue claims the task and becomes the actual owner of the task.

What happens when *people query* returns an empty set, i.e. in our example, the manager of the Marketing Area doesn't exist? Potential owners must be assigned explicitly using *nomination*, which is performed by a process administrator. In our example it means that if a manager of the Marketing Area is nominated after creation of "Vacation approval" task, this task will have to be manually assigned to the new manager.

This behavior generates other singular results. Suppose that neither Mr. Blue nor Mr. Black claim any task and they are both removed from their roles replaced by Mr. Yellow. Despite permanent organizational structure changes, Mr. Blue and Mr. Black continue to see approval tasks in their work list and Mr. Yellow doesn't see them unless process administrator manually replaces potential owners in the task.

WS-Human Task faces this problem using groups: if "people query" returns a group, persons can see tasks they have been assigned to as a consequence of their membership of a certain group. This *late binding* to the actual group members is very useful and in our example means that we have to define a group called Managers of Marketing Area.

Going on with abstractions, we would have to define a group for:

- each role and organizational unit
- each attribute value (skills, personal data, etc.) of organizational elements
- any combination of the above

A very difficult and heavy task, especially for continuously changing large organizations.

To solve this problem we need that absolute participants can be defined not only as persons or a group, but also in terms of organizational areas and roles, and we need those groups to be dynamically composed on attributes and corresponding values basis.

WS-Human Task identifies two patterns that need to be managed in order to compensate organization changes: *escalation* and *delegation*.

The escalation pattern applies when the workflow system attempts to progress a work item that has stalled by offering or allocating it to another resource. This automatic behavior can be adopted when a person is transferred and his/her tasks are assigned to his/her manager or upper level organizational unit manager.

The delegation pattern applies when a person allocates a work item previously allocated to him/her, to another person. For example, a manager can assign his/her tasks, or some of them, to another person of the same organizational unit.

These two patterns don't cover the case of *substitution* where is required that, in a well defined time interval, a person can see and use the task list of the other person he/she is replacing. Substitution can be applied not only for all activities, but also for some kind of process models, process instances or activity types and can be activated in two different ways:

- push substitution
- pull substitution

In the first one, organizational unit manager, for example, elects a person that replaces another one for a defined time interval: a typical use of this pattern is vacation management, when unit manager wants that substitute can see and execute tasks of the person currently on vacation.

In pull substitution, unit manager, for example, defines the person that replaces another one, but substitution remains inactive until the substitute pulls for substitution. A typical use of this pattern is sickness management: when a person is sick, he/she can ask his/her current substitute to pull for substitution, substitution becomes active and activities of the sick person can be started and completed by the defined substitute. When he/she recovers from sickness, substitution is released and becomes inactive.

Real life needs may be much more complex. Let's see for example what happens in a bank where people are daily transferred from one subsidiary to another one assigning them different roles.

Transfers can be definitive or temporary.

In the first case all the activities of a transferred person, related to his/her job in the old subsidiary, must be assigned to a manager of the old subsidiary or to a replacement list member.

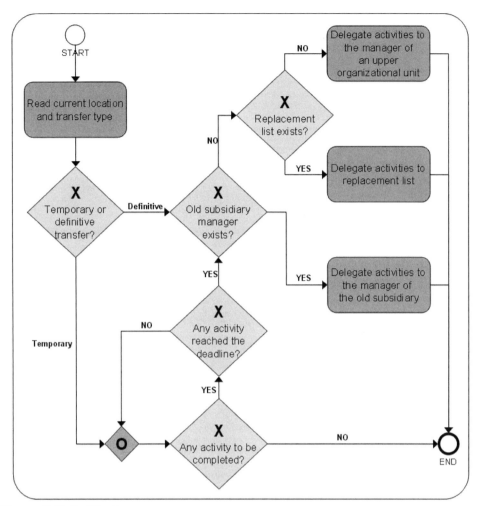

Figure 2 Substitution process

Transfers are managed on a dedicated Human Resource system, we have no way of triggering them and become active at user log on. This business case requires that a process is triggered at every user log on the application supported by the BPM platform.

Process involves delegation that must be called through Web Services or other API and must be stopped in case of temporary transfer, if person returns to its old subsidiary.

Figure 3 shows one possible scenario of this business case.

- Jack Red, operator of the Rome subsidiary, has three tasks in his personal task list.
- Jack Red is definitively transferred to the Bari subsidiary and his personal task list is delegated from the process to his old manager, Steve Green.
- Steve Green assigns former Jack Red's minor tasks to another operator directly from his task list interface.

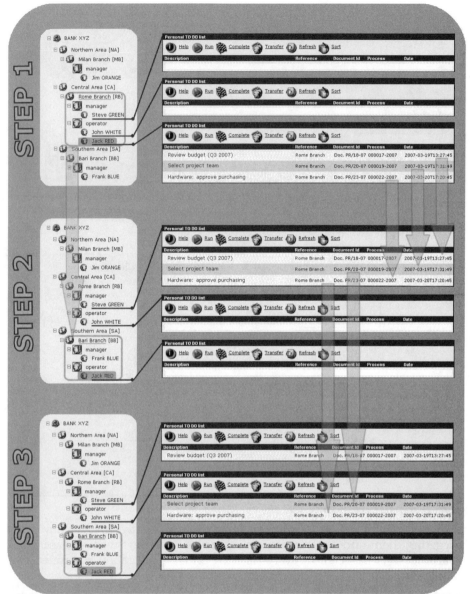

Figure 3. The update of personal task lists for a transfer business case

Beyond these examples there may be other relevant needs, such as:

- a tool that helps to analyze the impact of organizational structure changes (relation among organizational elements and their properties or abilities) on current process instances and process models
- a trigger that detects organizational structure changes that may influence processes.

The main issue is to intercept, understand and manage organizational structure changes, i.e. to streamline and improve the integration between organizational structure concepts/tools and BPM suites. In order to get such a result, a greater standardization of organizational concepts is strongly needed, but unfortunately nowadays this standardization lacks.

A step in this direction has been done with XPDL[4] introducing entities like role, organizational unit and human that can be described thorough an indefinite number of attributes. The attempt to identify and standardize basic attributes of a participant was already clear in "Process Definition Interchange Organisational Model"[5] explaining the hierarchical relation in organization structure through the organizational entities and respective attributes.

In order to integrate BPM platforms with HR systems, is necessary to generally standardize organizational attributes in a way similar to what xCIL standard[6] do about human entities. We think that a complete meta-model of participants attributes can significantly help in supporting this integration.

PROCESS MODEL CHANGES

One of the success factors of BPM suites is their ability of visual modelling business processes in order to generate software applications that automate them. Process instances inherit roles from process models, so is very simple to adapt software applications behaviour to organizational changes. Organizational changes may influence current instances not only impacting activities participants, but also other attributes and process topology.

The impact of organizational changes in process instances may be compared to unstructured events and BPM suite vendors provide a lot of techniques for managing them: workflow patterns (cancellation, multiple instance, force completion[7]), compensation flow[8], administrative settings of instances data, activity skipping and many other.

These solutions don't satisfy all possible cases: suppose we have an approval process like the following one:

And suppose that organizational changes cause the approval to be performed by two persons in specific cases.

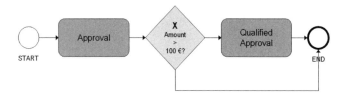

This change can be managed in a structured way only modifying the process instance. So we can conclude that for a wide and reasonably complete management of all possible changes of process instances, the same design functions available for process models are needed.

Changing process model or process instance implies many issues that can be described with the following patterns:
- create a new version of a process model with changes and apply them to currently running process instances or a subset of them;
- change a current process instance and apply them to parent process model creating a new version of it;

- change a current process instance and apply changes to all other currently running instances generated by the same process model or a subset of them.

While changes to processes and activities attributes can quite easily be applied to instances and models properly managing their versioning, in case of process topological changes, the issue is much more complex.

In the latter case, the good practice of splitting complex processes in a set of subprocesses is very helpful, re-applying something very similar to software engineering "information hiding" principle. In fact if changes can be applied to one single sub-process model, we can stop sub-process instances, compensate sub-process activities[8] and re-execute them: new sub-process instances are then started inheriting changes.

CONCLUSIONS

In this paper we explored some major cases related to the impact of organizational changes on running process. The proper and complete management of these questions is a key factor for the success of BPM technologies, but a *not-yet-reached* objective that requires the introduction of tools, concepts and *well-structured* approaches, first of all related to organizational structure management.

This is certainly a new frontier for Business Process Management suites innovation: the ability of adapting processes and software supporting their execution, to organizational changes is a key priority for any organization in a fast evolving world where business agility is crucial for competitiveness.

REFERENCES

[1] The Workflow Management Coalition, Terminology & Glossary, Document Number WfMC TC-1011, http://www.wfmc.org/standards/docs/TC-1011_term_glossary_v3.pdf, 1994-1999

[2] Matthias Kloppmann, Dieter Koenig, Frank Leymann, Gerhard Pfau, Alan Rickayzen, Claus von Riegen, Patrick Schmidt, Ivana Trickovic,
WS-BPEL Extension for People-BPEL4People,
http://download.boulder.ibm.com/ibmdl/pub/software/dw/specs/ws-bpel4people/BPEL4People_white_paper.pdf, July 2005.

[3] Ashish Agrawal, Mike Amend, Manoj Das, Mark Ford, Chris Keller, Matthias Kloppmann, Dieter König, Frank Leymann, Ralf Müller, Gerhard Pfau, Karsten Plösser, Ravi Rangaswamy, Alan Rickayzen, Michael Rowley, Patrick Schmidt, Ivana Trickovic, Alex Yiu, Matthias Zeller, Web Services Human Task (WS-HumanTask), Version 1.0
http://www.active-endpoints.com/documents/documents/1/WS-HumanTask-v1.pdf , June 2007

[4] Workflow Management Coalition, Workflow Standard, Process Definition Interface-XML Process Definition Language, Document Number WFMC-TC-1025, Version 2.00, http://www.wfmc.org/standards/docs/TC-1025_xpdl_2_2005-10-03.pdf, October 3, 2005

[5] The Workflow Management Coalition, Process Definition Interchange
Organisational Model, Document Number WfMC TC-1016-O,
http://www.wfmc.org/standards/docs/if19807o.pdf , 1994-1998

[6] OASIS, Extensible Customer Information Language (xCIL) Standard Description Document for W3C DTD/Schema, Version 2.0
http://www.oasis-open.org/committees/ciq/download.shtml, 31 May 2002

[7] N. Russell, A.H.M. ter Hofstede, W.M.P. van der Aalst, N. Mulyar,
Workflow Control-Flow Patterns: A Revised View,

http://www.workflowpatterns.com/documentation/documents/BPM-06-22.pdf, 2006

[8] Business Process Management Initiative (BPMI), Business Process Modeling Notation (BPMN) Version 1.0, http://www.omg.org/docs/bei/05-08-07.pdf, May 3, 2004

Human-Driven BPM:
the Missing Piece is People

Roberto Silva, SAP Latin America, Mexico

Roberto Silva, SAP Latin America, Mexico

INTRODUCTION

Business Process Management, or BPM, is a discipline that puts processes in the center of its universe. Its purpose is to assure continuous improvement of business performance inside a changing business ecosystem. BPM promises high performance based on process excellence as the driver for short-term problem resolution and long-term competitive advantages as well.

In this paper, my target group is composed of traditional companies that are operating as part of an ecosystem where the only constant is change. In this scope, BPM is a pervasive topic and one of the main business trends around the world. Today, these companies are running, planning or at least analyzing business-performance improvement initiatives based on BPM.

Unfortunately, it is very common to find that BPM is not well understood in these traditional companies. As a consequence, they are facing complex challenges and suffering from disappointing results. The main reason behind this observation is that people involved in these efforts (leaders, consultants, technologists, etc.) still think in term of business functions, and not in terms of business processes. This represents a large obstacle because functional thinking forces task-oriented behavior, whereas exactly the opposite behavior is required for BPM. BPM requires *teamwork*[1] instead of workgroups.

What is the difference between workgroups and teams? A workgroup is the form of working that has prevailed for many years in traditional companies. The work result is obtained by summing up individual contributions. Each member of a workgroup owns and shares subsets of information and has individual performance metrics and particular functional responsibilities. A team is a group of people that shares not only all the available information but also performance metrics. In BPM, a process team is the business performance unit that has a common set of objectives. These objectives are further related with other process teams, forming a hierarchic architecture of objectives. Working as workgroups is the best practice for human collaboration in business ecosystems with stable and predictable behavior. But workgroups are not the right working model in environments where the only constant is change.

People with a functional mindset, no matter what they do (even if they use the best BPM software technology and process-oriented applications), the benefits derived from their efforts will always be marginal and volatile from the business perspective (as a whole). In other words, the mentioned BPM promise will never be realized; and unexpected, inconsistent, unpredictable and unexplainable business results will remain the constant.

What is the solution? Target companies need to understand and act upon the human dimension of BPM. That is to say, their people need to shift their functional thinking and disciplinary-based behavior toward process thinking and systemic behavior respectively. I called this Human-Driven BPM. Let's get more insight about the challenges behind this needed shift.

THE PROCESS PARADOX

In general, BPM is seen merely as software solution that orchestrates business processes and automates workflows but it also has a human side that involves a new paradigm for work that has often been dismissed. A typical BPM project usually starts selecting a business process and specific BPM software with features like process modeling, simulation, orchestration, automation, monitoring, optimization, and management. The adoption problem arises later, after or during the solution implementation phase, as people still think in terms of functions and behave based on tasks with neither process vision nor business performance goals in mind. In other words, people with a functional mindset using a process-based software solution will deliver suboptimal results because they don't understand the multidisciplinary, dynamic, collaborative, open and holistic nature of a business process; I call this phenomenon *the process paradox*. Even in successful BPM technology-driven projects the business value will be marginal and/or volatile. Indeed, I've seen that most of these initiatives come to a close as a one-time-project.

Nowadays we can find excellent software solutions in the marketplace known as BPM suites (BPMS) that need to be selected carefully according to specific business needs. Not even making the "right" BPMS selection will assure project success nor long-term benefits if an organization is facing the process paradox. Why? Because real human practice change hasn't occurred yet. This is a big challenge for senior management, because it involves compromise, time and money investments, and innovation-based organizational transformation. It is a problem that reducing output (as operation costs decrease) is not enough anymore for being competitive in the long-term. They also need to increase their input in order to maintain market and financial success. Input increase means more value to customers, satisfying their expectations with no exception.

In order to be competitive in business ecosystems[2] with a rapid pace of change, a company must distinguish itself from its competition; "better" is not enough anymore, unique value propositions are required. For instance, leading companies defeat competition with more intelligent and aggressive approaches based on so-called blue ocean strategies[3]. For these companies competition doesn't matter and cost reduction is not the main driver because they are focused on value realization for customers, shareholders and employees in a balanced way. They have as foundation an agility-oriented enterprise architecture that shapes a culture of continuous innovation of value propositions and on-demand improvement of business capabilities. Basically, these market leaders have the installed capability of sustainable competitive-advantages development, they are agile!

In agility-oriented enterprise architectures, the value-driven business strategy is executed by an agile (responsive and adaptable) system of business processes. Business processes are the natural units for change synchronization, customer value realization, strategic objectives achievement, mission fulfillment and team performance management.

Traditional companies with the process paradox that operate in changing and competitive environments are *fragile*. Their rigid enterprise architecture and un-aligned, task-oriented and change resisting people, along with unadaptable software applications with embedded business rules, policy bureaucracy, implicit work procedures and individual/functional-driven performance management systems are some of the main obstacles for business agility.

BPM IS ALL ABOUT PEOPLE CHANGE

Let's focus on the missing piece in technology-driven BPM efforts: people. I will start discussing why BPM is about people change, and will continue going deeper into the human nature, the root cause behind change resistance and therefore the main reason for failures of organizational transformation programs.

Organizations that really practice BPM don't face the process paradox, because their people think in terms of processes and behave systemically. I have heard people that raise the question: "why is this process performance poor if it's already modeled, automated and deployed using BPMS"? The answer is simply and two-fold, but not obvious. First, what was really done with the BPMS was to work with the business process definitions and not with the business processes itself. Properly done, group of people collaborate according to process roles and share a mental model composed of common goals and metrics, that is to say, process-oriented teamwork. Second, if people just try but have not really adopted yet new processes practices, results won't be better all of a sudden. If an organization really wants to practice BPM, much more than just BPMS acquisition and process mapping and simulation will be needed in order to enjoy its promised benefits. I talk more about BPM benefits and impacts later in this paper.

Change management of process-driven team and individual practices is a critical requirement for BPM. We can talk about Human-Driven BPM when this requirement is considered and fulfilled in a BPM initiative. The very first kind of change that we need to target is the one at the individual level, that once achieved, will have a bottom-up butterfly effect[4] positively impacting team performance, strategic results, business processes value realization, and delivering against customer expectations. In big companies, the impact reaches higher levels or broader scopes. In many cases, the involved human shift is so significant that it is also visible at family and society levels. This is true in general wherever human nature is exposed to real changes.

In order to get an insight of the human change nature and the kind of challenges involved in a transformation program toward business-performance excellence, I'll describe the three human dimensions in a business context. I call the first dimension our spirit. In practice, human spirit can be seen as our essence composed by values, believes, conscience, identity and assumptions. The second dimension is our soul. A human soul can be seen as our will, driven by emotions, feelings, perceptions, expectations, thoughts, memories, personality, ideas and other mental aspects. The third dimension is our body. A human body can be seen as our attitude, composed by behaviors, communication skills, work orientation (task/results) and recreation, entertainment, exercise and feeding habits.

A very important issue about human beings is the fundamental need for balance between its three human dimensions in order to enjoy an integral life. Another relevant issue here is that people don't resist change but they resist to be changed. Having this in mind and according to this paper's scope, the natural question is why do organizations and specifically change-managers usually fail at human level? At this point the natural answer could be that managers are trying to change people practices the wrong way. This is correct but the analysis is still incomplete; the underlying problem is that organizations try to realize people change following the wrong approach. They try to achieve it outside-in because mostly they are not aware of the human dimensions and its relationship (see figure 1, on the next page).

A person resists to be changed because a desired result will never change his/her essence directly, doesn't work this way because is human design! Even if a person has only the will to change its attitudes according to specific desirable results, at the end will fail, because as humans we need to change from our very core, from our human spirit. In the context of a BPM effort, real human change has to start at the spiritual level and fundamental aspects have to be adapted accordingly to necessary attitudes that with lead to desirable results. The very first step is to become self-convinced about required changes. Going from functional to process thinking and from disciplinary (task-based) to systemic behavior, are two critical and mandatory human shifts for Human-Driven BPM. These shifts reduce hidden risks and foster value realization as expected by customers.

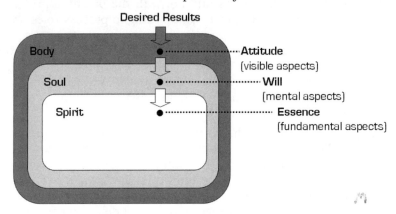

Figure 1. Wrong Direction for Human Change

The moment when an organization gets insight regarding these human aspects, is when the expected business results show up and the BPM promises become tangible. At this point is when everyone understands the value of human change managers and process managers. The right direction for real human change is inside-out (see Figure 2, on the next page). In BPM projects, real change starts at human spirit level having the corporate ethos[5] as the leading driver. Once a employee has changed part of its essence according to business needs, direction and coaching will be needed in order to realize the corresponding shifts at the soul level. At this point an intermediate level of change has been reached. The final phase of the process of human change will be completed driven by periodic evaluations and feedbacks about actual results against initial compromises – smart objectives[6] will be useful to avoid misunderstandings.

In order to be a practitioner of Human-Driven BPM a mandatory requisite is the holistic orientation that encompasses systemic behavior as a natural consequence of process thinking. In this paradigm, the whole is much more than its parts, or stated differently, the entire system is our focus and not its subsystems only. The optimization of the parts of the system will not result in the optimization of the whole. A critical success factor is the right selection of what is to be considered the entire system and the appropriate subdivision criteria. In Human-Driven BPM, the system is the business as a whole; a typical mistake is having a functional department or even a single business process as the system.

As an example, I am the head of sales department and select my area as the entire system along with its corresponding functional KPIs[7]. Naturally, sales people will only respond according to sales goals dismissing other department interests (like service delivery capacity planning) and affecting business goals as a consequence! This is typical functional thinking and behavior that results in unexpected, inconsistent, and unpredictable business results.

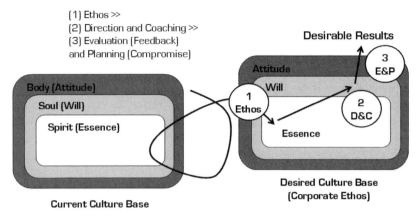

Figure 2. Right Direction for Real Human Change

AGILITY-ORIENTED ENTERPRISE ARCHITECTURE

To get more insight into human change and communication, business agility, and complexity management, let's take a closer look at the Enterprise Architecture Metamodel or EAM[8] (see Figure 3).

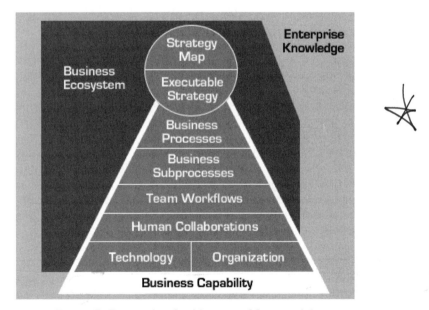

Figure 3. Enterprise Architecture Metamodel

Business agility is the domain addressed by the EAM. This metamodel is a generic blueprint composed by eleven related models. These models are generic abstractions of real structures and dynamics of changing organizations. An enterprise architect use the EAM as a business-model development framework that simplify their job regarding complexity management and human communications improvement. The purpose is to leverage human potential in decision making, change management, process improvement, strategy formulation and communication, people development, market analysis, business events monitoring, change impact traceability analysis, mergers and acquisitions, business process execution among many others.

The Enterprise Knowledge model lets us understand one of the most valuable set of intangible assets of an enterprise that include business rules, policies, guidelines (templates, procedures, tool mentors, roadmaps, etc.), models (patterns, frameworks, etc), and business practices like methods, techniques, standards and principles. Other intangible asset sets are human capital, business culture, trademarks, relationships with customers and partners, etc. I want to point out that normally more than the 75 percent of the average firm's market value is derived from its intangible assets[9].

The Business Ecosystem model is composed by natural agents of change (customers, owners, competitors, suppliers, partners, and others) and its relationships with enterprise components like processes, systems, employees and services. For example, when a customer matches one of his needs with a specific value offer (usually composed by a sort of services and products), a customer expectation is created. At business design time, the customer expectation creation is the expected event that drives the overall strategy formulation. At business execution time, this event represents the trigger that initiates business services and its corresponding realizations that are business processes. At the end, business processes realize customer value, meeting customer expectations; this is the foundation for business process excellence.

The Business Definition view is divided into two related models. The Strategy-Map model is an abstraction of the business strategy, and the Executable-Strategy model includes the relevant details that let us see how this strategy is supposed to be executed throughout a system of business processes. The Executable-Strategy model depicts the first level of the business process system architecture, that I call the *business process architecture*. In general, strategy managers don't have problems formulating mission and mapping its strategy (A very good and wide adopted framework for strategy formulation and visualization is Balanced Scorecard Strategy Maps[10]), a complex problem arises when they need to clarify how the mentioned strategy map will be put into reality. This is exactly what Human-Driven BPM is all about! This discipline makes "the customer expectations with no exception challenge" feasible by closing the business strategy-execution loop. In Human-Driven BPM, business process managers implement the business process architecture using BPMS technology enabling agile (responsive and adaptable) people to execute a visible strategy.

Business processes is about people. People are empowered by business knowledge and supported by enabling technology and the processes are aligned to the business strategy. This business strategy is driven jointly by business mission and value proposition. Using another perspective, agile people drive the development of agile teams that execute an agile system of processes. This system finally realizes a value-driven strategy, resulting in an agile business. Figure 3 outlines this concept and shows a comprehensive view called Business Capability[11]. This view includes relevant information about the executable strategy as a whole at a high level of abstraction that communicates the guiding mechanism for value creation, delivery and realization. This innovative view integrates elements from six different models into a holistic view that encapsulates business operations complexity by encouraging process thinking and systemic behavior. The basic idea is integrating and synchronizing processes, teams, organizations, technology, and knowledge into a responsive and adaptable unit called *business capability* that produces expected, consistent, and predictable business results. That is to say, this mechanism denotes the ability of one business to satisfy its customers' expectations.

The Organization model includes the concepts of performance and development units. Performance units are functional departments and process teams, and development units are competence centers and career centers. Every employee of each business should have one or more relationship with one or more component of each of these organizational units. For example, a process manager bears relation to the components "BPM career," "communication skill competence," "process engineering team," and "architecture team." In addition, he might also belong to a shared-service department called "business development."

The Technology model includes relevant details about the information technologies that are used directly by business users like tools, applications, databases, network workstations and business knowledge portals, between others. This business technology fosters innovation and enable business high performance when the involved people work as aligned teams and are well prepared to take advantage of its functionality.

BUSINESS PROCESS ARCHITECTURE

The business process architecture, or BPA, has five levels of abstraction that are organized as tiers, where the second level is the more specific that the first one and the third level is more specific than the second one, and so on. The executable strategy is its level zero. The business processes that realize this executable strategy conform the BPA level one. The relationship between these two higher levels constitutes the most important step in the enterprise architecture development process. In fragile organizations where these two higher levels are not well aligned, there exists something that I call *the business execution chasm*.

This chaotic situation is like a chasm that divides strategic and operational aspects. Nobody knows how the strategy is related with the work done on a daily basis. Often they do not even have a basic understanding of the business strategy or the overall processes where they are supposed to be an integral execution piece in. In fragile companies these processes are implicit inside peoples' minds, constituting a competitive disadvantage; because this knowledge can't be shared across the company. In other words, this implicit knowledge about current business processes and inherent work practices is not really part of the BPA. Consequently, it can't be considered as an intangible business asset. Therefore people are the missing piece in organizations that are trying to adopt BPM with the wrong approach. In these types of companies, the BPA (the central model of Human-Driven BPM) is hidden, invisible, or undocumented. They are immature and the execution chasm remains an integral part of its corporate culture.

A business has an executable strategy when an agile system of strategy-aligned business processes has been implemented. In order to be able to do so, process architects need to decompose each business process into subsystems called business subprocesses, which communicate relevant aspects of the business behavior at certain level of abstraction. For instance, business event handling and response triggering are visible here. Subprocesses are further subdivided into process team workflows (PTW). In theory, each business process is a business execution unit, but in practice, process team workflows are the ones. In a BPA, PTWs are the lowest level where business performance metrics are defined. It is at this level where synergy is given birth. This teamwork impacts the overall business strategy results bottom up by having a butterfly effect -whenever the BPA is well designed and effectively communicated.

Each team workflow is further subdivided into individual tasks. Each task can only be executed when a process role[12] is defined. Such a task in a team workflow is an atomic work unit. Even if this task is related to a work procedure, such a level of detail is not part of the business process architecture. In BPM, not only team workflows are automated, in many cases even the majority of its role tasks are automated by software services or composite applications under the umbrella of the so called SOA[13], the word-wide architecture trend in the software industry.

A manual task that was automated becomes part of a SOA implementation naturally. By "naturally" I mean that a service-oriented architecture in BPM is the natural way to structure supporting information technologies, because automation requirements are derived easily once a team workflow is modeled and deployed using a BPMS (for further details see next section). The functionality required to structure business software components and applications as part of service-based IT environments is already supported by all major software vendors. An automated task that doesn't need to interact with a person (playing a team role) is known as an automatic task otherwise it is an interactive task. The subset of all human-driven tasks that collaborate in order to achieve overall team workflow objectives are known as its human collaboration view. The collectivity of all human collaborations forms the level 5 of a BPA. In the same way, team workflows forms its level 4, and subprocesses forms its level 3.

As a summary of this section, a BPA allows business process architects to understand a complex system of business processes decomposing it in more manageable and easy to understand parts. Human collaborations constitute the core and represent the starting points for driving value creation, delivery and realization for end customers.

BUSINESS PROCESS ARCHITECTURE ENABLERS

In this section, I point out some enablers for BPA implementations and a brief description of BPM suites, SysML, BPMN, XPDL, and BPEL is given.

BPMSs use explicit process models to coordinate the interactions among people, systems and content as equally important aspects of work. This model-driven and process-thinking-based approach loosely couples the physical resources used at execution time from the design of the process, enabling agility. These BPM software solutions enable its users to see and directly manipulate the resources being coordinated. Explicit process models are far easier to change for process managers and software engineers than traditional applications, which use implicit approaches based on programming code. From the point of view of enterprise architects, a BPMS is the most important technology enabler not only for the BPA implementation but also for many challenges implied in business-process operation management. These include amongst others automated workflow execution and state management, real-time activity monitoring, event and exception handling, on demand improvements, human-task management, automated business-rules management, business-process innovation, process integration in B2X scenarios[14]. From the organizational point of view, a BPMS represents the mechanism that enables the integration and synchronization of all BPA components, including manual workflow tasks. From the point of view of IT departments, a BPMS is a platform that allows them to eliminate the business execution chasm and to foster implementation of business-driven SOA environments. In some cases IT returns the control of the business to business people, because business people can apply a great number of changes using the BPMS themselves when required by explicit processes without IT participation. In average, 80 percent of business change requirements are only related to business-rule evaluation and implementation. Taking into account that using a BPMS (with the business rule management feature supported), these rules are available for agile update because they are already extracted from software code and stored in a BPMS repository. Organized appropriately, those business change process instances will be completed in minutes or hours.

Systems Modeling Language (SysML) and Business Process Modeling Notation (BPMN) are two widely adopted standards that are very useful for human communications issues, both are maintained by The Object Management Group (www.omg.org). According to the OMG:

> SysML is a general-purpose graphical modeling language for specifying, analyzing, designing, and verifying complex systems that may include hardware, software, information, personnel, procedures, and facilities. In particular, the language provides graphical representations with a semantic foundation for modeling system requirements, behavior, structure, and parametrics. BPMN is a graphical notation that depicts the steps in a business process. BPMN depicts the end to end flow of a business process. The notation has been specifically designed to coordinate the sequence of processes and the messages that flow between different process participants in a related set of activities.

SysML can be adopted as a common visual language for the Enterprise Model as a whole and BPMN can be adopted as a specialized visual notation for the BPA modeling. There are many software offerings in the marketplace with certain support of BPMN and/or SysML.

XML Process Definition Language (XPDL) is the most widely deployed process definition language and XML-based BPM standard. XDPL is leveraged by a broad spectrum of software applications including ERP, CRM and call center, BI and BAM, process modeling and simulation, enterprise content management, as well as several of the leading workflow systems and BPMSs. XPDL is maintained by the Workflow Management Coalition (www.wfmc.org). According to the WFMC:

> The goal of XPDL is to store and exchange the process diagram, to allow one tool to model a process diagram, and another to read the diagram and edit, another to "run" the process model on an XPDL-compliant BPM engine (core of a BPMS), and so on. For this reason, XPDL is not an executable programming language like BPEL[15], but rather a process design format that literally represents the "drawing" of the process definition. Specifically, it has 'XY' or vector coordinates, including lines and points that define process flows. This allows an XPDL to store a one-to-one representation of a BPMN process diagram. For this reason, XPDL is effectively the file format or "serialization" of BPMN, as well as any non-BPMN design method or process model which use in their underlying definition the XPDL meta-model. BPEL and XPDL are entirely different yet complimentary standards. BPEL is an "execution language" designed to provide a definition of web services orchestration, specifically the underlying sequence of interactions, and the flow of data from point-to-point. For this reason, it is best suited for straight-through processing or data-flows vis-a-vis application integration.

SUMMARY AND CONCLUSION

Process thinking and systemic behavior are two critical success factors of any BPM effort, for short-term solution-implementation projects as well as for long-term transformation programs that are focused on the development of sustainable competitive advantages. If an organization wants to take advantage of the use of standards like SysML, BPMN, and XPDL and leverage the human potential using enabling BPM suites, its people need to be agile. They need to develop the ability to unlearn and relearn according to business change requirements.

In order to complete the first and critical shift towards human agility, people need to unlearn obsolete practices and learn a new way for value creation, delivery and realization inside changing work environments. This involves process thinking and systemic behavior. Relevant indicators of progress in this regards are effective human communication based on enterprise knowledge, agile technology adoption, and process-driven teamwork, all oriented towards customer value realization.

We can talk about *business agility* when an enterprise has developed and implemented aligned, responsive and adaptable business capabilities, when execution is carried out by technology-enabled process teams, which are driven by agile people, and when customer expectations are satisfied with no exception resulting in sustainable value.

BPM efforts that dismiss process thinking and systemic behavior are in reality not adopting BPM practices! In this paper I used the attribute *human-driven* in the discussion just to emphasize the importance of this dimension, but BPM is human driven by definition. Practitioners of BPM have the ability to make timely and consciously decisions based on facts under the umbrella of business capabilities that execute strategies for value realization.

The description of a BPM solution and transformation-program frameworks is out of the scope of this paper. Nevertheless, I want to point out that human change management is part of a broader discipline known as human capital management. It includes the critical shift in thinking and behavior discussed earlier but is not the only discipline related to BPM efforts. Other relevant examples are: business life-cycle management, product life-cycle management, customer expectation management, program and project management, business capability management and team life-cycle management, amongst other.

I conclude saying that BPM is a holistic and natural management model that is driven by *agile people* for the development and operation of growing and profitable businesses produced by responsive, adaptable and aligned capabilities that consistently achieve strategic objectives and sustain competitivity in changing business ecosystems.

REFERENCES AND GLOSSARY OF TERMS

[1] Further reading about teamwork and teams: The Wisdom of Teams, Jon R. Katzenbach and Douglas K. Smith, Harvard Business School Press.

[2] "A Business Ecosystem is an economic community supported by a foundation of interacting organizations and individuals--the organisms of the business world. This economic community produces goods and services of value to customers, who are themselves members of the ecosystem. The member organizations also

include suppliers, lead producers, competitors, and other stakeholders. Over time, they co-evolve their capabilities and roles, and tend to align themselves with the directions set by one or more central companies. Those companies holding leadership roles may change over time, but the function of ecosystem leader is valued by the community because it enables members to move toward shared visions to align their investments and to find mutually supportive roles." James F. Moore, Harvard Business Review in May/June of 1993.

3 For further information about Blue Ocean Strategy visit www.blueoceanstrategy.com

4 The Butterfly effect is a phrase that encapsulates the more technical notion of sensitive dependence on initial conditions in chaos theory. Small variations of the initial condition of a nonlinear dynamical system may produce large variations in the long term behavior of the system. For example, a ball placed at the crest of a hill might roll into any of several valleys depending on slight differences in initial position. The phrase refers to the idea that a butterfly's wings might create tiny changes in the atmosphere that ultimately cause a tornado to appear (or prevent a tornado from appearing). The flapping wing represents a small change in the initial condition of the system, which causes a chain of events leading to large-scale phenomena. Had the butterfly not flapped its wings, the trajectory of the system might have been vastly different (extracted from www.wikipedia.org).

5 A corporate ethos is the spirit of an organization that we could understand by analogy with the human spirit aspects already explained. In other words, a corporate ethos is the expected organizational culture (composed by important assumptions defined by the top management and founders) that must be developed as integral part of people and organizational development efforts.

6 Smart objectives are specific, measurable, achievable, relevant and time-bound

7 A KPI stand for Key Performance Indicator

8 A Metamodel is a model that encompasses guidelines for model development. It is a data model that represents a set of concepts within a domain and the relationships between those concepts. A metamodel helps architects to reason about the objects within that domain. In other words, a metamodel is a model that describes how to analyze and construct models that will be applicable and useful in predefined class of problems.

9 Extracted from Kaplan and Norton, Strategy Maps, HBS Press

10 Strategy maps are a way of providing a macro view of an organization's strategy, and provide it with a language in which they can describe their strategy, prior to constructing metrics to evaluate performance against their strategies (Extracted from www.wikipedia.org).

11 I define a Business Capability, in the context of BPM, as the ability to satisfy customer expectations with no exception through a strategy-focused system of processes. The processes are executed by technology-enabled process teams, which are integrated by agile people.

12 A process role is a set of responsibilities that people assume while executing a process.

13 Service Oriented Architecture, or SOA, represents a model in which functionality is decomposed into distinct units (services), which can be distributed over a network and can be combined together and reused to create business applications. These services communicate with each other by passing data from one service to another, or by coordinating an activity between two or more

services. The concepts of SOA are often seen as built upon, and the evolution of, the older concepts of distributed computing and modular programming (Extracted from www.wikipedia.org).

[14] B2X stand for process integration between a Business and X. For example, X can be C (a consumer), E (an employee), or B (another business).

[15] For further information about BPEL visit www.wikipedia.org. About a WS-BPEL that is a specification of the OASIS organization visit www.oasis-open.org.

The Rise of the Project Workforce

Managing Projects and People in a Flat World

Rudolf Melik, Tenrox, Canada

I think it's going to be one of the biggest middle-class jobs—collaborators. Collaborators are people who are good at working as part of global knowledge, manufacturing or supply chains.

- Thomas Friedman

ABSTRACT

Faster is the new fast in today's highly interconnected truly global economy. Project-driven businesses that rely upon a dispersed workforce are quickly finding out that their old way of doing business does not get the job done in the flat world. This paper offers a blueprint for combining workflow-driven project management and workforce management with traditional functions like accounting, payroll, and HR to provide real-time project status visibility, optimize resource utilization, and enable instant communication across multiple teams and time zones.

THE WORLD IS FLAT—AGAIN

In his seminal work: The World Is Flat (New York: Farrar, Straus and Giroux, 2006) author and "presentist" Thomas Friedman describes a highly integrated world where business is done instantaneously with billions of people across the planet. As a result of the lowering of trade and political barriers and the technical advances of the digital revolution, a new flat world has emerged in which a call center in the Philippines answers support questions from a distributor in England for software that was designed in California, coded in India, and tested in Ireland.

For some of us on the leading edge of global commerce, these developments may not come as a big surprise. But Friedman convinces us that the new flat world is no longer the stuff of futurists or presentations at the World Economic Forum. Outsourcing and collaboration are facts of life, and much more the norm than the insulated small manufacturer based in the heartland of the United States.

As organizations and executives find themselves with two feet planted firmly in a fully interconnected, truly global economy, one truth is evident for all enterprises; and particularly for project—or service—driven businesses that rely heavily on project teams and information workers:

> Our established ways of getting work done, of accounting for this work, of monitoring compliance, and of analyzing work in progress for intelligence that will help us do future work faster, better, cheaper, and smarter are through.

In his seminal work *Only the Paranoid Survive* [1] [then Intel Corporation CEO Andy Grove coined what would become the *de facto* phrase for points in time such as this: strategic inflection points. Strategic inflection points mark full-scale changes in the way business is conducted. The ways we work, the ways we compete, and

---

[1] New York, Random House, 1999

the ways we win require a new approach, a new outlook beyond simply making our existing systems bigger, better, faster. During strategic inflection points, businesses that "get it" and change, achieve unprecedented gains—those that do not, stumble and fade.

Driving our current strategic inflection point is the underlying social, economic, and world infrastructure transformation of what globalization guru, author, and Pulitzer Prize-winning New York Times columnist Thomas Friedman calls a "flat world." In a flat world, Friedman explained to *Wired* magazine, organizations compete on a "level, global, Web-enabled playing field that allows for multiple forms of collaboration without regard to geography or distance—or soon, even language."

Friedman goes on to tell us that while Fortune 500 firms are willing participants in this global business revolution, they are not driving it. Rather they are being pulled along by groups of highly innovative, widely dispersed project teams. Most of the individuals that comprise these teams are working from basements and boiler rooms, not skyscrapers. In essence, the new flat world is being driven by a corresponding flat hierarchy of small, co-equal teams interconnected by a series of co-dependent projects. And these teams are working fast!

Futurist, trends and innovation expert Jim Carroll concurs with Friedman and notes the increased pace at which change occurs in this new flat world. In his book, *What I Learned from Frogs in Texas* [2], he writes:

> As globalization and technological advances converge, competition is changing overnight, and product lifecycles often last for just a few months. Permanence has been torn asunder. We are in a time that demands a new agility and flexibility: leaders must have the skill and insight to prepare for a future that is rushing at them faster than ever before.

While star journalists like Thomas Friedman and Jim Carroll are free to chronicle the emergence of the flat world, it is left to the rest of us to figure out how to better manage and work in it, without falling off the edge. That's where this book comes in. It's a practical guide to organizing and getting work done in an environment that Friedman further describes as:

> More people than ever collaborating and competing in real time with more other people on more different kinds of work from more different corners of the planet and on a more equal footing than at any previous time in the history of the world. (p. 8)

Today's business systems are simply not designed to plan, schedule, manage, audit, and optimize work that gets done in a flat world. In fact, the origin of double-entry accounting actually dates back to the last time the world was flat: the days of Columbus. More modern versions of business automation tools such as enterprise resource planning (ERP), customer relationship management (CRM), and project management software want to impose a certain rigidity within business processes, and fail to address the dynamic interplay and constantly shifting relationship between projects and people, which occurs naturally in the flat world and characterizes today's business.

To help you navigate the flat world, this paper:
- reviews the market dynamics that are creating our flat world,

---

[2] Oblio Press, Toronto Canada, 2004)

- explores the new nature of work in this environment,
- highlights why today's business and IT systems fall short,
- introduces Project Workforce Management, a new set of Workflow driven disciplines and technology designed to manage people and projects in a flat world, and
- explains how you can connect project, talent and financial management applications using an underlying business process management platform.

NOTE: The contents of this paper are based primarily on chapters 1 and 7 of *The Rise of Project Workforce* by Rudolf [3].

MARKET DYNAMICS THAT CHALLENGE TRADITIONAL PROJECT MANAGEMENT

The following major market dynamics not only contribute to the flattening of the world, but also challenge the management capabilities of the processes and systems we use:

- Globalization: At the start of this shift, organizations moved simple tasks like assembly and manufacturing to developing countries where this work could be completed more economically. In globalization's current wave, organizations are outsourcing knowledge work as well. The Internet, fast networks and a globally connected workforce are the driving forces behind this trend.
- Regulatory scrutiny: As organizations have become more fragmented, they also have become subject to greater regulatory scrutiny. To comply, they need more thorough and expansive systems for assigning, tracking and managing accountability for the work being done. This oversight protects everyone: workers, customers, suppliers, the organization and its stakeholders.
- Flattened hierarchy: In a flat world, top-down decision-making is replaced by bottom-up empowerment. Widely-distributed companies cannot use an authoritative command/control structure. Instead, market leaders will find ways to remove the red tape shackles from their project teams and empower them to get work done and make local decisions.
- Fragmented enterprises: Today's work is defined by atomized segments that are delivered by specialized workers both inside and outside the company. Organizations assign work to internal or outsourced teams based on costs, available talent, the nature of the work, and customer expectations.

A FLAT WORLD DEMANDS COLLABORATION AND COOPERATION

The net result of a flat world is an overriding need for collaboration and cooperation. The problem is that companies are not really all that adept at collaborating; too many enterprises struggle with thinking innovatively about how they work, and fail to create processes and systems that support cooperative collaboration.

In *What I Learned from Frogs in Texas*, Jim Carroll reports the results of a survey by Collaborative Strategies LLC that revealed 32 percent of the time in a typical working week is spent on helping others resolve questions. Of these questions, 54 percent have been answered before, yet the answers are not recorded in any type of accessible knowledge base so that they can be institutionalized. Instead, organizations continue to waste time answering the same questions. This is despite

---

[3] New Jersey, John Wiley & Sons, 2007.

the fact that 81 percent of those in the survey believed it was important to share such knowledge.

Often, the desire to collaborate is not supported by processes and systems that make collaboration easy, or better yet, a natural part of the way work flows. Instead, entrenched roadblocks and business challenges get in the way.

- Employees are working very long hours to deliver projects, but management cannot report on the reasons why resources are so overloaded. As a result, management also lacks the insight to create innovative long-term solutions for balancing resource demand and resource availability.
- Businesses lack tangible measures of the value versus cost/effort of different internal departments.
- Manual data collection processes mean management receives reports on billable utilization and capacity planning after month end—too late to make corrections on work in process, and too late to take corrective action before initiating new projects.
- IT or engineering is unable to produce a report that shows the cost breakdown of effort across different types of projects—such as research and development, client and maintenance projects—so that work allocations can be optimized to meet the organization's goals.
- Business reporting comes "after the fact." Organizations do not have standardized processes and systems for capturing the details of work across the enterprise. They often use "pillars of disconnected data" that sometimes conflict. For example, they track time using spreadsheets, multiple information systems or multiple timesheet and expense reporting systems (one for payroll, another for project tracking and another for billable work). The information in these systems does not always agree. Managers use manual entry (such as merging spreadsheets) to integrate the data for reporting and decision-making—this consumes time and people resources, and often results in inaccuracies.
- Decentralized shared resource pools, spread across business units, cities, countries, and time zones, often have no systems to enable the real-time collaboration and data access their work requires.
- Compliance costs are escalating as regulations become more stringent, while the way work gets done becomes more fluid. The lack of process automation results in high additional costs for internal and external compliance audits and any process improvement initiative.
- Various departments and geographically dispersed resource groups use completely different or disconnected systems to manage the same processes, thus hindering collaboration and knowledge sharing.

NEW NATURE OF WORK

At the crossroads of a flat world and the heightened demand for collaborative organizations is the new nature of work. Today, work is increasingly differentiated, meaning it is compartmentalized into units of "subject matter expertise" delivered by collaborating specialized workers both inside and outside the company. While only a short while ago, just a small percentage of an enterprise's work was formed around collaborative projects and differentiated time, today, about more than half is, and the trend toward compartmentalization of work is expected to accelerate.

This shift in the way work gets done requires organizations to track "differentiated time and expenses," to allocate costs (whether or not they are billable) to the right projects, as well as to examine and justify spending and labor costs across both internal and external service units.

The empowered collaborative workforce has a substantial impact on how we track and measure work:

- Work is delivered or centered on an initiative or a project. Companies are able to quickly assemble a team of geographically dispersed, highly specialized professionals to execute a specific project. These teams are formed for varying durations depending on the nature of the project, and are dismantled just as quickly as initiatives are completed. Some have called this the "Hollywood Model" of work: bring together the best resources to make a movie, then disband and form other teams to make other movies.

- It is no longer sufficient to analyze customers, projects, employees and financial data as separate entities. These elements are too interdependent to be tracked by different executives, each using their own tools and policies for monitoring and reporting. A new global system of record is required that combines the customer, the talent, and the project.

TRADITIONAL SYSTEMS PREVENT PROGRESS IN A FLAT WORLD

"Inadequate" and "disconnected" describe most of the systems in use today. Traditional Enterprise Resource Planning (ERP) systems fail to provide a single system of record that unifies customer, project and workforce management. Whether or not they use an ERP system, most organizations (and all Global 2000 companies) have deployed multiple enterprise applications and heavy customizations, including but not limited to:

- Customer management systems, such as salesforce.com, Microsoft CRM, Sugar CRM
- Project scheduling and project collaboration software, such as Microsoft Project, Primavera
- Portfolio management solutions (such as Primavera, Planview or Computer Associate's Clarity) used by internal IT departments to prioritize projects, to conduct what-if-analysis, and to align projects with company objectives
- Portal development and document management software such as Microsoft's SharePoint or Captaris' Alchemy
- Time and attendance tracking software, whether ERP customizations or separate systems from companies such as Kronos or Workbrain
- Travel and entertainment expense tracking software, whether ERP customizations or systems from companies such as Concur
- Billable time tracking software, whether ERP customizations or separate systems such as Sage Carpe Diem
- Business process management software such as Ultimus or Lombardi to automate business processes that are not addressed in other enterprise applications

Often, these applications have their own databases, rules, and policies. Sometimes they are completely disconnected from the company's ERP, accounting, or payroll systems. Disconnected systems result in dozens and, in large corporations, easily hundreds of spreadsheets to track work; to import and export data; and to report on customers, projects, and workers. To further complicate matters, some of these applications are used on-demand (like salesforce.com) while others remain on-premise systems.

In addition, spreadsheet-based tracking and reporting is used as "cure all remaining gaps" approach that creates a blizzard of assorted and often conflicting data. Disconnected or manually integrated systems, a mish-mash of unapproved data, and a wild email exchange of spreadsheets leads to an environment that is ripe for revenue leakage, errors, fraud and systemic control weakness.

PROJECT WORKFORCE MANAGEMENT: A NEW SYSTEM FOR A FLAT WORLD

To operate effectively, businesses must combine:
- Human capital management,
- Project management,
- Business process management, and
- Cost/revenue accounting into a synthesized solution called Project Workforce Management.

The underlying business process management workflow in this system adapts to each process, project, business unit and organization. It automates accounting for time and expenses of a project workforce—both within the company and without, to include its service providers. The software can be configured to work the way the company does, and fundamentally empowers individuals and decentralized organizations.

Project Workforce systems enable companies to meet the cooperative collaboration challenges of a flat world. They establish a new "system of record" that interrelates the customer, the project and the workforce (talent) to identify interdependencies and to simplify priority setting and talent sourcing, while balancing project profitability with customer satisfaction. Customer Relationship Management systems (where the "customer" is the system of record), Project Management systems (where the "project" is the system of record), and Human Capital Management systems (where the "employee" is the system of record) cannot accommodate these interdependencies.

PROJECT WORKFORCE MANAGEMENT IDENTIFIES INTERDEPENDENCIES

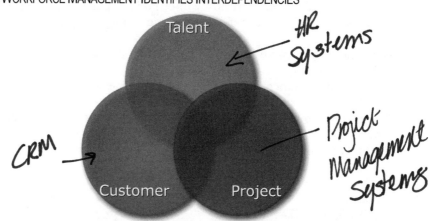

Figure 1 - Project Workforce Management links the customer, the project and the talent to create a global system of record.

The global "projectization" and fragmentation of work in the "flat world" has resulted in these business requirements which a Project Workforce Management solution fulfills:
- Project workforce management helps design and oversee the process itself, plus provides real-time visibility into "financial" implications. A Project Workforce Management solution provides the modules that link into a

single solution—a control "hub"—for total visibility and control. Examples include:

- Cost accounting for differentiated time and expenses
- Productivity analysis
- Budget-versus-actual comparisons
- Resource utilization trends, and
- Segmented reporting to fully understand the effectiveness and profitability of each separate project, resource group, and customer.

- Change is a constant. Project Workforce Management solutions make it easy for managers to change processes as they learn more about a project, resource group or customer. Process workflows are depicted graphically, and can be changed using simple "drag and drop" features. Organizations also can standardize these changes locally or worldwide if necessary.

- Work has been broken down into smaller pieces that sometimes overlap: business units, countries, outsourced teams, cost centers, and individual resources must collaborate, cooperate and handle more than one project at a time. A Project Workforce Management solution mirrors this reality by breaking down work and organizational structure into micro-components that can be tracked and summarized in any combination.

- A Project Workforce Management system provides an interactive environment for the real-time tracking and analyzing of project workforce data that complies with established policies and best practices, and enables immediate decision-making.

WORKFLOW: THE GLUE THAT CONNECTS PROJECTS AND PEOPLE TO BUSINESS PROCESSES

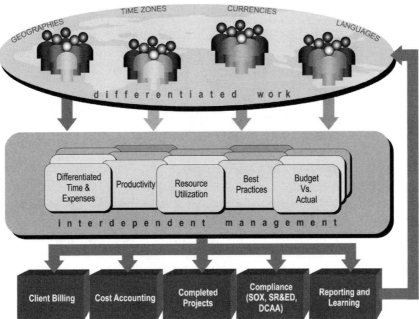

Figure 2 - Software is designed to plan, manage, track and report. Work differentiated in an interdependent and holistic way helps companies remain competitive and meet the significant challenges of today's flat world business environment.

Every project workforce activity is driven by an underlying business process. The workflow platform allows managers to model project, workforce, and financial processes; and subsequently to embed them into the software (Figure 2). This platform graphically represents work processes so that they can be designed, configured, and changed by authorized business process owners without requiring programming resources. The workflow interface enables users to visually define, control, track, and audit approvals, routing, role-based assignments and notifications. All business processes use the same workflow concepts and management interface. By leveraging the same visual framework and concepts, users experience a consistent interface that is easy to learn and use to manage any work process.

With a workflow-driven approach, managers and project contributors are designated a role within a business process. Unlike the rigidness of job titles, every project contributor can play different and multiple roles in various business processes. Using workflows to manage projects encourages workers to focus on their role for a given project or business process, instead of their title, rank or the department they belong to. Workflows break down the tribe psychology and corporate silos that leads to so much of the inefficiencies, waste and execution errors.

FUNCTIONS OF A PROJECT WORKFORCE MANAGEMENT SYSTEM

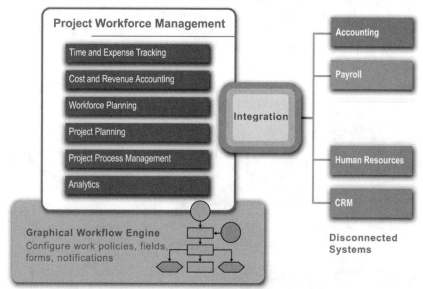

Figure 3 - The Components of a Project Workforce Management System

Project Workforce Management centrally manages project workforce related data, eliminating many of the spreadsheets used to track projects, time and labor, expenses, interdepartmental chargebacks, and billable work. Project Workforce Management encompasses and integrates:

- Time and Expense Tracking: Track all differentiated time and expenses billable or not.
- Cost and Revenue Accounting: Attribute all revenue (and charge back), spending and labor costs to specific projects, and establishes a formal charge back system for shared service departments such as IT and engineering. Formalizes and enforces a revenue accounting and recognition policy that is in compliance with regulations. Produce customer invoices, or chargeback to other business units, on a project basis for all billable

work, spending and labor costs; or invoices based on a pre-defined billing schedule.

- Workforce Planning: Handle competency and capacity planning. Optimally schedules your workforce by locating the most optimal available resources to accomplish specific roles in a project.
- Project Planning: Build a detailed project plan including the project's work breakdown structure and the project team. Assign resources to work on the tasks. Perform real-time earned value reporting and analysis.
- Project Process Management: Manage project processes, including project initiation, risk and issue reporting, and scope control using policy-based and enforced best practices.
- Analytics: Analyze consolidated, real-time and dynamic view of the company's projects, processes and workforce, with a special emphasis on reporting the financial perspective.

Project Workforce Management modules tightly integrate with accounting and payroll systems. The same reviewed and approved costs/expenses and differentiated time that are used to update and report on project status can also be used to process payroll, reimburse expenses, invoice for any billable work and spending, and update the accounting system with summary or detailed cost-revenue transactions.

THE WORKFLOW FOUNDATION

It's all about consistency. That's the way it has been forever. You can win the battles, but it doesn't matter unless you win the war.

- Jeremy Mayfield

E-mail and spreadsheets are so easy to use that most of us assume that they are an efficient way of organizing and recording work. Similarly, the personal contact we get from meetings gives us the feeling that they are the most effective way to collaborate.

However, in a company with more than just a handful of employees, the number of times requests are forwarded and escalated, the number of follow- ups, and the repetition of questions can easily add up to tremendous hidden costs, as well as frustration for employees, suppliers, and customers. E-mails, meetings, and conversations cannot be classified, sorted, and analyzed by project, task, or a resource group for tracking, auditing, and reporting purposes. Completing a work process requires that various people follow a pre-defined procedure, track their time and budgets, and capture all project information. These goals cannot be achieved cost effectively without using software that is specifically designed to manage work processes. The lack of a well-defined structure for guiding people through processes results in redundancies, inefficiencies, and mistakes.

The feature of Project Workforce Management that addresses these problems—and makes Project Workforce Management different from other solutions—is its workflow foundation. The workflow foundation drives, manages, and streamlines the flow of all project, workforce, and financial processes.

The workflow foundation automates many everyday work processes. This process automation enables executives to securely collaborate in real time with every member of the management team and all project contributors. Workflows also reduce the need for written procedures, follow-ups, and meetings. Training new staff on corporate policies and best practices is much faster and easier with self-service workflows and visually designed processes that guide new employees along the way—all of which leads to a significant reduction in mistakes, repetitive work, and administrative overhead.

A workflow management system completely defines, manages, and executes business processes using software. The sequence and progression of the work process is driven by the computer representation of the workflow logic. In an organization in which all staff is experienced and accustomed to the common way of "doing things," problems may have become invisible. As long as the procedures don't change and the staff remembers them, this flow may continue without a glitch. However, in the today's fast-changing business environment of today, even companies with well-established business models and processes need to reexamine, redefine, and re-engineer themselves constantly to remain efficient and competitive—this means "doing things" differently.

Traditional methods of documentation and staff training run the risk of having newly defined rules, policies, and methods that are not well understood or followed. Resistance to change might emerge because the staff is used to doing things the old way. These problems are only amplified in today's fragmented and remote workforce, where employees and project contributors can be anywhere, and in a highly regulated environment where companies face new compliance challenges. If a standard enterprise wide workflow system is used to manage projects, which is also linked to financials, and if that same workflow system guides the workforce through the proper steps to enforce the policies as well as audit the activities, then the results will be more predictable.

PROCESS DRIVEN PROJECT MANAGEMENT

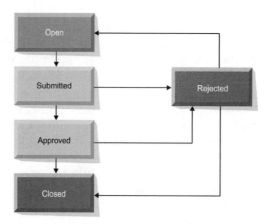

Figure 4 – A simple workflow

More and more businesses are starting to realize that a workflow system is applicable across their entire organization to manage any business process related to project and service delivery. The same solution can address the process automation needs of any project type including any IT, shared service, product development, or billable projects.

CIO Magazine's Research on Process Driven Project Management:

"The findings quantified distinctions between IT shops that live for the average and the few that take process leadership seriously. Elite IT performers weren't just two or three times better than median performers—they were seven or eight times better. High performers— roughly 13 percent of the 98 sampled—contributed on average eight times more projects, four and a half times more applications and software, four and a half times more IT services, and seven times more business IT changes. They implemented 14 more changes with half the failure rate."

An important difference between Project Workforce Management solutions and traditional project management is that the entire project/service delivery cycle is automated, controlled and audited using a workflow system. A graphical workflow interface provides visual definition, control, tracking and auditing of approvals, routing, role-based assignments and notifications. All Project Workforce Management processes are automated using the same user interface, concepts, and business logic. By leveraging the same visual framework, users experience a consistent and intuitive interface that is easy to learn and use to manage any project and workforce related business process.

WHICH WORK PROCESSES NEED WORKFLOWS?

Any nontrivial project, workforce, or financial process needs to be workflow managed. Project Workforce Management groups work processes based on their main usage area:

- Customer: Applies to a professional service organization or revenue-generating departments.
- Project: Applies to product development, IT, billable, and non-billable project and service delivery teams.
- Workforce: System of record is the employee (includes any consultants).
- Financial: System of record is a combination of customer, project, task, employee, or resource group for which the work is done, expenses incurred, and items purchased.

Project initiation, scope change, risk assessment, and issue tracking are some of the key project processes that must be managed in any project. The widely-known and rapidly growing Project Management Body of Knowledge [4](known as PMBOK) guide and certifications discuss the administration of these work processes as part of the project execution phase. However, the templates and solutions in PMBOK focus on capturing and documenting such events rather than the workflow to manage and institutionalize these project processes from start to finish. Treating these events as workflow-driven processes (in addition to treating them as documents and templates) provides visibility and transparency into their status at any stage. In fact, there is no mention of the need for a common standards-based workflow engine to manage all project, workforce, and financial processes. A more fundamental approach to work process management is required and it is the only way a company can achieve the consistency, automated compliance, transparency, and execution excellence that is so vital for any organization today.

The main Project Workforce Management processes, their interactions with each other and other enterprise software systems are shown in Figure 4.

1. [4] For more information visit http://www.pmi.org or http://www.wikipedia.org/wiki/Project_Management_Body_of_Knowledge

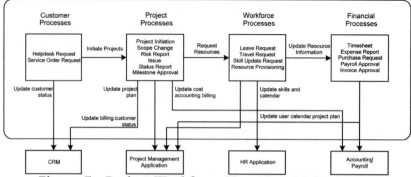

Figure 5 – Project Workforce Management Processes.

A COMMON LAUNCHING POINT FOR ALL EXPLORERS OF THE FLAT WORLD

The flattening of the world has created a strategic inflection point that organizations must address in order to survive: the need to accomplish, account for, monitor, analyze, and improve work in this new era of the Project Workforce.

Project Workforces encompass different teams of specialized subject matter experts both inside and outside of an organization that collaborate and cooperate. These teams achieve work that is differentiated, or compartmentalized, based on customer requirements, talent availability, and project scope, as well as business rules and objectives.

Traditional business management systems, which often exist in disconnected silos that provide narrow departmental or functional views, do not provide project workforces or business managers with the collaborative capabilities and integrated data they need to excel in this new business reality.

To address this need, Project Workforce Management systems have emerged. These systems bring together talent, work, and finances into one process-managed system with the following benefits:
- A common vantage point for all decision–makers
- Real-time views of projects, resource groups, actual progress, and issues
- More accurate decision making, since data is generated from approved, compliant, and automated processes.

In short, decisions that impact financial, team, and project performance are made faster with better information and in collaboration with stakeholders. In a flat world, an empowered project workforce can make faster localized decisions while gaining a global perspective.

While guides such as the "Project Management Body of Knowledge"[1] do a very good job of explaining the ideal project management concepts and techniques, they do not provide a road map to achieving differentiation or market advantage.

Purely methodology-based initiatives start with many good intentions and often end with compromises on quality, consistency, efficiency, or, worse yet, ineffective project controls. Project Workforce Management builds on the excellent disciplines and methodologies described in PMBOK. However, unlike the purely software-based enterprise project management and workforce management or educational tools such as PMBOK, Project Workforce Management is both a set of disciplines and workflow-driven tools combined with an unambiguous phased deployment road map that will help you achieve operational excellence.

XPDL-Enabled Cross-Product Exception Handling for WfMSs

Carlo Combi, University of Verona, Italy,
Florian Daniel, University of Trento, Italy, and
Giuseppe Pozzi, Politecnico di Milano, Italy

ABSTRACT

The effort invested by the Workflow Management Coalition in the interchangeability of process definitions has led to the definition of the XPDL language, a commonly acknowledged XML format for process definition. While XPDL effectively enables the cross-product portability of process definitions, the language has not been designed to also capture undesired behaviors that may arise during process execution, i.e. exceptions. Nonetheless, exceptions—especially those that are predictable at process definition time—do have semantics that are not negligible.

Our investigation of exception handling mechanisms in workflow management products has shown that a commonly accepted approach does not exist, and that, hence, a proposal for an exception-specific XPDL extension would probably not succeed. In this chapter, we describe our resulting idea of leveraging the products' very own extension mechanisms to enable cross-product exception definitions. The proposed approach operates at the conceptual level, formalizes exceptions in a fully XPDL-compliant fashion, and abstracts from product-specific details until process execution. Along with the description of our approach, we also discuss our experience with its effective portability across a few XPDL-compliant commercial and open-source workflow management products.

1 INTRODUCTION

Workflow management systems (WfMSs) enable the automated management of work that is typically executed by multiple roles (comprising both human actors and software applications) and whose flow is modeled according to one of the explicit process definition formalisms that have been developed over the last years. "Explicit" means that a process model expresses what is allowed or admissible during the execution of the actual work; other activities can simply not be enacted by the involved actors. All the semantics of the workflow are captured and suitably expressed in the process definition by means of basic modeling constructs such as tasks, roles, splits, joins, conditions, and so on.

Unfortunately, in general it is not easy—if not impossible—to explicitly capture all possible situations that may happen during the execution of a given process. Specifically, Eder and Liebhart [EL 1995] distinguish between exceptions and failures, which they further specialize into: *expected exceptions* (e.g., the impossibility to complete a payment activity), *unexpected exceptions* (e.g., the need to change the process definition during runtime), *basic failures* (e.g., a system crash), and *application failures* (e.g., a null pointer error). In addition to the model of the expected behavior of a WfMS, it is thus also necessary to specify how the system should react to the previous problems.

As failures are however out of the control of the WfMS, and unexpected exceptions cannot be predicted at process definition time, in this chapter we shall focus on expected exceptions[1], which can be considered part of the semantics of the overall process definition. Expected exceptions indeed deal with events that depend on the actual process in execution such as constraint violations over data managed by the process, or the start/end of a task or of a case, or a temporal deadline (e.g., for the completion of a task within a given timestamp), or an external event (e.g., a phone call from a customer to cancel the car reservation in a car rental company).

In order to successfully capture, manage, and execute exceptions, several efforts have been performed. We mention here WIDE [CCPP 1999] and other exception handling units [HA 2000], which are however tightly bundled inside the WfMSs and the process definition formalisms they have been developed for. As a consequence, there is no portability of exception specifications among different workflow management (WfM) products. The only way to obtain a portable and cross-product implementation of exception handling features is to map them onto the activity graphs.

In this chapter, we describe our experience with mapping exception handling features onto process or activity graphs. As our goal is to provide a portable definition of such exception handling features, we have opted for XPDL as process definition formalism [MNN 2005], also to assess its real support by current WfM products. The enriched process models we obtain from this mapping process still comply with the recommendations of XPDL and should successfully execute in XPDL-compliant WfMSs, provided that they enable a suitable customization of the system—a feature that is supported at different levels by all of today's WfMSs. We checked the portability of a normal process (one without embedded exception handling constructs) as well as that of the respective enriched process on some WfMSs declared to be XPDL-compliant. So far, we have considered Enhydra Shark, Bonita, Ascentn Agile Point, OBE, and WfMOpen, and results are interesting.

2 A REFERENCE EXAMPLE

Throughout this chapter, we shall make use of a reference example to better explain our approach. Consider Figure 1, which describes the *OrderManagement* process of a company trading in books called *RareBook* with very limited editions and accepting orders by its customers via telephone; payments can be done by credit card only.

After receiving an order, the *Sales Office* immediately checks the credit status of the customer's credit card. In case of overdraft, the order is declined. Otherwise, the *Sales Office* proceeds and checks the stock for the requested books. If all the products are available, the customer is notified of the immediate shipment, and the *Production* department provides for shipment. If, instead, not all the requested products are available, the *Sales Office* informs the user and asks for the approval of a delayed shipment. To accelerate the overall process, the *Production* department plans the production of the missing items in parallel, regardless of the user's decision, produces them and, if no cancellation is received, ships the complete order.[2]

---

[1] For simplicity, in the following we shall use the term *exception* to refer to the specific case of *expected exceptions*.

[2] Due to space restrictions, in this chapter we cannot exemplify the whole exception mapping procedure. For a more detailed discussion, the interested reader is referred to [CDP 2006].

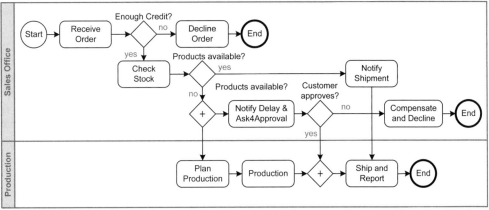

Figure 1 The OrderManagement process of the RareBook online book shop [CDP 2006].

For a better readability, in this chapter we shall use BPMN modeling constructs to express XPDL processes and activities, instead of providing unexpressive snippets of XPDL code. *Tasks* are represented as boxes, whose names describe the performed activity. *Transitions* are represented as directed arcs to connect process nodes, which, for routing purposes, may have associated a *condition* over workflow-relevant, application, or system data. Each process definition has one *start* and one *end* task, depicted by thin or thick circles, respectively. *Gateways* are represented as diamonds; condition gateways also have an associated textual condition, while *AND* gateways are diamonds that contain a + symbol.

3 Defining Exceptions

Expected exceptions in WfMSs deal with events that may occur during the enactment of a case. In order to successfully complete the execution of a case that has been affected by an exception, optional conditions may be tested and, possibly, some actions can be performed. Typical performed actions include the activation of a specific task or of a new case, the roll-back or compensation of the tasks already completed for that case, the re-assignment of a task to a new actor, etc.

Expected exceptions are generally classified according to their triggering event, i.e. to the event that raises the exception. As in [CCPP 1999], triggering events are classified as:

- *Workflow events*: events such as the start/end of a task/case may trigger an exception;
- *Data events*: the insertion, deletion, or update of a value of a workflow variable may trigger an exception, e.g., to monitor whether constraints defined over that workflow variable are violated or not;
- *Temporal events*: the occurrence of a specified timestamp, as well as the expiration of a deadline (e.g., for the completion of a task/case) or the periodic occurrence of timestamps (e.g., to perform a complete backup of the archives every Monday morning at 3:30 a.m.) may trigger an exception [CP 2004];
- *External events*: the occurrence of events raised by external applications (e.g., if the water level inside a basin raises above a specified maximum level) may trigger an exception which requires an intervention by the WfMS.

Properly dealing with such kinds of exceptions typically requires that the process execution continues with a deviation from the normal flow of execution, allowing the WfMS to respond to the exception. The semantics of expected exceptions are not negligible when specifying a new process definition.

While very few WfMSs come with a proper exception management unit, several efforts have been performed in order to define tools and languages for exception handling. As a reference, in our approach we consider the Chimera-Exception language [CCPP 1999], which, although quite complex, enables one to define exception handling triggers that are able to manage several types of events and of actions. The language reflects the above classification of events and provides an adequate set of process-specific actions to deal with typical exceptions in WfMSs. Also, the language is characterized by an adequate level of abstraction, i.e., it is completely product-independent and remains at a conceptual level, and is thus particularly suited as basis for our cross-product exception handling approach.

Referring to the example of the *RareBook* agency of Section 2, we consider here the following Chimera-Exception trigger (*CustomerCancel*), which is activated whenever a customer calls in to cancel his/her book order, causing the abnormal interruption of a respective case of the process *OrderManagement*:

```
define trigger CustomerCancel for OrderManagement
   events     modify(Cancel)
   condition  OrderManagement(O),
              occurred(modify(Cancel),O),
              O.Cancel="Yes"
   actions    startTask("CompensateAndDecline")
end
```

The meaning of the trigger *CustomerCancel* is as follows. The trigger is defined for the *OrderManagement* process only, which means that the trigger is a so-called process-specific trigger whose validity is confined to that specific process. The trigger reacts to a data event over the workflow-relevant data field *Cancel*, which is a process variable that is set to "No" as long as no cancellation has occurred; we assume that in the moment a users calls in to cancel an order, *Cancel* gets set to "Yes". The condition first defines an object *O* of type *OrderManagement*, which is used to identify the specific instance of *OrderManagement* in which the event has occurred. Then, the condition checks whether the new value of the *Cancel* variable equals "Yes", in which case the trigger enacts its action; otherwise, no action is performed. The action consists in the enactment of the task *CompensateAndDecline*, which can be seen in Figure 1 and causes the cancellation of the running case.[3] In this example, a task already existing in the normal process specification is enacted; it could be the case that an ad-hoc task has to be enacted, to be performed either by the exception handler or by another agent.

4 MAPPING EXCEPTIONS TO XPDL

The mapping of triggers like the previous *CustomerCancel* trigger from Chimera-Exception to XPDL occurs along two orthogonal dimensions, one that is *process-independent* and one that is *process-dependent*:

- The support for the basic expression evaluation and expression composition functions, as well as the support for the enactment of Chimera-

---

[3] The full syntax of the Chimera-Exception language is out of the scope of this chapter, but the interested reader is invited to read [CCPP 1999].

Exception's set of workflow actions, requires the provisioning of a set of basic sub-processes that can be reused across multiple process definitions. These sub-processes form a library of basic exception handling features, whose internal implementation typically varies from product to product. Sub-processes are process-independent.

- The actual mapping of the exception handling logic, instead, is process-dependent, as it requires intimate knowledge of the process structure in order to be able to correctly expand the original process graph with exception handling constructs according to the nature of the trigger to be mapped. The expansion of the process graph uses and combines basic sub-processes into macros and patterns in order to achieve an expressive power that is equivalent to the one of Chimera-Exception.

Due to the very tight interactions between the basic exception management constructs (the sub-processes) and the workflow engine of the host WfMS in order to suitably capture events and to enact actions, the development of the library of basic sub-processes typically requires intimate knowledge of the host WfMS. The knowledge of a process designer who is skilled in using the host WfMS however largely suffices to perform this task.

The mapping of the exception handling constructs onto the actual process graph enables one to define and manage expected exceptions even in WfMSs which do not feature an own exception management unit. According to the characteristics of the considered exception (i.e., its triggering event, its synchronicity or asynchronicity with respect to the normal flow of work, the number of process models affected by the exception—to mention few of them), several mapping techniques are required [CDP 2006].

In general, mapping events and actions into the process definition leads to less efficient and sometimes hardly readable schemata. To alleviate process designers from the inherent complexity of enriching existing process definitions with exception handling constructs by hand, we have developed a suitable compiler, which enables the designer to model the *plain* process as usual, to specify the exceptions to be handled in form of Chimera-Exception *triggers*, and to automatically compile the trigger definition into the *enriched* process definition. Process designers, thus, do not have to deal with the complexity of the enriched process graph. The enriched process definition produced by the compiler is still runnable by the host WfMS, provided that the necessary sub-processes have been customized.

Figure 2 depicts the logic of how to obtain the enriched process definition. The compiler requires in input the plain process definition in XPDL and a text file containing the Chimera-Exception rules to be compiled. Starting from the developed XPDL macros, patterns, and sub-processes, the compiler then enriches the plain process definition with exception handling constructs by adding a proper exception handling swim lane into the process definition. After the compilation, an optimizer prunes auxiliary nodes from the enriched process, which are required during the compilation process. Finally, the whole mapping process produces in output the enriched XPDL process definition and a report of the compilation/optimization process.

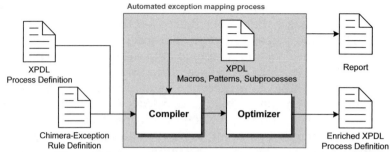

Figure 2 Compiling Chimera-Exception rules into enriched XPDL process definitions.

Let us now consider the example exception defined in Section 3. The exception is asynchronous with respect to the actual process flow since its time of occurrence cannot be known a priori: in fact, there is no relationship between the state of the running case and the timestamp at which the customer calls in to cancel the order. The exception is also process-specific, meaning that it relates to all the instances of the schema *OrderManagement*, only.[4] The only way of enriching a process model, enabling it to manage asynchronous exceptions, is that of starting immediately at case start time an exception handler that periodically checks for the raising of the exception. If the exception occurs, it can be captured at periodical time instants, which enables the WfMS to properly react. The mapping of such an asynchronous exception is performed by means of an additional swim lane, i.e., *Exc. Handler,* which contains the necessary exception handling logic. The result of the compilation of the trigger from Section 3 into the process definition of Figure 1 is shown in Figure 3.

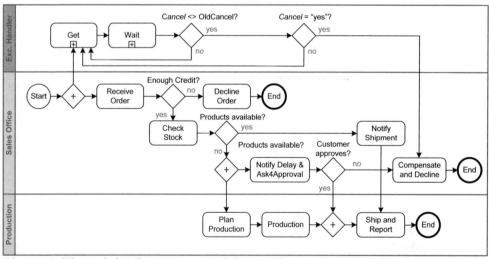

Figure 3 The original process model (see Figure 1) enriched with exception handling constructs. The compilation process automatically added the Exc. Handler swim lane.

---

[4] Other exceptions may also be cross-process, meaning that they may affect instances of different schemata (e.g., when an agent leaves, he/she may be involved in the executions of several cases from different process models, and all these cases will have no executing agent).

Let us analyze in detail the contents of the *Exc. Handler* lane. In order to check whether the data event of the exception has occurred, the *Get* sub-process reads the workflow variable named *Cancel* and stores its value in the temporary workflow variable *OldCancel*. The sub-process *Wait* then inserts a temporal delay *D*, i.e., the temporal interval that must expire between two subsequent readings of the same workflow variable to check for modifications. The actual comparison of the two values of the *Cancel* variable is performed by the *OR* split "Cancel <> OldCancel?", which compares the current value of *Cancel* with its previous value stored in *OldCancel*. The outgoing arc that goes back to the *Get* sub-process is executed if the two values are the same, meaning that no change has been detected; instead, the other outgoing arc that goes to the next *OR* split is executed if a change in the workflow variable has been detected. This concludes the event detection logic for the mapped trigger. The final *OR* split in the *Exc. Handler* lane represents the mapping of the condition part of the trigger. It checks whether the new value of *Cancel* is "Yes", in which case the *Compensate and Decline* task is executed (the action of the trigger); otherwise, the event detection logic continues polling the *Cancel* variable.

The so enriched process definition (from Figure 1 to Figure 3) is now capable of monitoring the occurrence of the data event *modify(Cancel)*, of checking the respective condition, and of enacting the *Compensate and Decline* task as required by the trigger in Section 3. It is worth noting that choosing an adequate polling interval to monitor the occurrence of data events is a critical task: in fact, too high a value of *D* introduces an average detection delay of $D/2$, which can be critical for some real-time applications; too small a value of *D*, even if reducing the detection delay, introduces an additional workload into the host WfMS. Fixing a suitable polling interval is thus a trade-off between the two considerations; a meaningful value can be configured before starting the compilation process.

5 Executing Processes on XPDL-Compliant WfMSs

In order to validate our exception mapping methodology, we tried to execute both the plain and the enriched process definitions on some XPDL-compliant WfMSs. We considered only systems that declare to be capable of directly executing XPDL process definitions or, however, of importing XPDL process definitions.[5] More precisely, the website of the Workflow Management Coalition[6] lists several WfMSs with the required characteristics. Some of these WfMSs are open source and available for free, while some others are not. Among the first ones, we chose and performed our tests on Enhydra Shark (version 2.0), WfMOpen (version 2.1), Bonita (version 3.0), and OBE - Open Business Engine (version 1.0); among the latter ones, we chose Ascentn Agile Point Server (version 4.01), which has been kindly provided to us by the vendor.

In order to perform the tests over the five different WfMSs, we needed five separate installations that could not interfere with each other. This was achieved by installing each WfMS on a separate virtual machine: we used several VMware virtual machines, one running Windows 2000 for Enhydra Shark, for OBE, and for WfMOpen, one running Windows XP for Bonita, and one running Windows 2003 Server for Ascentn Agile Point (these were strong installation requirements by the considered WfMSs). As our goal was to test the overall approach and the portabil-

---

[5] In this chapter, we always refer to XPDL version 1.0. For an overview of XPDL versions, the interested reader could refer to [Shapiro 2006].

[6] http://www.wfmc.org/standards/xpdl.htm

ity of plain and enriched process definitions, we did not take into account the performance of the different systems; this also justifies the use of virtual machines to run the systems.

The *OrderManagement* process model of the *RareBook* agency described in Section 2 has been modeled with the open source workflow editor Enhydra JAWE, which allows the graphical editing of process definitions and supports XPDL as native file format. According to its developers, JAWE does not make use of any proprietary XPDL extensions and, hence, provides a fully compliant implementation of XPDL.

Very few changes (ideally no changes) were expected when porting the plain process from one XPDL-compliant WfMS to another XPDL-compliant WfMS. On the other hand, the porting of the enriched process was expected to require more efforts, also due to the additional product-specific modules (macros, sub-processes) that are required. The following considerations do not represent a thorough scientific investigation, but rather represent a straight-forward experience report that highlights the problems and difficulties that we have encountered during our first test phase.

5.1 Implementation of Basic Sub-processes

One could expect that sub-processes (like *Get* and *Wait* in the considered example) are defined once for all as XPDL library. Unfortunately, as their internal execution logic typically requires a tight integration with the WfMS, i.e. they are WfMS-dependent, it is not possible to provide a universal library of exception handling sub-processes. Therefore, for each of the systems considered, we implemented a minimum set of sub-processes, in order to support a few tests and, in particular, the example described in this chapter. We were able to provide a small library of exception handling sub-processes with consistent interfaces across the libraries for each of the systems.

5.2 Execution Tests

As a first proof of validity of the proposed approach, we only used Enhydra Shark. We loaded the plain process model into Enhydra Shark and successfully run it. Next we specified the exception of Section 3 in a text file, compiled it into the enriched process model of Figure 3, and successfully run it again, leveraging the Shark-specific library of sub-processes. To our satisfaction, executing both versions of the process did not require any noteworthy interventions in the respective process definitions.

The next tests dealt with porting the plain process model from Enhydra Shark to the other WfMSs. We successfully imported the process model into WfMOpen and back. When we tried to import the respective process model into OBE and Bonita, we experienced some difficulties with both the WfMSs in reading the XPDL file designed with Enhydra JAWE. Thus, we had to adjust the XPDL file and to slightly redesign the plain process in both OBE and Bonita: main changes concerned the translation between basic data types (enumerative, string etc.), date formats (month/day/year, day/month/year), roles of agents. Subsequently, we also experienced difficulties when importing the plain process into Ascentn Agile Point, and we redesigned the process for Ascentn Agile Point: these importing difficulties relate to mismatching tags in the file format. To complete the test of porting the plain process model across the chosen WfMSs, we tried to port each product-specific process model to all the other WfMSs, but again in some cases readjusting and partial redesigning were still needed.

At this point, we had four XPDL files (Enhydra Shark and WfMOpen shared the same file), describing the same process model of Figure 3 but in four different XPDL implementations. According to the mapping methodology described in Section 4 and starting from the four different definitions of the plain process model, we were however able to obtain four enriched process definitions that could be executed on the five systems. However, in this case, we had to adjust the output of the compiler according to the specific XPDL dialect, just as we had to adjust the plain process definition in the first place. Nonetheless, the actual mapping of the exception definitions from Chimera-Exception to the single XPDL dialects of the chosen products works, and the resulting enriched processes execute correctly.

Due to the described difficulties, we are now considering to provide the rule compiler with suitable drivers (i.e., language customizers) for each of the encountered XPDL dialects.

6 DISCUSSION AND OUTLOOK

In this chapter we described our experience with the automatic enrichment of existing process definitions with inline exception handling constructs. Exceptions are specified as triggers in Chimera-Exception, an event-condition-action language developed in the context of the WIDE project [CCPP 1999]; process definitions are formalized in XPDL. A suitable compiler enables the automated translation of exception definitions from Chimera-Exception into XPDL, and WfMSs are equipped with a common library of supporting sub-processes, which provide for the necessary execution support for enriched process definitions and enable the actual portability of the proposed approach.

The results achieved so far with this cross-product exception handling approach can be summarized as follows:

- The mapping technique is robust when moving from an XPDL process definition to its enriched version;
- It is possible to provide product-specific implementations of the basic sub-processes that are at the basis of the execution of enriched processes (at least for the five WfMSs considered in this chapter);
- Enriched processes execute correctly and still have a good performance in terms of usage of system resources and execution (till now, this is only a subjective evaluation).

As the previous section has shown, we could however not achieve the initially expected level of portability among different XPDL-compliant WfMSs. While XPDL, on the one hand, was the enabling factor that led us to conceive the described approach, on the other hand, it is also its main limiting factor. Indeed, our "naive" portability tests (just save/export and load/import tests) for both the plain and the enriched version of a process definition revealed the existence of different dialects of XPDL in the tested WfMSs, which prevent even generic process definitions from really being portable among the systems.

In order for XPDL to succeed on the market of WfMSs, it seems thus of utmost importance that vendors fully comply with the language specification proposed by the Workflow Management Coalition, and that they avoid as much as possible the use of proprietary XPDL extensions. It is not necessary that products use XPDL as native file format, but—although this might prevent the optimal use of a given system's features—we believe the provided import and export functions should concentrate on XPDL-compliant constructs, only. If a process designer wants to use XPDL, he/she will be aware of and accept the possible limitations, but he/she will also be sure that process definitions effectively are portable.

In this chapter, we informally described the difficulties we encountered in testing our exception handling approach. In our future work, instead, we shall try to better understand the nature of these difficulties so as to formalize them in a more detailed manner and to be able to propose concrete solutions. Also, we intend to systematically evaluate the execution performance of plain and enriched processes in terms of workload, robustness, and speed.

7 ACKNOWLEDGEMENTS

This work has been partially funded by the Department of Computer Science, University of Verona and by the Department of Electronics and Information, Politecnico di Milano.

8. REFERENCES

[CCPP 1999] Casati, F., Ceri, S., Paraboschi, S., & Pozzi, G. (1999). Specification and Implementation of Exceptions in Workflow Management Systems. ACM Transactions on Database Systems, 24(3), 405-451.

[CDP 2006] Combi, C., Daniel, F., & Pozzi, G. (2006). A Portable Approach to Exception Handling in Workflow Management Systems. In R. Meersman & Z. Tari (Eds.), OTM Conferences (1), LNCS 4275 (pp. 201-218). Montpellier, France: Springer Verlag.

[CP 2004] Combi, C., & Pozzi, G. (2004). Architectures for a Temporal Workflow Management System. In H. Haddad, A. Omicini, R. L. Wainwright, & L. M. Liebrock (Eds.), Proceedings of SAC'04 (pp. 659-666). New York: ACM Press.

[EL 1995] Eder, J., & Liebhart, W. (1995). The Workflow Activity Model WAMO. In Proceedings of CoopIS'95 (pp. 87-98).

[HA 2000] Hagen, C., & Alonso, G. (2000). Exception Handling in Workflow Management Systems, IEEE Transactions on Software Engineering, 26(10), 943-958.

[MNN 2005] Mendling, J., Nuemann, G., & Nuttgens, M. (2005), A Comparison of XML Interchange Formats for Business process Modelling, Workflow Handbook 2005, Edited by Layna Fischer, Future Strategies Inc., Lighthouse Point, Florida.

[Shapiro 2006] Shapiro, R. M. (2006) XPDL 2.0: Integrating Process Interchange and BPMN, Workflow Handbook 2006, Edited by Layna Fischer, Future Strategies Inc., Lighthouse Point, Florida.

The Road to XPDL 2.0 Case Study

Justin C Brunt, WfMC Steering Committee and TIBCO Software Inc., United Kingdom

BACKGROUND

The road to XPDL 2.0; this inspiring story charts its journey from a proprietary process definition language to an open standard. This is also, by necessity, a very personal perspective because my involvement in XPDL was due to the fact that I worked for the respective organizations that supported the emerging standard from its earliest days. Now as WfMC's Vice Chair of the Steering Committee representing TIBCO within WfMC, I can speak only from my own experience in working on XPDL, using TIBCO as the case study whose narrative echoes the course taken by most WfMC members and vendors in this industry. It's a fascinating story often researched by academics tracking the origins of an industry standard and is, in essence, WfMC's *own* XPDL story. While many chapters in our annual Handbook are about user implementation case studies of our standards, we seldom offer a peek at how they started and evolved.

This chapter thus documents TIBCO's journey to XPDL 2.0 and relates some of the challenges along the way and some of the eventual advantages associated with the move to XPDL 2.0.

INTRODUCTION

As a founder and long-term contributing member of the WfMC, TIBCO embraced the original XPDL 1.0 specification and implemented it in TIBCO iProcess™ Modeler, the company's Windows-based modeling tool.

TIBCO iProcess Suite, with its origins in Staffware's BPM and workflow products and consistent with other workflow and BPM products at the time, provided a proprietary solution to persisting and exchanging process definitions. However, with the advent of TIBCO's new Eclipse-based modeling tool TIBCO Business Studio™, with its support for BPMN 1.0, XPDL 2.0 was the natural choice for persisting and exchanging process definitions.

As with other established workflow and BPM products the origins of TIBCO iProcess™ Suite pre-date workflow or BPM standards. Indeed, iProcess Suite's ancestors can be traced back to the second half of the 1980s, well before the Workflow Management Coalition (WfMC) was founded in 1993.

Even in those early days it was evident to us that the ability to exchange process definitions was an important factor. Therefore, in the absence of an open standard, a proprietary solution was created.

In the more than 20 intervening years since the original Staffware workflow product was created, workflow, BPM, and related standards have progressed considerably. The WfMC's XML Process Definition Language (XPDL) has gained popularity with approximately 70 known implementations[1]. At the time of writing the

---

[1] A list of known XPDL implementers can be found at
http://www.wfmc.org/standards/xpdl.htm

WfMC is completing version 2.1 of the specification and is aiming to release it formally during the first half of 2008. Although originally intended as an execution language, some product authors have chosen WS-BPEL[2] (Business Process Execution Language) as a basis for exchanging business process definitions.

What follows is an overview of how process definition persistence and interoperability of the product line that has become TIBCO iProcess Suite has progressed hand-in-hand with the evolution of the WfMC's XPDL right up to the present day.

CHANGING REQUIREMENTS

In the early days of workflow there were fewer reasons to exchange process definitions than there are today. The main reasons included:

- Promoting workflows between environments such as between development and test and between test and production.
- Providing technical support with copies of process definitions to enable diagnosis of problems that had occurred.
- In local government-related installations there were cases of different local government authorities providing workflow definitions they had created for legislative compliance to other authorities to ease their adoption of the legislation in question. At the time I considered this a very entrepreneurial approach for organizations that are normally considered to be fairly staid.

Since these early times the reasons to exchange process definitions have expanded to include:

- Exchanging process definitions between specialized modeling tools and workflow design tools.
- Providing process definitions along with historical workflow and business data to analytics tools to allow the analysis of process and organizational efficiency as well as processing trends. This is an example of both the need for some organizations to use "best of breed" products as part of their overall solution as well as the growing number of product components that sometimes make up a particular vendor's BPM suite.
- Expanding on the example above, there are cases where ready-made or substantially complete processes are sold to end user organizations to accelerate their ability to automate commonly occurring processes typically in vertical markets.
- With the explosion in the number of workflow and BPM product — combined with end user reorganizations, changes in platform and supplier strategy, and takeovers and mergers — there is a growing need to be able to migrate processes from one BPM product to another. A similar situation exists in some organizations where there are multiple enterprise modeling tools used across departments (e.g. Casewise, ARIS, Proforma). In these cases there is a desire to preserve the existing investment in models that have been created. This drives a requirement for the exchange of process definitions even if it is uni-directional.

These reasons can be summarized in the process design ecosystem shown below.

---

[2] OASIS, Web Services Business Process Execution Language Version 2.0, April 2007, http://docs.oasis-open.org/wsbpel/2.0/OS/wsbpel-v2.0-OS.pdf

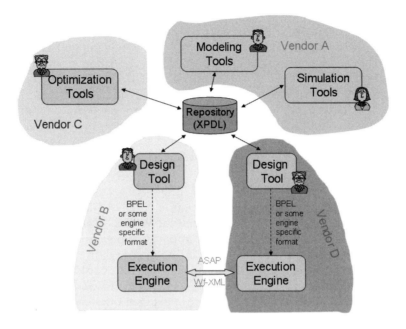

Figure 1—Process Design Ecosystem

As I mentioned earlier, prior to the existence of an open standard for process definition, the ancestors of iProcess Suite and virtually every other workflow or BPM
tool on the market adopted a proprietary solution to enable process definitions to
be exchanged. The process definition exchange format in iProcess, which pre-
dated the emergence of XML, was text-based and we economically named the
XFR Format (Transfer Format). The XFR Format was documented and provided
on request to customers and partners. Being text-based it was relatively easy to
interpret and a number of specialized conversions appeared, typically between
modeling tools and the XFR Format. I was always surprised that some conversions were achieved without our documentation. If only they'd asked; they would
have found it much easier with the documentation that we'd have readily provided! This marked the start of the requirement for true interoperability between
products produced by different vendors.

EVOLUTION HAS BEGUN

In 1998 the WfMC with a working group led by Robert Shapiro published a specification for process definition interchange[3]. You'll often find us WfMC old-timers
refer to this as Interface 1 as this corresponds to the first of the five interfaces defined in the WfMC's Workflow Reference Model[4] which was constructed by largely
David Hollingsworth and long time chair of WfMC, Jon Pyke. This format was
commonly known as Workflow Process Definition Language (WPDL). WPDL was a
text-based process definition language. Whilst the specification was still under

---

[3] Workflow Management Coalition Interface 1: Process Definition Interchange process Model,
WfMC TC-1016-P, 1998.

[4] Workflow Management Coalition, The Workflow Reference Model, WFMC-TC-1001, January
1995

development, we engaged a computer science graduate[5] studying for his master's degree to determine on behalf of Staffware the viability of converting processes defined in XFR Format into WPDL. His resulting master's thesis concluded that by and large there was a good match between the constructs offered by both formats. Indeed he even created a utility to prove that an export from XFR Format to WPDL was achievable. However, the timing of WPDL's publication coincided with the emergence of XML as an extensible language to be used for describing documents to be exchanged. XML offered clear advantages for describing process definitions along with the ability for implementers to provide their own extensions to describe process constructs that were unique to their own workflow or BPM products. With this in mind, the WfMC with a working group led by Mike Marin and Robert Shapiro started work on an XML-based process definition interchange language XPDL[6] . XPDL 1.0 was published in 2002[7].

With the advantages XML provided, adoption of XPDL 1.0 by workflow and BPM vendors was much greater than it had been for WPDL. Staffware was one of the early adopters and provided an XPDL 1.0 import/export capability for its process modeling tool. On its own, the existence of this facility didn't provide much of an advantage within iProcess Suite, since the XFR Format could still be used to exchange process definitions within the suite. However, it was the potential for exchanging process definitions with software packages outside iProcess Suite that we firmly believed would generate the most interest and benefit for our users. We weren't alone in our view; my WfMC Technical Committee co-members who were largely our competitors in their day jobs shared this view that the ability to exchange process definitions between tools would help the growth in acceptance of workflow and BPM.

XPDL provides all of the key constructs that are used by the majority of BPM products. This includes provisions for both human- and system-centric activities (integration, web services, etc.) including associated attributes such as participants. It also includes the ability to define sub-processes to promote both reuse and ease of understanding and maintenance. On the other hand, product authors who choose to use WS-BPEL as their method for persisting process definitions are faced with the challenges of representing other activity types, such as those listed above, given that BPEL is primarily concerned with the orchestration of web services. Of course these limitations are well known and the proposed WS-Human Task[8] and BPEL4People[9] specifications are expected to ultimately fill many of these gaps. The 1.0 versions of these specifications have been drawn up by a number of vendor organizations, but until the specifications are adopted by recognized standards bodies they cannot be regarded as open standards.

---

[5] Christian Kjaeldgaard, Master's Thesis in Mechatronics, Department of Machine Design, The Royal Institute of Technology, Stockholm

[6] Major contributors to XPDL 1.0 included Roberta Norin, Mike Gilger and Seth Osher

[7] Workflow Management Coalition: Workflow Process Definition Interface – XML Process Definition Language, version 1.0, WFMC-TC-1025, October 2002.

[8] Web Services Human Task (WS-HumanTask), Version 1.0, June 2007, Active Endpoints Inc., Adobe Systems Inc., BEA Systems Inc., International Business Machines Corporation, Oracle Inc., and SAP AG.
http://www.ibm.com/developerworks/webservices/library/specification/ws-bpel4people/

[9] WS-BPEL Extension for People (BPEL4People), Version 1.0, June 2007, Active Endpoints Inc., Adobe Systems Inc., BEA Systems Inc., International Business Machines Corporation, Oracle Inc., and SAP AG.
http://www.ibm.com/developerworks/webservices/library/specification/ws-bpel4people/

It is inevitable that there will be some process constructs that are unique to a particular product or weren't considered as core requirements for XPDL. For example, XPDL 1.0 doesn't provide support for how a process diagram should be represented graphically, but it does define the relationship between all the process entities. The WfMC envisaged such situations when designing XPDL, so there is provision in the specification for implementers to include their own extensions to describe such additional or different process constructs. After all, every product vendor needs a mechanism to represent their unique selling points. The fact that XPDL is XML-based means that XSLT can be used to transform one XPDL dialect into another (or even a non-XPDL but XML-based process definition language such as IDS Scheer's AML[10]). iProcess Suite's XPDL import/export functionality supports the ability for XSLT[11] (XSL[12] Transforms) files to be "plugged in" to pre- or post-process import and export respectively. Hence users of iProcess Suite now have the ability to exchange process definitions with modeling tools or other process centric software packages as appropriate.

A NEW MODELING NOTATION CHANGES THE PERSPECTIVE

While the WfMC was busy with XPDL 1.0, a new group, Business Process Management Initiative (BPMI.org) which is now merged with the Object Management Group (OMG) had emerged and was also concerned with BPM related standards. One of their initiatives was to develop a common graphical modeling notation to describe business processes: Business Process Modeling Notation (BPMN)[13]. Although BPMN specifies graphical details of how a process definition should be drawn, along with associated attributes, it does not specify a mechanism for storing a process diagram so it could be retrieved for further editing or exchanged with other tools. In order to provide a standardized mechanism to persist a diagram drawn using BPMN, again with the working group led by Robert Shapiro and Mike Marin the WfMC extended XPDL to provide support for BPMN, resulting in XPDL 2.0[14].

BPMN has been adopted by more than 40 products with the number of adopters continuing to grow. As such it has become a widely recognized notation for describing business processes. TIBCO, with its new Eclipse-based process modeling tool TIBCO Business Studio, is one of these adopters.

---

[10] ARIS Platform, White Paper – April 2006, Overview of interfaces to ARIS 6.1x/6.2x/7.0x

[11] XSLT, XSL Transformations Version 1.0, W3C November 1999, http://www.w3.org/TR/xslt

[12] XSL, Extensible Stylesheet Language Family, http://www.w3.org/Style/XSL/

[13] Business Process Management Initiative (BPMI), Business Process Modeling Notation (BPMN), Version 1.0, May 2004. The OMG subsequently released a formally adopted version of this specification: Business Process Modeling Notation (BPMN) Specification, Final Adopted Specification, dtc/06-02-01, February 2006.

[14] Workflow Management Coalition Workflow Standard, Process Definition Interface – XML Process Definition Language, WFMC-TC-1025, Version 2.0, October 2005. Contributors included Tim Stephenson, Wojciech Zurek, Sasa Bojanic, Gangadhar Gouri, Keith Swenson and Justin Brunt.

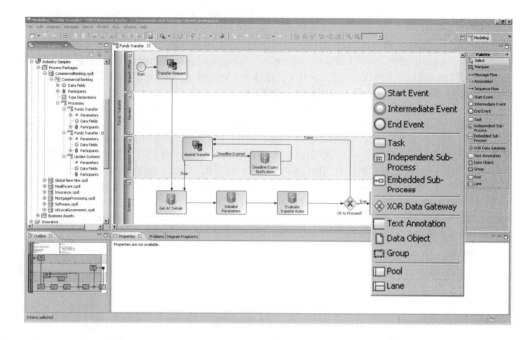

Figure 2—Example: TIBCO Business Studio

Since TIBCO, in common with other implementers, adopted BPMN before XPDL 2.0 was available a choice had to be made about how to persist the process models described with BPMN. Because TIBCO was already a supporter of XPDL, the choice was made to map the BPMN to XPDL 1.0 with appropriate extensions to support the graphical notation. A similar mapping had already been achieved with TIBCO's existing modeling tool; therefore this exercise was reasonably straightforward. I share the sentiments that are outlined in the introductory sections of the BPMN specification that the advantage to users, is that they can capture business processes using a notation that was not proprietary and can be readily communicated among the stakeholders (e.g. process owner, business analyst, process implementer). Because the diagrams were persisted in the same dialect (same extensions) of XPDL 1.0, they could be readily imported by TIBCO's existing process design tool.

Once XPDL 2.0 was available, we were happy that Business Studio was able immediately to adopt it as its primary format for persisting process models defined with BPMN. We liked that a key feature of XPDL 2.0 is that it provides standardized support for persisting BPMN diagrams. BPEL does not provide this capability, so other mechanisms need to be employed if BPEL-based process definitions are to preserve the layout information of BPMN diagrams. Not only does XPDL 2.0 provide the support for BPMN diagrams but also incorporates solutions to feedback from implementers about additional constructs they had independently implemented.

What I find rewarding is that because so many people had implemented these constructs as extensions, there was sufficient evidence to indicate that they should be supported as part of the core specification rather than leaving it to implementers to provide their own solutions such as how value is assigned to data elements (Workflow Relevant Data). By enabling process diagrams to be described using a common format across a number of different tools, the resultant XPDL

2.0 files contain less vendor-specific extensions thus increasing the opportunity for successfully exchanging business processes between different tools. Here at TIBCO we acknowledge that there will continue to be unique constructs within our own and other tools' implementations of XPDL, so we ensured Business Studio also includes the ability to tweak the process models it imports and exports using XSLT.

The thing that now makes everything worthwhile — from my perspective — is the ability to exchange process definitions with as little effort as possible between different tools that will provide users with the greatest benefits from XPDL. Without this ability, XPDL might as well be another proprietary process definition format. The WfMC and a number of interested modeling tool providers have conducted some preliminary interoperability tests using six simple process definitions defined in BPMN 1.0.

In this scenario, modeling tool providers are asked to define the six processes using their own modeling tool and then submit the resulting XPDL files so that other tool providers can see whether they can import XPDL generated by other tools. Although these process samples are simple they have helped to highlight differences in interpretations of the XPDL specification and errors in implementations. Any ambiguities that have been highlighted have been fed back to form input to the XPDL 2.1 specification and implementers have been able to correct problems in their implementations.

There has been reasonable success with this exercise as process definitions have been successfully exchanged between a number of modeling tools. Sometimes one direction has been more successful than another, but progress has been made.

The next stage is to define more complex processes that are more representative of real life business processes. These will use a higher proportion of the BPMN vocabulary and will thus use more of the constructs in XPDL.

We have seen that there is interest in achieving conformance from tool providers, end users as well as the analyst community. In particular, Bruce Silver has provided considerable input to the WfMC XPDL team during the creation of XPDL 2.1 in an effort to get closer to achieving the conformance goal. It is hoped that partnerships like this that are enhancing the efforts of the BPM standards producers will continue.

END OF THE ROAD?

As the field of BPM progresses so do the BPM standards. Implementers of XPDL 2.0 have provided feedback based on their experiences in implementing the standard. The OMG has been busy producing BPMN 1.1, which consists largely of clarifications of version 1.0 but also includes a new variation on a process construct (Signal Event) and some other changes that need to be reflected in XPDL. The WfMC has updated XPDL to incorporate implementer feedback and the relevant parts of BPMN 1.1[15]. The result of these endeavors will be XPDL 2.1, which should be published in the first half of 2008.

Of course, new versions of tools like Business Studio will be released to reflect the changes in both BPMN 1.1 and XPDL 2.1. By actively keeping up with develop-

---

[15] Business Process Modeling Notation, Specification, dtc/07-06-03 BPMN FTF 2 Convenience Document, June 2007, http://www.omg.org/docs/dtc/07-06-03.pdf. This document is a pre-release version of the BPMN 1.1 specification that is publicly available.

ments in XPDL and BPMN, vendors like TIBCO are ensuring that their tools are as up to date as possible and are in line with other tools such that users of multiple tools can use the same visual process vocabulary across different tools and have the greatest chance of successfully exchanging business processes between them.

At present, only XPDL 2.x provides a standardized way to persist a process diagram defined using BPMN. However, over time, alternatives solutions will likely appear, notably in the form of the OMG's BPDM[16] and BPMN 2.0[17]. BPMN 2.0 is also likely to introduce further modeling constructs that will then need to be supported by XPDL so this specification will continue to evolve to keep up with both the modeling notation and other advances in BPM.

Being instrumental in growing a major industry standard like XPDL gives me great personal satisfaction, knowing that we're achieving great things here at WfMC. More importantly TIBCO benefits as a result.

As BPM progresses, I'm certain that the associated standards will evolve providing enhanced interoperability capabilities and benefits for organizations choosing to implement BPM projects.

---

[16] Business Process Definition Metamodel (BPDM), Object Management Group. This specification is not yet released but a beta version is available at http://www.omg.org/technology/documents/br_pm_spec_catalog.htm.

[17] Business Process Modeling and Notation (BPMN) 2.0, Request for Proposal, OMG Document/BMI2007-06-05, http://www.omg.org/docs/bmi/07-06-05.pdf. One of the aims of BPMN 2.0 is to merge BPDM and BPMN to give a single specification for the definition of process models and how they can be persisted and interchanged.

Section 2

Standards and Technology

Integration of Workforce Management with a Business Process Management Suite

Robert M. Shapiro, Global 360, USA

ABSTRACT

BPM Systems have promised the capability of managing business process improvement for the enterprise. Yet they have failed to offer an integrated solution to resource management, despite the fact that this is critical to the profitability of many businesses. We describe below a typical use case for such integration.

A large bank has a Wholesale Lock Box division. The overall staff utilization for this division seems low in comparison with benchmark studies of similar banks.

The work load by position (role) and time period (e.g. every fifteen minutes) is exported from the BPM audit trail/analytics to the workforce management scheduler (WFM scheduler). The scheduler, using the staff database which contains skill set, availability preferences and minimum/maximum hours per day and week, generates an optimum staff schedule.

This schedule may shift the work load and have negative effect on critical KPIs[1]. The schedule is imported to the BPM simulator. A new set of statistics for staff utilization is generated (along with other KPIs such as end-to-end cycle time and cost.)

The process is repeated, by exporting the new work load information to the WFM scheduler, generating a new schedule which is then fed back to the simulator. The process stops when staff utilization cannot be improved further.

We describe the details of this integration and the potential ROI[2] for a real-world back-office banking application[3].

INTRODUCTION

In this paper we describe the integration of two technologies:
- A Workforce Management System with a scheduler.
- A BPM suite with integrated analytics, process modeler and simulator.

In the sequel we describe details of the scheduler and the inter-related inputs and outputs of both the scheduler and the simulator.

The approach described can be used both in situations where the business process being studied has been implemented using a BPM engine (enactment or workflow) as well as systems where the sequence of steps is controlled entirely by human operators. In the former case, the starting data for the scheduler is obtained from the BPM suite analytics. Otherwise the data is obtained by separate analysis of historical data or projections (based on statistics or simulation or both).

---

[1] Key Performance Indicator

[2] Return On Investment.

[3] Case study of Wholesale Lock Box Process provided by Meta Software Corporation.

A detailed discussion of BPM analytics is outside the scope of this paper. Here we include an architectural overview.

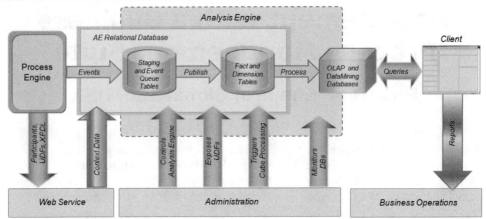

We assume the Simulator makes use of the same analytics.

OVERVIEW OF SCHEDULER

A Workforce Management Scheduler assigns detailed schedules to the staff of an organization. It uses two input sets:

- Work load drivers that define how much work has to be done in each time period and what skills are required to perform the work.
- Resource characteristics that define staffing availability, preferred work hours, work rules, salaries and so forth.

The scheduling algorithm creates a schedule for each resource, trying to precisely match the work load. The result is generally not perfect. In some time periods there is more staff than is needed; in other time periods there is less. The algorithm has to contend with holiday and vacation schedules, minimum and maximum shift lengths, hours per week, skill sets and so forth.

Understaffing in a time period implies that some work will not be completed. Schedulers usually do not propagate the incomplete work. It is treated like a dropped call in a Call Center. Overstaffing represents excess resource availability in a time period and offers the opportunity for cost savings by better scheduling. A scheduling program usually provides some measure of the 'fit' of a schedule based on the understaffing and overstaffing.

WORKFORCE MANAGEMENT SCHEDULER

Inputs

Staff requirements by role and time period	Workload demand. Historical Data or Projections (based on simulation).
Roles	For each person, what positions (roles) they can fill.
Availability	Preferred work hours, possible work hours.
Proficiency	Performance measure for each role.
Minimum and maximum work hours	Per day, week and month.
Break rules and Holiday schedules.	

Input Example: Availability of an individual staff person.

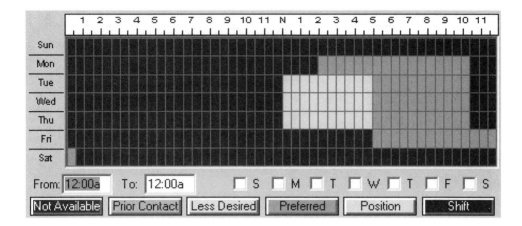

Input Example: Basic Employee Data, Roles, Work Hour requirements: In the example the last name reflects position/role.

KEITH Proof_BITSSORT_

(Employee)

Basic Information

Last Name	Proof_BITSSORT_
First Name	KEITH
SS Number	121
Hire Date	01-01-2000
Seniority Date	01-01-2000
Break Set	FullTime Break Rule *(BRFULL)*
Department	BITS *(BITS)*
Costing Set	COST 1 (COST1)
Employee Class	Employee Class 1 (EMP CLASS1)
Eligible for Overtime	Yes

Positions

1. BITS Sorter *(STAFF BITSSORTE)* in BITS
2. PMO Clerk *(STAFF PROOFPMO)* in PMO
3. 1st Floor Receiving *(PROOFRECE1ST)* in Receiving
4. 2nd Floor Receiving *(PROOFRECE2ND)* in Receiving

Scheduler Information

Status	parttime (0)
Minimum Span	dayminpart (4.00)
Maximum Span	daymaxfull (10.00)
Minimum Weekly Hours	0.00
Hours Desired	32.00
Maximum Weekly Hours	36.48

Heuristic Scheduler   *Example Using Neural Net Technology*

Match Resource Supply to Workload Demand:

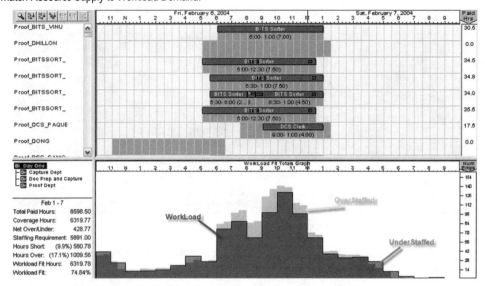

Generate Schedule:

Adams, DawnJacinta				1/9/2006 to 1/15/2006 Paid Hours: 40.00
Monday	1/9/2006	10:00 pm - 6:00 am	Check Keying	
			Break: 11:45 pm - 12:00 am (15 min.) *Lunch: 2:00 am - 2:30 am (30 min.)* *Break: 4:00 am - 4:15 am (15 min.)*	
Tuesday	1/10/2006	10:00 pm - 6:00 am	Supplemental Keying Level 1	
			Break: 12:00 am - 12:15 am (15 min.) *Lunch: 2:00 am - 2:30 am (30 min.)* *Break: 4:00 am - 4:15 am (15 min.)*	
Wednesday	1/11/2006	10:00 pm - 6:30 am	Supplemental Keying	
			Break: 12:00 am - 12:15 am (15 min.) *Lunch: 2:00 am - 2:30 am (30 min.)* *Break: 4:00 am - 4:15 am (15 min.)*	
Thursday	1/12/2006	10:00 pm - 2:00 am	Supplemental Keying Level 2	
			Break: 12:00 am - 12:15 am (15 min.)	
	1/12/2006	2:00 am - 6:30 am	Check Keying	
			Lunch: 2:00 am - 2:30 am (30 min.) *Break: 4:00 am - 4:15 am (15 min.)*	
Sunday	1/15/2006	9:00 pm - 11:30 pm	Supplemental Keying	
	1/15/2006	11:30 pm - 1:30 am	Check Keying	
			Break: 11:30 pm - 11:45 pm (15 min.)	
	1/15/2006	1:30 am - 6:30 am	Supplemental Keying	
			Lunch: 1:30 am - 2:00 am (30 min.) *Break: 3:00 am - 3:15 am (15 min.)*	

OVERVIEW OF SIMULATION TECHNOLOGY

The typical simulator for making predictions in a BPMS environment is a discrete event simulator. Preparation of a simulation run is commonly referred to as a scenario. The scenario consists of:

- The set of processes to be simulated. The process definitions may be represented in a format that supports process interchange, such as XPDL[4]. Process definitions may be created by a diagram editor that is part of the BPM system, or by an independent tool such as a BPMN[5] editor. Process definitions provide information about the activities performed, the routes taken, the rules impacting which routes and activities to perform, and the

---

[4] XML Process Definition Language, developed by WfMC.

[5] Business Process Modeling Notation, developed by BPMI and OMG.

resources (human and automated) used to perform the activities. A scenario can include one or many processes for a simulation run.

- Incoming Work (Arrivals). Each scenario must involve work to be processed. The description includes information about when the work arrives, as well as all appropriate attributes of the work (e.g. region, amount, size) that may have an impact on processing.
- Resources, Roles and Shifts: As work is routed to activities in a process, resources are required to perform the activity. Resources may be human resources; they may be pieces of equipment; or they might simply be application systems. Roles are often used to describe the function performed and the skill required. Specific resources are then described as performing defined roles. The availability of Resources and Roles can also be controlled by using Shift information.
- Activity Details: In order for the simulator to reflect the real-world processing of a business process, additional information is often appended to the scenario. How long an activity takes to process is not defined in a Process Definition, but is included in the scenario information (historical data collected by the analytics may be the source of this information). This and many other details can be expressed as a single integer or a complex expression involving the attributes of the work and/or the use of distribution functions for randomness. Other information appended for simulation might include routing information which tells the simulator under what conditions certain routes are taken. Routing information can come from rules that exist in the process definition, but it is often amended with percentages that, based on historical activity, reflect the likelihood of a certain outcome or path.

A simulation run generates new data for the analytics engine. This can then be viewed or extracted for various purposes.

WORKLOAD ANALYSIS BY SIMULATION OF BUSINESS PROCESS

Inputs:

Work Item Arrival Data	
Actual	Arrival rates for work items, based on historical data. Includes key attribute values.
Forecast	Projected arrival rates, including key attribute values.
Human Resource Data	
Roles	Defines the process activities (Tasks) the person can perform.
Availability	Scheduled work hours. Includes breaks, holiday and vacation information.
Proficiency	Skill rating for each job position.
Salary	Hourly Rate.
Equipment Data	Equipment could be, for instance, Check Sorter in Check Clearing operation.
	Type
	Role
	Quantity

	Throughput
Parameter Data (activity details)	
Activity Durations	How long each activity (Task) takes. May be characterized by a distribution.
Decision point distributions (%)	For each decision in that process, the probability of each outcome.

Business Process To Be Simulated   Illustration using BPMN (only part of Business Process Diagram)

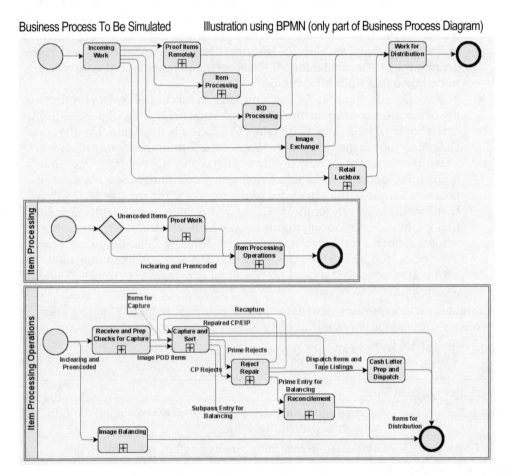

This Business Process diagram is only a small part of the Process. The top level shows Retail Lock Box as one of the sub-processes, without providing and further detail. The actual wholesale lock box process is proprietary information.

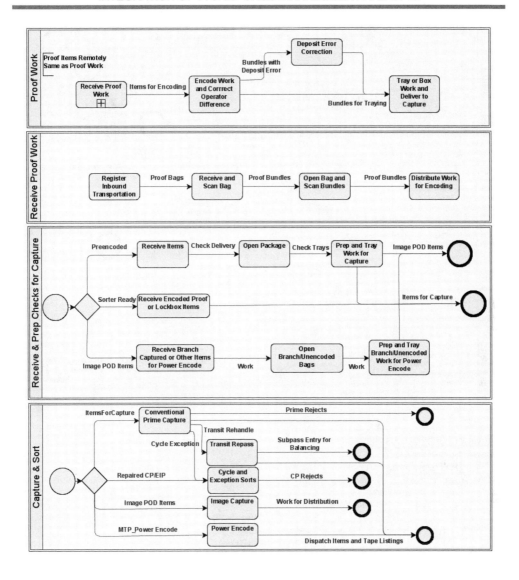

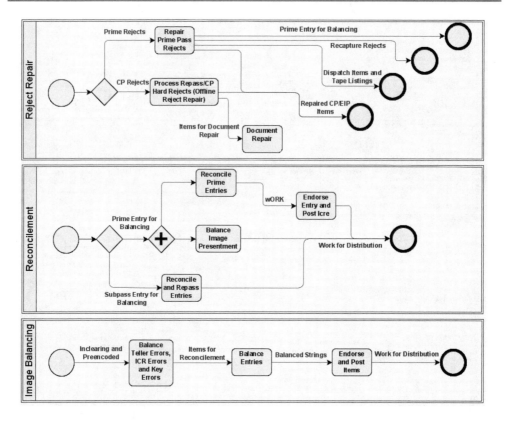

Overview of Sub-Process Hierarchy

Process Enterprise Payments

- Proof Items Remotely
- Item Processing
  - o Proof Work
    - Receive Proof Work
      - Register Inbound Transportation
      - Receive and Scan Bag
      - Open Bag and Scan Bundles
      - Distribute Work for Encoding
    - Encode Work and Correct Operator Difference
    - Deposit Error Correction
    - Tray or Box Work and Deliver to Capture
  - o Item Processing Operations
    - Receive and Prep Checks for Capture
      - Receive Items
      - Open Package
      - Prep and Tray Work for Capture
      - Receive Encoded Proof or Lockbox Items
      - Receive Branch Captured or Other Items for Power Decode
      - Open Branch/Unencoded Bags
      - Prep and Tray Branch/Unencoded Work for Power Encode
    - Capture and Sort
      - Conventional Prime Capture
      - Transit Repass
      - Cycle and Exception Sorts
      - Image Capture
      - Power Encode
    - Reject Repair
      - Repair Prime Pass Rejects
      - Process Repass/CP Hard Rejects

- Document Repair
- Reconcilement
  - Reconcile Prime Entries
  - Balance Image Presentment
  - Reconcile and Repass Entries
  - Endorse Entry and Post ICRE
- Cash Letter Prep and Dispatch
- Image Balancing
  - Balance Teller Errors, ICR errors and Key Errors
  - Balance Entries
  - Endorse and Post Items
- IRD Processing
- Image Exchange
- Retail Lockbox

Simulation Outputs (generated by the analytics and using OLAP[6])

Staff requirements by role and time period	For each time period, how many people are required for each role.
Staff utilization by period	
Equipment utilization by period	
Cycle time deadline and holdover reports	Percent satisfying SLA[7] for end-to-end cycle time.
Unprocessed volume by period	
Work in Progress Report by period	
Work arrival profile report	Arrival volume by period
Activity summary report	

Output Example: To-Be Staff Utilization:

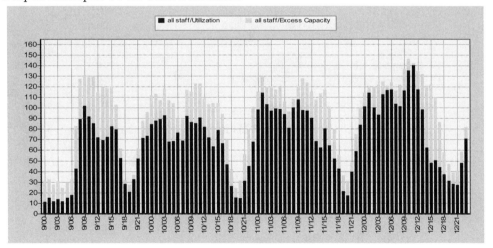

---

[6] OnLine Analytical Processing

[7] Service Level Agreement

Output Example: To-Be Work In Progress:

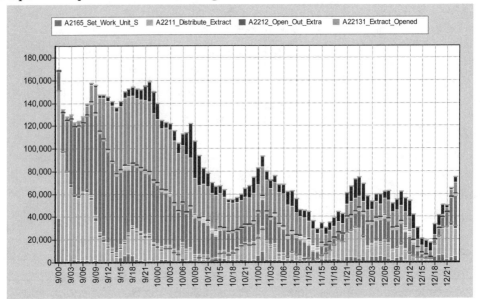

POSSIBLE ROI: USING SIMULATION/WFM SCHEDULER ON WHOLESALE LOCK BOX PROCESS

Current Productivity

- Productivity is reflected as total items per total paid hours. FTE = Full Time Equivalent.
- Wholesale Lock Box Operation for one region of major bank:

Volume Base	2,971,163
Production FTE	397.7
Management and Production Support FTE	33.2
Total Staff	430.9
WLB Items per Paid Hour	**41.0**
WLB Items per Paid Hour (excl. mgmt.)	**44.5**
Current Labor Utilization Rate	70%

- The current productivity of 41 WLB items per hour is equivalent to median benchmark productivity.
- Based on the current productivity profile the simulation model computed a labor utilization rate of 70% including paid time off (PTO).

Simulation Model FTE Requirements

- Model FTE compared to current FTE:

Model Production FTE Requirements	276.7
PTO Factor - 20%	55.3
Note: We are aware that the current PTO is 10% but have used the more conservative 20% number	
Total Model FTE	**332.0**
Current Production FTE	**397.7**
Total Scheduling Opportunity	**65.7**

Current Production FTE	397.7
1st Wave FTE Reduction Target	32.9
Revised Production FTE	364.8
Management and Production Support FTE	33.2
Total Staff	398.0
WLB Items per Paid Hour	**44.4**
WLB Items per Paid Hour (excl. mgmt.)	**48.5**
Projected Labor Utilization Rate	76%
Current Production FTE	397.7
1st Wave FTE Reduction Target	32.9
2nd Wave FTE Reduction Target	32.9
Projected Production FTE	332.0
Management and Production Support FTE	33.2
Total Staff	365.2
WLB Items per Paid Hour	**48.4**
WLB Items per Paid Hour (excl. mgmt.)	**53.3**
Projected Labor Utilization Rate	83%

- The model FTE target is a long-term end state goal.
- Based on experience working with similar customers, it is more realistic to implement the scheduling opportunity in two waves.

First Wave Opportunity
- The first wave productivity target is slightly better than the benchmarking 66th percentile.

Second Wave Opportunity
- The longer term goal should be the end-state Model FTE target.
- The second wave productivity target is slightly less than the benchmarking 85th percentile.

Review of Opportunity
- Paid hour benefit:

Annualized Paid Hour Benefit	Annual Fully Loaded Salary	Saving Opportunity
32.9 FTE	$ 29,276	$ 963,186

- Overtime reduction benefit

Annualized OT Benefit	Annual Salary	Total Cost	Saving Opportunity
38.7 FTE @ Straight Time	$ 22,872	$ 885,146	
38.7 FTE @ Time and a Half	$ 34,308	$ 1,327,720	$ 442,573

Total combined benefit – $1,405,759

SUMMARY

We have described the integration of two technologies: Workforce Management Scheduling and Business Process Management. The integration involves back-and-forth feeds of data between the two.

One typical use pattern would be as follows:

- The BPM system has been in operation for a while. The analytics component has collected statistics about work arrival patterns, resource utilization, work-in-progress and activity loads.
- The appropriate data, staff requirements by role and time period (Workload demand), is extracted from the analytics and fed to the scheduler. The scheduler has other inputs that characterize the staff resources.
- These include for each person their roles, availability, proficiency, minimum and maximum work hours. Also included are 'break rules' and holiday schedules.
- The scheduler generates a best-fit schedule that matches the Workload demand to the staff, minimizing the understaffing/overstaffing according to adjustable criteria. The algorithm may be based on neural nets or some other constraint-based optimization technique.
- The new resource schedule is passed back to the simulation component of the BPM system. A scenario is created based on the set of business processes being studied, work arrivals (derived from the analytics), the new resource schedule and activity details (also determined from the analytics).
- The simulation run generates a new set of data which includes an updated version of Workload demand, along with other information about the effect of the new staff assignment. This data includes:
  - Staff utilization
  - Equipment utilization
  - Cycle time SLA report
  - Unprocessed volume
  - Activity summary report
- The scheduling optimization loops back to step 4 until no further improvement is possible.

We have described in some detail the characteristics of the inputs and outputs of the two systems. We have also briefly overviewed the two technologies.

Finally, we have presented an example of applying this approach to a back office banking process: wholesale lockbox operation. The example, based on a case study, analyses the potential ROI for changing the staffing of an existing operation.

This approach appears to be most suited to situations where the business process being executed is well structured (rather than ad hoc), the work item arrivals can be characterized as repeatable patterns and the total resource pool to be scheduled is large. Under these circumstances it is not unusual to achieve a 10 to 20 percent reduction in staff costs.

Department of Defense Suspense Tracking

Charles Joesten, ICOR Partners LLC, USA

ABSTRACT

Nearly every Department of Defense (DoD) agency, department, command, and activity, regardless of service provided or operational mission, manages work commitments for routine and ad hoc tasks known as "taskers." Taskers are directives or action items required by some higher authority that involve numerous process steps and activities that result in a response. The due date of a tasker is the "suspense" and tracking the tasker steps and resulting response throughout the entire lifecycle requires extraordinary effort. In the DoD organizational structure and protocol, taskers are directed and delegated to subordinates down the chain of command until at some point, a subject matter expert or support resource performs the required tasks and submits a response back up the chain for approval or acceptance. Taskers initiate or influence the majority of work and DoD workforces are expected to complete the tasks regardless of budget or staffing requirements. The volume of work continues to increase as resource levels continue to shrink, so manual-intensive and paper-based processes put tremendous constraints on the effectiveness, accuracy, and timeliness of actions and responses. Leveraging workflow improvements and technology to streamline and provide visibility to the tasker management and suspense tracking process is critical to improve the readiness, responsiveness and productivity of DoD organizations.

INTRODUCTION

This case analyzes the tasker management and suspense tracking process of the Commander in Chief, U.S. Pacific Fleet (CINCPACFLT or CPF) during an initiative to implement solutions to improve headquarters readiness and improve the allocation of constrained resources. CPF intended to address several business practice issues, explore improvement options, and implement technical solutions to improve headquarters operational effectiveness, streamline administrative functions, and lower costs of doing business. The case describes tasker and suspense process issues found at CPF, as well as integrated solutions developed and implemented to manage command taskers, route work products for approval, and track suspenses throughout the tasker lifecycle. Finally, lessons learned from CPF translate to other agencies and potential solutions for managing taskers and suspenses amidst the emergence of enterprise integration and transformation.

COMMANDER IN CHIEF, U.S. PACIFIC FLEET

As the largest fleet in the U.S. Navy, the Pacific Fleet's area of responsibility covers the Pacific, Indian, and Arctic Oceans and in the late 1990s had approximately 190 ships, 1,400 aircraft, and 200,000 Sailors, Marines, and Civilians.[1] Admiral

---

[1] Admiral Archie Clemins' statement to the U.S. House of Representatives Armed Services Committee, Readiness Subcommittee, April 21, 1999.

Archie Clemins, the Commander in Chief, U.S. Pacific Fleet (CINCPACFLT) from November 7, 1996 to October 8, 1999,[2] was the chief architect of the Navy's Information Technology for the 21st Century (IT-21) initiative. This initiative was a high-visibility investment in IT by the Navy to improve warfighter readiness and capability through enhancements in enterprise infrastructure, fleet information management, and resource effectiveness. The unique approach proposed by Admiral Clemins was to focus on the functional and tactical levels to align products and solutions to the architectural and strategic levels. Essentially, solutions came from the bottom up where implementations came from the top down. To ensure funding at the lower echelons, CPF helped the Navy creatively pull from a variety of existing programs to fund the IT-21 behemoth.

While substantial investments began to enhance both at sea and ashore IT infrastructure, the CPF headquarters staff at the Makalapa Compound in Pearl Harbor, HI, faced challenges with initial ashore tactical improvement projects. The headquarters staff of approximately 750 military and civilians was responsible for managing approximately 17 percent of the entire Pacific Fleet and 10,000 workstations.[3] They were the first to implement the Admiral's plan in an effort that began in January 1998, the results of which provide the basis for this analysis.

TASKER PROCESS INITIATIVE

To emphasize the importance of tactical improvements to support the strategic mission, CPF assembled a small contract team to support the Admiral's vision through process analysis and solution recommendations within each of the headquarters' directorates. CPF directed the contract team and directorates to examine business operations, look for trends and inefficiencies across directorates, prioritize areas for potential improvement, and develop solutions using existing tools to address the highest priority issues.

Perhaps the most proliferate of the process areas identified was Workflow Management because it was performed by everyone on the staff, regardless of rank, directorate, or function. At CPF, the entire lifecycle of a tasker and the tracking of its suspense included:

- originating—receiving assignments and initiating taskers,
- routing—routing taskers, work products, and responses,
- delegating—delegating taskers to subordinates,
- responding—generating a response and supporting documents,
- coordinating—reviewing and approving responses,
- tracking—tracking suspense and response status, and
- archiving—saving a permanent record of completed deliverables.

The following sections describe specific processes and practices found at CPF in the late 1990s. Generally, the tasker lifecycle was manual and suspense tracking cumbersome, putting additional pressure on already-constrained resources.

TASKER MANAGEMENT AND SUSPENSE TRACKING

The workflow of a tasker and its related suspense tracking are familiar processes across DoD organizations. Taskers and suspenses themselves are unique and ad hoc, where identical requests, lifecycle durations, and responses are rare. Varying levels of automation, technical facilitation, human intervention, policy, and proto-

---

[2] CPF website, www.cpf.navy.mil.

[3] "Navy's IT-21 plan steams ahead with global intranet," Government Computer News, December 15, 1997.

col also contribute to the uniqueness of every single tasker and suspense. The following descriptions and scenarios portray root causes of frustration and utilization of excessive CPF resources to field command taskers.

Anatomy of a Tasker

Several different directorates make up the organizational structure of the headquarters command at CPF, each managing a specific function that serves the fleet (operations, maintenance, manpower and personnel, etc.). Not surprisingly, directorates managed work in their respective stovepipes, where workflow, cycle time, deliverable quality, communications, and resource allocation were typically directorate-specific. A lack of standardization or strict adherence to command-wide procedures contributed to duplication of effort, miscommunication, and ineffective cross-directorate collaboration. Figure 1 shows the lifecycle of a generic tasker, but each step had multiple sub-process steps.

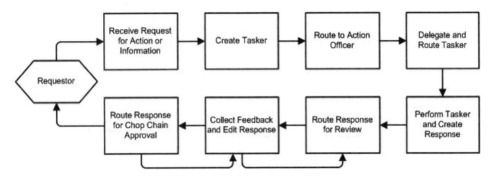

Figure 1. The tasker workflow process.

Cycle time discoveries within steps, directorate practices, and staff work-arounds to broken processes began to amplify the need for a command-wide solution to workflow management. The key participants in the CPF tasker and suspense process include the:

- **Requestor**—someone directing or requesting action or information that requires a response.
- **Front Office/Tasker Originator**—the front office staff supports the Admiral and directorate Flag Officers. The front office receives directives or requests to perform actions that result in a deliverable or response. It originates a tasker and assigns one or more Action Codes/Officers to take action, includes Supporting Codes/Officers, adds a serial number, and sets the "suspense." The front office archives the completed tasker and supporting response material upon coordination and approval.
- **Action Code/Officer**—a code refers to the designation of each directorate. A tasker is assigned to an Action Code, the Director, who then tasks one or more Divisions or Action Officers, who are responsible for tasker completion.
- **Supporting Code/Officer**—a directorate not directly responsible for completion of the tasker, but receives it for informational purposes or for informal input. Similar to a courtesy copy recipient of an email, a Supporting Officer working on a tasker outside of their reporting structure would require a copy to their ranking Supporting Code (their direct commander or boss).

- **Delegate**—a resource delegated a tasker from a ranking superior to take responsibility for action on it and its response package.
- **Reviewer**—someone providing an informal review of a deliverable or response before its submission through channels.
- **Approver**—a reviewer who provides an approval or disapproval of a deliverable or response, makes comments, and forwards the tasker on to the next reviewer in the "chop chain."

The key components of a tasker include:

- **Tasker Number**—a serial number generated and managed by the front office (for CPF taskers) or directorates (if subordinate command coordination requires separate tracking).
- **Originator Name/Organization**—information about the originator of the tasker like command, code number, and email address.
- **Origination Date**—date of the generation of the tasker.
- **Suspense Date**—the due date for a tasker response. The suspense includes activities and actions until the delivery of a response (hopefully before the suspense date).
- **Action Code/Officer Information**—command code and email address of the Action Code/Officer responsible for the tasker.
- **Supporting Code/Officer Information**—command codes and email addresses for any Supporting Codes/Officers on the tasker.
- **Priority**—basic prioritization of the tasker (high, medium, or low).
- **Response Scope and Format**—the level of detail and format of the tasker response: email, white paper, presentation, etc.
- **Response**—the answer, case, data, recommendation, assessment, or other information provided to respond to the tasker request. All reference materials, regardless of media, routed back to the requestor to support the tasker.
- **Comments**—input or clarification provided by participants in the generation, review, or approval of the tasker.
- **Classification**—clarification as to whether the tasker or response was Classified or Unclassified. At CPF, users tracked taskers on either Classified or Unclassified networks respectively, but the majority of taskers were Unclassified.

Work Inputs and Triggers

The primary inputs to work at CPF related to data calls or requests for information, initiated mostly by sources external to the command but also by internal sources. External triggers included higher DoD or Navy echelons in Washington, D.C., other DoD commands or agencies, other Navy commands or subordinates, political officials, or even the public. External triggers were typically directed to the CPF front office, which in turn sent taskers to the directorates. Methods of communication included official DoD messages, email, postal mail, verbal requests, or interpreted actions from inquiries during official meetings. Internal triggers included actions required by the flag officers or any other commander of the headquarters staff, whether or not it related to external taskers. The CPF Automated Message Handling System (AMHS) filtered Official DoD email upon arrival. The AMHS filtered email by user profile and automatically forwarded correspondence based on filtering criteria. However, outdated profiles and inaccurate criteria created duplication of effort, confusion, and delayed suspenses.

A typical scenario was for a director to find the email inbox full of several hundred new emails at the beginning of each day. As Figure 2 shows, numerous triggers send incoming work or data requests to the front office or directly to an Action Officer. Typically, official taskers come to the front office and informal taskers go to Action Officers directly. Given the number of directorates and functions within each of those directorates, the workflow permutations were exponential.

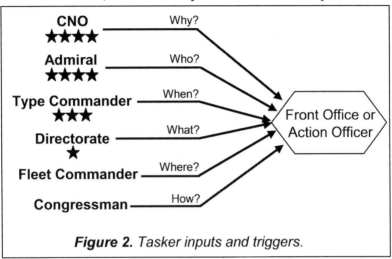

Figure 2. Tasker inputs and triggers.

The first few hours of each day required sifting through the voluminous emails to determine priority, responsibility, scope, deliverable format, suspense dates, and required coordination. The first few steps taken by a recipient fielding a data call were critical in the workflow process and were direct impacts to cycle time and response quality back to the requestor. Because of the volume of requests, backlog, delays, miscommunications, errors, and rework were routine.

Tasker Assignment, Delegation, and Routing
The front office was the central point of contact for all CPF taskers. The front office determined if the tasker was the responsibility of CPF, a directorate, a subordinate command, or a completely different command or agency and routed it there if necessary. Assuming the request came to CPF successfully, the front office added available information including priority, originator information, Action Codes, Supporting Codes, scope, and suspense dates. The front office would task the necessary directorates, who would task one or more divisions, who would task the appropriate Action Officers.

Frequently, multiple directorates' input was required to provide a comprehensive response, requiring coordination among directorates or Action Officers. Coordination across several directorates, with one Action Code consolidating several Action Officers' input, required even more effort given the manual processes and limited visibility into suspense progress. When the front office assigned cross-directorate taskers, the practice was known as "shotgun" tasking. Like a shotgun blast, a tasker was blasted to many different directorates at the same time making it difficult for the Action Code to know which Action Officers were working on what.

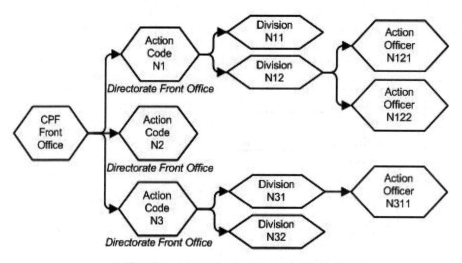

Figure 3. *"Shotgun" assignment of a tasker.*

Figure 3 depicts a shotgun tasker. The CPF front office in this scenario has tasked three separate directorates who in turn have delegated the tasker to subordinate divisions. Finally, the divisions assign the tasker to Action Officers. The N1 and N3 directors, as Action Codes, delegated the tasker to their respective direct division reports. Divisions N12 and N31 delegated the tasker to their respective Action Officers. Decisions made on scope and format interpretations by each Action Officer increased overall cycle time and workload, particularly if they did not collaborate with others working on the tasker. The shotgun approach caused increased volume, confusion, miscommunication, and duplication of effort. Action Officers send the tasker to multiple delegates, or even across directorates, and with few mechanisms or constraints to facilitate and monitor work performed, frustration ensued. Even in less extreme cases of "serial" routing, when taskers were assigned and delegated serially through a single directorate, problems still existed due to limited visibility into suspense status.

Tasker Action, Coordination, and Response Generation

Ultimately, some Action Officer in the delegation chain took responsibility for action on the tasker and performed the work necessary to prepare the response. The Action Officer personally, or with tasked staff members, helped gather the information, prepare the response, and assemble the response package. Sometimes the Action Officer routed the tasker to another colleague ("horizontally") for informational purposes or perspective on the response, but many times verbal or email collaboration sufficed.

Most actions and communications were manually intensive, with Action Officers forwarding taskers via email but work documents and information via paper format to a physical "inbox." Disruptions and bottlenecks arose when staff overwhelmed by their own duties or out of the office altogether brought the inbox handoffs to a grinding halt. Often work products made it to a contributor or two and would then find an electronic or physical inbox recipient out of the office. It was difficult for Action Officers or midstream delegates to track down the response packages for status on progress. Frequently participants up the delegation chain realized status only when a response package returned for review or approval. The completed responses usually consisted of printed material including the original tasker, response deliverable, and supporting data or other documentation. Action Officers assembled responses into a folder with an attached routing slip that listed the names of the people required to review or approve the response.

Tasker Response Package Review

Once a work product was generated in response to a tasker, it was routed for review and then ultimately for approval. As in the delegation of taskers and the routing of tasker information in the assignment stages of the process, the review and approval processes were also marred with manual steps, bottlenecks, and poor visibility into the status of the response.

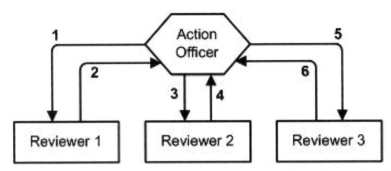

Figure 4. Serial review routing of a tasker response package.

Figure 4 shows one process used for routing work products for review before submitting them as finished products for approval and return to the original requestors. In a "serial" review, the Action Officer routed the response package to Reviewer 1 and awaited a response from that reviewer before proceeding (as steps 1-6 in Figure 4 indicate). The response from Reviewer 1 was to concur with the work product or action recommended, provide comments or edits to the response package, or reject the response package altogether (although rejection was more likely evident in a formal chop chain). Upon receiving the response, comments, or edits from Reviewer 1, the Action Officer could either make changes to the response package and re-route it to Reviewer 1, or collect responses from other reviewers before making collective changes to the response package. The latter would allow future reviewers to see what changes previous reviewers recommended. Again in Figure 4, after receiving responses from the first review, the Action Officer proceeded to route the response package to the second review by Reviewer 2. The same process steps of routing, waiting, receiving, and updating occurred for as many reviewers as the Action Officer assigned. The Action Officer could correct the work package with a new version and then reroute the new work package through the entire review process.

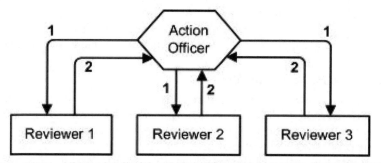

Figure 5. Parallel review routing of a tasker response package.

Another possible review process for an Action Officer was to send a tasker response package to multiple reviewers simultaneously. In this "parallel" review, shown in Figure 5, all reviewers received the response package at the same time, reviewed it, and provided concurrence, comments, or edits back to the Action Officer. The Action Officer in this process only waited as long as the longest reviewer response, making corrections upon receiving individual responses or after receiving all responses. In a parallel route, reviewers had no visibility into other reviewers' comments. When the response package had been edited to the satisfaction of the Action Officer, the package was routed into the approval process know as the "chop chain."

The "Chop Chain" and Approval

The formal routing of the final tasker response package was the "chop chain" because each person in the chain of command approved or provided their "chop" before the Action Officer submitted the final response package to the front office, who ultimately submitted it to the original requestor. In most routes, the chop chain followed the opposite direction of the original tasker delegation—the tasker came down through command channels and then the response went back up. The chop chain could be agonizing for the Action Officer because it potentially became a perpetual "do loop" where competing opinions or draftsmanship took work products or response packages through endless and repetitive iterations. Rank, classification, visibility, or sensitivity could all lead to more scrutiny on the finished response product.

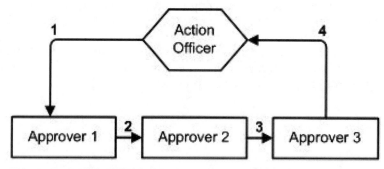

Figure 6. Successful approval of a tasker response package.

Similar to the tasker review route, the chop chain route primarily used a folder with the original tasker, response products, and related documents inside. A routing slip listed the names of the approvers in the chop chain and each signed and crossed off their names if they approved the response package before manually forwarding it to the next inbox. If the response package met the expectations of each approver, it routed through the chop chain and ultimately back to the Action Officer. Approvers sometimes added comments to the response, which the Action Officer incorporated before submitting the finalized package to the front office. Figure 6 shows a chop chain with a tasker response package approved successfully. Upon approval, the response package worked its way through the chop chain in a serial route, each additional approver likely more senior in the command structure.

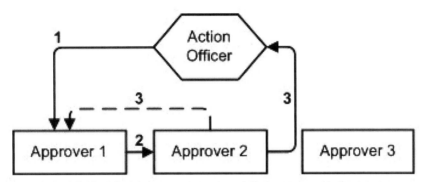

Figure 7. Disapproval of a tasker response package.

Like some review routes, the chop chain made the Action Officer's life difficult. If someone in the chop chain disapproved the response package, it routed back to the Action Officer for correction and notified the previous approvers. Reviewers in the chain could leave markups or comments on changes required. Once corrected, the Action Officer resubmitted the response package into the chop chain from the beginning. Figure 7 shows an unsuccessful chop chain route where Approver 2 disapproved the response package and routed it back to the Action Officer for correction. Notification was sent to Approver 1 (the dashed arrow), but Approver 3 had no participation or visibility to the chop chain without an approval from Approver 2.

Grammatical errors, content scope, or data omission warranted disapprovals, as did conflicting opinions or subjective review criteria. The Action Officer experienced significant delays in submitting a response without knowing how to assemble a package that could navigate the chop chain successfully.

At the close of the tasker process, the front office received the final response package, submitted it to the requestor and closed the tasker. Finally, the front office or responsible directorate's administrative staff archived the response package using the serial number as a reference.

Suspense Tracking

Tracking the tasker during the suspense was difficult for all participants. As Action Officers, reviewers, and approvers manually routed the response package from inbox to inbox, it was nearly impossible to determine progress, status, or package whereabouts. As suspense dates approached, Action Officers often searched from office to office to track down their response packages, only to find them stalled in an inbox whose owner was on travel or leave. In those cases, Action Officers delegated the review to another colleague in the same office, further delaying the suspense.

Even electronically routed response packages were difficult to track because of the lack of a formal workflow system. Email traditionally followed a point-to-point route to one or many recipients, making visibility into the suspense limited without direct correspondence from recipients. Action Officers had great difficulty reporting on progress and in rare cases, the front office initiated taskers to get status on other taskers.

SUSPENSE TRACKING SOLUTION

After extensive analysis into the tasker process, workload impacts, and suspense monitoring requirements, the contractor team at CPF designed, built, and implemented a tasker management and suspense tracking solution. The primary goal for this system was to manage all command taskers, improve cycle time of responses, streamline the collaboration of participants, and provide greater visibility into status and progress.

Workload Management System

The solution to the tasker management and suspense tracking problems at CPF was the Workload Management System (WMS). In an effort to leverage existing tools of CPF per guidance from Admiral Clemins, the WMS integrated with the existing Microsoft Exchange and SQL Server platforms. Custom forms used in Microsoft Outlook offered the same look and feel of regular email, but offered standardized and comprehensive templates and procedures for initiating, routing, managing, and tracking suspenses and response packages related to taskers.

The front office initiated taskers by populating a WMS tasker form, indicating which Action and Supporting Codes or Officers were required to perform the action. Once the front office entered the tasker information and saved the form, it automatically routed to those selected via Exchange's Active Directory handling. The WMS used Exchange and Active Directory to send automated status notifications to participants while a tasker was in transit. Action Officers accessed the tasker form, which appeared in an Outlook folder as a new task and either delegated it to someone else or began to work on the response. Participants saved response products as attachments to the tasker form within Outlook, leaving a running history of actions performed on the response. Action Officers initiated review and approval routing from within the tasker form, selecting the appropriate coordination participants or even using a predetermined, "canned," route. Those initiating recurring review routes saved participant lists for future use without having to select the individual participants each time. During reviews or chop chains, reviewers added comments into the form or onto the response deliverable, helping the Action Officer identify who made what comments. Approval determinations prompted automated emails to participants that provided results and justifications. Lastly, the WMS routed final responses back up the chain to the front office for submittal and archival.

The WMS facilitated the entire routing process through Microsoft Exchange handlers, directed all participants to the same form and contents, and leveraged functionality of Exchange, Outlook, and Active Directory. This approach helped deliver tremendous advantages to the CPF staff for automating taskers and tracking suspenses.

Cycle Time Improvement

In the legacy process, the required tasker due date directly influenced the cycle time of responses to taskers, and typically this was non-negotiable. A tighter deadline resulted in increased staffing to complete the tasker response. In an environment where workload was increasing, but the number of available resources was decreasing, improving cycle time was essential. Automating the manual nature of delegation, routing, and approval significantly reduced cycle time for the entire lifecycle of a tasker. More importantly, Action Officers and other participants had increased visibility into the status of the suspense.

Suspense Visibility

The approach to improving visibility to the lifecycle of taskers was to extract taskers, suspenses, and related communication from regular email channels and control them more rigorously in the single, dedicated system. Users managed and updated taskers in a completely separate folder within the Microsoft Outlook interface. This reduced staff time sifting through emails and searching for work in progress. Greater visibility into the tasker suspense provided the greatest savings in CPF staff effort. Direct visibility into the response routing, review, and approval provided Action Officers with more timely information on the whereabouts of a response package and better expectations on progress toward meeting the suspense dates.

Collaboration

By establishing more rigid procedures for processing taskers in a single system, all participants could more interactively delegate, route, develop, review, and approve taskers and response packages. Instead of numerous and repetitive emails circulating throughout the command, the WMS was the single repository for pending taskers, works in progress, and archived responses. Standardization in the tasker and suspense process, as well as business rules for establishing tasker scope and responsibility built into the WMS, reduced participant confusion and duplication of effort. With suspense information readily available in the system, users could become more proactive and less reactive in obtaining information about command activities. Instead of continually searching for response whereabouts, automated status notifications provided location information to participants.

LESSONS LEARNED AND RESULTS

Leveraging existing tools and implementing more rigorous workflow processes helped CPF get the tasker management and suspense tracking issues under control and manage resources more efficiently. Extensive system, process, and training documentation provided guidance in the transition from manual and paper-based processes to automated and electronically managed processes. With respect to business tools, the WMS helped the CPF email culture migrate from sorting through the trivial many to focusing on the vital few. CPF leveraged processes and tools that followed the rigid command protocol but flexibly supported the dynamic nature of numerous and mostly ad hoc work streams.

Integrated Workflow Management

The first positive impact the WMS provided was relief to Directors and Action Officers from email inbox management. Once Action Officers helped improve AMHS filtering profiles and tasker-related communications were migrated to the WMS, the overload of email traffic greatly diminished. Though moving taskers to the WMS initially looked like moving email from one inbox to another, users soon realized dramatic savings in time and effort. Instead of opening, reading, and mentally prioritizing each email in the inbox looking for taskers, users could open the WMS folder to see the comprehensive collection of clearly labeled and initially prioritized taskers. Additionally, Action Officers would only see taskers that they had or needed to take action on. The standardized WMS forms streamlined the workflow through the entire lifecycle and provided better visibility to participants during the suspense. By basing the solution on existing tools, other capabilities provided value and facilitated collaboration throughout the command. For example, Microsoft Outlook capabilities like the "Out-of-Office" setting, automated email rules, dynamic customizable forms, automatic archiving using public folders, and calendaring functions provided tremendous time savings, ease of use, and facilitated command-wide collaboration.

Business Rules

Where improved processes or systems could not streamline workflow, business rules helped provide continuity to operations. The WMS provided standardization to tasker management and suspense tracking, but human factors and manual steps unavoidably still existed. For example, to alleviate suspense bottlenecks created by staff on leave, a business rule for use of the "Out-of-Office" function rerouted taskers to other delegates or immediately back to the sender instead of sitting on a desk and halting progress. From another perspective, command announcements were vital sources of information to the staff, but other mechanisms of disseminating the information established "information pull" capabilities instead of constant "information push" email overload. For information on Morale, Welfare, and Recreation events or Navy newsletters, websites provided easy access without cluttering the inbox with a barrage of emails. Special administrative web pages provided staff members in charge of disseminating information the ability to quickly and easily publish content without relying on email. Finally, during the routing of response packages, built-in business rules helped reviewers and approvers provide information on specific changes made to documents in the package, clarification to approval or disapproval, or general comments to the Action Officer. Facilitating the capture of this information in the WMS forms with drop down menus and checklists made editing work documents easier and captured critical evidence of response participation, input, and signoff.

Scalable and Iterative Releases

CPF took a top-down approach to the implementation of the WMS, starting at headquarters, moving to the type commands, and finally to one battle group in a limited capacity. This was the most cost-effective approach to institutionalize the new processes and address issues as close to the source of the problems as possible, as the tasker process is top-down and the headquarters seemingly controls everything below. The next steps included implementation of the WMS at the subordinate type commands, using instances of the tool at each of the three sites as well as the same processes and business rules. One drawback of the WMS was that it required a thin client to access each Exchange server, making it a site-specific tool. Until CPF developed the next version, a more easily scalable web-based version built two years later, business rules addressed the handoffs between commands. Action Officers noted the command-specific serial numbers in their tasker forms when performing a handoff in order to track the suspense across the WMS firewall.

Measurable Benefits

In 1998, there were only a few rudimentary instances of web "portals" at CPF and benchmarks in the web-based Navy were few if any. Even in commercial business, web-based applications were in their infancy although they experienced exponential growth in the following few years. With very few, and expensive, commercial-off-the-shelf (COTS) choices, CPF chose to leverage the technology investments already in place, although with some custom configuration. Incredibly, the team researched, designed, built, and deployed the WMS, training 80 percent of the staff, in a mere eight months. Tailoring legacy technology to accommodate familiar processes made transition to the WMS straightforward and more user-friendly. The cost of ownership per seat was a fraction of what any available system could offer. Additionally, the instances of the WMS implemented at the CPF subordinate commands, and later at other commands such as the Commander in Chief, U.S. Naval Forces, Europe (CINCUSNAVEUR) and the Office of Naval Research (ONR), required only limited additional funding for minor patches, upgrades, and deployment team activities. The Navy owned the WMS code, so the per seat cost of ownership overall decreased substantially with each new site deployed.

CPF estimated an annual return on investment of 35 percent for the Solution Provider Initiative overall. The Workload Management System resulted in savings of nearly 50 percent of Action Officers' time by reducing effort spent tracking down taskers.[4] Initial savings due to improved productivity, reduction in non-value activities, and increased collaborative decision-making were on an order of magnitude of 18,000 staff hours per month.[5]

CONCLUSION

Relationships and interfaces among people, processes, and technologies directly influenced tasker management and suspense tracking improvements at CPF. By addressing very specific and tactical process problems for workflow management, new efficiencies provided visibility into strategic objectives for the headquarters staff. Critical success factors for the CPF tasker management and suspense tracking solution were:

- dynamic routing—accommodating all recurring and ad hoc permutations of a tasker, as well as any attachment format,
- visibility—allowing anyone to track the tasker suspense at any stage,
- notification—using technology to push out status and deadline information,
- automation—using technology features and visibility to reduce or eliminate routing choke points,
- incremental releases—implement incremental instances of a new tool to build groups of experienced users that lead to critical mass,
- business rules—establish process boundaries and controls that technology cannot accommodate, and
- training—develop a robust training suite of tools easily accessible by users though the web portal.

---

[4] Admiral Archie Clemins' statement to the U.S. House of Representatives Armed Services Committee, Hearing on Information Superiority, February 23, 1999.

[5] "Knowledge Management: Unlocking the Potential of Our Intellectual Capital," Alex Bennet, former DON CIO, Deputy Chief Information Officer for Enterprise Integration, Winter 2000.

These successes also resonated with other DoD, Federal Government, and commercial organizations. In the late 1990s more application vendors emerged with robust web-based solutions for document and content management. Many of the content management vendors enhanced their software or acquired other applications to offer initial business process and workflow management capabilities. Despite some feature-rich functionality of web portals to manage documents and content, the early workflow management systems were not tailored to DoD processes and were expensive, if not impossible, to customize. Workflow engines became more dynamic and powerful, allowing workflow-specific vendors to create user interfaces for novice programmers or proficient users to create their own workflow templates that the engines ran when triggered. More DoD-specific workflow solutions appeared, but the expense of purchasing the software and paying integrators was a barrier to entry for most government organizations.

The trend of relying on government-off-the-shelf (GOTS) software continued, as evidenced in 2001 when the U.S. Air Force contracted the development of a suspense tracking system specifically for workflow and tasker management. Other DoD agencies have tried similar approaches using expensive commercial packages, but none necessarily specific to workflow management. The challenge of realizing quantifiable returns on investments to automate tactical or administrative processes will continue, but building on improvements from the lowest process levels helps achieve early successes and drive value throughout an organization, eventually to the strategic mission.

Process Discovery through Process Mining

John Hoogland, Pallas Athena International, The Netherlands

INTRODUCTION

Just imagine that you had a tool that would model your process models for you, would also automatically give you baseline measurements of your process and would simplify your process analysis by adding case specific data to reveal why some cases take longer to process than others. Hard to imagine? The future is probably closer than you think.

Process discovery combined with process mining offers the possibility to create process models and mine process data from logs of existing information systems in your organization. Research results on this subject have led to the first implementation of process discovery and process mining in commercial software[1].

Much of the research on process mining is done by a research group from the Information Systems department of the Eindhoven University of Technology led by Prof.dr. W.M.P. van der Aalst. This research group invented much of the technology that was built into this commercial BPM suite[2].

HOW DOES PROCESS MINING WORK?

In order to understand the concept of process mining, it is important to realize that information systems form an approximation of reality. Information systems are driven by the models of the business processes they support, whilst at the same time, constant interaction takes place between a business process and the underlying information system. For example, most systems assume that certain processes occur within an organization and that specific activities are performed in a meaningful order. However, they allow users to deviate, to a certain extent, from these processes to provide the necessary flexibility. Independent from the way in which an information system is used, events are logged. An event is a particular action that is performed at a specific point in time. Depending on the context, events logs are also called database transactions, audit trail events, or simply management information.

Most contemporary information systems, including Workflow Management, Case Management, Enterprise Resource Planning, and Customer Relationship Management systems, support standard logging capabilities for registering events that have happened in an organization. As a consequence, a wealth of historical data from legacy and operational systems is usually available. This is the very data we are looking for when we want to apply process mining.

Process discovery

Figure 1 illustrates the capabilities of the process mining component. A process definition of an invoice process is automatically discovered from an information system's log. The actual implementation of the mining component is based on a

---

[1] BPM Suite by Pallas Athena (www.pallas-athena.com).

[2] Many publications on the subject can be found on www.processmining.org

combination of a heuristic algorithm and a genetic algorithm[3]. The discovery process converges towards a process definition that keeps getting better every iteration step, and finally results in a process definition that accurately and objectively describes the actual, underlying invoice process. In addition, a powerful feature is available that allows you to filter out parts of the information system's log, e.g. exceptional or erroneous behavior, in order to abstract from diverting elements and focus on what is important to you.

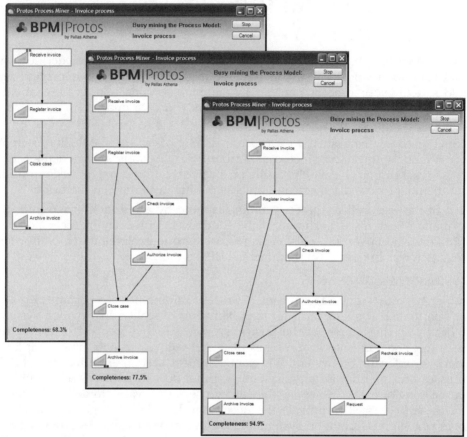

Figure 1: Discovery of an invoice process model. Three iterations steps are shown to illustrate incremental construction of the mined process

Simulation

A process definition that is discovered with process mining can be opened in the modeling component of the BPM Suite for further analysis or redesign. One attractive possibility is that you use this process definition to compare alternative simulation scenarios. The process mining component strongly supports this by automatically mining all kinds of simulation parameters in the process definition. This means that you get simulation parameters like processing times and cost for free, which allows you to perform realistic and accurate simulations.

---

[3] More details and background about these algorithms can be found at the website www.processmining.org

Animation

Mining also allows you to perform detailed analysis using a variety of animations. By doing so, a unique insight is obtained into the execution of your business process. Figure 2 shows an SLA analysis of the invoice process that was discovered (see Figure 1). This analysis is animated by a flash movie.

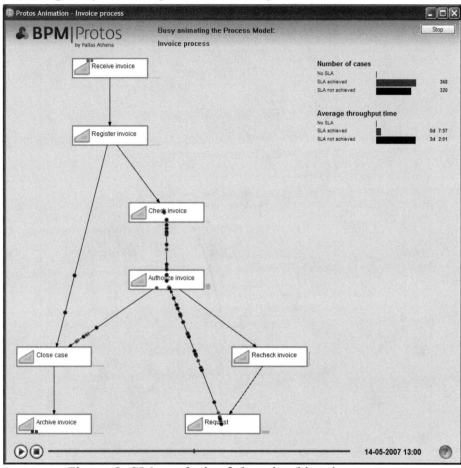

Figure 2: SLA analysis of the mined invoice process

The information about invoices in the information system's log is projected onto the invoice process definition as small moving dots. Each of these dots represents an invoice that runs through the process. The timeline at the bottom of the screen shows exactly where an invoice was located at a specific moment in history. The color of a dot instantly shows whether the SLA was met or failed for that invoice. Moreover, this information is quantified by showing the exact number of invoices that were met or failed and their respective average throughput times. This is just one of many examples of how an animation using the process mining component provides a window into the past showing where and when bottlenecks have occurred, where process compliance rules were broken, and even for which individual cases a break-down occurred.

PROCESS MINING IN A BPM APPROACH

BPM system vendors usually place their software within some kind of methodological or functional framework to explain its features or its business value. To explain the business value of process mining, we will show the BPM approach of

Pallas Athena and see how we relate process mining to other steps in our BPM lifecycle.

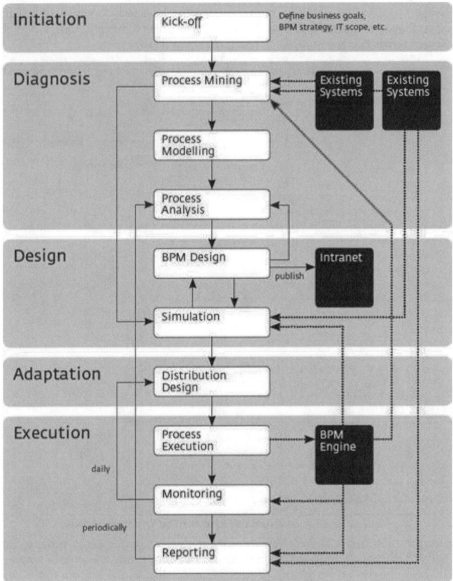

Figure 3 BPM lifecycle as supported by BPM Suite

As you can see in Figure 3, process mining is placed early in the BPM lifecycle. Process mining will improve your analysis and design phase the first time a particular process is analyzed in detail and even before you have implemented a process support system. However, after implementation of your process support system, it will again improve the analysis for further process improvements or other adaptations of the BPM system. We will describe the role of process mining in both stages: the first time you develop your process support system and the adaptation phase

DIAGNOSIS AND DESIGN PHASE, FIRST TIME AROUND

In cases where process discovery from existing information systems is feasible, it will save time and effort in later phases; in particular in the analysis phase and in proving the value of the new process support system.

Then, how does it speed up process analysis?

Process mining gives process definitions for free based on historical data. By doing so, process mining accelerates the process definition and process analysis phases. In the process definition phase, an analyst has to construct a detailed business process accurately describing the execution of tasks and routing of work in order to specify the workflow. In many cases, it will take days to weeks for a process analyst to map such a process. Usually, some kind of process description, e.g. in writing or in some flowchart, will be available as input. While analyzing existing process descriptions and interviewing key players in the process, the analyst will soon find out that they are outdated, disputable and incomplete. Furthermore, the process operators that are interviewed will tend to give disproportional attention to individual cases that stand out, because they are harder to handle. This will cause regular cases to be overlooked. Finally, it is most unlikely they will reveal to any analyst shortcuts, alternative ways of working and creative solutions to problems, which are not compliant, let alone fraudulent. Mining however will detect such deviations. In general, analysis of models only makes sense if they are an adequate reflection of reality. And most man-made models simply do not reflect reality sufficiently, especially not for quantitative analysis.

Process mining can dramatically improve the results of the process modeling and the process analysis phase. A process model mined from existing information systems will usually show more execution paths, will show what execution paths are taken more frequently, will show exceptions, and may show the data that process decisions are based on. Most importantly however, the process description is based on reality. It is an image of real transactions that have been going on in an organization and will help convince project stakeholders that the outcome of the analysis is objective.

Can it also perform baseline measurements?

Providing these measurements should be process-related, yes it can. Data of throughput times, execution times, resource consumption and cost may be derived from the system. Of course, sufficient data about timestamps, activities and resources should be available in the log. People who have ever been involved in baseline measurement projects will know how time-consuming these projects can be, especially if no process support system is in place and measurements can only be done by hand. In that case too, without process mining in place, the underlying model for these measurements will be inadequate, which will result in inaccurate measurement data.

Most time-based measurements will be based on interpretation. There are several traditional ways to perform process measurements when there is no process data available from process-based systems. Interviewing several process participants and asking them how long processing individual steps will take is one of them. A second possibility is to attach a document on the cover of dossiers and have every process participant fill in the timestamp when he received, started working on, and ended processing the dossier. A third possibility is to have an analyst sit beside several process participant and measure the time they need for processing "their" activities. There probably are other methods that may even provide better data. Anyhow, process mining should be taken into consideration as a quicker solution that will provide more objective baseline measurement data.

And what about organizational info?

In addition to process models, process mining can discover several other types of models. Based on metrics like the hand-over of work from one operator to the next, social networks and organizational structures can be discovered that show dependencies and interactions between departments, roles, functions, groups, users, etc. Moreover, information such as reporting lines and the distributions of work to users can also be revealed.

Typical results of process mining are the identification of heavily interacting departments in an organization, hierarchical relations between roles, and that specific persons are always working together as a team.

REDESIGN AND ADAPTATION - INTRODUCTION

If, after the analysis and design phase, the BPM system is in place to support the execution of the designed process, detailed process execution information will be available for redesign or on-the-fly adaptation of the system. Recent sales-talks of many BPM vendors and of the SOA movement often focused on easy adaptation to changing circumstances. However, this kind of adaptation usually still refers to changing the definition side of BPM, in which models, interfaces and data interact to allow proper execution of the business processes. A problem of this definition side is, however, that it is rigid by nature. Because of the tight interaction between the models, applications and data, changing either may affect the system as a whole. Implementing changes to the definition part of BPM systems therefore requires time; desired changes will not be implemented instantly but should be tested accurately.

However, there also is a need for implementing changes on-the-fly; in particular changes to the distribution of work or for business rules affecting the quality of the products created. To allow for instant agility, some BPMS vendors have been able to separate their *work distribution* and *business (process) rules* from their process design, which should allow real-time configuration.

Let's see how process mining can help in both the redesign phase where existing BPMS models need to be changed and in the adaptation phase where the operational side of the BPMS can be configured by an operational manager to immediately react to changing situations.

REDESIGN PHASE

When entering this phase, it will be useful to first mine the BPM system's log. The resulting process model will give insight in the real execution of the process. This exercise will be a great starting point for identifying bottlenecks. To give you some ideas of the added value this analysis could offer:

- Available aggregated process data will be automatically linked to the resulting mined model and the model will be instantly ready for simulation. This means that if only small changes are made to the process, simulation may be used to calculate the effects the changes may have to process performance like waiting times, throughput times, execution times, resource occupation and cost
- Mining might show that some modeled branches of the process model are never taken. These parts could be deleted for simplification of model execution

- Combining the mined process with case-specific data, which usually is done, often shows a correlation between data characteristics and process characteristics. Process animation will usually play an important part in this type of analysis. Mining exercises may come up with the following observations:
  - Additional checks are only done when cases are handled by specific persons
  - Department A takes more time handling similar requests than department B
  - Throughput times agreed in service level agreements for specific customers are never met
  - The four-eyes principle is not supported in 10 percent of all financial checks
  - Specific groups of people work more closely together and seem to form a social network
  - High risk cases take much longer to execute than low risk cases because of long waiting times for activities executed by highly specialized personnel

This is just a small set of possible results of process mining exercises. It shows added value of process mining in specific fields of research like social network analysis and conformance checking.

Within a BPM cycle process mining is of high value. It captures the actual execution of a process in models that reveal bottlenecks, situations that should not occur according to process definitions, and other irregularities. It does this in an objective manner and presents the result in a clear and present way that is very persuasive. Process mining often acts as an eye opener by providing convincing insight into specific process details, which have already been present but were difficult to pinpoint. Therefore, process mining gives you the ammunition to convince others and make them face the facts.

ADAPTATION PHASE

The adaptation phase in the BPM cycle shown in Figure 3 supports change of the operational side of the BPM system without having to change the definition side. This particularly applies to work distribution or business rules. Especially operational managers will want to immediately react to changing circumstances. Usually they will only get this opportunity after the problem has occurred. With a process mining dashboard, they would be able to monitor what's going on or even predict future bottlenecks. Of course this means the BPM system should be flexible enough to handle the changes asked for by the middle managers. Operational agility is key; a challenge only few process support systems can confront.

Example

Let's illustrate this with an example. An insurer that divides all processing of claims to regional teams suddenly sees a rise of incoming claims. This is signaled on the BAM dashboard the BPM system offers. By mining the process with the updated log, process mining discovers that the claims came in from one particular region. Because the resulting model will also contain all simulation parameters, a simulation can be run immediately. Based on the current workload at activities early in the process, the simulation model predicts that the workload for the eastern regional team will triple, which will lead to throughput times four times longer than agreed. The middle manager will now have sufficient time to react by adding additional resources to the eastern regional team or simply by creating a new temporary worklist that is shared with other teams and results in a redistribution of claims.

This example demonstrates that combining the power of process mining, business intelligence, and simulation allows you to forecast future workload, and expected throughput or processing times. A dashboard could even signal a potential exceeding of threshold values. The forecast can be trusted, because it is based on real management information obtained from system logs and a real process with simulation parameters that are mined from (previous versions of) the same log.

CASE STUDY: PROCESS MINING AT A LARGE EUROPEAN AIRLINER

This case study is about a very successful European airliner carrying more than 80 million passengers yearly and consistently showing strong financial performance. Recently, the airliner was born out of an enormous challenging merger. The integration of IT and IT departments especially required coordination, management attention and creativity. The new IT department has a strong focus on performance. Almost all aspects of the operation are monitored. Every month an extensive Balance Score Card is produced indicating the overall performance within the various IT processes.

One of these processes is carried out by the IS department. Amongst many other things, The IS department takes care of change and incident handling, related to the internal IT systems. The IS department deals with approximately 35.000 incidents per year, varying from users who have forgotten their password, to hanging PCs or crashing servers. More than 60 percent of the incident handling is subject to Service Level Agreements, requiring most incidents to be solved within three days.

The registration of calls and handling of the incidents are logged.[4] After initial registration, calls are routed to the appropriate department for solving. About 12 specialized teams are involved in solving incidents. Many use dedicated systems for actual solving the problem, but they log the outcome in the management service application as well. This system issues warnings whenever SLA deadlines are about to be crossed.

In June 2007 it became discernible, that due to an increase of incidents, the SLA obligations were impossible to match. The BSC reports clearly indicated that regardless of the type of incident, the IS department was performing way under expectations, with about 60 percent of the calls being solved after the SLA deadline. The BSC report did however not give clear indications to what caused the delays; let alone how to solve them. After consulting various team managers, IS was under the impression that many delays were caused by calls being routed to the wrong handling team, due to insufficient information when issuing the call and lack of knowledge at the call handlers. As a consequence calls needed to be rerouted and re-investigated, extra information needed to be supplied and the short SLA deadline had then already passed. The airliner therefore planned to invest in an artificial intelligence and knowledge based system, in order to more accurately route the calls to the appropriate team for solving.

Being one of their most innovative customers, just about the same time Pallas Athena had contacted the airliner to beta-test their new BPM process mining module. The IS department suggested the Peregrine logs were mined, in order to

---

[4] Supported by Peregrine, a service management solution acquired by HP in 2005

gain even more insight in the incident handling process. Within two hours the Peregrine information was extracted, using existing interfaces used by the BSC reporting system. After mining the raw Peregrine data of the incident handling process was accurately turned into a process map, showing all distinctive steps. A second mining was done to visualize the routing of cases between the various teams. The mined period was one year, ending in June 2007.

The result of this process mining exercise was overwhelming and totally unexpected.

In three areas we did not only gain insight into the actual process, but the generated results demonstrated that processes, bottlenecks and cause of problems were different to what was assumed.

1. First of all, the idea that many of the problems were caused by inadequate initial routing appeared to be incorrect. Although rerouting does occur, it seems to be a *result* of too many bottlenecks, instead of the cause. Furthermore, it showed that the vast majority of calls (95 percent) are routed between the same two departments.

2. Secondly, the mined process demonstrated that—especially in case of complaints—the official procedure was not always followed. The actual process was not compliant to the formal processes.

3. Thirdly, the real cause of problems was outside of IS. The introduction of a new system generated too many incidents that could not be handled by the available staff. As a consequence, for each call, at least three warnings were issued by Peregrine that the SLA deadline for that call was not going to be met. Handling this enormous amount of warnings in itself caused bottlenecks as well. At least 25 percent of the time spent on calls had to do with responding to SLA warnings and postponing them.

Not only did the process mining give better insight in the incident process itself, as a side affect it became clear that in order to get control on the execution of their processes the airliner requires a much more process oriented approach and tooling. Silosystems responsible for horizontal or vertical support of processes are just not capable of giving the operational managers adequate tools to detect problems in a process oriented way, let alone to give tools for solving them.

As a result of the mining study the airliner is now investing in the introduction of BPM into its organization. Peregrine will still be used for registration and handling of incidents, but on top of this BPM software will be added in order to really control and manage operational processes. This BPM layer will play a central role in the airliner's software architecture.

CONCLUSION

Process mining techniques allow for extracting information from event logs. For example, the audit trails of a workflow management system or the transaction logs of an enterprise resource planning system can be used to discover models describing processes, organizations, and products. Moreover, it is possible to use process mining to monitor deviations (e.g., comparing the observed events with predefined models or business rules in the context of SOX).

Process mining will first of all improve the speed of process analysis because it automatically generates process models from the past, your system logs. Secondly, it will link information from the log to the mined process model. This allows to instantly analyze the process, e.g. by observing process animations to find out how specific case-characteristics influence case-routing or processing times. You may also want to calculate improvement scenarios through simulating the process model. Simulation parameters will be mined automatically together with the process model. Simulation can also be used to forecast operational bottlenecks that might arise so they can be prevented instead of repaired.

Process mining will be useful in several stages of a BPM lifecycle; in designing your processes, in analyzing your design, in improving and redesigning your processes, and in forecasting operational behavior. In short, process mining allows you to capitalize on the past, optimize the present and anticipate the future.

Analysis of Most Common Process Modelling Mistakes in BPMN Process Models

Tomislav Rozman, Gregor Polančič, Romana Vajde Horvat, University of Maribor, Slovenia

ABSTRACT

The purpose of this article is to present the most common patterns of mistakes, misunderstandings and proposed solutions, which resulted from the analysis of more than two thousand process models designed using BPMN notation.

The approach, used in our research was a multiple case study of graphical process models drawn using Business Process Modelling Notation (BPMN), created by students of information systems study programme. Most important finding of our research is that we have identified 15 most common BPMN process model anti-patterns. Most of them represent wrong usage of BPMN's connecting objects. Less notable is wrong usage of other BPMN's objects.

Results of our research could have direct positive implications on learning habits of process analysts and on faster learning of correct process modelling. Findings could also be used for the improvement of process modelling tools and finally to improve the students skills. The findings are useful for all types of stakeholders in education and businesses, who deal with business process management.

INTRODUCTION

Business process modelling is becoming increasingly important activity in all types of organisations, especially as a part of larger initiatives—Business Process Management. One of main purposes of process modelling is to ensure at least repeatability of organisation's processes [1].

Process modelling is especially valuable and unavoidable when implementing quality management systems in organisations. In addition, it can be extremely useful as a part of software development cycle, especially in early phases of software development projects, where behaviour of target domain is analysed and requirements are being gathered.

Latest information technology evolution is heading towards process models as the core drivers of the distributed computing [2]. In addition, the web services technologies stack contains process modelling and synchronisation (choreography) languages on its highest level [3].

Until now, business process modelling was often neglected, mainly due to the gap between business requirements for information systems (process models) and inability of automated execution of the process models. The development of the latest XML-based languages for process description [4] and execution [5] and process engines is enabling the execution of the business process models already.

Nevertheless, information system developers and business analysts do not have sufficient knowledge about the detailed process modelling, because in the last decades, there was the need only for rough process models, which were performed manually.

It is well known that poor quality of process models can cause poor quality software requirements resulting in a poor information system. Therefore, greater emphasis should be put on the business process modelling education.

In the recent years, many modelling techniques were used for process modelling and many of them were not appropriate as a teaching method for process modelling. The process modelling technique, which is appropriate for students, should be easy to learn, it should hide the unnecessary details of process model and it should be broadly accepted. At University of Maribor, newer process modelling techniques such as BPMN [6] were introduced in the curriculum of Information Systems course [7].

Students at the Faculty of Electrical Engineering and Computer Science are taught how to model business and software processes. The goal of practical lectures of process modelling is to teach students how to design business and software development process models. In the last six years, many experiences about process modelling were gathered.

The BPMN notation was chosen for theoretical and practical lectures for classes "Standards and quality" and "Organisation and management of information systems projects", because it offers a graphical notation with the support of all important process concepts (process, activity, event, routing, merging, synchronisation, messages, roles and so on), which can be used to model various kinds of discrete processes. Another reason for choosing this notation was that the specification of the notation defines standardised mappings to the process execution languages, currently for BPEL4WS [5] and XPDL [4].

Currently, there are many commercial tools being developed, which shows the overall adoption of the notation in the industry is increasing. Although BPMN notation is ontologically most complete notation currently available [8,9], it does not prevent us to design bad process models, including syntactical, semantic and pragmatically errors. During last six years, we gathered the most frequent mistakes created by students. We have analysed over two thousand process models and extracted 15 most important and frequent process anti-patterns and proposed solutions for them.

SIMILAR WORK

The term anti-pattern is not new. It is often called a pitfall, or, set of classes of commonly-reinvented bad solutions to problems. They are studied as a category so they can be avoided in the future, and so instances of them may be recognized when investigating non-working systems [10].

Similar definition has been used in a book [11]: Anti-patterns are commonly repeated bad practices, or, roadblocks, which prevent successful delivery and are directly caused by lack of understanding of the problem.

To our knowledge, currently no such work described here can be found in accessible literature. Other researchers describe process patterns from different contextual and abstraction levels.

For example, a great work of authors [12] identifies a set of generic workflow patterns, which can be used to test the capability and completeness of process modelling languages or tools regardless of the notation used. Those patterns are grouped as control flow patterns, resource patterns, data patterns and exception handling patterns.

Our work differs from above-mentioned that we identified process modelling anti-patterns, which are specific to the BPMN notation and often occur when an inexperienced analyst uses a tool without the verification capabilities.

Nevertheless, our anti-patterns are somehow similar to control-flow and data patterns [12], because most of our anti-patterns describe incorrect connectedness of activities, events and organizational structures.

Other authors, such as [13,14] describe possible process management pitfalls, which should be avoided. In the context of process modelling, the author warns the analysts not to exaggerate with the details and completeness of the process models. Author's work describes pitfalls from the human resources point of view and does not identify mistakes in the process models.

Other patterns, found in the literature, such as design patterns [10], are not directly related to our work.

RESEARCH METHOD

In order to answer the stated research question "What are the most common mistakes when modelling business process diagrams using BPMN notation?", we decided to perform a multiple case study research based on data collected during the curriculum. The process models, designed by students were gathered and systematically analysed from 2002 to 2007. Corresponding to data collection and data analysis, exploratory research approach was chosen, which allows collecting the data prior to the definition of the research question [15-17].

Within the curriculum, the process models are designed during practical lectures by students of fifth (higher programme) and eighth semester (university programme) of information systems study programme. Total duration of Information systems study programme is six (higher programme) or nine semesters (university programme). Students in both groups receive equal knowledge about the BPMN topic. The learning process of BPMN includes the following steps.

Students learn about the theory of process modelling during theoretical classes. The practical lectures take 45 hours. Based on textual requirements, each student designs five process models using computer aided software engineering tool. This tool (Microsoft Visio or Dia plug-in) allows students to design process model. However, neither of the tools syntactical or semantically validate created models. Additionally, students design process models during the exam. The models are stored in a configuration management system, which simplifies evolution of models and identification of plagiarism. The quality of designed models is validated by teaching assistants using rules defined in BPMN 1.0 specification. Finally, the validated and updated versions of process models are committed back in configuration management system. There are roughly 30 students for each class for each year, which makes totally around two thousand process models designed in last six years.

To ensure validity of the case study, the triangulation principle [15-17] should be used: The case should be examined by multiple observers, data sources and theories or methods. Corresponding to the triangulation principle, process models were analysed by two teaching assistants and one assistant professor. Additional, multiple process models were analysed, which ensures data sources validity. The study (analysis of process models) was repeated multiple times in each study year, after each process model finished by students.

The validity of our case study could only be threatened by the fact that the case should be observed from different viewpoints (theories or methods) and we are fully aware of this issue.

The study followed the procedure: After each process model designed by students, the process model was inspected and problematic patterns were identified and recorded. This step was repeated for each process model.

Wrong usages of the BPMN notation were classified as syntactical mistakes. Process models with wrong meaning were classified as semantically mistakes. Process models, which were not understandable or ambiguous, were classified as pragmatic mistakes. 'Anti-Patterns' evolved when similar mistakes repeated over multiple cases of process models. Those patterns were incrementally added to the 'Most common process modelling mistakes' document, which will be used in next year's curriculum to prevent most common mistakes.

FINDINGS: MOST COMMON ANTI-PATTERNS OF PROCESS MODELLING AND PROPOSED SOLUTIONS

Improper use of BPMN syntax rules and general modelling principles can cause low process modelling performance in the sense of correctness.

During the practical lessons of process modelling we noticed that some process model patterns cause problems and are not used in the right way. Most frequent patterns of such mistakes were gathered and are presented in this chapter.

Each process pattern is described in the following way: first, problem is formulated in a form of process anti-pattern and classified according to the type of mistake. Type of mistake can be syntactical, semantic or pragmatic. Second, the severity and implications are discussed. Implications can be deadlocks, un-reachability of some process parts, unnecessary complications and so on. Third, the solution is proposed in a form of correct process pattern.

Examples are drawn using BPMN notation. Patterns represent only parts of process models. Dots (...) represent hidden parts of the process models, which are not necessary for pattern understandability. Patterns from 1 to 8 represent improper use of BPMN's connecting elements. Patterns from 9 to 15 represent improper use of other BPMN's elements, such as events and activities.

Pattern 1. Activities in one pool are not connected

Problem: A common mistake in this case is that activities in one pool are not connected with sequence flow (see Pool B on Fig. 1). When multiple pools are modelled, only message flows can be used to connect different pools. Within each pool a separate flow should be defined. Most frequent reason for this type of mistake is that students perceive multiple pools as one process or dependent processes and think that message flows between pools can be used instead of sequence flows.

Possible practical impacts: In the organization, which is represented by Pool B (Fig. 1) the dependency of the activities is not defined. These could lead to non-performing of the task D. In case that there are several non-connected activities, the sequence of performing them is also unknown.

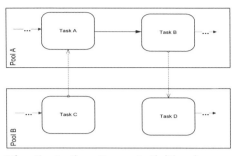 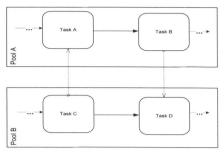

Fig. 1. Anti-pattern: Activities in one pool are not connected

Fig. 2. Correct pattern

Type of error: This is a syntactical error and pragmatic error; students think that sequence flow between task C and task D is not required.

Implications: Process model is not valid. Direct implication of this mistake is that part of the process model is not reachable (Activity D).

Proposed solution: The modelling should be performed in a way that pools are modelled independently, without thinking about the connection between pools. All process elements in one pool should be fully connected using sequence flow, according to the BPMN specification. This step should be repeated for all pools.

Lastly, message flows, intermediate message events and data objects should be added. Example of the solution is presented below (Fig. 2).

Pattern 2. Process does not contain a start event

Problem: Although start event is optional (according to BPMN specification), its usage is recommended, especially for complex processes, where it is difficult to localize process starts (Fig. 3).

Possible practical impacts: If the starting event is missing most probably in an organization it will be unclear when or where to start performing the process. It could happen that the process is not performed at all.

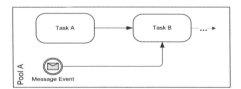 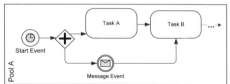

Fig. 3. Anti-pattern: Process does not contain a start event

Fig. 4. Correct pattern

Type of error: This is pragmatic error, not syntax error, according to the BPMN specification.

Implications: The understandability of the process model is lowered, because it is not clear where the process starts.

Proposed solution: The start event should be added (Fig. 4), to make the understanding of the process model easier. If necessary, a combination of routing elements should be added also. If the pool contains sequential and simple process then the start event is not needed.

Pattern 3. Process does not contain an end event

Problem: If the process doesn't contain an end event, it is not clear when the process ends, for example: Does the process on (Fig. 5) ends when Task B and C are finished? The answer is "probably, but not necessary".

Possible practical impacts: In an organization, process performers' work may stall, because they don't know how to react when tasks B and C (Fig. 5) are finished. Other dependent processes may be delayed also.

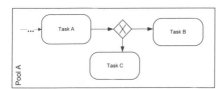 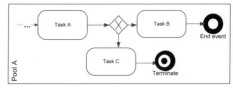

Fig. 5. Anti-pattern: Process does not contain an end event

Fig. 6. Correct pattern

Type of error: This is a pragmatic error, because it is not clear when the process in Pool A ends.

Implications: The understandability of the process model is lowered, because it is not clear when the process ends.

Proposed solution: Process ends should be explicitly modelled to specify when the process ends. For example, the whole process on (Fig. 6) ends when the task C is finished (see terminate event).

Pattern 4. Sequence flow crosses process boundary

Problem: The sequence flow crosses sub-process boundary. Inexperienced analysts often don't perceive sub-processes as independent units.

Possible practical impacts: In an organization, sub-process is often treated as 'batch of activities', which is started at the first activity, which is treated as the beginning, not in the middle of the sub-process. In case of following incorrect sequence flow, process performers might skip the task C (Fig. 7).

Fig. 7. Anti-pattern: Sequence flow crosses process boundary

Fig. 8. Correct pattern

Type of error: This is a syntax error, according to the BPMN specification.

Implications: Process model is not valid. There are no other serious implications, but understandability is lowered and process model does not conform to the specification.

Proposed solution: Re-combine activities and connect wrong sequence flow to the boundary of sub-process (Process X Fig. 8). When teaching students process modelling, comparison with Java programming language methods is useful and helps students to understand the proposed solution. When programming in java, calls of the statements within the class' methods are not allowed also, only calls to the whole objects' methods.

Pattern 5. Sequence flow crosses pool boundary

Problem: Improper use of flow objects often occurs in combination with pattern 1. In this case (Fig. 9), activities from different pools are connected with the sequence flow, which is not allowed in this case. Interaction between pools should be designed using message flows only.

Possible practical impacts: The process performer from the Pool A may think that passing the control to the organization B, no action is needed, for example sending documents, emails, contracts and so on. This situation can cause the Task F is not performed at all.

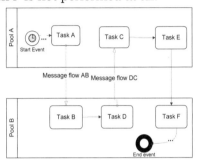 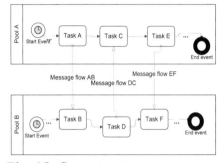

Fig. 9. Anti-pattern: Sequence flow crosses pool boundary   **Fig. 10.** Correct pattern

Type of error: This is a syntax error, according to the BPMN specification.

Implications: Process model is not valid. Two independent processes are being made dependent using sequence flow.

Proposed solution: The message flow should be used instead of sequence flow (Fig. 10).

Pattern 6. Gateway receives, evaluates or sends a message

Problem: A common mistake when using gateways is that a gateway receives or sends a message (Fig. 11). The most common cause for this type of error is that it is wrongly assumed that the incoming message influences the decision and that a gateway alternative or output can directly result in a message flow. However a gateway cannot produce, receive or evaluate data, which is also evident from BPMN's Message flow rules. A similar mistake appears when association flows are used.

Possible practical impacts: Process performers may think that messages can trigger the decisions or can be result of the decision, which is wrong. Direct impact could be unwanted waiting for the message before the decision is taken during the process execution.

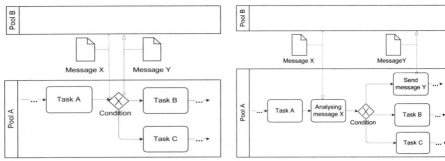

Fig. 11. Anti-pattern: Gateway receives, evaluates or sends a message

Fig. 12. Correct pattern

Type of error: This is syntactical error and semantic error; students think a gateway can receive and produce messages.

Implications: The most critical implications of this anti-pattern are missing activities which should receive or produce messages. Beside, while gateway alternatives are not modelled correctly this usually implies further sequence flows.

Proposed solution: New activities should be included in the model, which receive, evaluate or produce messages (Fig. 12).

Pattern 7. Intermediate events are placed on the edge of the pool

Problem: Students often model pool interfaces as intermediate events placed on the pool's boundary, which is not correct (Fig. 13).

Possible practical impacts: Process performers may think the intermediate message events can be triggered anytime during the process, which can cause unwanted execution of the activities in the process.

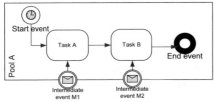

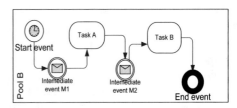

Fig. 13. Anti-pattern: Intermediate events are placed on the edge of the pool

Fig. 14. Correct pattern

Type of error: Syntactical error.

Implications: Event is not reachable within the pool.

Proposed solution: Intermediate events should be modelled within the pool and fully connected (in and out sequence flows). Only then they are reachable and represent delays in the process (Fig. 14).

Pattern 8. Hanging intermediate events or activities

Problem: Activities or events within the pool do not contain incoming sequence flows (Fig. 15).

Possible practical impacts: Some activities in the organization may never be performed. Triggering of the intermediate events can cause unwanted performing of activities.

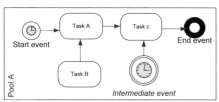

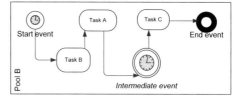

Fig. 15. Anti-pattern: Hanging intermediate events or activities

Fig. 16. Correct pattern

Type of error: This semantic mistake leads to the non-reachability of the activities.

Implications: Activity is not reachable.

Proposed solution: The process model should be rearranged and fully connected (Fig. 16). The meaning of the process should be examined when rearranging sequence flows.

Pattern 9. Each lane in the pool contains start event

Problem: Although this situation is allowed (according to BPMN), we've found that it can cause a lot of ambiguity when reading the process model (Fig. 17).

Possible practical impacts: Process performers may think the processes in the organization are independent, which may not be true. The processes can also be started at the wrong time.

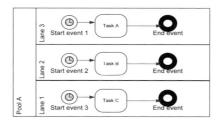

Fig. 17. Anti-pattern: Each lane in the pool contains start event

Type of error: This is a pragmatic error.

Implications: The model is ambiguous.

Proposed solutions: There are several possibilities how to resolve this case. First possibility (Fig. 18 - left) is that the process includes only one start event and sequence the activities. Second possibility (Fig. 18 – right) is that the process includes one start event, event based decision, intermediate events and parallel activities. Or, the processes in lanes can be modelled as processes in separate and independent pools. The correct solution depends on semantics of the process model.

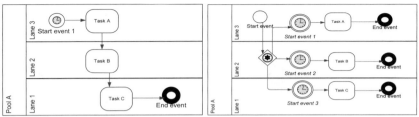

Fig. 18. Two possibilities of correct patterns

Pattern 10. Incorrect use of time events

Problem: Intermediate time events have two basic purposes - acting as a delay mechanism when used between sequence flows and acting as an exception (duration) when attached to the boundary of task or sub-process (Fig. 19). These two purposes are often interchanged.

Possible practical impacts: Process performers may interrupt the execution of the activity at the wrong time, or, the execution of the next activity may be delayed.

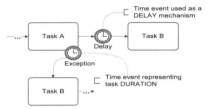

Fig. 19. : Anti-pattern: Incorrect use of time events

Type of error: This is a pragmatic error; students want to model a duration mechanism, but they model a delay instead; and opposite.

Implications: The most critical implication of this anti-pattern is unwanted delay in a business process.

Proposed solution: There is no recipe for solving this type of problem because both types of models are syntactically correct. The students should learn how does the meaning of the intermediate event change when using in different locations in the process model.

Pattern 11. Sequence and message event represent data flow

Problem: Similar to time events, intermediate message events are used as delay or synchronisation mechanism. When an intermediate message event is placed within a sequence flow it will continue when a message (explicit or implicit) arrives from a participant and triggers the event. However, students often wrongly use intermediate message event as a mechanism for sending messages (data) from previous task to following task (Fig. 20).

Possible practical impacts: In the organization, if process performer follows wrong process model, the execution of some activities may be delayed and document, which should flow between the activities may not be created at all.

Fig. 20. Anti-pattern: Sequence and message event represent data flow

Fig. 21. Correct pattern

Type of error: This is a semantic error; students think to model a message or data flow. Instead, they model a delay mechanism.

Implications: The process if forced to stop. Therefore a part of the process will not be able to execute until the message arrives.

Proposed solution: Instead of using intermediate message event, the document or data flow as presented below (Fig. 21) should be used.

Pattern 12. Event is used as a message flow source

Problem: Events are often used as sources of message flows. According to BPMN message flow rules this is wrong and can be explained with the fact that only activities can produce messages (Fig. 22).

Possible practical impacts: In the organization, the process performer who follows the incorrect process model may think that he or she should produce a document at some point in the process, instead of waiting for the message. The situation can cause ambiguity and unnecessary work of the process performer.

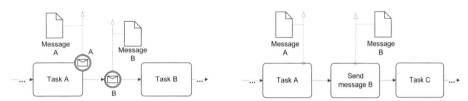

Fig. 22. Anti-pattern: Event is used as a message flow source

Fig. 23. Correct pattern

Type of error: According to BPMN specification, this is a syntactical error.

Implications: Missing activities which actually produce messages.

Proposed solution: If message event is placed on the activity boundary it should be deleted. The message should be connected directly to the activity. If message event is placed between the sequence flows it should be replaced with an activity (Fig. 23).

Pattern 13. Improper use of flow elements

Problem: Different states of the activity are often incorrectly modelled as separate activities. This includes the receiving of the messages. However these types of activities usually complicate the process (Fig. 24).

Possible practical impacts: In the organization, the process performer who follows the incorrect process model may be confused, because states of the activity are represented as separate activities.

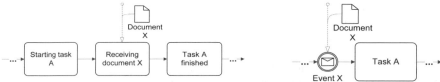

Fig. 24. Anti-pattern: Improper use of flow elements

Fig. 25. Correct pattern

Type of error: The anti-pattern represents semantic and pragmatic errors. The models are often confusing and complex.

Implications: Non-understandable models.

Proposed solution: The states of an activity are not required because the sequence flow indicates if an activity starts (incoming sequence flow) or ends (outgoing sequence flow). To model intermediate message events explicitly is a better solution. In case of multiple incoming message flows the event based gateway and the appropriate combination of intermediate events should be used. (Fig. 25).

Pattern 14. Starting timer placed instead of intermediate timer

Problem: This is a small but very frequent mistake using starting timer instead of intermediate one. We believe that time events are often misused because of the inner circle which represents the clock symbol (Fig. 26).

Possible practical impacts: Because this is syntactical error, we think that it would not cause any significant problems during process execution.

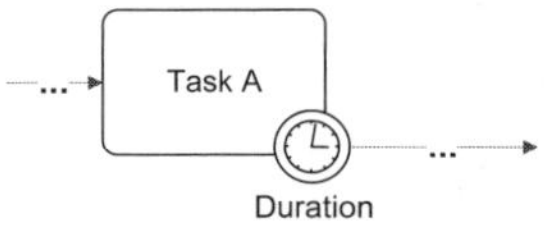

Fig. 26. Anti-pattern: Starting timer placed instead of intermediate timer

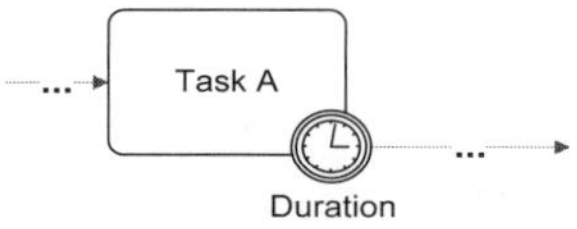

Fig. 27. Correct pattern

Type of error: This is a syntactic error.

Implications: Syntactically wrong model.

Proposed solution: Start timer should be replaced with intermediate timer event as presented on Fig. 27.

Pattern 15. Exception flow is not connected to the exception

Problem: Analysts often model task exception using intermediate event, but the sequence flow remains connected to the task, which is syntactically correct, but semantically wrong, if we want to represent the activity, which is performed after the exception is triggered.

Possible practical impacts: This type of process model mistake could cause serious problems in the organization. If the activity which is currently performed is interrupted, no compensation activity would be performed because of wrong connections.

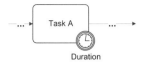

Fig. 28. Anti-pattern: Exception flow is not connected to the exception

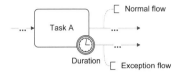

Fig. 29. Correct pattern

Type of error: This is a semantic error.

Implications: Wrong meaning of the process model, especially if read by other person than original author. Also, it is not clear if a sequence flow is missing or it is just wrongly connected directly to the activity.

Proposed solution: Correct flow should be modelled. If the analyst wants to represent the exception flow, then the sequence flow should be connected to the intermediate event (Fig. 29).

CONCLUSIONS

In this paper we presented unique collection of most common process modelling mistakes or anti-patterns which occurred most often within the process models designed by a large group of information system students.

If the process models with identified anti-patterns would be performed in the organizations, several implications could occur. These practical implications include unwanted delays in the process performance, non-execution of the activities or simply ambiguity which could hinder the process performers at their work. Therefore, process modellers should have knowledge about anti-patterns, which would prevent their appearance in the process models.

Results of our research leaded to the following activities. Firstly, the learning materials for students are being improved, where examples of mistakes in process models are emphasized. A one page (A2) poster, containing BPMN symbols and anti-patterns has already been designed[1], as a kind of student's 'cheat sheet', to prevent the process modelling mistakes in the first place. Second, the results of our research can also indicate how inexperienced process analysts perceive BPMN notation and process modelling principles. This could lead to further improvements of the BPMN and other business process modelling notations.

Another insight that we gained is that the anti-patterns should be implemented in the process modelling tool as 'on-the fly' verification and validation mechanism of process models. Verification of syntax-checking mechanisms is not difficult and it is implemented in many existing modelling tools. A bigger problem, which remains still an open issue in the research domain is, how to check the semantics and understandability of process models.

REFERENCES

1. SEI. Capability Maturity Model(R) Integration, CMMISM for Software Engineering, Version 1.1., CMU/SEI-2002-TR-029. http://www.sei.cmu.edu/publications/documents/02.reports/02tr029.html . 2002. SEI. 4-6-2005.

---

[1] Available from http://bpmn.itposter.net

2.   Rozman I, Juric MB, Golob I, Hericko M: Qualitative and quantitative analysis and comparison of Java distributed architectures. Software-Practice & Experience 2006; 36:1543-1562.

3.   Smith H, Fingar P: "Business Process Management (BPM): The Third Wave." Meghan-Kiffer Press, 2003.

4.   WfMC. XML Process Definition Language. http://www.wfmc.org/standards/XPDL.htm . 2005. 3-2-2006.

5.   IBM, BEA, Microsoft, et al. Business Process Execution Language for Web Services version 1.1. http://www-128.ibm.com/developerworks/library/specification/ws-bpel/ . 2005. 6-12-2005.

6.   BPMI. Business Process Modeling Notation, (1.0). http://www.bpmi.org/bpmn-spec.htm . 2004. 1-11-2004.

7.   Rozman T, Vajde RH, Rozman I. Experiences with business process modeling notation in educational process. IBIMA2003. E-Business and organizations in the 21st century : Proceedings of the 2003 International business information management conference , 310-315. 2003. Cairo, Egypt.

8.   Recker J, Indulska M, Rosemann M, Green P. Do Process Modelling Techniques Get Better? A Comparative Ontological Analysis of BPMN . 16th Australasian Conference on Information Systems. 16th Australasian Conference on Information Systems . 2005. 16th Australasian Conference on Information Systems.

9.   Rosemann M, Green P, Indulska M: A Reference Methodology for Conducting Ontological Analyses. Lecture Notes in Computer Science 2004; 3288:110.

10.   Gamma E, Helm R, Johnson R, Vlissides J: "Design Patterns: Elements of Reusable Object-Oriented Software." Addison-Wesley Professional, 1995.

11.   Brown WJ, McCormick HW, Thomas SW: "AntiPatterns in Project Management." John Wiley & Sons, 2000.

12.   van der Aalst WMP, ter Hofstede AHM, Kiepuszewski B, Barros AP: Workflow patterns. Distributed and Parallel Databases 2003; 14:5-51.

13.   Rosemann M: Potential pitfalls of process modeling: part A. Business Process Management Journal 2006; 12:249-254.

14.   Rosemann M: Potential pitfalls of process modeling: part B. Business Process Management Journal 2006; 12:249-254.

15.   Tellis W: Introduction to Case Study. The Qualitative Report 1997; 3.

16.   Tellis W: Application of Case Study Methodology. The Qualitative Report 1997; 3.

17.   Tellis W: Results of Case Study on Information Technology at a University. The Qualitative Report 1997; 3.

The Temporal Perspective: Expressing Temporal Constraints and Dependencies in Process Models

Denis Gagné, Trisotech, Canada
André Trudel, Acadia University, Canada

ABSTRACT

We characterize the temporal perspective of workflow specifications through a series of 31 temporal constructs that may occur when defining a process model. This characterization is independent of any specific modeling formalism or approach. We precisely define each temporal construct and when possible, provide a formal temporal account of these constructs based on Allen's interval algebra. Our characterization not only provides a basis and objective means to evaluate the temporal expressiveness of various formalisms and tools, but can also open the way to the integration of formal validation tools, such as constraint satisfaction or theorem proving systems, to verify temporal satisfiability of the workflow specification. As an example of the application of the proposed framework, we present a brief discussion of the suitability of BPMN and Gantt Charts for business process modeling from the temporal perspective.

1. INTRODUCTION

Business processes require the coordinated execution of individual activities to achieve a common business goal. A process model (or workflow specification) formally describes the structure of the workflow and how these atomic activities are coordinated and enacted by software systems named Workflow Management Systems (WfMS) [1] or by software suites named Business Process Management Suites (BPMS). These generic software systems normally support both the definition and the enactment of process models.

Process modeling is the task of creating process specifications. Several formalisms (e.g. BPMN [2], BPEL [3], UML [4], YAWL [5]) have been suggested for modeling business processes from various perspectives and for various purposes. The notion of perspectives in process modeling was addressed by Jablonski and Bussler [6]. More recently, the Workflow Pattern Initiative [7] reframed the notion of process modeling perspectives via a series of workflow pattern frameworks.

The various pattern frameworks from the Workflow Pattern Initiative provide a collection of generic recurring process constructs. Each pattern framework captures a different perspective such as control [8, 23], data [9], resources [10], and exceptions [11]. One important perspective missing from this list is the temporal perspective.

Time is a critical dimension of process modeling as it is directly related to customer satisfaction and cost reduction. The speedy delivery of goods or services has a direct impact on customer satisfaction. Furthermore, time optimization is often a very effective cost reduction strategy for an organization.

The temporal perspective contributes to both the definition and the enactment of a workflow specification. When defining a workflow, the temporal perspective allows the modeler to explicitly specify temporal constraints and dependencies to ensure that all temporal requirements of the process are met. At enactment time, the temporal perspective of the workflow specification leads to the ability to precisely schedule a process and its resources.

We characterize the temporal perspective of process modeling by providing a series of generic recurring temporal constructs. This characterization is independent of any specific modeling formalism or approach. We precisely define each temporal construct and when possible provide a formal temporal account of these constructs based on Allen's interval algebra [12]. Allen's interval algebra is the most popular in Artificial Intelligence. Although the management of time in the context of business processes has been studied (e.g. [13, 14, 15, 16, 17, 18, 19, 20, 21, 22]), previous work does not address all the temporal constructs studied in this paper. Furthermore, although Allen's interval algebra has been applied to many application areas, it has not received much attention in the business process community. To the best of our knowledge, only Lu et. al. [22] use Allen's algebra as the basis for flexible business process execution via constraint satisfaction.

Our characterization of the temporal perspective for workflow specifications provides a basis and objective means to evaluate the temporal expressiveness of various formalisms and tools. Also it opens the way to the integration of formal validation tools, such as constraint satisfaction or theorem proving systems, to verify the temporal satisfiability of the workflow specification.

The remainder of this paper is organized as follows. After providing a brief overview of Allen's interval algebra, we present our characterisation of the temporal perspective via various temporal constructs. We first identify and define the temporal components that capture the elapsed time occurring during the enactment of a process or an activity and then introduce Temporal Dependencies and Constraints. As an example of the application of the proposed framework, we present a brief discussion of the suitability of BPMN and Gantt Charts (as portrayed by Microsoft Project) for business process modeling from the temporal perspective.

2 ALLEN'S INTERVAL ALGEBRA

The most popular temporal reasoning approach in Artificial Intelligence is due to Allen [12]. Allen's approach is based on intervals and the 13 possible binary relations between them. The first relation is "precedes" which is represented by the letter "p". Interval A precedes interval B if A ends before B starts, and is written as "A{p}B". If A precedes B, then it is also the case that B is preceded by A. This inverse relation for precedes, "preceded by", is represented by "pi". The precedes relation is drawn in the top left of figure 1. This precedes diagram represents both "A{p}B" and "B{pi}A".

The other relations are meets (m), overlaps (o), during (d), starts (s), finishes (f), and equals (e). As with precedes, each of these relations has an inverse which is represented by appending an "i" to the relation symbol: mi, oi, di, si, and fi. The inverse of equals is equals. We refer to the 13 relations by their basic labels and they are all shown in figure 1.

Allen's interval relations are mutually exhaustive. For example, given two intervals, exactly one of the 13 relations will hold between them. It is impossible to have none or, two or more relations true between two temporal intervals.

Often, there is uncertainty as to exactly which relation holds between two intervals. For example, supper may be before or after going to the movies. We write this as: (supper p movies) xor (supper pi movies). Since exactly one of "p" or "pi" will be true, we use an exclusive-or (i.e., "xor"). A shorthand notation for the above formula is: supper{p,pi}movies. In general, the relation between two intervals is allowed to be any subset of I = {p,pi,m,mi,o,oi,d,di,s,si,f,fi,e} including I itself.

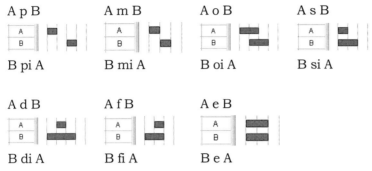

Fig. 1. Allen's 13 relations

We extend Allen's approach with points. We represent a temporal interval A by its endpoints written as (A-, A+). For example, the interval A = (1, 10) has a left endpoint A- = 1, and right endpoint A+ = 10. All intervals are convex (i.e., there are no gaps in the interval). We define the function *length(A)* to be the length of interval A.

The underlying temporal structure is assumed to be discrete, linear, and totally ordered. An example of such a structure is the integers.

3. THE TEMPORAL PERSPECTIVE

In this section, we introduce generic recurring temporal constructs from the temporal perspective and precisely define each temporal construct. When possible, we capture their temporal semantics with one or more logical formulas. This serves as a template for representing the general constructs.

In our formulas, we use the convention that capital letters, except for I, are constants and represent the specific temporal intervals during which activities take place. For example, the constant A represents the unique temporal interval over which the activity labeled A takes place. If activity A happens before activity B we write A{p}B.

Recall that I is not an activity, and represents the set of 13 possible interval relationships. For example, if a construct does not place any restrictions on activities C and D, we can write CID.

Variables range over temporal intervals and are specified with Greek letters (e.g., α, β).

We consider processes and subprocesses to be compound activities (i.e., they can be broken down into lower levels of detail through a set of sub activities [2]). Assume a process or subprocess A contains activities A_1, A_2, ..., A_n. Each activity A_i occurs during A:

$$A^- \leq A_i^- \leq A_i^+ \leq A^+ \qquad (1)$$

Non trivial processes may contain many activities which depend on one another. We will refer to the process or activity that depends on the other process or activity as the *Successor*, and the process or activity it depends on as the *Predecessor*.

During its enactment, a process or an activity will be instantiated and will take place over a certain period of time. We often refer to a process instance as a *Case* and to an activity instance as a *Task*. We represent the Case or Task instantiation, start and completion times with the constants *instantiation-time*, *start-time* and *finish-time* respectively. Note that these constants represent a time point and not an interval.

We now introduce a series of temporal components of interest from the temporal perspective. The 31 temporal constructs are shown in Table 1. The last two columns will be discussed at the end of the paper. In the following subsections, we precisely define each temporal construct and when possible, provide a logical specification using Allen's algebra.

Table 1. Expressing the temporal perspective in BPMN and MSProject. ☑ Directly expressible. ◪ Indirectly expressible. ? Inconsistent documentation. A blank entry represents not expressible.

Category	Code	Name	BPMN	MSProject
Time Points	ATP	Absolute Time Point	☑	☑
	PTP	Periodic Time Point	☑	☑
	RTP	Relative Time Point	?	
Intervals	TT	Transfer Time		
	QT	Queue Time		
	WT	Wait Time		
	Lag	Lag Time	?	☑
	Lead	Lead Time		☑
	ST	Set Up Time		
	PT	Processing Time		☑
	VT	Validation Time		
	RT	Rework Time		
	DT	Downtime		
	Duration	Duration		☑
	Cycle	Cycle Time		
	Idle	Idle Time		
Interval Duration	MaxD	Maximum Duration		◪
	MinD	Minimum Duration		
	ED	Estimated Duration		☑
Dependencies	FS	Finish-to-start	☑	☑
	FF	Finish-to-finish		☑
	SS	Start-to-start		☑
	SF	Start-to-finish		☑
Inflexible Constraints	MSO	Must Start On		☑
	MFO	Must Finish On		☑
Flexible Constraints	ASAP	As Soon As Possible	◪	☑
	ALAP	As Late As Possible		☑
	FNET	Finish No Earlier Than		☑
	FNLT	Finish No Later Than		☑
	SNET	Start No Earlier Than	☑	☑
	SNLT	Start No Later Than		☑

3.1 TIME POINTS

When modeling a process, we usually need to specify time points or intervals of interest to the model. *Time Points* can be specified as *Absolute* (e.g., Tuesday April 11), *Periodic* (e.g., every Monday, 16:00hrs) [16] or *Relative* (e.g., 2 days after start).

3.2 INTERVALS

Interval size can either be explicitly specified as a duration, or implicitly derived from the interval's endpoints. In Figure 2, we depict generally accepted temporal components that capture the elapsed time occurring during the enactment of a sequence of activities or processes. Rectangles in Figure 2 represent temporal intervals. The other symbols (e.g., stars and arrows) represent time points. Note that the duration of the temporal components of a *Case* will be the sum of the durations of all the temporal components of its *Tasks*. In the remainder of this sub-section, we precisely define each temporal component in Figure 2 and present an axiomatization when possible.

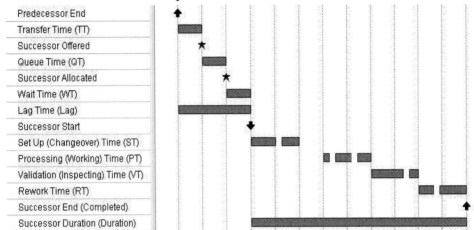

Fig. 2. Temporal components of a sequence of activities

At the point in time labeled *Successor Offered* in Figure 2, the Successor is offered to a single resource or to multiple resources [10]. We refer to the time between the end of the Predecessor and the offering of the Successor as the *Transfer Time*. The Transfer Time occurs over the interval TT. It may be the case that the Successor is offered at the same time as the Predecessor is completed. In such a case, there is no Transfer Time. If the Successor is offered to multiple resources, the Successor may spend time waiting for a resource to claim it. At which point in time, the Successor will become *Allocated*. The delay between the Successor being offered and the Successor being allocated is called the *Queue Time*. The Queue Time occurs over the interval QT. When the Successor is offered to a single resource, the offered time point and the allocated time point coincide and thus no Queue Time is incurred. The time between the Successor being allocated and it being actually started is called the *Wait Time*. The Wait Time occurs over the interval WT. It may be the case that the Successor is started at the same time that it is allocated, in which case no Wait Time is incurred. The *Lag Time* is the delay between the end of the Predecessor and the start of the Successor. It is the sum of the Transfer Time, Queue Time and Wait Time. The Lag Time occurs over the interval LAG. If there is a LAG, its length is equal to *Lag-Time:*

$$(\exists\ \alpha.\ \text{LAG}\{e\}\alpha) \rightarrow \text{length(LAG)} = \textit{Lag-Time} \qquad (2)$$

In formula (2) above, we use "LAG{e}α" in the antecedant to specify that the interval LAG is equal to an already existing interval α (i.e., LAG occurs). Technically, we cannot specify "LAG" by itself in the antecedent because it is a constant. If there is no LAG interval, then Lag-Time defaults to a value of zero:

$$(\neg\exists\ \alpha.\ \text{LAG}\{e\}\alpha) \rightarrow \textit{Lag-Time} = 0 \qquad (3)$$

We have similar formulas for the intervals TT, QT, and WT:

$$(\exists\ \alpha.\ \text{TT}\{e\}\alpha) \rightarrow \text{length(TT)} = \textit{Transfer-Time} \qquad (4)$$

$$(\exists\ \alpha.\ \text{QT}\{e\}\alpha) \rightarrow \text{length(QT)} = \textit{Queue-Time} \qquad (5)$$

$$(\exists \ \alpha. \ WT\{e\}\alpha) \rightarrow length(WT) = \textit{Wait-Time} \qquad (6)$$

$$(\neg\exists \ \alpha. \ TT\{e\}\alpha) \rightarrow \textit{Transfer-Time} = 0 \qquad (7)$$

$$(\neg\exists \ \alpha. \ QT\{e\}\alpha) \rightarrow \textit{Queue-Time} = 0 \qquad (8)$$

$$(\neg\exists \ \alpha. \ WT\{e\}\alpha) \rightarrow \textit{Wait-Time} = 0 \qquad (9)$$

The total lag time is the sum of the transfer, queue, and wait times:

Lag-Time = Transfer-Time + Queue-Time + Wait-Time (10)

If there is a transfer time, it happens at the beginning of the Lag interval:

$$(\exists \ \alpha. \ TT\{e\}\alpha) \rightarrow TT\{s,e\}LAG \qquad (11)$$

Since there may not be any transfer or wait time, the queue time can potentially occur anywhere within Lag:

$$(\exists \ \alpha. \ QT\{e\}\alpha) \rightarrow QT\{s,d,f,e\}LAG \qquad (12)$$

The wait time can only happen at the end of the Lag:

$$(\exists \ \alpha. \ WT\{e\}\alpha) \rightarrow WT\{f,e\}LAG \qquad (13)$$

Additionally, if we have transfer and queue times, they must follow each other:

$$(\exists \ \alpha, \beta. \ [TT\{e\}\alpha \ \& \ QT\{e\}\beta]) \rightarrow TT\{m\}QT \qquad (14)$$

Similarly for queue and wait times:

$$(\exists \ \alpha, \beta. \ [QT\{e\}\alpha \ \& \ WT\{e\}\beta]) \rightarrow QT\{m\}WT \qquad (15)$$

If there are transfer and wait times, and no queue time, then the transfer and wait times meet:

$$(\exists \ \alpha, \beta, \neg\exists \ \gamma. \ [TT\{e\}\alpha \ \& \ WT\{e\}\beta \ \& \ QT\{e\}\gamma]) \rightarrow TT\{m\}WT \qquad (16)$$

The *Set Up Time* is the time expended prior to performing the actual work (e.g. lookup files, setup machines, etc.). In manufacturing this time is often referred to as *Changeover Time*. The Set Up Time occurs over the interval ST. The *Processing Time*, also referred to as the *Working Time*, is the time actually spent doing the work at hand. The Processing Time occurs over the interval PT. In the course of completing the Successor, a resource may spend time reviewing or inspecting the work done (*Validation Time*) and may even correct or redo some of the work (*Rework Time*). In manufacturing, Validation Time is often referred to as *Inspecting Time*. Note that we are referring here to validation/inspection and rework done by the same resource within the same Case or Task. As opposed to, for example, having another resource inspecting the work, this would constitute another process or activity. The Validation Time and the Rework Time take place over interval VT and RT respectively. In the course of completing the Successor, it may be *Suspended* and then later *Resumed*. The *Downtime* is the time elapsed between the Successor being Suspended and then Resumed. The Downtime occurs over interval DT. Downtime can occur between the intervals ST, PT, VT, and RT. For example in Figure 2, there is Downtime between ST and PT. There can also be Downtime within the ST, PT, VT, and RT intervals. For example in Figure 2, each has been suspended and resumed at least once. There can be arbitrarily many Downtime sub-intervals within ST, PT, VT and RT. Therefore, all the intervals ST, PT, VT, RT, and also DT can potentially be non-convex (i.e., a collection of intervals). Non-convex intervals cannot be directly represented in Allen's algebra. Future work will involve extending the algebra to deal with these intervals.

The *Successor Duration* is the elapsed time between the *Successor Start* and *End* points. The *Successor Duration* occurs over the interval *Duration*. The length of *Duration* is the sum of the lengths of the intervals ST, PT, VT, RT, and DT. Since the latter intervals are all convex, we cannot at this time provide axioms for *Duration*.

We refer to the time between *Predecessor End* and *Successor End* as the *Cycle Time* (sometimes also called the *Elapsed Time*). The Cycle Time is the sum of the Lag Time and the Duration. The Cycle Time occurs over interval CYCLE:

(∃ α. CYCLE{e}α) & length(CYCLE) = *Cycle-Time*   **(17)**

The *Idle Time* is the sum of the time within the cycle that is not dedicated to processing the item (i.e., length(*Cycle*) – length(*PT*)). Once again, *Idle Time* can potentially be non-convex and we do not represent it in Allen's algebra.

Studies have shown that Processing Time -where actual work is performed- can be remarkably low in the total Cycle Time. In addition, only a small portion of that amount is actually value-added time. Hence, each of the temporal components enumerated above are often scrutinized, and the subject of temporal optimization. The Lean methodology is known for addressing problems of time reduction in various processes [24].

3.3 INTERVAL DURATION

Although interval duration can be inferred from the time points, temporal dependencies, and constraints of the workflow specification, it is sometimes simpler to directly specify the duration of an interval. Two aspects of interval duration are of interest as constraints, namely the Maximum and Minimum duration. For example, we may want to model statements like: the acceptance process must last (at least/at most) 6 days. A *Maximum Duration* (MaxD) or *Minimum Duration* (MinD) can be directly specified as a constraint for a process or an activity or any other temporal components (e.g., MaxD = 6 for the acceptance process).

Another aspect of interval duration that is often used for simulation or, as a threshold in process and activity monitoring is the *Estimated Duration* (ED). The Estimated Duration is not a temporal dependency or constraint that regulates the enactment of business processes but is nevertheless a ubiquitous aspect of the temporal perspective of workflow specification.

In the following subsections, we differentiate between *Temporal Dependencies*, which are temporalities implied by the interrelationship between processes or activities, and *Temporal Constraints* which are time values specified for a process or an activity. Temporal dependencies and constraints are in effect scheduling parameters that must be met by the enactment of the process specification.

Note that it is possible for a collection of processes or activities to have, or not have, interrelationships among them and thus no Temporal Dependencies. In either case, the processes or activities may or may not have Temporal Constraints specified.

3.4   DEPENDENCIES

A *Temporal Dependency* is a relationship between two processes or activities in which one process or activity depends on the start or finish of another process or activity in order to begin or end. There are four types of Temporal Dependencies between a Predecessor and Successor:

Finish-to-start (FS),

Start-to-start (SS),

Finish-to-finish (FF), and

Start-to-finish (SF).

Temporal Dependencies can be further constrained with delays called Lead and Lag Time. *Lag Time* which was introduced above (e.g., in Figure 2) can also be used as a constraint to specify a delay between the finish of the predecessor and the start of the successor. For example, we need a delay between the finish of the activity "Paint wall" and the start of the next activity "Hang pictures" to allow the paint to dry. A Lag time can be specified as a duration. For example, if "Paint wall" has a 4 day duration, specifying a Lag time of 1 day would result in a 1 day delay to allow the paint to dry before starting the activity "Hang pictures".

Lead Time causes the overlap of the successor and predecessor. In this case, the successor starts before the predecessor finishes. Lead time is useful when the successor requires a head start. It is usual to specify Lead time as negative lag, such as "-1" day. For example, for the activities "Construct walls" and "Plaster walls," we can use lead time to begin "Plaster walls" when "Construct walls" is half done.

As a constraint, Lag can be specified either by its length or relative to two tasks. In the following formulas, we represent the lag as a binary function. The function *lagBT(A,B)* returns the lag between tasks A and B. For example, a lag of 5 between tasks A and B is written as lagBT(A,B)=5. If lagBT(A,B) is negative, it represents a lead time.

Finish-to-start (FS)

A Finish-to-start temporal dependency between predecessor A and successor B means that B cannot start until A finishes. For example, the activity "Submit Paper" cannot start until "Write Paper" finishes. This is the most common type of temporal dependency.

$$\text{lagBT(A,B)=0} \rightarrow \text{A\{p,m\}B} \tag{18}$$

$$\text{lagBT(A,B)>0} \rightarrow \text{[[B$^-$ - A$^+$ $\geq$ lagBT(A,B)] \& A\{p\}B]} \tag{19}$$

$$\text{lagBT(A,B)<0} \rightarrow \text{[[B$^-$ $\geq$ (A$^+$ - | lagBT(A,B) |)] \& A|B]} \tag{20}$$

Start-to-start (SS)

A Start-to-start temporal dependency between predecessor A and successor B means that B cannot start until A starts. For example, if A is "Pour foundation" and B is "Level concrete," "Level concrete" cannot begin until "Pour foundation" begins.

$$\text{lagBT(A,B)=0} \rightarrow \text{A\{p,m,o,fi,di,s,e,si\}B} \tag{21}$$

$$\text{lagBT(A,B)>0} \rightarrow \text{[[B$^-$ - A$^-$ $\geq$ lagBT(A,B)] \& A\{p,m,o,fi,di\}B]} \tag{22}$$

$$\text{lagBT(A,B)<0} \rightarrow \text{[[B$^-$ $\geq$ (A$^-$ - | lagBT(A,B) |)] \& A|B]} \tag{23}$$

Finish-to-finish (FF)

A Finish-to-finish temporal dependency between predecessor A and successor B means that B cannot finish until A finishes. For example, if A is "Add wiring" and B is "Inspect electrical," "Inspect electrical" cannot finish until "Add wiring" finishes. Note that with a Finish-to-finish dependency, B can finish later than A's finish time.

$$\text{lagBT(A,B)=0} \rightarrow \text{A\{p,m,o,fi,s,e,d,f\}B} \tag{24}$$

lagBT(A,B)>0 → [[B$^+$ - A$^+$ ≥ lagBT(A,B)] & A{p,m,o,s,d}B]   (25)

lagBT(A,B)<0 → [[B$^+$ ≥ (A$^+$ - | lagBT(A,B) |)] & AIB]   (26)

Start-to-finish (SF)

A Start-to-finish temporal dependency between predecessor A and successor B means that B cannot finish until A starts. This temporal dependency type can be used for just-in-time scheduling up to a milestone or the project finish date to minimize the risk of an activity finishing late if its dependent activities slip.

lagBT(A,B)=0 → [A I-{pi} B]   (27)

lagBT(A,B)>0 → [[B$^+$ - A$^-$ ≥ lagBT(A,B)] & [A I-{pi,mi} B]]   (28)

lagBT(A,B)<0 → [[B$^+$ ≥ (A$^-$ - | lagBT(A,B) |)] & AIB]   (29)

3.5 CONSTRAINTS

Temporal Constraints can be specified to control the start or finish time of a Process or an Activity. These temporal constraints can be inflexible (*i.e.* tied to a specific value) or flexible (*i.e.* not tied to a specific value).

3.5.1 INFLEXIBLE TEMPORAL CONSTRAINTS

An *Inflexible Temporal Constraint* ties a process or an activity to a specific time point. The inflexible temporal constraints are:

Must Start On (MSO) and

Must Finish On (MFO).

Inflexible Temporal Constraints override any process or activity dependencies and restrict a process or an activity to a specified time. For example, an activity with a Must Start On (MSO) constraint for April 16 and a temporal dependency to another activity will always be scheduled for April 16 whether its predecessor finishes early or late. The inflexible temporal constraints are described below.

Must Start On (MSO)

This temporal constraint indicates the exact time (i.e., *Time-Point*) at which a process or activity A must be scheduled to begin. Other scheduling parameters such as temporal dependencies, lead or lag time and delay cannot affect scheduling the process or activity unless this requirement is met.

A$^-$ = Time-Point   (30)

Must Finish On (MFO)

This temporal constraint indicates the exact time (i.e., *Time-Point*) at which a process or activity A must be scheduled to be completed. Other scheduling parameters such as temporal dependencies, lead or lag time, and delay cannot affect scheduling the process or activity unless this requirement is met.

A$^+$ = Time-Point   (31)

3.5.2 FLEXIBLE TEMPORAL CONSTRAINTS

A *Flexible Temporal Constraint* does not specify a specific time point for a process or an activity, but rather imposes scheduling upper and lower bounds. The flexible temporal constraints are:

As Soon As Possible (ASAP),

As Late As Possible (ALAP),

Finish No Later Than (FNLT),

Start No Later Than (SNLT),

Finish No Earlier Than (FNET), and

Start No Earlier Than (SNET).

Flexible Temporal Constraints work in conjunction with temporal dependencies to make a process or activity occur as soon or as late as the process or activity dependency will allow. For example, a successor activity with an As Soon As Possible (ASAP) constraint and a finish-to-start dependency will be scheduled as soon as the predecessor activity finishes.

Constraints with moderate scheduling flexibility restrict an activity from starting or finishing before or after a specified time point. For example, a successor activity with a Start No Later Than (SNLT) constraint of June 15 and a finish-to-start dependency can begin any time its predecessor is finished up until June 15, but cannot be scheduled after June 15.

The flexible constraints are described in detail below.

As Soon As Possible (ASAP)

If an activity A is assigned an As Soon As Possible constraint, the enactment scheduler instantiates the activity as early as it consistently can. No additional time restrictions are put on the activity. This is the default constraint used (or assumed) by most process modelers when specifying workflows. Note that an activity will not be instantiated prior to the process (Case) being instantiated (i.e., *instantiation-time*).

minimize(A⁻) & A⁻ ≥ *instantiation-time* (32)

As Late As Possible (ALAP)

This constraint is analogous to the ASAP constraint, but relative to the end of the Case. If an activity A is assigned an As Late As Possible constraint, the activity is scheduled as late as it consistently can, given other scheduling parameters. No additional time restrictions are put on the activity. If activities are scheduled from the Case *finish-time*, the enactment scheduler will determine how late the Case can start and still finish by the specified Case *finish-time*.

maximize(A+) & A+ ≤ finish-time (33)

Finish No Later Than (FNLT)

This constraint indicates the latest possible time point (i.e., *Time-Point*) that activity A is to be completed. It can be scheduled to finish on or before the specified time point. A predecessor activity cannot push a successor activity with an FNLT constraint past the constraint time point.

A+ ≤ Time-Point (34)

Start No Later Than (SNLT)

This constraint indicates the latest possible time point (i.e., *Time-Point*) that activity A can begin. The activity can be scheduled to start on or before the specified time point. A predecessor activity cannot push a successor activity with an SNLT constraint past the constraint time point.

A- ≤ Time-Point (35)

Finish No Earlier Than (FNET)

This constraint indicates the earliest possible time point (i.e., *Time-Point*) that activity A can be completed. The activity cannot be scheduled to finish any time before the specified time point.

A+ ≥ Time-Point (36)

Start No Earlier Than (SNET)

This constraint indicates the earliest possible time point (i.e., *Time-Point*) that activity A can begin. The activity cannot be scheduled to start any time before the specified time point.

A- ≥ Time-Point (37)

4   EXPRESSING TEMPORALITIES IN BPMN AND GANTT CHARTS

In this section, we present a brief discussion of the expressibility of BPMN and Gantt Charts (as portrayed by Microsoft Project) for business process modeling from the temporal perspective.

4.1 BPMN

The Business Modeling Notation (BPMN) [2] is an OMG standard which allows workflow modellers to depict workflow specifications in an easily understandable graphical representation. Although BPMN has been shown to be quite expressive with respect to other perspectives [7, 25], it is limited in its ability to express temporal dependencies and constraints.

In a BPMN process diagram, a sequence flow depicts a Finish-to-start (FS) temporal dependency between a predecessor and a successor due to the fact that in BPMN an activity is instantiated and assumed started as soon as it receives the token from a sequence path. Although not explicit, the sequence flow implies an As Soon As Possible (ASAP) constraint on the successor.

Absolute and Periodic Time Points (ATP, PTP) are directly expressible in BPMN using the Timedate and TimeCycle attributes of Events with a Timer trigger. Although no BPMN attribute allows the expression of Relative Time Points (RTP), the BPMN specification provides example diagrams annotated with relative time points (e.g., Figure 3). Note that figure 3 does not capture the notion of a Finish No Later Than (FNLT) constraint as such, since a BPMN boundary Intermediate Event can only lead to an Alternate flow.

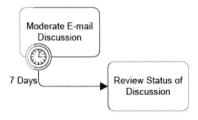

Fig. 3. BPMN example from p.44 of [2]

It is possible to depict a Start No Earlier Than (SNET) flexible constraint using an Intermediate Timer Event using the TimeDate attribute (see figure 4). Similarly, (as per above specification inconsistency) an expected delay, which corresponds to a Lag Time, can be depicted in BPMN using an Intermediate Event with a Timer Trigger using a duration or relative time point.

Fig. 4. A SNET and Potentially Lag Time in BPMN

4.2 GANTT CHARTS

Microsoft Project (MSProject) [26] is a product within the Microsoft Office Suite that allows the user to specify, plan and schedule various types of projects. MSProject is not a process modeling tool *per se*, as it cannot capture some of the basic constructs of process models such as decision (or-split) and loops. Nevertheless, MSProject can still be used to model certain simple classes of processes. For example, we can capture in MSProject all activities related to the opening of a new store. We can then use this MSProject file as a franchise template by instantiating the series of coordinated activities captured in the MSProject file for all future store openings.

A Gantt chart (as exemplified by MSProject) is an appropriate graphical representation for the temporal perspective. Many of the temporal dependencies and constraints can directly be depicted with a Gantt chart.

A summary of the temporal expressiveness of BPMN and MSProject, and a comparison between them appears in Table 1.

5. CONCLUSION & FUTURE WORK

Time is a critical dimension of business processes as it is directly related to customer satisfaction and cost reduction. The speed at which an organization delivers goods or services has a direct impact on customer satisfaction. Furthermore, time optimization is often an effective cost reduction strategy for many organizations. This important perspective is nevertheless lacking attention from current process standards initiatives.

In this paper, we provided a characterization of the temporal perspective of process modeling by providing a reference series of 31 generic recurring temporal constructs. For our temporal formalism, we chose Allen's which is the most popular in Artificial Intelligence. This characterization is independent of any specific modeling formalism or approach, and allows process models to be compared in a more meaningful manner on the basis of formal semantics.

Thus our characterization of the temporal perspective for workflow specifications provides a basis and objective means to evaluate the temporal expressiveness of various formalisms and tools. Also it opens the way to the integration of formal validation tools, such as constraint satisfaction or theorem proving systems, to verify the temporal satisfiability of the workflow specification.

As an example of the application of the proposed framework, we presented a brief discussion of the suitability of BPMN (an OMG specification) and Gantt Charts (as portrayed by Microsoft Project) for business process modeling from the temporal perspective. Gantt Charts have been found to be a suitable graphical representation for depicting the temporal perspective of process models.

These results have been used in a workflow management system which is currently under development. As a direct result of our deeper understanding of BPMN and MSProject's temporal semantics, we were able to semantically parse MSProject files as process model inputs and then visualise the process model via a BPMN depiction.

Allen's algebra only applies to convex time intervals (i.e., intervals containing no gaps). Future work will extend the algebra so that simple relationships can be specified between non-convex intervals. Specifically, we need to represent the relationship between two non-convex intervals. For example, one is before the other. Also, given two non-convex intervals, we need to represent the relationship between two sub-intervals where each is taken from one of the non-convex intervals. This will then allow us to represent the non-convex intervals Set Up, Processing, Validation, Rework, Down, and Idle times from Figure 2.

Future work will also involve using a constraint satisfaction system to automatically check the temporal consistency of a process. Given a process, we first capture its temporal attributes and constraints using the axioms presented in this paper. The resulting formulas are then input to the constraint satisfaction system which can detect inconsistencies. This exercise will also validate the soundness, feasibility, and usefulness of our proposed axiomatization.

REFERENCES

1. WFMC.: The Workflow Reference Model. WFMC-TC-1003, 19-Jan-95, 1.1, WfMC, (1995)
2. OMG.: Business Process Modeling Notation (BPMN) Specification. Version 1.0, OMG report: dtc/06-02-01, OMG, (2006)
3. OASIS.: Web Services Business Process Execution Language Version 2.0. OASIS report: wsbpel-specification-cd_Jan_25_2007, OASIS, (2006)
4. OMG.: Unified Modeling Language: Superstructure Specification. Version 2.1.1,. OMG report: formal/2007-02-03, OMG, (2007)
5. W.M.P. van der Aalst and A.H.M. ter Hofstede.: YAWL: Yet another workflow language. Information Systems, 30(4):245–275, (2005)
6. S. Jablonski and C. Bussler. Workflow Management: Modeling Concepts, Architecture, and Implementation. International Thomson Computer Press, London, UK, (1996).
7. Workflow Patterns home page, retrieved March 24, 2007: http://www.workflowpatterns.com/
8. van der Aalst, W.M.P., ter Hofstede, A.H.M., Kiepuszewski, B., Barros. A.P.: Workflow Patterns. Distributed and Parallel Databases 14(3) (2003) 5-51
9. Russell, N., ter Hofstede, A.H.M., Edmond, D., van der Aalst, W.M.P.: Workflow Data Patterns. QUT Technical report, FIT-TR-2004-01, Queensland University of Technology, Brisbane (2004)
10. Russell, N., ter Hofstede, A.H.M., Edmond, D., van der Aalst, W.M.P.: Workflow Resource Patterns. BETA Working Paper Series, WP 127, Eindhoven University of Technology, Eindhoven, (2004)
11. Russell, N., van der Aalst, W.M.P., ter Hofstede, A.H.M.: Workflow Exception Patterns. In: Dubois, E., Pohl, K. (eds.): Proceedings of the 18th International Conference on Advanced Information Systems Engineering (CAiSE'06). Lecture Notes in Computer Science, Vol. 4001. Springer-Verlag, Berlin Heidelberg New York (2006) 288-302
12. Allen, J.F.: Maintaining Knowledge about Temporal Intervals. Communications of the ACM 26 (1983) 832-843
13. C. Combi and G. Pozzi.: Architectures for a Temporal Workflow Management System. In Proceedings of the 2004 ACM Symposium on Applied Computing (SAC'04), Nicosias, Cyprus, (2004)

14. C. Combi and G. Pozzi.: Task Scheduling for Temporal Workflow Management System. In Proceedings of the Thirteenth International Symposium on Temporal Representation and Reasoning (TIME'06), IEEE, (2006)

15. C. Combi and G. Pozzi.: Towards Temporal Information Workflow Systems. In A. Olivé et al. (Eds.): ER 2002 Ws, LNCS 2784, pp. 13-25, Springer-Verlag, Berlin Heidelberg New York 2003.

16. C. Combi and G. Pozzi.: Temporal Conceptual Modelling of Workflows. In I.-Y Song et al. et al. (Eds.): ER 2003, LNCS 2813, pp. 59-76, Springer-Verlag, Berlin Heidelberg New York, (2003)

17. J. Eder, W. Gruber and E. Panagos.: Temporal Modeling of Workflows with Conditional Execution Paths, Database and Expert Systems Applications, Int. Conf., Springer, (2000) 243–253

18. J. Eder, and E. Paganos.: Managing Time in Workflow Systems. In Workflow Handbook 2001, Layna Fischer (Ed.), Future Strategies Inc., USA, (2001)

19. A. Meyer, S. McGough, N. Furmento, W. Lee, S. Newhouse and J. Darlington.: ICENI Dataflow and Workflow: Composition and Scheduling in Space and Time. In Proc of UK e-Science All Hands Meeting 2003, EPSRC, (2003)

20. A. Meyer, S. McGough, N. Furmento, W. Lee, M. Gulamali, S. Newhouse and J. Darlington.: Workflow Expression: Comparison of Spatial and Temporal Approaches. Workflow in Grid Systems Workshop, GGF-10, Berlin, (2004)

21. J.L. Zhao and E.A. Stohr.: Temporal Workflow Management in a Claim Handling Systems. In Georgakopoulos D. et al. (Eds.): Proceedings of the international joint conference on Work activities coordination and collaboration (WACC '99) . ACM Press, New York, NY, (1999) 187-195

22. R. Lu, S. Sadiq, V. Padmanabhan, and G Governatori.: Using a Temporal Constraint Network for Business Process Execution. In G. Dobbie and J. Bailey, editors, Proceedings of the 17th Australian Database Conference(ADC2006), volume 49 of Conferences in Research and Practice in Information Technology (CRPIT). Hobart, Australia, (2006)

23. N. Russell, A.H.M. ter Hofstede, W.M.P. van der Aalst, and N. Mulyar.: Workflow Control-Flow Patterns: A Revised View. BPM Center Report BPM-06-22, BPMcenter.org, (2006)

24. Lean Enterprise Institute home page, retrieved April 4, 2007: http://www.lean.org/

25. P.Wohed, W.M.P. van der Aalst, M. Dumas, A.H.M. ter Hofstede, and N. Russell.: On the Suitability of BPMN for Business Process Modelling. S. Dudstdarr, J.L. Fiadeiro, and A. Sheeth (Eds.): BPM2006, LNCS4102, pp161-176, Springer-Verlag, Berlin Heidelberg New York, (2006)

26. Microsoft Project, Online Documentation. Retrieved April 2, 2007. http://office.microsoft.com/enca/assistance/CH790018101033.aspx

How to Implement the Automation of the *Omnipresent* 'Distributed Treatments' in BPMS

Dr. Juan J. Trilles, AuraPortal BPMS, Spain

ABSTRACT

The **Distributed Treatments** represent an important part of the enterprise activities, being present in many procedures such as purchase cycles, customer requests, incoming service calls, claims handling, invoicing and many other, as well as in a good part of all processes related to the activities performed by Government Agencies.

Being so pervasive, the automatic handling of Distributed Treatments through Processes in a BPMS is a very desirable goal. Unfortunately, however, in many situations, a well designed automation requires the seamless participation of several linked processes of different kinds. But the automatic control of different processes in cohabitation, including the transference of selective information among them, is far from a trivial subject. As a matter of fact, it can carry a high degree of complexity, representing an insurmountable challenge for many BPMS product offerings.

INTRODUCTION

The concept of Distributed Treatments has been created to handle homogeneous pieces of information (called Lines) that, although generated by the same or similar processes, need for each one, specific treatments along their lifecycle, be within the same process or requiring the implication of several different interrelated processes.

One typical example of Distributed Treatments involves the processes generated by a customer asking for several different products in one single order. It frequently happens that part of the ordered goods are to be obtained (i.e. manufactured), through a given production line, other goods are to be obtained through different lines, others can be taken directly out of the warehouse and finally there may be goods that are to be obtained through subsequent purchasing to external suppliers. In other words, there may be different 'Supply Channels' and each requested good must undergo the treatments foreseen in the channel that corresponds to it. In order to automate the whole procedure, several flow threads with different paths must be automatically activated—one for each supply channel—and all phases in each thread must be efficiently handled including the control of expected and unexpected exceptions. And all that taking into account that, at the end, the goods requested must be shipped altogether to the customer.

Another typical example is a purchase cycle in which an employee requests goods or services to be supplied, either from the company warehouse or by means of orders sent to external providers, all that, subject to the mandatory approvals. This example is the one followed in the present work to illustrate the concepts and operational procedures defined and explained here.

GROUP OF FIELDS, CONTAINERS, CAUSAL AND DERIVATIVE PROCESSES

The term **Group of Fields (GF)** is used to define a set of fields that are treated together. They are handled by means of a table with columns and rows. Each column represents a field like price, quantity, line status, attached documents, a given calculation from other columns, etc., whereas each row represents one single register or entrance of the set of columns generated in the process. This register is called 'Line'.

The system must allow that, when a Group of Fields is used in a form (either a Task Form or a Message Form), not all the fields (columns) need to be shown. The process designer should decide which fields must appear in each case.

Also not all Lines (registers) need to be always present. Only those Lines that meet certain conditions as specified by the designer are to be shown in each particular instance. This filtering of the Lines contained in a Group of Fields is achieved by means of system tasks. The filtered contents are then lodged in **Containers**, each one containing the Lines that meet the corresponding filtering conditions.

A procedure covering complex distributed treatments generally involves more than one process. The procedure follows the life of each and every Line, within a Group of Fields that travels across a number of processes in order to receive the adequate treatments until the whole circuit or lifecycle of the Line is exhausted.

For example, let's imagine a request for a good or service that is originated in a given moment and that, together with other requests for other gods or services originated in different moments, must undergo the approval by a committee of officers that meet periodically to review a number of different requests. In this case, there must be a process for the requestor to enter the request (one process for each request) and a process of a different class that will receive the requests and, when considered appropriate, will present the set of requests received to the committee for revision and approval.

The Processes where the requests are generated are called the **Causal Processes**. The processes that receive flow deviations from Causal Processes are called **Derivative Processes**. Among the Derivative Processes, there are two different behaviors:

- **Single Derivative**, meaning that a process of this kind is generated each time the flow is deviated from the Causal Process in order to continue the treatments to be applied to the Line coming from the Causal Process.
- **Confluential**. In this case, one single process (already running) may receive successive Lines coming from different Causal Processes in order to administer the adequate treatments to the aggregated Lines.

Both behaviors are illustrated in the following figure.

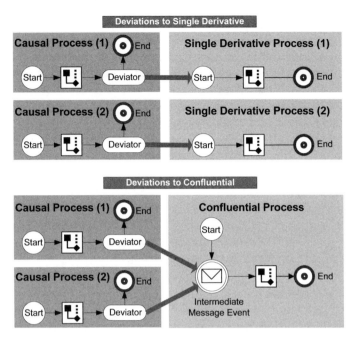

Also, the Confluential Processes may treat the arriving Lines in one of the two following manners.

- **Continuous Treatments**. The incoming Lines are treated one by one as they enter the Confluential Process that remains open all the time until the responsible decides to end it and substitute it by a new one of the same class.
- **Batch Treatments**. In this case, the Confluential Process does not treat the incoming Lines one by one but instead it waits until a number of them (a batch) from Causal Processes have entered, then closes new entrances and treats the batch altogether.

The following figure shows the classification of processes in relation to its role in Distribution Treatments.

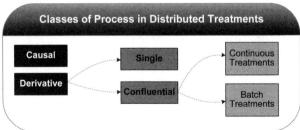

AN EXAMPLE

To illustrate the concepts related to Groups of Fields and their Containers in Distributed Treatments, an example of a Purchasing System is presented as follows.

Company: Modern Buildings Inc.

It is assumed that any Purchase cycle is initiated by a requestor (an employee with enough permission) that fills in a multi-line request form, containing mixed types of goods that may require different supply channels and different treatments depending on the nature of each good.

The Model must contemplate:
- The inclusion of two approvals (one related to the request's contents and another related to the monetary amount of the request).
- The procurement of the goods requested following the appropriate supply channel for each good, and
- The delivery of goods to the Requestor.

All that must be controlled within a global system that handles the requests, not in a linear manner but in a combination of series and parallel treatments including the grouping of Lines coming from different Causal Processes to optimize the company's resources and the permanent observation and control, for each Line, of the performance of all phases involved in the whole procedure.

OPERATIONAL PROCEDURES

The following assumptions are considered.
- All requests are made by means of a Goods Request form available to employees (requestors) in accordance to their access permission. When a Good Request form is filled in, a message is created by the system. This message triggers a procedure, involving different classes of process, for obtaining the requested goods and delivering them to the requestor. This frequently, although not always, implies the generation of purchasing orders to external suppliers.
- All purchases are carried out by the **Purchase Department**. However, there are three (they could be more) different purchasing procedures or supplying channels depending upon the kind of good requested:
  - **Regular Supply Channel**. This channel implies that the purchase order is sent to certified suppliers that regularly provide certain goods and therefore no Requests for Quotation (RFQ) sent to different suppliers are needed for purchasing actions. However, a minimum quantity of goods is necessary to issue a purchase order. One or more internal requests originated inside the company arrive to the Purchasing Department that will wait until the accumulation of requests reach the minimum number of units required for issuing the purchase order.
    - This channel is adequate for items like regular construction materials, PCs, cellular telephones, etc.
  - **Contractual Supply Channel**. This channel accomplishes the acquisition of the requested goods by means of a contract with a particular supplier previously selected from a set of candidates that have received a Request for Quotation (RFQ).
    - This channel is used for equipment and other goods that represent important expenditures and require comparisons among quotations from different suppliers.
  - **Warehouse Supply Channel**. This Channel provides goods to the Requestor directly out of the Warehouse.
    - This channel is used for goods like stationary and other office materials normally available from the warehouses.

CLASSES OF PROCESS INVOLVED

In this approach, one Causal Process and three Derivative Processes, one Confluential and two Single Derivative, are used as follows.

- Class: **Goods Request** (Causal Process). Every time an employee requires one or more goods he/she will fill in a form called 'Goods Request Form' that will initiate a Process of this Class.
- Class: **Regular Supply** (Confluential Process). One process of this class is permanently running and receiving, in an Intermediate Message Event, the requests (Lines) generated in the Goods Request processes (Causal Processes). In a given moment, the process stops admissions from Causal Processes and generates a new process of the same class. The decision about when to stop new admissions is made by the responsible of the Purchase Department. The requests from the Causal Process will arrive via the web service generated by a system task of the type DEVIATOR. An observer (the executor of a personal task, probably the Purchase Manager), will permanently watch in his 'Observatory Task' the new entrances of requests and the status of the phases (Ordered, Received, Delivered) undergone by them. From this observatory he will also make decisions about cancelling lines and stop admissions.
- Class: **Contractual Supply** (Single Derivative Process). A process of this kind will be initiated every time a request for goods that must be purchased following the 'contractual' supply channel (as explained above) is filled in within a Goods Request process (Causal Process). The Contractual Supply process will take care of the treatments foreseen for the Lines deviated from a single Causal process (Goods Requests). The creation of the Contractual process will be made through a DEVIATOR.
- Class: **Warehouse Supply** (Single Derivative Process). This process provides goods out of the warehouse when requested internally via a deviation from the Causal process. This is a Single Derivative process that behaves in a similar manner as the one explained above.

Depending on the type of good requested in the Causal Process, which in turn determines the supply channel, the flow will be deviated to one or another Derivative Process (Single or Confluential) as mentioned above.

The following image illustrates the inter-relation and deviations among the 4 class of processes.

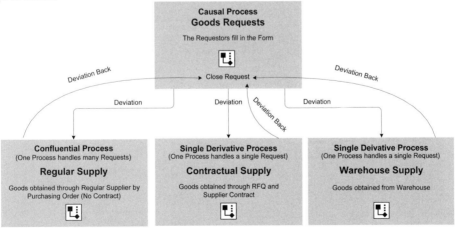

MODEL DIAGRAMS FOR THE FOUR CLASSES OF PROCESSES INVOLVED

The following four diagrams exhibit the models designed for each one of the four classes of process involved in this example.

It can be seen that the first class of process (Goods Requests) is the Causal Process and the other three are the Derivative Processes, one of confluential nature (Regular Supply) and two of single derivative nature (Contractual Supply and Warehouse Supply).

After the model diagrams are shown, brief explanations about the flow travelling inside each class of process will be found.

The explanations given are general, meant to give a shallow view of the approach proposed here. The space limitation inherent to a work of this nature prevents from entering into details about the definition of the objects constituting the process models, therefore, the focus has been placed on the operating structure and flow deviations among processes using Groups of Fields, Containers and System Tasks.

CLASS OF PROCESS MODEL: GOODS REQUESTS (CAUSAL)

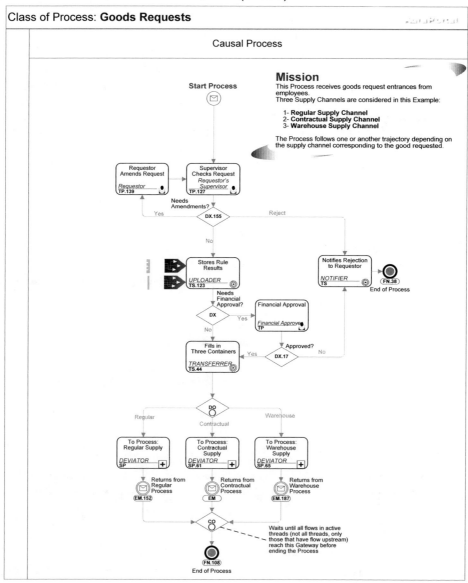

Class of Process Model: Regular Supply (Confluential, Continuous Treatments)

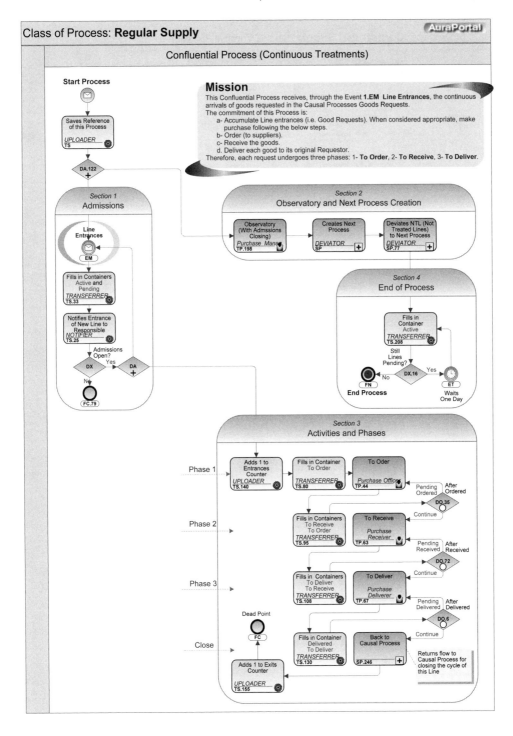

Class of Process Model: Contractual Supply (Single Derivative)

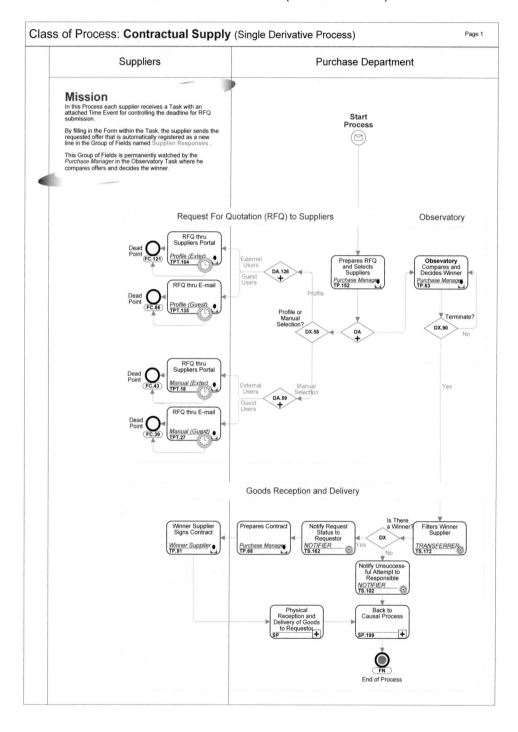

Class of Process Model: Warehouse Supply (Single Derivative)

Class of Process: Warehouse Supply

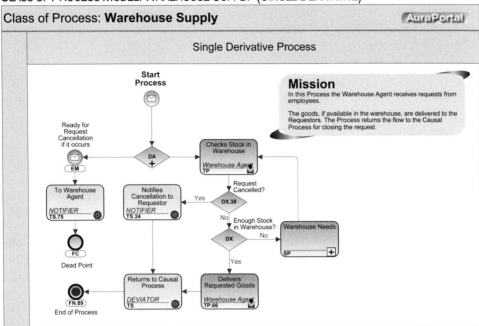

The explanations concerning the above models follow.

Goods Requests (Causal)

One process of this class is created when an employee with enough permission (Requestor) fills in the 'Request Form' entering one Line for each good requested. This is therefore the Causal Process. A quick explanation of the Diagram follows.

The flow reaches the Task 'TP.127" where the Supervisor of the Requestor checks the request and either approves it, rejects it or recommends amendments. Once the request is approved in its contents, it must undergo the financial approval in case the total amount of the request surpasses a limit specified in the Business Rule 'IR.100'.

If approved, the flow reaches the System Task 'TS.44' of type TRANSFERRER. This task prepares three containers: Regular, Contractual and Warehouse, each one defined to lodge, respectively, the Lines corresponding to goods to be obtained by each one of the channels: Regular, Contractual and Warehouse.

When the three Containers are prepared, the Gateway 'DO' splits the flow in one, two or three threads, one for each required channel, connected with the respective Subprocess that will deviate such flow to the corresponding Derivative Processes (Single or Confluential). When all Derivative Processes returns the flow back, the Process ends.

Regular Supply (Confluential, Continuous Treatments)

A Process of this Class is permanently open and ready to receive entrances of new Lines through the Message Event 'EM'. The entrances are made by means of DE-VIATORS from the Causal Process. In the present example, the DEVIATOR is the System Task 'TS.61' located in the Diagram of the Causal Process 'Goods Requests'.

When a new Line enters this Process, the Containers are filled by means of the TRANSFERRER 'TS.33' and a NOTIFIER ('TS.25') informs the Responsible (the Purchase Manager) about the Line Entrance. Then the flow reaches the Gateway 'DX' that checks whether the Line Admissions is still open or not.

If it is not open, the flow stops in the Event 'FC.79' and therefore the Message Event 'EM' will not receive new flow, preventing the Process from receiving new Lines. The just entered Line will not be treated in this Process. Instead it will be deviated later to the Next Process to undergo its treatment.

If the Line admission is open, the flow will reach the Gateway 'DA' which splits it into three branches: One will feed the Event 'EM' so that new Lines can be received from Causal Processes. Another one will carry flow to the Task 'TP.198' that allows the Observer to control the progress of all phases and also allows for closing the Line admissions when the Observer wishes so, hence triggering the Creation of a Next Process, the deviation of the Not Treated Lines (NTL) to such Process and the preparation of the End of the present Process. Finally, a third branch reaches the specific treatments to be applied to the Lines entered following the established Phases: To Order, To Receive and To Deliver.

The Process will end when, after closing the Line admissions, all Lines that have entered the Phases of treatment are duly treated, as can be seen in 'Section 4 End of Process' of the Diagram. Obviously the Process cannot reach the End Event suddenly when the executor decides so, because any Process End implies that all Tasks are immediately cancelled. This would produce the undesirable effect of preventing the unfinished Line Phases from continuing and finalizing their lifecycle.

Contractual Supply (Single Derivative)

A Process of this Class is created when the flow of the Causal Process is deviated to the Start Event in the 'Contractual Supply' Class of Process.

Once started, the Purchase Manager executes the Task 'TP.152' where he/she analyzes the requested items in the Lines deviated (the ones in the Container for Contractual Channel) and prepares the corresponding Request For Quotations (RFQ) that will be sent to each one of the suppliers that are invited to send an offer. The suppliers are selected, either manually or by indicating a 'Profile' that contains a previously defined selection of suppliers, including altogether external and guest users.

In case the Profile selection is used, the Process engine detects which users are external and which users are guests, and consequently creates one Task 'TPT.104' for each 'external user' through the External Portal corresponding to each user and also creates one Task 'TPT.135' for each 'guest user' using Email messages.

Whatever the selection method (manual or Profile), each supplier receives a Personal Task with attached Time Event (TPT) asking him/her to prepare the offer. When the supplier terminates the Task or the Time Event exhausts, the flow exits the Task and reaches a dead point. The documents with the offers are saved in the Panel and therefore they are available and accessible from other Tasks.

The 'TP.63' is an Observatory where the Purchase Manager controls all aspects related to the Line treatment, meaning the analysis of all documentation involved, including the RFQ sent to suppliers and their responses, the scoring of their offers and the final appointment of a winner.

Once the winner is appointed, the Process enters into its second part where the activities related to the purchase order, the contract with the supplier, the reception of the purchased goods and the goods deliverance to the Requestor are carried out. These activities are shown in the Diagram (objects: 'DX', 'TS.102' 'TS.162', 'TP.68', 'TP.91' and 'SP'). Once this Derivative Process has performed all its duties, the System Task 'TS.97' returns the flow to the Causal Process and reaches its end.

Warehouse Supply (Single Derivative)

When a request is made in the Causal Process and the flow is deviated to initiate a Process for handling the Warehouse Supply Channel, a Process of this Class is created. Therefore, there will be a Process of this Class for each request containing goods to be obtained through the Warehouse.

Once the Process starts, the flow splits in two threads, one to receive a message of cancellation in case it is produced, and another sending a personal Task to the Warehouse Agent for checking the availability of the requested goods in the warehouse.

If there is enough availability of the requested goods, they are delivered to the Requestor. Otherwise, the Subprocess 'SP' will take care of the procurement of the needed goods from the suppliers to refill the warehouse.

If there is a cancellation (promoted by a Message Form available for that purpose), the Warehouse Agent is informed and the process ends.

Conclusion

The automation of the pervasive Distributed Treatments in BPMS calls for a set of robust mechanisms involving flow deviations among processes of different classes and the corresponding transference of information. To do that, the use of Group of Fields and Containers is essential. The modern BPMS conception, where shared spaces for confluent processes are available and the use of web services for transferring information among different processes and databases is a must, may provide a right solution to this challenge.

The Representation of Dynamic, Context-Informed Workflow

H. Dominic Covvey, Donald D. Cowan, Paulo Alencar, William Malyk, Joel So, David Henriques and Shirley L. Fenton, University of Waterloo, Canada

ABSTRACT

In this chapter, we analyze the nature of dynamic workflow processes, show the limitations of classic techniques in representing these processes, and articulate a new model for representing and processing workflows and a framework for incorporating workflow context into the workflow representation.

INTRODUCTION

Although much has been done on the representation of workflow in business settings, two challenges are still the focus of current research: (1) the representation of workflow in highly variable (dynamic) settings, and (2) the incorporation of contextual knowledge into workflow representations in an explicit, declarative form. Properly addressing the latter challenge would enable the automated evaluation of workflows, i.e., the assessment of a workflow relative to objectives and constraints. Regarding the former, many processes in complex environments are dynamic, such as in healthcare, our focus. Dynamic environments typically involve considerable human interaction resulting in a high degree of variability in scenario outcome. In healthcare settings there are many decision makers (e.g., the patient, family, and physicians), kinds of decisions, events and a multitude of reactive, subsidiary workflows (e.g., those that deal with the occurrence of specific events) that often require a quick revision of the course of action. Operational and treatment protocols have been introduced in an attempt to regularize workflow, but the needs of care, the great variety of situations and individuals, the exigencies of the moment (such as equipment failure), and the nature of human beings frustrate attempts at regularization, often resulting in protocols being labeled as "cookbook medicine" and being abandoned. While event sequences in healthcare processes may abide by loose constraints, they are largely non-deterministic. Therefore, it is difficult, if not impossible, to fully prescribe workflow in such environments. Instead, workflow must be dynamic, self-adapting and evolving at run-time, in order to match the dynamicity of the environment.

Traditional workflow technology by its very (static) nature supports a finite set of scenarios. In fact, traditional workflow is understood to support, at best, the union of any/all atomic workflow patterns described by van der Aalst [1]. Examination of these patterns underscores the limited ability of traditional workflow technology to support highly dynamic environments. That is, the majority of workflow patterns that traditional workflow representations can support are unequivocally static in nature—they are prescribed at design-time and cannot deviate without generating an exception at run-time. Of the 20 workflow patterns described by van der Aalst, there exist six that implement some degree of run-time variability and could arguably be used to support some scenarios in dynamic environments.

However, available workflow platforms that support these patterns are often incomplete, unsatisfactory, or even non-existent. In fact, a feature comparison of 15 commercially available WFMSs reveals that no pattern listed above that *may* be able to address dynamic scenarios is supported by more than two of the fifteen reviewed products, and no single product supports all listed patterns. [1]

Other attempts at supporting high-dynamicity with traditional workflow include the use of *exception* and *compensation* constructs to handle run-time unpredictability and variability. This still requires some design-time prescription and is *semantically* flawed: *valid* run-time events (albeit unforeseen at design-time) are treated as *exceptions.*

Our work embraces the reality of the complexity and variability of healthcare processes and re-conceptualizes workflow as a dynamic process. We have studied and analyzed the nature of highly complex and variable care processes and have applied concepts from software engineering, database theory, work analysis, workflow engineering and physics towards the development of a radically new way of representing healthcare processes that we believe is able to address the true human-machine interactive nature and complexity of these processes. Furthermore, this representation can also be used for context-based reasoning.

In this chapter, we analyze the nature of dynamic workflow processes, show the limitations of classic techniques in representing these processes, and articulate a new model for representing and processing workflows and a framework for incorporating workflow context into the workflow representation.

ON THE CONCEPT OF DYNAMIC WORKFLOW

To arrive at a viable solution for the problem of dynamic workflow support, we must define exactly what "dynamic workflow" means. First, we distinguish the notion of workflow *scenario* (the real-world environment and processes) from workflow *application* (the computer-encoded form of a workflow scenario):

- A workflow scenario is the real-life, physical-world occurrence of what a workflow application attempts to model and manage.
- A scenario is what is *actually* happening—an occurrence (or execution) of a scenario is a scenario *instance.*
- An application is a *computer-model* of what is actually happening.
- Sometimes, the application *becomes* the scenario (or the two merge—e.g., electronic procurement scenarios automated by workflow applications).

By separating application from scenario, we can make these distinct claims:

1. Workflow scenarios range from static to dynamic.
2. Workflow applications are prescribed (pre-fabricated) or dynamic (assembled).
3. The workflow problem space is defined by the overlay of workflow applications on workflow scenarios.

Workflow scenarios range from static at one extreme to dynamic at the other (Figure 1). In static scenarios, all instances of scenario execution are substantially similar, both in terms of the work performed (the "what" and "why") and the specifics involved (the "who," "when," "where" and "how"). In dynamic scenarios, on the other hand, each instance of scenario execution performs the same work, that is, the goals ("what" and "why") of the work are satisfied, but the specifics of each instance may vary ("who," "when," "where," "how") from instance to instance. Therefore, we classify a workflow scenario as (highly) dynamic when there is a (high) degree of variability (in tasks, sequence, actors, etc.) and unpredictability from instance to instance, to achieve the same work.

Static Scenario   **Dynamic Scenario**

(Decreasing variability)   (Increasing unpredictability)

Figure 1: Static and Dynamic Scenarios

Traditional workflow technologies enable prescribed workflow applications. That is, workflow is prescribed at design-time to model a reasonably static scenario that, at run-time, is supported by the prescribed workflow application. Dynamic workflow applications, on the other hand, must dynamically assemble workflow at run-time, in response to the dynamic scenario that it models. As discussed, this is not enabled by traditional workflow technologies.

To rationalize the workflow problem space further, we need an additional classification of workflow applications. Specifically, workflow applications can be divided into two classes (see Figure 2):

Proactive workflow:
- Workflow application is *proactively applied* to scenario execution
- Application relies on design-time completeness for run-time efficacy—anything not defined during design-time becomes a run-time exception
- Examples: workflow automation, workflow facilitation—these are *scenario enablement* workflow applications and are proactive in nature

Retroactive workflow:
- Workflow application is *retroactively realized* from scenario execution
- Application relies on run-time analysis for *next-iteration* design-time efficacy—anything not captured during run-time will be omitted at *next* design-time
- Workflow is after-the-fact
- Examples: workflow mining, workflow reengineering—these are *scenario discovery* workflow applications and are retroactive in nature

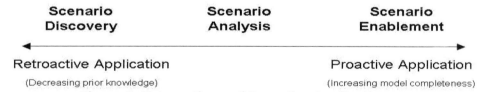

Scenario Discovery	**Scenario Analysis**	**Scenario Enablement**

Retroactive Application   **Proactive Application**

(Decreasing prior knowledge)   (Increasing model completeness)

Figure 2: Retroactive and Proactive Applications

Some workflow applications reside somewhere between. These are *scenario analysis* workflow applications and have both proactive and retroactive elements. Examples include workflow-based decision support systems (e.g. CareFlows in hospitals), process tracking, process diagnostics, and workflow simulation.

Now consider an overlay of the workflow application scale atop the workflow scenario scale as shown in Figure 3. This provides a clear view of the workflow problem space:

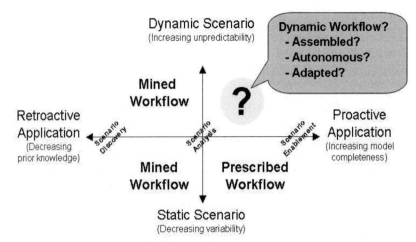

Figure 3: Overlay of Applications and Scenarios

This overlay of concepts reveals a relationship between workflow scenario and workflow application and suggests that *prescribed* workflow and *mined* workflow (both of which can be achieved by *traditional* workflow technologies) can address much of the workflow problem space:

Prescribed workflow:
- Workflow application run-time behaviour is defined entirely at design-time based on prior knowledge of the scenario
- Any scenario deviation is treated as an exception case

Mined workflow:
- Workflow application (model) is unknown at design-time and instead is derived from data collected during scenario execution (run-time), or after many instances of scenario execution
- Derived workflow could become prescribed workflow at next iteration of workflow development

However, the upper-right quadrant of Figure 3 (proactive workflow application in dynamic workflow scenarios) cannot be addressed by traditional workflow technologies. The overlay view suggests that *dynamic workflow* can be defined as the proactive application of workflow in highly-dynamic environments. More precisely, we define dynamic workflow (application) as a class of proactive workflow applications that use techniques beyond those of traditional workflow (i.e., prescription and mining) to enable (or model) highly dynamic workflow scenarios. We also suggest that dynamic workflow may perhaps be implemented by techniques such as run-time workflow assembly, autonomous workflow inference, or adaptive workflow (e.g. rules-based). The basis for these suggestions and potential solution designs are discussed throughout this chapter.

REPRESENTING AND EXECUTING DYNAMIC WORKFLOW AND CONTEXT

Workflow is usually described by connecting services or tasks in a programmatic format such as a workflow language, flowchart or other type of sequencing mechanism. Thus, prescribing a workflow in a dynamic environment could require a protocol or "program" of immense complexity as one tries to ensure that all possible choices and their sequencing are captured in advance. Further, changing such a protocol is extremely difficult manually or automatically. In addition, annotating the services with context is possible but not easily implemented. This section contains a description of an innovative approach to implementing workflow, which, based on experience to date, provides a way to support dynamic configuration and context.

The approach used in our research to capture workflow and include dynamic services and context, and which has been used to describe over 40 service-oriented information systems [2], is based on the work by Jackson and Twaddle [3]. Workflow is represented using an entity-relationship (E-R) model [4] which is then transformed into a relational database. Thus, the control structure and all the information about the services are captured in a data structure which can be easily modified and then either compiled or interpreted into a workflow "program." The Jackson and Twaddle approach is outlined and then extended to include dynamic relationships among tasks/services and context.

Entities

Following the Jackson/Twaddle model, the first step in producing an E-R workflow representation is to develop a data model in terms of entities that are central to the description of the business processes. In a medical laboratory context the data model could consists of entities such as admissions-clerk, patient, technician, physician, test-order and test-equipment to name a few examples. These entities have corresponding entries in the information system database related to the medical facility in which the laboratory is located.

Lifecycles, Stages and Services

Each entity in an operational information system has an associated lifecycle. Each lifecycle goes through a number of sequential stages and each stage contains a number of services or tasks that are applied to the entity. A simple example of a lifecycle is the one associated with an individual where the stages are birth, life and death and the tasks or services are related to each of those stages. Of course the life stage itself can be subdivided into stages (sub-stages) by decades or some other convenient criteria.

In a medical test situation a patient has a lifecycle as he/she proceeds sequentially from the admission stage, to the testing stage and finally to the interpretation stage where the results of the test are explained and decisions are made about further actions. At this point, the lifecycle in the medical facility for the patient ends as he/she is discharged or passed on to a new lifecycle for further testing or treatment. The diagram in Figure 4 provides an illustration of these relationships. Although not shown in Figure 4, services can be executed sequentially, conditionally or repeatedly. Parallel execution is also possible through the splitting (fork) and merging (join) of services.

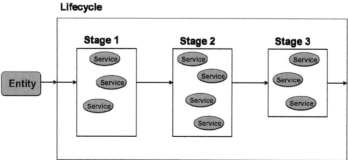

Figure 4: Workflow/Business processes as lifecycles, stages and services

All stages in a lifecycle must be completed, but not all tasks in each stage must be executed. For example, during the testing stage several different types of testing equipment could be chosen. Each task is associated with an equipment-type and represents the administration of a different test and thus only one task is chosen and completed. Although stages can not be skipped, they can contain a skip-this-stage task. For example, if a patient does not complete the admission stage, then skip-this-stage would be executed in all subsequent stages.

Tasks/services are interdependent in that the application of one service may have to wait for the completion of services in other stages or lifecycles associated with other entities. For example, if in the lifecycle associated with a piece of equipment the equipment is in use, then the testing service related to a patient lifecycle that uses this equipment may not be started.

Up to this point the services are all interconnected through control flow (sequence, condition, repetition, fork and join). However, it is possible to introduce dynamic services into the model that can be chosen based on the current context. These dynamic services are not directly connected into the control structure, but are chosen as the workflow progresses and the context is determined. For example, once a test is to occur, there may be several machines that could provide the needed testing service. Choosing the specific test-equipment could occur dynamically based on machine or operator availability, or type of test. This concept of dynamic execution of workflow is amplified as more details of the model are provided.

Workflow as an Entity Relationship and Database Model

Workflow or business process models can be represented as a program structure connecting services, but the lifecycles, stages, services and interdependencies can also be represented by an E-R model based on the diagram in Figure 4. Although not identical, entity-relationship models can be further mapped into a relational database where the concepts in the system (entity, lifecycle, stage and service) and the relationships among them each correspond to a table.

Each entity has one corresponding lifecycle (one-to-one); each lifecycle can have multiple stages (one-to-many) and each stage can have multiple services (one-to-many). The relationships among the services can further be annotated to include sequence (pre-conditions and post-conditions), choice, repetition, fork and join. Note that pre-conditions and post-conditions can be used with dynamic services to specify services that must be performed before or after the selected service.

Thus, except for the code associated with services, workflow is represented as a large data-structure. Note that the location of code related to the service can also be entered in the table or could be directly stored in the database as an embedded procedure. Such a data structure makes it possible to present the entire process in a graphical format, thus supporting a significant degree of visualization.

The relationship between lifecycles, stages, and services in a workflow or business-process model can be modified by changing a data structure rather than a program structure. Modifying workflow is easier, because the abstractions corresponding to the workflow or control structure are clearly identified. Another benefit of our approach is that end-users can easily be shielded from these details using a visual interface. In addition, E-R models can be easily represented by XML tagged structures thus allowing the development of a declarative domain specific language for describing workflow.

The declarative representation of the workflow can be transformed into other representations such as BPEL [5], UML [6] or XMI [7] through transformations defined in languages such as XSL/XSLT [8]. This approach has been demonstrated in [9] where XML-based declarations for agents were transformed into code written in the programming language C.

This workflow model associates services with entities similar to object-oriented approaches where methods are associated with objects. The difference is that the services are also related to each other through a workflow structure and the services are loosely coupled to each other and to the related entity.

Complex Entities

To this point we have described workflow in terms of entities, lifecycles, stages, and tasks or services. Each entity can itself be quite complex. For example, if the entity is a house, it can be composed of other entities such as floor, walls, roof, appliances, rugs and furniture. The entities used to compose the house depend on the function of the information systems being developed. For example if the system describes building the house, then the entities would be floor, walls, roof, etc, whereas furnishing the house would involve rugs and flooring, furniture, and appliances. Each entity composing the house would have its associated services and there would be dependencies specified between these services. We do not discuss this composition approach further in this paper but just describe it to show how a workflow-based information system might be constructed.

Making the Workflow Model into an Operational System

Workflow has now been converted to a data structure where only one type of component, the atomic service or task, encapsulates the work to be done. The remainder of the data structure captures the relationships and dependencies among tasks. We now define a workflow machine or engine (compiler or interpreter) that is capable of traversing the workflow data structure in the proper sequence including dealing with dependencies. As the machine travels over the data structure, it can either interpret, or compile the data in the structure into code which can then be launched once the entire compilation is complete.

The services can be manual, meaning there is a requirement for human intervention as in completing a form, or automatic as in processing a credit card payment. The workflow engine shown in Figure 5 is driven by a set of rules. The rules, which produce more complex behaviors, are composed from three basic forms of command for the workflow engine. By simple changes to the semantics of these three rules, the engine can act either as an interpreter or compiler. The workflow that is being described in this paper would be interpreted because at least some of services are dynamic; they are chosen based on current context.

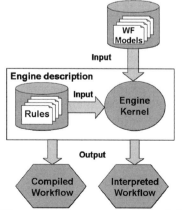

Figure 5: The workflow engine/machine

Adding Context to Workflow

Workflow service models can be applied to connect services and express service flows [10], and to determine a transition from one service to another according to contextual information that is dynamically generated from various sources.

Context is defined in the Merriam-Webster dictionary as "the interrelated conditions in which something exists." This definition implies that this concept is only meaningful with respect to an entity. An entity is, in general, an object, person, or place considered relevant to the interaction between user and application. For our purposes, context depends on the user, his/her environment and potentially an observer [11]. In our approach, context can be seen as any information that can be used to characterize and help interpret the situation in which the workflow execution is taking place, including the information concerning user and service interaction.

Contexts can be generally classified under several categories. Jang and Woo [12], Munoz et al. [13] and Satyanarayana [14] describe examples of different context classifications.

Some general examples of context are: identity, spatial information (e.g., location, orientation, speed, acceleration), temporal information (e.g., time of the day, date, and season of the year, schedule, agendas, availability of equipment, personnel), environmental information (e.g., temperature, air quality, and light or noise level), social situation (e.g., who you are with, and people that are nearby), resources that are nearby (e.g., accessible devices, and hosts), physiological measurements (e.g., blood pressure, heart rate, respiration rate, step count, muscle activity, and testing results), activity (e.g., talking, reading, walking and running), financial information (e.g., budget restrictions), and legal constraints (e.g., regulations to be followed) [15].

Specifically, workflow context can be described as attributes for entities that can then be associated with the service applied to those entities, and can be defined, more formally, as a general tuple that may include the following elements:

<User-Information, Spatial-Information, Temporal-Information, Environmental-Information, Application-Information, Social-Information, Resource-Information, Physiological-Information, Activity-Information, Financial-Information, Legal-Information, Business-Deliverables>.

The context attributes constrain each step of the workflow execution. For example, depending on the temporal information concerning the availability of a specific piece of equipment, this equipment may or may not be used in a workflow to perform certain tests.

Capturing workflow as a data structure supports the addition of context services. Context can be characterized as attributes of the services in the accompanying database table. Availability of equipment can be characterized as a table containing repetitions of each equipment identifier with the different time intervals where the equipment is available or unavailable. A similar table can be created for personnel such as radiologists or technicians. Budget information can be associated with personnel and equipment and incremented or decremented to indicate how much has been spent for a specific test. Of course such budget information can be related back to the departmental or organizational budgets which are the contexts for this budget.

Documentation about safety regulations or business processes associated with equipment could be displayed automatically when the equipment is selected for operation. As equipment or personnel are selected for operation, a record can be kept which forms a history. Such an account could be used to monitor and ensure that the load among equipment and people is shared equitably or in the case of equipment could be used to indicate a need for maintenance.

Thus each stage can be decomposed into services whose sequence is fixed, and into those chosen based on context. The workflow engine described in an earlier section can account for this context.

TOWARDS SUPPORTING DYNAMIC WORKFLOW

To practically support dynamic workflow, we need to be concerned with how scenario dynamicity impacts workflow application and what is needed to support increasing variability and unpredictability. Based on our definition of dynamic workflow, we defined three top-level requirements for dynamic workflow support atop traditional workflow technology:

1. Design-time representation of variability and unpredictability— introduction of a "dynamic section" construct that allows design-time stochastic workflow model and workflow mining configuration
2. Run-time integration and invocation of services for event collection and analysis (based on workflow mining configuration) and workflow inference (based on stochastic model) within dynamic sections
3. Seamless run-time mode-switching between prescribed sections (traditional) and dynamic/assembled sections

While it is feasible to augment extensible *traditional* workflow technologies to address these three requirements (and therefore support dynamic workflow), there is ongoing debate over the merits of extending a traditional workflow platform or language to support dynamic workflow versus building a new platform from the ground-up with dynamic workflow as a core capability. One perspective is that building atop existing commercial platforms (such as BPEL-based products or Microsoft's Windows Workflow Foundation) may help accelerate adoption of workflow technology in highly dynamic environments, such as those in Healthcare.

> "Only when a standard workflow language does not meet requirements of a scientific workflow and such a language cannot be extended to meet requirements (or extensions are too complicated) should a new workflow language be created." [16]

A WORKFLOW ENGINE FOR EXECUTING DYNAMIC WORKFLOW

To address the representation of dynamic Real World processes (i.e., a *workflow scenario*, as defined in the section "On the Concept of Dynamic Workflow"), we have designed an approach involving service selection and real-time composition of services into workflow instances (See Figure 6). In this approach, we consider the activities that are carried out within a workflow to be services. Example services include such activities as a receive-patient service, a register-patient service, a produce-report service, etc. These services are pre-defined and may themselves be composed of more granular services. These services can be provided by a services-server on request by the workflow generation engine. Services have pre-conditions (other services that must be executed before this service) and post-conditions (other services that must be executed after this service).

To choreograph these loosely-coupled services that comprise a workflow, a service selection unit is incorporated that can select services both statically (sequential prescription) and stochastically (by way of inference). An inference-engine based service selection mode selects services (the next activity in a workflow) based on the decisions of the participants in a workflow as well as on historical data collected from past instances. If a selected service indicates that it must be preceded by another service, this other service will be selected and executed, otherwise the first service will be executed, and so on. In this probabilistic model, services are selected at run-time based on three key criteria: available contextual knowledge of the *current* workflow instance, statistical knowledge collected and mined from *previous* workflow instances, and composition rules and constraints—a rules-engine. This rules-engine allows enforcement of service sequencing based on temporal dependencies, data availability, business rules, and role restrictions.

As mentioned, services can also be sequentially invoked, thus providing backwards compatibility with classic prescribed workflow models. A workflow instance continues selecting services (prescriptively and stochastically) until it has addressed all the required services to complete the process. In highly dynamic environments, workflows may possibly enter a state where the next appropriate activity is absolutely unknown and cannot be inferred. This may occur during times of process discovery or reengineering within an organization. To address this, we incorporate workflow mining services. A workflow mining service can record data from the current workflow instance and subsequently examine previous instances of whole workflows to guide the selection of services until participant decisions redirect the workflow. This forms a closed-loop feedback cycle with the inference-engine used for service selection.

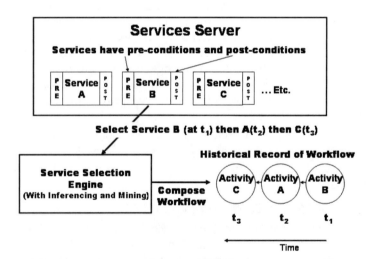

Figure 6: Service Selection and Workflow Composition

WORKFLOW VISUALIZATION

Classic workflow representation techniques typically provide the ability for a designer to step through workflows. This commonly manifests itself in the ability to traverse flowcharts or process maps. In reality workflow occurs in a spatial environment that has known properties (room capacity, hallway flow rate, etc.) that can impact its execution. This information is not available in current representation techniques, and would be of use in analyzing workflow execution via simulation (e.g., to determine queue lengths and relate it back to room capacity) in order to optimize it. Given this, we recognized that the spatial environment is a context of workflow and developed an approach whereby workflow descriptions are projected into a spatial environment. This has involved the selection of a leading object-oriented representation of spatial environments (IFC, http://www.iai-international.org/Model/IFC(ifcXML)Specs.html) and the integration of a workflow representation tool with the Arena simulation package (http://www.arenasimulation.com). This will support the presentation of workflows mapped into a floor plan, and the processing of workflow characteristics using Arena's simulation processing tools.

VISUALIZATION OF WORKFLOW AND REPRESENTATION OF SPATIAL CONTEXT

Classical representations (flow charts, process maps) provide intuitive workflow visualization but provide few options for describing the relationship between a workflow and its physical environment. This relationship places constraints on workflow, such as the throughput limitations and holding space capacities. Understanding these constraints and their relation to the execution of workflow is valuable in visualization and helpful when analyzing the effectiveness of workflows in different environments.

The physical environment is a contextual dimension of workflows carried out "in the real world". Accordingly, such workflows have spatial requirements. To model these we require a representation of the environment. Two predominant representations: geometric data models (GDMs) and building data models (BDMs). The majority are GMDs; objects defined as collections of Cartesian points and lines. GDMs are limited analytically as the objects possess no properties aside from geometric information such as the load bearing limits of walls. Any additional properties added to objects in GDMs are done ad hoc with no common rules. On the other hand, BDMs utilize an object-oriented approach in which building objects are defined as common objects (walls, doors, spaces, etc.) with defined property sets. Though geometric coordinates are one of these property sets, the focus of BDMs is on defining the space as a collection of objects rather than just lines and points. In general BDMs offer better interoperability.

A building data model of particular interest is the Industry Foundation Classes (IFC). IFC is a data standard that was created to provide an alternative to proprietary object-oriented vendor models. It has been incorporated into several commercial applications and has been used in projects by the US Army. The purpose of IFC is to define all possible objects involved in the design and construction phases of building a facility. Continual revisions to the standard are attempting to meet this goal and so the list of possible objects expands.

IFC, like most BDMs, defines facility objects as well as the unused space. Unused space refers to space in which the free movement of physical objects can occur as unconstrained by building objects that impose a physical barrier. The workflow is executed in this unused space or, as we have defined it, the work-available space.

The work-available space differs from the projection of the workflow onto the spatial environment. The work-available space and the workflow are separate entities and require separate definitions. A workflow exists as an abstract entity until it is executed at which time it gains real world properties. As an abstract entity it still possesses requirements that may be different from that of the facility it is to exist in. In other words, we cannot assume that the facility is ideal and matches the workflows; the spatial representation of the workflow and the work-available space are not necessarily equal.

Based on our definitions, the visualization of a workflow is a projection onto one of its dimensions. In this case, the physical characteristics of a workflow, such as activity-spatial requirements and size of objects traveling between processes, are a projection onto a facility space constrained by the space of rooms, hallways and doors. IFC was created for the architecture community for the purposes of design and construction of a facility, not to plan its future use. The incorporation of workflows into IFC required some consideration; workflows were defined in IFC using existing IFC elements.

Using simulation we can compare the properties of the workflow to the constraints of the facility. Based on the definition of space in IFC, we know information such as its capacity as defined by the physical limitations of the space. This can be compared to the output from the simulation of the expected queue sizes under various conditions to observe the expected interaction between workflow and the environment. In this approach, the simulation output can be compared to facility design specifications to determine the viability of a workflow in a given space.

RELATED WORK

Several approaches presented in the literature introduce context and situation models. Costa et al. have introduced a context model and a rule-based approach to detect high-level situations that are specified using a combination of UML class diagrams and OCL constraints [17]. Work on ontology-based context modeling and reasoning using OWL is presented in [18]. Approaches to the development of context-aware and pervasive applications were described in [19]. In contrast to these approaches, our focus is on context-oriented dynamic workflows as services and on a database-oriented realization of a service framework.

A number of approaches to the representation and realization of dynamic workflow have been also proposed. Workflow languages such as BPEL4WS [20], WSFL [21], and XLANG [22] do not consider context information as transition constraints of services.

A situation-adaptable workflow system was described in [23] that can support service demands generated dynamically in a business process. This system can dynamically handle a user's requests using open-ended adaptation techniques. Our approach relies on context attributes to constrain service executions within a database-oriented realization.

FollowMe is a framework that combines a workflow-based application model and a context model based on the ontology concept [24]. uFlow is a ubiquitous workflow framework to support context-aware service based on workflow scenarios [25]. These two frameworks do not consider a method to handle user's service demands during service processing. An approach for dynamic adaptation for a user's situation information in a context-aware workflow system is described in [26, 27]. The focus of this approach is on dynamic workflows restricted by a user's situation attributes in ubiquitous computing applications.

RELEVANCE AND VALUE

There is growing awareness of the importance of capturing, understanding, and improving workflow if the benefits of investments in information and communications technologies are to be realized. Classic, rigid workflows, however, are too constraining to address the complexity and variability of workflows in healthcare environments. In order to be able to address the dynamic nature of healthcare workflows, a means of representing this type of workflow in "computationally tractable" form is essential. This work will ultimately enable us to approach our goal of being able to represent the full richness of workflows like those in health care, at least semi-automatically to evaluate workflows and to optimize them within the many constraints in which they are performed. Finally, the approach we have used to representing healthcare workflow has provided a key capability in developing new systems architectures that enable the reduction of barriers to end-user adaptation of systems to satisfy changing requirements.

ACKNOWLEDGEMENTS

This work has been support by the Natural Sciences and Engineering Research Council of Canada (NSERC) and by Agfa. The unflagging support of the Computer Systems Group at the University of Waterloo is also gratefully acknowledged.

REFERENCES

1. van der Aalst W.M.P. *et al.*, "Workflow Patterns". *Distributed and Parallel Databases,* Volume 14, Issue 1, pp. 5-51.

2. D.D. Cowan et al "Software System Generation from an Enterprise Service Model" David R. Cheriton School of Computer Science Report (CS-2007-04) http://www.cs.uwaterloo.ca/research/tr/2007/(last accessed May 21, 2007).

3. Michael Jackson and Graham Twaddle "Business Process Implementation: Building Workflow Systems." Addison-Wesley, 1997.

4. Chen, P. P.-S. "The Entity-Relationship Model: Toward a Unified View of Data", ACM Transactions on Database Systems, 1, Vol 1, pp 9-36, 1976.

5. Business Process Execution Language for Web Services version 1.1 http://www-128.ibm.com/developerworks/library/specification/ws-bpel/ (last accessed May 21, 2007).

6. Rumbaugh, J., Jacobson, I., Booch, G., The Unified Modeling language Reference Manual Addison Wesley 2004.

7. XML Metadata Interchange (XMI), v2.1 (last accessed May 21, 2007) http://www.omg.org/technology/documents/formal/xmi.htm.

8. Extensible Stylesheet Language (XSL) http://www.w3.org/Style/XSL/ (last accessed May 21, 2007).

9. P.S.C. Alencar, T. Oliveira, D.D. Cowan, D. Mulholland. "Towards Monitored Data Consistency and Business Processing Based on Declarative Software Agents, Software Engineering for Large-Scale Multi-Agent Systems—Research Issues and Practical Applications," Garcia, A., Lucena, C. et al. (Eds), Lecture Notes in Computer Science (LNCS), vol. 2603, pp. 267-284, Springer, 2003.

10. Workflow Management Coalition: The Workflow Reference Model, Document number TC00-1003, 1995.

11. Bazire, M., Brézillon, P., Understanding Context Before Using It, CONTEXT 2005, Lecture Notes in Artificial Intelligence, vol. 3554, pp. 29-40, 2005.

12. Jang, S., Woo, W., Ubi-UCAM, A Unified Context-aware Application Model, Lecture Notes in Artificial Intelligence, vol. 2680, pp. 178-189, 2003.

13. Munoz, M. *et al.*, Context-aware Mobile Communication in Hospitals, IEEE Computer, vol. 36, no. 9, pp. 38-47, 2003.

14. Satyanarayana, M., Challenges in Implementing a Context-aware System, Editorial, IEEE Transactions on Pervasive Computing, pp. 2-4, July-September 2002.

15. Murthy, V., Krishnamurthy, E., Contextual Information Using Contract-Based Workflow, Proceedings of the Second Conference on Computing Frontiers, pp.236-245, ACM Press, 2005.

16. Taylor, I.J. *et al.*, *Workflows for e-Science,* London: Springer-Verlag London Limited, ISBN 1-84628-519-4, pp. 213, 2007.

17. Costa, P. *et al.*, Situation Specification and Realization in Rule-Based Context-Aware Applications, DAIS 2007, International Federation of Information Processing, Lecture Notes in Computer Science, vol. 4531, pp. 32-47, 2007.

18. Wang, H. *et al.*, Ontology-based Context Modeling and Reasoning using OWL, Proceedings of the 2nd IEEE Annual Conference on Pervasive Computing and Communications Workshops (PERCOMW04), pp. 18-22, 2004.

19. Henricksen, K., Indulska, J., Developing Context-Aware Pervasive Computing Applications: Models and Approach, Journal of Pervasive and Mobile Computing, vol. 2, no. 1, pp. 37-64, Elsevier, 2006.

20. Andrews, T., Curbera, F., Golan, Y., Business Process Execution Language for Web Services, BEA Systems, version 1.1., 2003.

21. Leymann, F., Web Services Flow Language (WSFL 1.0), IBM, 2001.

22. Thatte, S., XLANG Web Services for Business Process Design, Microsoft Corporation, 2001.

23. Vieira, P., Rito-Silva, A., Adaptive Workflow Management in WorkSCo, 16th International Workshop on Database and Expert Systems Applications (DEXA05), pp. 640-645, 2005.

24. Li, J., *et al.*, FollowMe: On Research of Pluggable Infrastructure for Context-Awareness, 20th International Conference on Advanced Networking and Applications (AINA06), vol. 1, pp. 199-204, 2006

25. Ghezzi, C., Mandrioli, D., Incremental Parsing, ACM Transactions on Programming Languages and Systems, vol. 1., no. 1, pp. 55-70, 1979.

26. Cho, Y. *et al.*, Toward Dynamic Adoption for a User's Situation Information in a Context-Aware Workflow System, ICCS 2007, Lecture Notes in Computer Science, vol. 4489, pp. 236-243, Springer-Verlag, 2007.

27. Han, J. *et al.*, Context-Aware Workflow Language based on Web Services for Ubiquitous Computing, ICCSA 2005, Lecture Notes in Computer Science, pp. 1008-1017, 2005.

Section 3

Appendices

WfMC Structure and Membership Information

WHAT IS THE WORKFLOW MANAGEMENT COALITION?

The Workflow Management Coalition, founded in August 1993, is a non-profit, international organization of workflow vendors, users, analysts and university/research groups. The Coalition's mission is to promote and develop the use of workflow through the establishment of standards for software terminology, interoperability and connectivity among BPM and workflow products. Comprising more than 250 members worldwide, the Coalition is the primary standards body for this software market.

WORKFLOW STANDARDS FRAMEWORK

The Coalition has developed a framework for the establishment of workflow standards. This framework includes five categories of interoperability and communication standards that will allow multiple workflow products to co-exist and interoperate within a user's environment. Technical details are included in the white paper entitled, "The Work of the Coalition," available at www.wfmc.org.

ACHIEVEMENTS

The initial work of the Coalition focused on publishing the Reference Model and Glossary, defining a common architecture and terminology for the industry. A major milestone was achieved with the publication of the first versions of the Workflow API (WAPI) specification, covering the Workflow Client Application Interface, and the Workflow Interoperability specification.

In addition to a series of successful tutorials across the U.S., Asia and Europe, the WfMC spent many hours over 2007 helping to drive awareness, understanding and adoption of XPDL. As a result, it has been cited as the most deployed BPM standard by a number of industry analysts, and continues to receive a growing amount of media attention.

In "Open Formats and Transparency in Business Process Definition" published in the Enterprise Open Source Journal, WfMC Executive Director Nathaniel Palmer discusses the merits of XPDL as means for ensuring process definition transparency and portability. XDPL is being adopted as a requirement for BPM workflow RFPs, with the most recent examples cited as a large federal government project and that of a telecommunications firm.

WORKFLOW MANAGEMENT COALITION STRUCTURE

The Coalition is divided into three major committees, the Technical Committee, the External Relations Committee, and the Steering Committee. Small working groups exist within each committee for the purpose of defining workflow terminology, interoperability and connectivity standards, conformance requirements, and for assisting in the communication of this information to the workflow user community.

The Coalition's major committees meet three times per calendar year for three days at a time, with meetings usually alternating between a North American and a European location. The working group meetings are held during these three days, and as necessary throughout the year.

Coalition membership is open to all interested parties involved in the creation, analysis or deployment of workflow software systems. Membership is governed by a Document of Understanding, which outlines meeting regulations, voting rights etc. Membership material is available at www.wfmc.org.

COALITION WORKING GROUPS

The Coalition has established a number of Working Groups, each working on a particular area of specification. The working groups are loosely structured around the "Workflow Reference Model" which provides the framework for the Coalition's standards program. The Reference Model identifies the common characteristics of workflow systems and defines five discrete functional interfaces through which a workflow management system interacts with its environment—users, computer tools and applications, other software services, etc. Working groups meet individually, and also under the umbrella of the Technical Committee, which is responsible for overall technical direction and co-ordination.

WORKFLOW REFERENCE MODEL DIAGRAM

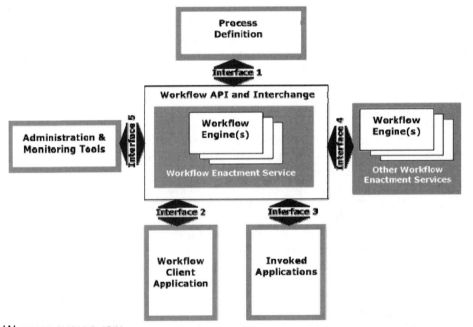

WHY YOU SHOULD JOIN

Being a member of the Workflow Management Coalition gives you the unique opportunity to participate in the creation of standards for the workflow industry as they are developing. Your contributions to our community ensure that progress continues in the adoption of royalty-free workflow and process standards.

MEMBERSHIP CATEGORIES

The Coalition has three major categories of membership per the membership matrix following. **All employees worldwide** are welcome to attend all meetings, and will be permitted access to the *Members Only* area of our web site.

Full Membership is appropriate for Workflow and Business Process Management (BPM) vendors, analysts and consultants. You may include up to three active members from your organization on your application and these may be replaced at any time by notifying us accordingly.

	Full Member	Associate /Academic Member	Individual Member	Fellow (by election only)	Visitor
Annual fee	$3500	$1500	$500	$0	$100 per day
Hold office	Yes	Yes	Yes	Yes	No
Nominate somebody for office	Yes	Yes	No	No	No
Committee membership	Yes	Yes	Yes	Yes	Observer
Voting right on standards	Yes	Yes	Active Participants only	Active Participants only	No
Voting right on WfMC.org business	Yes	Current officers only	Current officers only	Current officers only	No
Company reps in Meetings without visitor fee	4 (transferable)	1 (transferable)	individual only	individual only	Fee required

FULL MEMBERSHIP

This corporate category offers exclusive visibility in this sector at events and seminars across the world, enhancing your customers' perception of you as an industry authority, on our web site, in the Coalition Handbook and CDROM, by speaking opportunities, access to the Members Only area of our web site, attending the Coalition meetings and most importantly within the workgroups whereby through discussion and personal involvement, using your voting power, you can contribute actively to the development of standards and interfaces.

Full member benefits include:

- Financial incentives: 50 percent discount all "brochure-ware" (such as our annual CDROM Companion to the Workflow Handbook, advertising on our sister-site www.e-workflow.org), $500 credit toward next year's fee for at least 60 percent per year meeting attendance or if you serve as an officer of the WfMC.
- Web Visibility: a paragraph on your company services/products with links to your own company website.
- User RFIs: (Requests for Information) is an exclusive privilege to all full members. We often have queries from user organizations looking for specific workflow solutions. These valuable leads can result in real business benefits for your organization.
- Publicity: full members may choose to have their company logos including collaterals displayed along with WfMC material at conferences / expos we attend. You may also list corporate events and press releases (relating to WfMC issues) on the relevant pages on the website, and have a company entry in the annual Coalition Workflow Handbook
- Speaking Opportunities: We frequently receive calls for speakers at industry events because many of our members are recognized experts in

their fields. These opportunities are forwarded to Full Members for their direct response to the respective conference organizers.

ASSOCIATE AND ACADEMIC MEMBERSHIP

Associate and Academic Membership is appropriate for those (such as IT user organizations) who need to keep abreast of workflow developments, but who are not workflow vendors. It allows voting on decision-making issues, including the publication of standards and interfaces but does not permit anything near the amount of visibility or incentives provided to a Full Member. You may include up to three active members from your organization on your application.

INDIVIDUAL MEMBERSHIP

Individual Membership is appropriate for self-employed persons or small user companies. Employees of workflow vendors, academic institutions or analyst organizations are not typically eligible for this category. Individual membership is held in one person's name only, is not a corporate membership, and is not transferable within the company. If three or more people within a company wish to participate in the WfMC, it would be cost-effective to upgrade to corporate Associate Membership whereby all employees worldwide are granted membership status.

FELLOWS

The WfMC recognizes individuals from within its existing membership who have made sustained and outstanding contributions to WfMC objectives far and above that expected from normal member representation.

VISITORS

We welcome visitors at our meetings; it is an excellent opportunity for you to observe first hand the process of creating standards and to network with members of the Coalition. Your role will be as an observer only, and you are not eligible for a password, or for special offers available to WfMC members. You must pre-register and prepay your Visitor attendance fee. If you decide to join WfMC within 30 days of the meeting, your membership dues will be credited with your visitor fee.

HOW TO JOIN

Complete the form on the Coalition's website, or contact the Coalition Secretariat, at the address below. All members are required to sign the Coalition's "Document of Understanding" which sets out the contractual rights and obligations between members and the Coalition.

THE SECRETARIAT

Workflow Management Coalition (WfMC)

Nathaniel Palmer, Executive Director,
99 Derby Street, Suite 200
Hingham, MA 02043
+1-781-923-1411 (t), +1-781-735-0491 (f)
wfmc@wfmc.org.

WfMC Membership Directory

ADOBE SYSTEMS INC.
Full Member
345 Park Avenue, San Jose CA 95110, USA
Ashish Agrawal, Senior Product Manager
Tel: [1] 408-536-6262
ashish@adobe.com
Adobe revolutionizes how the world engages with ideas and information. Adobe recently launched LiveCycle Enterprise Suite (ES) is a family of servers and tools for automating external-facing business processes and closing the engagement gap. It enables organizations to automate tasks such as data capture and dissemination, process management, digital rights management, and document generation. It also changes the way organizations think about how they automate the processes that directly or indirectly touch customers, partners, and suppliers. LiveCycle ES drives a new way to develop applications specifically for end users who abandon shopping carts, do not complete forms, or become frustrated with automated ways of interacting with organizations. These engagement applications are enabled through a blend of LiveCycle ES, leveraging Adobe Portable Document Format (PDF) and Flex™ technologies that put a whole new type of interface based on Adobe Flash® on outward-facing applications. LiveCycle ES is the only solution that offers a comprehensive platform for customer engagement, blending industry-leading tools and services with best-in-class partner solutions and enterprise standards to transform business processes that extend to customers, partners, and suppliers.

ADVANTYS SOLUTIONS LTD.
Full Member
1250 Rene Levesque West, Suite 2200, Montreal, Quebec, H3B 4W8 Canada
Alain Bezancon, President
Tel: [1] 514-989-3700
alain.bezancon@advantys.com
Since 1995 ADVANTYS provides organizations worldwide with a range of innovative, powerful, robust, affordable and easy-to-use web based software through a practical approach to technology. ADVANTYS' solutions are used daily by hundreds of customers worldwide to automate processes, publish web sites, collaborate and develop web applications. Today's ADVANTYS' flagship product is the Workflow Gen BPM / Workflow software already deployed by more than 250 clients internationally. The Workflow Gen BPM / Workflow software is fully web based and enables the end users to complete and monitor processes online. .Net Web Forms and PDF forms can be used as electronic forms. The design and implementation of the workflows are realized online via a graphical mapping interface without programming. The Workflow Gen BPM / Workflow software is based around a practical technical solution integrating tried and tested development standards. Workflow Gen's scalable architecture, and its ability to incorporate additional development, provides for easy integration with existing databases and applications including Microsoft Sharepoint and SAP. Workflow Gen is available in 10 languages and distributed in 30 countries.

AIIM INTERNATIONAL
Full Member
1100 Wayne Avenue, Suite 1100, Silver Springs, MD, 20910 United States
www.aiim.org
Betsy Fanning, Director, Standards & Content Development
Tel: [1] 301-755-2682 / Fax: [1] 301-587-2711
bfanning@aiim.org
AIIM International is the global authority on Enterprise Content Management (ECM). The technologies, tools and methods used to capture, manage, store, preserve and deliver information to support business processes. AIIM promotes the understanding, adoption, and use of ECM technologies through education, networking, marketing, research, standards and advocacy programs.

APPIAN CORPORATION
Full Member
8000 Towers Crescent Drive, 16th Floor, Vienna, VA. 22182 United States www.appian.com

Malcolm Ross, Director of Product Management
Tel: [1] 703-442-1080
malcom.ross@appian.com
Founded in 1999 and headquartered in Vienna, VA, Appian is the first business process management (BPM) company to deliver advanced process, knowledge management, and analytics capabilities in a fully-integrated suite. Designed to extend the value of your existing systems, Appian's process-centric, context-driven solutions align business strategy with execution, and drive quantifiable improvements in business performance. Fortune 500 companies, government agencies, and non-governmental organizations have deployed Appian's award-winning platform–Appian Enterprise–to gain unprecedented visibility and control over their strategic business processes and enable customers to make better-informed decisions about their business.

BEA Systems
Full Member
2315 North First St., San Jose, California, 95131 United States
www.bea.com
Linus Chow, Principal Engineer
Tel: [1] 703-203-2178
linus.chow@bea.com
BEA Systems, Inc. (NASDAQ: BEAS) is a world leader in enterprise infrastructure software. BEA delivers the unified SOA platform for business transformation and optimization in order to improve cost structures and grow new revenue streams. BEA AquaLogic™ BPM Suite, an integrated component of BEA's SOA platform, is a market leading software suite that allows enterprises to integrate modeling, execution and measurement of end-to-end business processes involving complex interactions between people and IT systems. BEA customers across the world have achieved greater efficiency, control and agility by using AquaLogic BPM Suite to optimize the business process lifecycle and improve alignment between business and IT.

Bizmann System(s) Pte Ltd
Associate Member
73 Science Park Drive, #02-05, CINTECH I, Singapore Science Park I, Singapore 118254
www.bizmann.com
Ken Loke, Director
Tel: [65] 65-62711911
kenloke@bizmann.com

BOC Information Technologies Consulting Ltd.
Full Member
80 Haddington Road, Dublin 4, Ireland
www.boc-group.com
Margit Schwab, Managing Director
Tel: [353] 1-6375-240/ Fax: [353] 1- 6375241
Margit.schwab@boc-ie.com
The BOC Group is a software and consulting house specializing in IT-based Management Approaches. From its offices in six different countries and its Headquarters in Vienna, the BOC Group operates on a world-wide basis with Europe as its core market. Anticipating markets needs, the BOC Group offers expertise in Strategy Management by using the Balanced Scorecard concept, product ADOscore®, in Business Process Management based on the Business Process Management System Meta-Modelling concept, ADONIS®, in Supply Chain Management using the SCOR® concept, ADOlog® and in IT Architecture and IT Service Management by using, current concepts like ITIL®, ADOit®. The BOC Group performs projects and offers solutions in the banking, insurance, telecommunication, health care, public administration sectors as well as in the fields of E-Learning and Knowledge Management providing its customers with competence optimizing their processes, identifying their IT potentials, better utilizing their knowledge assets and deployment of their human and IT resources.

Brainware Strategies Consulting Gmbh
Associate Member
Sonnengass 15 Grafenstein, Carinthia, A-9131 Austria
Roel Krageten
Tel: [43] 664.3070865
brainware@brainware-at.com

CACI PRODUCTS COMPANY
Full Member
Advanced Simulation Lab, 1455 Frazee Road Suite #700, San Diego, CA 92108, US
Mike Engiles, SIMPROCESS Product Manager
Tel: [1] 703-679-3874
mengiles@caci.com
CACI Product's Company simulation software will address a wide variety of industries and applications. Determining which product is right for your application depends on the requirements and ultimate goal of your project. Our 40+ years of experience is at your disposal. SIMPROCESS® is hierarchical integrated process simulation software that combines Process Mapping, Flow Charting, Discrete Event Simulation, and ABC (Activity Based Costing) in a single easy to use tool. SIMPROCESS® provides non-programmers with ready-made blocks for building logic-based business models, while the underlying language allows experienced programmers to customize and add their own logic. SIMPROCESS® is designed for organizations that need to analyze varied scenarios and to mitigate the risk associated with dynamically changing environments. Whether you are modeling processes that take nanoseconds or days, SIMPROCESS® utilizes Java and XML technologies providing you with the necessary power and flexibility to meet your needs.

CAPTARIS, INC.
Full Member
10085 N.E. 4th Street, Suite 400, Bellevue, WA, 98004 USA
www.captaris.com
Dan Lucarini, Senior Director, Marketing
Tel: [1] 303-930-4405
danlucarini@captaris.com
Captaris, Inc. is a leading provider of software products that automate business processes, manage documents electronically and provide efficient information delivery. Our product suite of Captaris RightFax, Captaris Workflow and Captaris Alchemy Document Management is distributed through a global network of leading technology partners. RightFax is a proven market leader in enterprise fax server and electronic document delivery solutions. Alchemy gives organizations the power to manage and use all of their fixed content – including images, faxes, email, PDFs, and COLD – throughout the information lifecycle management (ILM) stages, with an integrated and scalable set of tools that are easy to deploy and even easier to use. And Workflow provides easy, flexible and integrated business process workflow for organizations, enabling productivity, accountability and compliancy.

CONSOLIDATED CONTRACTORS INTL. COMPANY
Associate Member
62B Kifissias, Marroussi Athens Attiki 15125 Greece
www.ccc.gr
Aref Boualwan, Product Manager
Tel : [30] 6932415177
aboualwan@ccc.gr

CORDYS
Full Member
Cordys Headquarters, Vanenburgerallee, 33882 RH PUTTEN, The Netherlands
www.cordys.com
Jon Pyke, Chief Strategy Officer
Tel: [44] 1932264636
jpyke@cordys.com
Cordys provides an industry-leading Business Process Management Suite (BPMS) to Global 2000 companies. Cordys' unique SOA-based solution enables customers to design, execute, monitor and improve business processes more rapidly, with better performance, and with greater adaptability than any other available solution. Companies from major industries worldwide have selected Cordys to support business performance improvement because business executives can continually optimize IT systems in real-time within a code-free environment. Headquartered in the Netherlands, Cordys is a global company with offices throughout the Americas, Europe, China and India.

DST SYSTEMS, INC.
Full Member

330 W. 9th Street, Kansas City, Missouri 64105 United States
www.dstawd.com
Bob Puccinelli, Director of Marketing AWD
Tel: [1] 816-843-8148 / Fax: [1] 816-843-8197
rjpuccinelli@dstawd.com
AWD® (Automated Work Distributor™) is a comprehensive business process management, imaging, workflow, and customer management solution designed to improve productivity and reduce costs. AWD captures all communication channels, streamlines processes, provides real-time reporting, and enables world-class customer service. For more than a decade, AWD has been improving processes in industries including banking, brokerage, healthcare, insurance, mortgage, mutual funds, and video/broadband. Today, AWD is licensed by more than 400 companies worldwide with nearly 140,000 active users. AWD is provided by the DST Technologies subsidiary of DST Systems, Inc. In business since 1969, DST Systems was ranked as one of "America's Most Admired Companies" by Fortune magazine for 2006.

FLOWRING TECHNOLOGY CO. LTD.

Associate Member
12F, No.120, Sec.2, Gongdao 5th Rd., Hsinchu City, 300 Taiwan
www.flowring.com
Chi-Tsai Yang, VP and CTO
Tel: [886] 3-5753331 / Fax: [886] 3-5753292
jjyang@flowring.com

FUJITSU SOFTWARE CORPORATION

Full Member
1250 E. Arques Avenue, Sunnyvale, CA 94085, United States.
www.fujitsu.com/interstage
Keith Swenson, Chief Architect
Tel: [1] 408-746-6304 (877) 372-8787) / Fax: [1] 408 746-6344
kswenson@us.fujitsu.com
Ranked as a leader in the Application Infrastructure Software market, the Fujitsu Interstage BPM Suite helps companies build SOA-enabled BPM applications by bringing business and IT professionals together to design, simulate, automate, analyze, and optimize business processes. Fujitsu's Process-Driven Approach to SOA using Interstage Business Process Manager, together with CentraSite, Fujitsu's SOA registry and repository, successfully brings business and IT professionals together. This top-down approach allows for collaboration on translating real business models into optimized, executable business processes while letting an organization reuse their existing Visio process maps, IT infrastructure and other SOA assets to reduce operational costs and maximize business agility and efficiencies. With $43 billion in annual revenues, Fujitsu is the third largest global IT Company. Its Interstage offerings are the enabling technologies of choice for companies building applications that can be shared across the enterprise to lower operating costs, accelerate business processes and react quickly to changing market requirements. For more information, visit www.fujitsu.com/interstage.

GLOBAL 360, INC

Full Member
2911 Turtle Creek Blvd. Suite 1100 Dallas, TX 75219
www.global360.com
Robert M Shapiro, Senior Vice President, Research
Tel: 1-617-823-1055
robert.shapiro@global360.com
Insight 360 is Process Intelligence for BPM, providing bottom-line BPM benefits without the risk and cost of a BI project, and without relying on a competing application infrastructure that attempts to obviate existing investments. While most BPM Suites are not designed to address the management of processes that lie outside of their direct control, Insight 360 is unique because it offers an independent layer that can integrate with BPM Suites and other applications for providing end to end process visibility and alignment. Insight 360 benefits are focused in four distinct areas: Visibility, Alignment, Efficiency, and Agility.

HANDYSOFT GLOBAL CORPORATION

Full Member
1952 Gallows Road, Suite 200, Vienna, VA 22182, USA
www.handysoft.com

H.J. Lee Caffrey, Vice President, Product Management
Tel: [1] 703-442-5690/ Fax: [1] 703-442.5650
hjlee@handysoft.com
HandySoft Global Corporation is leading the way for companies worldwide to develop new strategies for conducting business through the improvement, automation, and optimization of their business processes. As a leading provider of Business Process Management (BPM) software and services, we deliver innovative solutions to both the public and private sectors. Proven to reduce costs while improving quality and productivity, our foundation software platform, BizFlow®, is an award-winning BPM suite of tools used to design, analyze, automate, monitor, and optimize business processes. By delivering a single-source solution, capable of improving all types of business processes, HandySoft empowers our clients to leverage their investment across whole departments and the entire enterprise, making BizFlow the Strategic Choice for BPM.

HITACHI LTD., SOFTWARE DIVISION
Full Member
5030 Totsuka-Chou, Tosuka-Ku, Yokohama, 2448555, Japan
Makoto Yoshimura, Senior Manager
Tel: [81] 45 826 8161 / Fax: [81] 45 826 9050
Makoto.yoshimura.zh@hitachi.com
Hitachi offers a wide variety of integrated products for groupware systems such as e-mail and document information systems. One of these products is Hitachi's workflow system Groupmax. The powerful engine of Groupmax effectively automates office business such as the circulation of documents. Groupmax provides the following powerful tools and facilities: A visual status monitor shows the route taken and present location of each document in a business process definition. Cooperative facilities between servers provide support for a wide area workflow system Groupmax supports application processes such as consultation, send back, withdrawal, activation, transfer, stop and cancellation. Groupmax is rated to be the most suitable workflow system for typical business processes in Japan and has provided a high level of customer satisfaction. Groupmax workflow supports the Interface 4.

INSTICC
Associate Member
Av. D. Manuell I, 27A - 2ºEsq. Setabul 2910-595, PT
www.insticc.org
Joaquim Filipe, PhD
Tel: [351] 265-520-184 / Fax: [351] 265-520-186
jfilipe@insticc.org

IVYTEAM-SORECOGROUP
Associate Member
Alpenstrasse 9, P.O. Box CH-6304, Zug, Switzerland
www.ivyteam.ch
Tel: [44] 41-417108020
Heinz.lienhard@ivyteam.ch

K2
Full Member
4042 148th Ave NE, Redmond, WA 98052, USA
www.k2.com
Josh Swihart
Vice President, Corporate Marketing
Tel: [1] 303-552-0628
josh@k2.com
K2 provides the platform for a new generation of users to collaboratively assemble dynamic business applications from reusable items. K2-based solutions are deployed by a growing number of the global Fortune 100, and since the release of its first software in 2000, K2 has helped clients in more than 40 countries increase profitability and productivity. K2 is a business unit of SourceCode Technology Holdings, Inc., based in Redmond, Washington, and has offices in Australia, Canada, China, France, Germany, Singapore, South Africa, the United Kingdom and the United States. SourceCode and K2 are registered trademarks or trademarks of SourceCode Technology Holdings, Inc., in the United States and/or other countries.

METASTORM

Full Member
500 East Pratt Street, Suite 1250, Baltimore, MD 21202, USA
www.metastorm.com
Doug Gruber
Director, Sales Consulting
Tel: [1] 443-874-1300
dgruber@metastorm.com
With a focus on enterprise visibility, optimization, and agility, Metastorm offers market-leading solutions for Enterprise Architecture (EA), Business Process Analysis & Modeling (BPA) and Business Process Management (BPM). As an integrated product portfolio, Metastorm Enterprise™ allows organizations to maximize business results by unifying strategy, analysis and execution. Metastorm is the only solution provider to bring together these critical disciplines on a single software platform to enable an understanding of enterprise architecture and strategy, accurate impact and opportunity assessment, effective process execution, and accelerated value realization for organizations worldwide. For more information on powering strategic advantage with Metastorm Enterprise, visit www.metastorm.com.

NEC SOFT LTD.

Full Member
1-18-6, Shinkiba, Koto-ku, Tokyo, 136-8608, JAPAN
www.nec.com
Yoshihisa Sadakane, Sales and Marketing Senior Manager
Tel: [81]3-5569-3399 / Fax: [81]3-5569-3286
sadakane@mxw.nes.nec.co.jp
NEC Soft is a subsidiary of NEC Corporation, Japan's leading IT firm. NEC Soft, Ltd. has been providing solutions, mainly System Integration & System Services, Software Development, and Sales of Software Packages & Information Processors, and creating reliable partnerships with our customers for over 30 years since it was established. By offering total, unified services with separate business domains, NEC Soft's Total Services dynamically support the value creation customers seek.

OBJECT MANAGEMENT GROUP, INC.

Association Member
140 Kendrick Street, Bldg A, Suite 300 Needham, MA. 02494 United States
Jamie Nemiah
www.omg.org
Tel: [1] 781-444-0404
nemiah@omg.org

OPENWORK

Full Member
Via Conservatorio 22, Milano, 20122 Italy
www.openworkBPM.com
Francesco Battista, Marketing Director
Tel: [39] 02-77297558 / Fax: [39] 0805833115
francesco.battista@openworkBPM.com
openwork® is a pure Independent Software Vendor concentrating all efforts exclusively on its openwork Business Process Management suite. openwork features an original methodology that makes use of daily business, non-technical language and approach, introducing high-abstraction tools to map, share and maintain organizations shape and working rules. Those agile tools also allow to reflect organizations evolutions, keeping them always aligned with changing business needs. openwork is then able to act as an interpreter of graphic representation of organizations shape and working rules, enabling paper manual processes to become alive into finalized real-world web applications, integrated with other existing IT systems. openwork is the final solution of a crucial problem: modeling business organizations and processes, getting at the same time suitable fitting-like-a-glove BPM web applications, cutting down low added-value activities, technical complexity and costs. openwork suite including also Workflow Management, Document Management and Business Activity Monitoring capabilities has already been used to build hundreds of complete solutions for customer companies of any sector and size.

PEARSON TECHNOLOGY
Associate Member
1 Lake Street, 3F18, Upper Saddle River, NJ 07458
www.pearson.com, www.openworkBPM.com
Yonah Hirschman, Sr. Business Analyst, Digital Content Management Group
Tel: [1] 201-236-7836 / Fax: [1] 201-236-7024
Yonah.Hirschman@pearson.com

PECTRA TECHNOLOGY, INC.
Full Member
2425 West Loop South – Suite 200, Houston TX 77027, USA
www.pectra.com
Federico Silva, Marketing Manager
Tel: [1] 713-335-5562 / [54] 351-410-4400, ext 9309
fsilva@pectra.com
PECTRA Technolgy's award-winning Business Process Management system, PECTRA BPM
Suite, is a powerful set of tools enabling discovery, design, implementation, maintenance,
optimization and analysis of business processes in the organizations. PECTRA BPM Suite
automates processes and critical tasks generating optimum levels of operational effectiveness.
It fulfills all requirements demanded by today's organization, quickly and efficiently. Furthermore, it increases the return on previous investments made in technology by integrating all
existing applications. PECTRA incorporates the follow concepts: BAM (Business Activity Monitoring); WORKFLOW; EAI (Enterprise Application Integration) and B2Bi (Business to Business
Integration). Also, its functionality PECTRA BPM Mobile, allows every user to execute tasks
from any mobile device in a very simple way, through an interface designed on Services Oriented Architecture (SOA). PECTRA BPM Mobile increases organizations productivity through
fast access to information, providing dynamism and synchronization to the operations. PEC-
TRA BPM Suite increases productivity, saving time and reducing costs in any organization.

PEGASYSTEMS INC.
Full Member
101 Main Street, Cambridge, MA 02142 United States
www.pegasystems.com
Dr. Setrag Khoshafian
Vice President of BPM Technology
Tel: [1] 617-866-6407
Setrag.khoshafian@pega.com
Pegasystems (NASDAQ: PEGA), the leader in Business Process Management, provides software to drive revenue growth, productivity and agility for the world's most sophisticated organizations. Customers use our award-winning SmartBPM® suite to improve customer service, reach new markets and boost operational effectiveness. Our patented SmartBPM technology makes enterprise applications easy to build and change by directly capturing business
objectives and eliminating manual programming. SmartBPM unifies business rules and processes into composite applications that leverage existing systems -- empowering businesspeo-
ple and IT staff to Build for Change®, deliver value quickly and outperform their competitors.
Pegasystems' suite is complemented by best-practice frameworks designed for leaders in financial services, insurance, healthcare, government, life sciences, communications, manufacturing and other industries. Headquartered in Cambridge, MA, Pegasystems has offices in
North America, Europe and Asia. Visit us at www.pega.com.

PERSHING LLC
Associate Member
19 Vreeland Road, Florham Park, NJ 07932, United States
www.pershing.com
Regina DeGennaro, VP – Process Management Applications
Tel: [1] 973-360-2631
rdegennaro@pershing.com

PROJEKTY BANKOWE POLSOFT
Full Member
Plac Wolnosci 18, Poznan, 61-739 Poland
Boguslaw Rutkowski, Solution Architect
Tel: [48] 61-8599311/ Fax: [48] 61-8516995

boguslaw.rutkowski@pbpolsoft.com.pl
Projekty Bankowe Polsoft Company is part of Sygnity Group, one of the biggest IT services and software vendor for industry and public sectors in Poland. PB Polsoft offers BPB Workflow technology, highly scalable standard-based workflow system with strong EAI capabilities, especially for Web Services, rich process and form (XForms) modeling tools as well as set of components for building workflow client portal applications based on java portlet technology. BPB Workflow was developed in J2EE technology and can be used as both an embedded or a standalone server working in EJB container. It has well defined Java WAPI and Web Services interface and offers web-based administration and modeling tools. The workflow engine is cluster aware and has robust build-in process fail-over and recovery capabilities.

SAVVION
Full Member
5104 Old Ironsides Drive, Suite 205, Santa Clara, California 95054, United States
http://www.savvion.com
Tel: [1] 408-330-3400
Dr. Phanendra Garimella, Vice President, Product Development
Tel: [1] 408-330-3400
bgarimella@savvion.com
Savvion is the leading provider of business process management (BPM) software that improves business performance and reduces costs. Savvion has a proven track record of turning process improvement ideas into real-world solutions quickly, often in as few as 30 days, and delivering a return on investment as high as 300%. More than 300 global business enterprises, public service agencies, and systems integration firms, including 20 of the Fortune 100, use Savvion systems to manage their business. Savvion is recognized by Intelligent Enterprise as one of the most influential companies in information technology today, and is cited as a leader by independent research firms. To start down the path of process improvement, download the Savvion Process Modeler available for free at www.savvion.com/startnow. Or visit the Savvion's www.ProcessXchange.com , where people can connect with a community of interest devoted to business process management.

STFC
Associate Member
Rutherford Appleton Laboratory, Harwell Science and Innovation Campus, Didcot OX11 0QX, United Kingdom
www.stfc.ac.uk
Trudy Hall, Project Manager
Tel: [44] 0-1235-445100
t.a.hall@rl.ac.uk

TELECOM ITALIA S.P.A
Associate Member
Via G. Reiss Romoli 274, Torino, Italy 10148
Giovanna Sacchi
Tel: [0039] (01) 12288040
giovanna.sacchi@telecomitalia.it

TIBCO SOFTWARE, INC.
Full Member
3303 Hillview Avenue, Palo Alto, CA 94304 USA
http://www.tibco.com/software/process_management/default.jsp
Justin Brunt, Sr. Product Manager
Tel: [44] 0-1793-441300 / Fax: [44] 0-1793 441333
jbrunt@tibco.com
TIBCO digitized Wall Street in the '80s with its event-driven "Information Bus" software, which helped make real-time business a strategic differentiator in the '90s. Today, TIBCO's infrastructure software gives customers the ability to constantly innovate by connecting applications and data in a service-oriented architecture, streamlining activities through business process management, and giving people the information and intelligence tools they need to make faster and smarter decisions, what we call The Power of Now®. TIBCO serves more than 3,000 customers around the world with offices in 40 countries and an ecosystem of over 200 partners. Learn more at http://www.tibco.com.

UNISYS CORPORATION
Full Member
1000 Cedar Hollow Road, Malvern, PA 19335, USA
www.unisys.com
Shane C. Gabie, MBA, Director Technology Research
Tel: [1] 610-648-2731 / Cell: [1] 610-316-0930 / Net: 358-2731
Shane.Gabie@unisys.com
Unisys Corporation (NYSE: UIS) is a worldwide technology services and solutions company. Our consultants apply Unisys expertise in consulting, systems integration, outsourcing, infrastructure, and server technology to help our clients achieve secure business operations. We build more secure organizations by creating visibility into clients' business operations. Leveraging the Unisys 3D Visible Enterprise approach, we make visible the impact of their decisions – ahead of investments, opportunities and risks. For more information, visit www.unisys.com.

W4 (WORLD WIDE WEB WORKFLOW)
Full Member
4 rue Emile Baudot, 91873 Palaiseau Cedex, France
www.w4global.com
Philippe Betschart, CTO
Tel: [33] 1-64531760 / Fax: [33] 1-64532898
Philippe.Betschart@w4global.com
W4, one of the leading European software vendors specialized in Business Process Management, supplies more than 270 customers, serving more than 1 million users. For more than 10 years W4 has been widely acclaimed for its expertise in Human Centric BPM. Whatever the particular need, there is a package available allowing customers to take full advantage of W4 technology. W4 BPM Suite is a complete package, from modeling to monitoring, dedicated to the enterprise process automation. This BPM package is managing the automation of complex work processes involving high volumes of users, connections to applications and integration to the IT. Process can be both support (finance, HR...) and company-specific (new product launch, modification requests...). W4 BPM Suite provides an easy tool for modeling their processes and generate the presentation layer (application) for both Java and .NET environments. It also offers managers reporting and supervision functionalities.

WORK MANAGEMENT EUROPE
Associate Member
Postbus 168, 3830 AD Leusden, The Netherlands
www.wmeonline.com
Cor H. Visser, Managing Director
Tel: [31] (33) 433 2223 / Fax: [31] (33) 433 2224
cvisser@wmeonline.com

WORKPOINT
Full Member
407 N. 117th Street, Omaha, NE 68154, USA
www.workpoint.com
Tel: +1-402-964-1996 / Fax: +1-402-964-1967
Ruth Nimrod, CTO
rnimrod@workpoint.com
BPM with Torque--IT environments requiring high performance and high throughput need more than a standard BPM engine, they need a BPM engine with torque. Workpoint is world-class BPM that is differentiated from any other solution on the market today. To date, Workpoint is the only BPM solution with two native engines, offering both a native Microsoft® .NET version and a pure Java™ J2EE version. These interoperable engines, along with component architecture provide maximum performance and scalability enabling organizations to seamlessly automate, manage and optimize dynamic, high volume business processes across the enterprise. With its powerful, stateless runtime engine, Workpoint is BPM that manages processes throughout the entire lifecycle. It's BPM with torque.

WfMC Officers 2008

STEERING COMMITTEE

Chairman	Jon Pyke	Fellow, UK
Vice Chairman (Europe)	Justin Brunt	TIBCO, UK
Vice Chairman (Americas)	Keith Swenson	Fujitsu Computer Systems, USA
Vice Chairman (Asia-Pacific)	Yoshihisa Sadakane	NEC Soft, Japan

TECHNICAL COMMITTEE

Chair Emeritus	David Hollingsworth	Fujitsu Software, UK
Committee Chair	Keith Swenson	Fujitsu Computer Systems, USA
Vice Chairman	Robert Shapiro	Global 360, USA
Vice Chairman (Asia-Pacific)	Dr. Yang Chi-Tsai	Flowring, Taiwan
Vice Chairman (Europe)	Philippe Betschart	W4, France

EXTERNAL RELATIONS COMMITTEE

Chairman	Ken Mei	Fellow, USA
Vice Chairman (Europe)	François Bonnet	W4, France
Vice Chairman (Americas)	Bob Puccinelli	DST Systems, USA
Vice Chairman (Asia-Pacific)	Dr Kwang-Hoon Kim	BPM Korea, South Korea
SECRETARY / TREASURER	Cor Visser	Work Management Europe, Netherlands
INDUSTRY LIAISON CHAIR	Shane Gabie	Unisys, USA
USER LIAISON CHAIR	Charlie Plesums	Fellow, USA

WfMC Country Chairs

ARGENTINA
Federico Silva
PECTRA Technology, Inc.
USA: +1 (713) 335 5562
ARG (BA): +54 (11) 4590 0000
ARG (CBA): +54 (351) 410 4400
fsilva@pectra.com

AUSTRALIA & NEW ZEALAND
Carol Prior
Alphawest
Tel: +61 2 9263 5888
Carol.Prior@alphawest.com.au

BRAZIL
Vinícius Amaral
iProcess
Phone: +55 51 3211-4036
vinicius.amaral@iprocess.com.br

FRANCE
Raphaël Syren
W4 Global
Tel: + (331) 64 53 17 65
raphael.syren@w4global.com

GERMANY
Tobias Rieke
University of Muenster
Tel: [49] 251-8338-072 -
istori@wi.uni-muenster.de

ITALY
Francesco Battista
openwork
Tel: +39 3355794429
francesco.battista@openworkBPM.com

JAPAN
Yoshihisa Sadakane
NEC Soft
Tel: +81-3-5569-3399
sadakane@mxw.nes.nec.co.jp

KOREA
Kwanghoon Kim, Ph.D.
Department of Computer Science
Kyonggi University
kwang@kgu.ac.kr

PORTUGAL
Dr. Joaquim Filipe
INSTICC
Tel.: +351-265.520.184
jfilipe-at-insticc.org

POLAND
Boguslaw Rutkowski
PB Polsoft
Tel: +48 61 853 10 51
Boguslaw.Rutkowski
@pbpolsoft.com.pl

SINGAPORE & MALAYSIA
Ken Loke
Bizmann System (S) Pte Ltd
Tel: +65 - 6271 1911
kenloke@bizmann.com

SOUTH AFRICA
Marco Gerazounis
TIBCO Software Inc.
Tel: +27 (0)11 467 3111
mgerazou@tibco.com

SPAIN
Elena Rodríguez Martín
Fujitsu España Services S.A.
Tel. +34 91 784 9565
ermartin@mail.fujitsu.es

THE NETHERLANDS
Fred van Leeuwen
DCE Consultants
Tel: +31 20 44 999 00
leeuwen@dceconsultants.com

TAIWAN
Erin Yang
Flowring Technology Co. Ltd.
Tel: +886-3-5753331 ext. 316
erin_yang@flowring.com

USA (WEST)
Bob Puccinelli
DST Systems
Tel: +1 816-843-8148
rjpuccinelli@dstsystems.com

USA (EAST)
Betsy Fanning
AIIM International
Tel: 1 301 755 2682
bfanning@aiim.org

WfMC Technical Committee

Working Group Chairs 2008

WG1—PROCESS DEFINITION INTERCHANGE MODEL AND APIS
Chair: Robert Shapiro, Fellow
Email: rshapiro@capevisions.com

WG2/3—CLIENT / APPLICATION APIS
open

WG4—WORKFLOW INTEROPERABILITY
Chair: Keith Swenson, Fujitsu Computer Systems, USA
Email: kswenson@us.fujitsu.com

WG5—ADMINISTRATION & MONITORING
Chair: Michael zur Muehlen, Stevens Institute of Technology
Email: mzurmuehlen@stevens.edu

WG ON OMG
Chair: Ken Mei, WfMC Fellow
Email: kmei@wfmc.org

CONFORMANCE WG
Chair: Michael zur Muehlen, Stevens Institute of Technology
Email: mzurmuehlen@stevens.edu

WGRM—REFERENCE MODEL
Chair: Dave Hollingsworth, Fujitsu
david.hollingsworth@uk.fujitsu.com

WG9—RESOURCE MODEL
Chair: Michael zur Muehlen, Stevens Institute of Technology
Email: mzurmuehlen@stevens.edu

WfMC Fellows

The WfMC recognizes individuals who have made sustained and outstanding contributions to WfMC objectives far and above that expected from normal member representation.

WfMC FELLOW—FACTORS:

- To be considered as a candidate, the individual must have participated in the WfMC for a period of not less than two years and be elected by majority vote within the nominating committee.
- Rights of a WfMC Fellow: Receives guest member level of email support from the Secretariat; pays no fee when attending WfMC meetings; may participate in the work of the WfMC (workgroups, etc), may hold office.

Martin Ader
France

Robert Allen
United Kingdom

Mike Anderson
United Kingdom

Wolfgang Altenhuber
Austria

Richard Bailey
United States

Justin Brunt
United Kingdom

Emmy Botterman
United Kingdom

Katherine Drennan
United States

Layna Fischer
United States

Mike Gilger
United States

Michael Grabert
United States

Shirish Hardikar
United States

Paula Helfrich
United States

Hideshige Hasegawa
Japan

Dr. Haruo Hayami
Japan

Nick Kingsbury
United Kingdom

Klaus-Dieter Kreplin
Germany

Mike Marin
United States

Emma Matejka
Austria

Dan Matheson
United States

Ken Mei
United States

Akira Misowa
Japan

Roberta Norin
United States

Sue Owen
United Kingdom

Jon Pyke
United Kingdom

Charles Plesums
United States

Harald Raetzsch
Austria

Michele Rochefort
Germany

Joseph Rogowski
United States

Michael Rossi
United States

Sunil Sarin
United States

Robert Shapiro
United States

Dave Shorter
(Chair Emeritus)
United States

David Stirrup
United Kingdom

Keith Swenson
United States

Tetsu Tada
United States

Austin Tate
United Kingdom

Cor Visser
The Netherlands

Rainer Weber
Germany

Alfons Westgeest
Belgium

Marilyn Wright
United States

Michael zur Muehlen
United States

Author Biographies

Our sincere thanks go to the authors who kindly gave their time, effort and expertise into contributing papers that cover methods, concepts, case studies and standards in business process management and workflow. These international industry experts and thought leaders present significant new ideas and concepts to help you plan a successful future for your organization. We also extend our thanks and appreciation to the members of WfMC Review Committee who volunteered many hours of their valuable time in the selection of the final submissions and who helped guide the content of the book.

PAULO ALENCAR

[palencar@csg.uwaterloo.ca]
Research Associate Professor, University of Waterloo.
DC2597B, 200 University Ave. W., Waterloo, Ontario, N2L 3G1, Canada
Paulo Alencar is a professor in computer science. He is a member of the Waterloo Institute for Health Informatics Research and a member of the Workflow Research & Knowledge (WoRK) Research Group. Professor Alencar's research, teaching and consulting activities span a variety of areas in Software Engineering, including software architectures, software design, and formal methods. He is the principal or co-principal investigator of various projects in the Computer Systems Group. NSERC, CSER, CITO, IBM (CAS), Sybase, Siebel, i-Anywhere Solutions and Bell have supported his research. Dr. Alencar has a BSc (Brazil), MSc (Brazil), and a PhD (Pontifical Catholic University, Brazil in cooperation with the University of Karlsruhe, Germany).

DAVID ATWOOD

[datwood@gov.bm]
Director of e-Government, Government of Bermuda.
40 Church Street, Hamilton, HM NX, Bermuda.
David Atwood, Director of e-Government for the Government of Bermuda, David Atwood directs a team of consultants and vendors on the development of the Bermuda Government Portal (www.gov.bm) and the Government's Business Process Improvement initiatives. These activities require Mr. Atwood to serve as a liaison between various Government compartments to foster cross-departmental collaboration and IT-enabled service improvement. Prior to serving as the Director of e-Government, Mr. Atwood held several posts within Bermuda Government's Information Technology Office. Mr. Atwood speaks at various conferences and seminars on issues surrounding e-Government and improving collaboration across government departments and ministries.

JUHEE BAE

[baejh@kr.ibm.com]
Software Engineer,
IBM, Korea
MMAA Bldg, Dogok2-dong, Gangnam-gu, Seoul, 135-700, Korea.
JuHee Bae working for digital media solution team of Ubiquitous Computing Lab (UCL), IBM Korea.

FRANCESCO BATTISTA

[francesco.battista@openworkBPM.com]
Marketing Director, openwork
Via Conservatorio 22, Milano 20122, Italy.
Francesco BATTISTA is a Computer Science graduated, since 1994 he worked for Procter & Gamble as Management Systems Project Manager in Italian and international projects, than moved to major IT consultancy companies with account and project management responsibilities for process reorganizations involving SAP and web technologies. Since 2004 Francesco is Marketing Director for openwork, the Italian BPM company, leading also corporate communications. Published author, he is WfMC Chairman for Italy and active speaker in BPM related events.

GIANPIERO BONGALLINO

[gianpiero.bongallino@openworkBPM.com]
Research & Development Specialist, openwork
Via delle Violette, 12, Modugno - Bari 70026, Italy.
Gianpiero Bongallino is a Computer Science graduated, Gianpiero is specialized in Intelligent System, A.I., and Software Engineering. For openwork, the Italian BPM company, he contributed since 2005 to Document Processing tools development, including image recognition & processing, automation, digital sign, server/client integration and enterprise application design. Gianpiero is also part of the openwork research team for Workflow Standards and Software Design.

PETER BOSTROM

[pbostrom@bea.com]
Federal CTO, BEA Systems, Inc.
3015 Nicosh Circle, 2204 Falls Church, VA, USA
Peter Bostrom has over two decades of technology industry experience in a wide variety of technical and executive management positions in both innovative, venture backed start-ups and large enterprise software companies. Currently, Mr. Bostrom serves as the Federal CTO for BEA Government Systems. He works with BEA customers throughout the U.S. Federal Government as well as with state, local and municipal organizations facing the dual challenges of budget constraints and increased demand for responsiveness from their IT assets. Previously, Mr. Bostrom worked in the same capacity at TIBCO Software. Mr. Bostrom has served in leadership positions on numerous technical committees, user groups, and as an advisor to several technology companies. He is a frequent speaker on technology topics around the country. Mr. Bostrom served in the 1st Battalion of the U.S. Army's 75th Ranger Regiment and the 11th Special Forces Group. He holds a BA in International Affairs from The American University in Washington, DC with a focus on U.S. Defense and Security Policy, as well as Middle East studies.

JUSTIN BRUNT

[jbrunt@tibco.com]
Senior Product Manager, TIBCO Software.
4 Apple Walk, Kembrey Park, Swindon, Wilshire, United Kingdom.
Justin Brunt is Senior Product Manager for TIBCO's BPM product suite, TIBCO iProcess™ Suite. He has been involved with Business Process Management for over 14 years initially as Director of Development for Staffware plc and latterly as Director of Research. Following the acquisition of Staffware by TIBCO Justin took his current product management role. Prior to joining Staffware, Justin held senior software development roles with Logica and Siemens. During his BPM and Workflow career Justin has been involved in the development of BPM related standards. Throughout this time he has been involved with the WfMC and held the position of Vice Chair (Europe) of the WfMC's Technical committee between 2002 and 2006 prior to his current position as Vice Chair [Europe] of the steering committee. He is also a Fellow of the Workflow Management Coalition. Justin also represents TIBCO in the OMG's BPM related initiatives.

LINUS CHOW

[linus.chow@bea.com]
Co-Chair WfMC Public Sector Chapter
Principal Systems Engineer, BEA Systems, Inc.
3015 Nicosh Circle, 2204 Falls Church, VA, USA
Linus Chow is the Co-Chair of the WfMC Public Sector Chapter and a Principal Systems Engineer for BEA systems. He has over 15 years of leadership and management experience in information technology internationally with over 8 years in workflow, BPM, and SOA. He has played crucial roles in expanding the growth of BPM and workflow adoption first in the US and then internationally from Australia to Switzerland. Currently, Linus leads the adoption of BPM/SOA solutions for Public Sector customers promoting the WfMC and its standards and best practices. He is a published author and an active speaker on the Best Practices of BPM and SOA frequently engaging with AFCEA, WfMC,

BPMI, IQPC, AIIM, Brainstorm, and other industry organizations. A decorated former US Army Officer, Linus has an MBA, a MS in Management Information Systems, and BS in Mathematics.

ALFREDO CISTERNA

[acisterna@pectra.com]
Product Manager,
PECTRA Technology, Inc., USA
2425 West Loop South, Suite 200, Houston, Texas. USA
Alfredo Cisterna is responsible for the planning, developing, and marketing efforts for PECTRA BPM Suite. Also, guides the inbound oriented product definitions and all the stages of the product lifecycle. Moreover, he is responsible for all the activities performed in the interest of delivering the different releases of PECTRA BPM Suite to market. Alfredo joined PECTRA Technology in June, 2003, as a BPM consultant to collaborate with the Consulting Services Department of PECTRA Technology in Latin America. In January 2006, he moved to the software factory of PECTRA Technology located in Argentina, carrying out coordination activities for the development of PECTRA BPM Suite. In March 2007, he became Product Manager of PECTRA BPM Suite. Before joining PECTRA Technology, Alfredo worked as BPM Consultant for different companies. A graduate from the IES Collage, in Systems Analysis, Alfredo has taught and participated in seminars on the development and impact of Information Technologies worldwide, especially about Workflow, Business Process Management and Service Oriented Architecture. He is 27-years old and is fluent in Spanish and English.

CARLO COMBI

[carlo.combi@univr.it]
Professor, Department of Computer Science, University of Verona.
Verona, strada le Grazie 15, I-37134 Verona, VR, Italy.
Carlo Combi is full professor and head of the Department of Computer Science at the University of Verona, Italy. He teaches the classes of Database and Information Systems. Carlo Combi received an M.Sc in E.E. in 1987 and a Ph.D. in 1993 from Politecnico di Milano, Italy, respectively. His main research interests include temporal databases, data warehouses and semi-structured data, workflow management systems. Carlo Combi is co-author with prof. Giuseppe Pozzi of a paper entitled "Architectures for a Temporal Workflow Management System", presented at the SAC conference, 2004: the paper has been ranked inside the monthly top 10 downloads from the ACM digital library for the last 36 months.

DOMINIC COVVEY

[dcovvey@uwaterloo.ca]
Professor, University of Waterloo.
DC3333, 200 University Ave. W., Waterloo, Ontario, N2L 3G1, Canada.
Dominic Covvey is a Professor and the Founding Director of the Waterloo Institute for Health Informatics Research at the University of Waterloo. He also leads the Workflow Research & Knowledge (WoRK) Research Group. His research is in the representation and analysis of healthcare workflow, the definition of competencies and curricula in Health Informatics and the design of the Electronic Health Record. Dominic is a Fellow of the American College of Medical Informatics and of the Healthcare Information and Management Systems Society, a senior member of the IEEE, and a certified Information Systems Professional.

DONALD D. COWAN

[dcowan@uwaterloo.ca]
Professor, University of Waterloo
DC3333, 200 University Ave. W., Waterloo, Ontario, N2L 3G1, Canada.
Donald D. Cowan is Distinguished Professor Emeritus at the University of Waterloo (UW) and holds adjunct professor appointments in both the David R. Cheriton School of Computer Science and the Department of Biology. He is also the Director of the Computer

Systems Group, a software engineering research group, a member of the Waterloo Institute for Health Informatics Research and a member of the Workflow Research & Knowledge (WoRK) Research Group at UW. His research is in software engineering directed toward lowering technology barriers to the design, implementation, evolution and maintenance of complex enterprise software systems with a particular focus on Web 2.0 and 3.0. He is a member of the ACM, IEEE and the Canadian Information Processing Society.

FLORIAN DANIEL

[daniel@dit.unitn.it]
Post-doc researcher, University of Trento.
Via Sommarive 14, I-38050 Trento, TN, Italy.
Florian Daniel is a post-doc fellow at the University of Trento, Italy, and the Politecnico di Milano, Italy. In 2006 he worked as visiting researcher in HP Labs, Palo Alto, California. His research interests include conceptual modelling and design of Web applications, adaptively and context-awareness in Web applications, component-based Web application development, and business process management. Florian Daniel holds a Ph.D. in Information Technology from Politecnico di Milano and a Master in Computer Engineering from Politecnico di Milano.

KARL DJEMAL

[karl.djemal@citi.com]
Vice President/Senior Business Analyst
Global Equity Middle Office, 390 Greenwich Street, New York, NY 10013, U.S.A.
Karl Djemal has worked in technology for the last 18 years in the financial sector, with roles that range from the developer, architect, project leader and manager.
At Citi for the last 3 years, he has been using Agile on projects that he has lead and has helped promote Agile Development. He recently transferred to work for the business as a Senior Business Analyst where he focuses more on BPM and introducing Agile Practices in the way the business collaborates with technology.

SHIRLEY L. FENTON

[sfenton@uwaterloo.ca]
Managing Director, University of Waterloo.
DC3333, 200 University Ave. W., Waterloo, Ontario, N2L 3G1, Canada.
Shirley Fenton (BES, MA) is the Managing Director and member of the Waterloo Institute for Health Informatics Research at the University of Waterloo (UW). She is also a Research Associate of the Computer Systems Group and a member of the Workflow Research & Knowledge (WoRK) Research Group at UW. Her research is in health informatics, the representation and analysis of healthcare workflow, communities of practice, innovative Internet applications, and community information utilities/portals. She is a member of COACH.

DENIS GAGNE

[dgagne@trisotech.com]
CEO, Trisotech.
3100 Cote Vertu, B380, Montreal, Quebec, H4R 2J8, Canada.
M. Gagne is responsible for the solutions and technology vision at Trisotech. He has led Trisotech through the process of developing unique services and product propositions and provided leadership in plotting out Trisotech's market strategy. M. Gagné's current research interest focus on technological and know-how innovation in the fields business process management and business transformation.

RAJA HAMMOUD

[rhammoud@adobe.com]
Group Product Marketing Manager, Enterprise & Developer Business Unit, Adobe Systems, Incorporated
345 Park Ave., San Jose, California, USA.

Raja Hammoud is a Group product marketing manager responsible for the business and marketing strategy for Adobe's business process management (BPM) technology. Raja joined Adobe in 2007 after serving as senior director of product management at web-Methods for 7 years. webMethods is an enterprise software provider of integration, SOA and BPM solutions. While at webMethods, Raja managed multiple products through their entire life cycle. Most notably, Raja successfully led webMethods in the BPM market, by setting a solid BPM product roadmap, and driving its execution across product development, marketing, sales and professional services. With over 10 years experience, Raja has served with Eastman Chemical Company, Ventro, and webMethods in positions encompassing software development, quality assurance, implementation, product management, and marketing. Raja Hammoud graduated with high distinction from the American University of Beirut with degrees in Computer Science and Mathematics.

DAVID HENRIQUES

[dhenriqu@uwaterloo.ca]
Graduate Student, University of Waterloo
DC3333, 200 University Ave. W., Waterloo, Ontario, N2L 3G1, Canada
David Henriques is a Masters student at the University of Waterloo working with the Waterloo Institute for Health Informatics Research (WIHIR). He is a member of the Workflow Research & Knowledge (WoRK) Research Group. His research is in applied health informatics specifically in studying the visualization of health care workflows in physical environments.

JOHN HOOGLAND

[john.hoogland@pallas-athena.com]
CEO, Pallas Athena International
Piet Joubertstraat 4, Apeldoorn, 7315 AV, The Netherlands.
For more then 20 years John has been involved in many workflow and BPM projects, with operational experience with most of today's workflow management and BPM tools. Both in the research and business field he was involved in the development of many workflow management products and BPM implementations. John is the driving force behind the Case Management philosophy, aiming to provide flexibility in both design and execution of processes, essecially in human centric environments. As CEO of Pallas Athena International, John is responsible for the development of the BPM | suite by Pallas Athena. As such, he introduced process mining technology as an integrated part of the current BPM offering of Pallas Athena.

CHARLES JOESTEN

[cjoesten@icorpartners.com]
Director, ICOR Partners, LLC
3101 Wilson Blvd., Suite 500, Arlington, Virginia, 22201, USA.
Charles Joesten has delivered business process management solutions to Department of Defense (DoD) and Federal Government agencies for nearly two decades. As a certified Project Management Professional (PMP), Charles leverages industry standards and principles to establish process rigor and workflow efficiency that translate into operational value. He is a key manager and practitioner on numerous engagements in areas of operational strategy, enterprise transformation, and performance measurement. Notable DoD and Federal Government clients include the Department of Homeland Security Immigration and Customs Enforcement (DHS ICE), the U.S. Army Installation Management Command (IMCOM), the U.S. Air Force Research Laboratory (AFRL), Arnold Engineering Development Center (AEDC), Commander in Chief U.S. Pacific Fleet (CINCPACFLT), Commander Naval Surface Forces U.S. Pacific Fleet (COMNAVSURFPAC), and the Office of Naval Research (ONR). Commercial clients include Southern New England Telephone, Pratt & Whitney, Sodexho Marriott, Morgan Stanley Dean Witter, and Nextel Communications. As a Director with ICOR Partners, LLC, Charles is responsible for client engagement delivery, quality assurance, subject matter expertise, and methodology enhancement. Prior to joining ICOR Partners, Charles served in senior management roles with Grant Thornton, LLP, CACI, Inc., American Management Systems, Inc., Ernst & Young,

LLP, and PricewaterhouseCoopers, LLP. Charles holds a Bachelor of Arts in economics from Vanderbilt University and a Master of Business Administration in strategy and business process reengineering from George Mason University.

DR. SETRAG KHOSHAFIAN

[setrag@pega.com]
VP of BPM Technology, Pegasystems Inc.
101 Main St., Cambridge, MA, USA.
Dr. Setrag Khoshafian is Vice President of BPM Technology for Pegasystems Inc. Dr. Khoshafian is a recognized BPM pioneer and thought leader who has done R&D, innovation, and productization in a number of domains including Business Process Management, Service Oriented Architectures, Business Intelligence, Collaborative Computing, Database and Content Management, and Object Orientation. Dr. Khoshafian's vision of enterprise software is captured in his recent book *Service Oriented Enterprises*. This vision combines a service-focused way of doing business with the latest BPM technology for a fresh approach in which each party or participant sees itself as a service provider as well as a service consumer integrated through BPM. Service Oriented Enterprises shows how Business agility could be achieved through BPM and focuses on the emerging architecture of service orientation. Dr. Khoshafian holds a PhD in Computer Science from the University of Wisconsin-Madison.

SALVATORE LATRONICO

[salvatore.latronico@openworkBPM.com]
BPM Consultancy Director, openwork
Via Conservatorio 22, Milano 20122, Italy.
Salvatore LATRONICO – co-Founder and BPM Consultancy Director, openwork Physics graduated, he is one of the founders and inventors of openwork, the Italian BPM company born in 1998. Starting from methodology and architecture definition, he always played a basic role in the evolution of the openwork BPM suite both for theoretical & high abstraction tools definition and technical matters. Salvatore is now BPM Consultancy Director for openwork, coordinating all BPM projects resources: published author, he is active speaker in BPM related events.

CHRIS LAWRENCE

[ergonology@iafrica.com]
Business Architecture Consultant, Old Mutual South Africa.
PO Box 66, Cape Town 8000, South Africa
Chris Lawrence has designed and implemented solutions in the UK, US and Southern Africa over a 30-year career in IT, after studying philosophy at Cambridge and London Universities. In 1996 he left England for Cape Town to co-found Global Edge, a strategic business-enablement competency in support of financial services group Old Mutual's international expansion. He is now an independent business architecture consultant, specializing in business process architecture and holistic delivery and transition methodologies. He speaks and facilitates workshops in South Africa, the UK and US, gives seminars at UK universities, and writes for international publications. His book *Make work make sense* articulates the process-based delivery approach he developed for Global Edge. In 2004 its theory was adopted as the 'Old Mutual Business Process Methodology' (OMBPM).

DAERYUNG LEE

[drlee@kr.ibm.com]
Software Engineer,
IBM, Korea
MMAA Bldg, Dogok2-dong, Gangnam-gu, Seoul, 135-700, Korea.
DaeRyung Lee is working for digital media solution team of Ubiquitous Computing Lab (UCL), IBM Korea.

WILLIAM J. MALYK

[bmalyk@csg.uwaterloo.ca]
Graduate Student, University of Waterloo
DC3334, 200 University Ave. W., Waterloo, Ontario, N2L 3G1, Canada.
William Malyk is a PhD candidate in David R. Cheriton School of Computer Science at the University of Waterloo. He is also a member of the Computer Systems Group, the founding leader of the Waterloo Institute for Health Informatics Research (WIHIR) Student Group and a member of the Workflow Research & Knowledge (WoRK) Research Group. In 2006, William received a Master of Mathematics degree in Computer Science, his thesis topic was Dynamic Workflow for the Healthcare. His current research involves workflow-driven system generation, health informatics and the conceptualization of aspect-oriented workflow.

RUDOLF MELIK

[rudolf@tenrox.com]
CEO, Tenrox.
600 Boulevard Armand-Frappier, Laval, Quebec, Canada.
Rudolf has been a successful entrepreneur, professional speaker, and author with more than twelve years of field-proven experience in project and workforce management, regulatory compliance, and business process automation. A former software engineer, he co-founded Tenrox in 1995, where he has served as the CEO since the company's inception. He helped build Tenrox into a respected international software company with clients in more than fifty countries. He is also the author of industry white papers, a book on professional services automation, and a second book, The Rise of the Project Workforce, Managing People and Projects in a Flat World (www.projectworkforcebook.com). He lives with his wife and two children in Montreal Canada. He holds a bachelor's degree in electrical engineering from McGill University.

PATRICK MORRISSEY

[pmorrissey@savvion.com]
Senior Vice President of Marketing and Business Development, Savvion.
5104 Old Ironsides Drive, Santa Clara, California, USA.
Patrick Morrissey is responsible for all aspects of marketing at Savvion including the development of the company's brand and marketing strategy, corporate communications, product, field and customer marketing. With over 15 years experience in marketing, Morrissey most recently served as Vice President of Marketing for planning and enterprise performance management (EPM) at Business Objects. During his four-and-a-half years with the company, it grew from $400 million to more than $1 billion dollars in revenue. Prior to Business Objects, Morrissey held positions at Scient and McCann Erickson, where he demonstrated expertise in leading organizations to build brands and drive revenue. He has a B.A. in Political Science from the Iowa State University.

NATHANIEL PALMER

[nathaniel@wfmc.org]
President, Transformation+Innovation and
Executive Director, Workflow Management Coalition
99 Derby Street, Suite 200, Hingham, MA 02043, USA.
Nathaniel Palmer is President of Transformation+Innovation, as well as the Executive Director of the Workflow Management Coalition. Previously he was Director, Business Consulting for Perot Systems Corp, and also spent over a decade with Delphi Group as Vice President and Chief Analyst. He is the author of over 200 research studies and published articles, as well as "The X-Economy" (Texere, 2001). Nathaniel has been featured in numerous media ranging from Fortune to The New York Times. He is on the advisory boards of many relevant industry publications, as well as the Board of Directors of Association of Information Management (AIIM) NE, and was nominated to represent the Governor of Massachusetts on the Commonwealth's IT Advisory Board.

GREGOR POLANCIC

[gregor.polancic@uni-mb.si]
Teaching Assistant at Faculty of Electrical Engineering and Computer Science, University of Maribor.
Smetanova 17, Maribor, SI-2000, Slovenia.
Gregor Polancic is a teaching assistant and PhD student in the field of software engineering and information systems. His work and research interests include business process and workflow modeling, web application development, software frameworks, research methods and collaboration technologies. He has been involved in several commercial, open source and research projects in the field of business process modeling. He is also the author of BPMN Poster and Research Methods Poster (www.itposter.net).

GIUSEPPE POZZI

[giuseppe.pozzi@polimi.it]
Associate professor, Politecnico di Milano - Dipartimento di Elettronica e Informazione.
via Anzani 42, Como, Co 22100, Italy.
Giuseppe Pozzi is associate professor of Computer Engineering at the Politecnico di Milano, Italy, where he teaches the classes of Database Systems and of Workgroup and Workflow Systems. He received a M.Sc in E.E. in 1986 and a Ph.D. in 1992 from Politecnico di Milano, respectively. His main research interests include temporal databases, workflow management systems, and temporal information in workflow systems.
Giuseppe Pozzi is co-author with prof. Carlo Combi of a paper entitled "Architectures for a Temporal Workflow Management System", presented at the SAC conference, 2004: the paper has been ranked inside the monthly top 10 downloads from the ACM digital library for the last 36 months.

JON PYKE

[jpyke@cordys.com]
Chief Strategy Officer and Executive Vice President, Cordys BV.
PO Box 118, Putten, Gelderland, 3880 AC, The Netherlands.
Jon is the Chief Strategy Officer and executive Vice President for Cordys BV. Cordys was founded in 2001 and came to market with a completely new genre of BPM technology. Dubbed BPM 2.0 (or total BPM) Cordys has rapidly become a global force in the market and has built an impressive list of blue chip clients around the world in a very short space of time. As an individual, Jon demonstrates an exceptional blend of Business/People Manager; a Technician with a highly developed sense of where technologies fit and how they should be utilized. Jon is a world recognized industry figure; an exceptional public speaker and a seasoned quoted company executive. Prior to joining Cordys, Jon was the CTO and Executive Vice President for Staffware Plc, where he was responsible for product development and overall executive responsibility for product strategy, positioning, public speaking etc. Finally, as a main board director he was heavily involved in PLC board activities including merges and acquisitions, corporate governance, and board director of several subsidiaries. Jon's final piece of work for Staffware was to conceive, design and oversee the development of the IProcess Engine. Staffware was sold to Tibco in 2004.
Jon has over 30 years experience in the field of software development. During his career he has worked for a number of software and hardware companies as well as user organizations. Jon has written and published a number of articles on the subject of Office Automation, BPM and Workflow Technology. More recently Jon has Co-Authored a book covering both technical and business aspects of BPM. The book is published by Cambridge University Press and is called – Mastering you Organization's Processes. Jon co-founded and is the Chair of the Workflow Management Coalition He is an AiiM Laureate for Workflow – and was awarded the Marvin Manheim award for Excellence in workflow in 2003.

NEIL RADEN

[neil@smartenoughsystems.com]

Principal, Smart (Enough) Systems LLC
Santa Barbara, California, USA.
Prior to co-founding Smart (Enough) Systems, Neil Raden was the founder of Hired Brains, a research and advisory firm in Santa Barbara, CA, offering research and analysis services to technology providers and venture capitalists as well as providing consulting and implementation services in Business Intelligence and Analytics throughout North America and Europe. Hired Brains, and its predecessor company, Archer Decision Sciences, have been in business for over 20 years, providing services to many of the Global 2000 companies. Mr. Raden began his career as a casualty actuary with AIG in New York before moving into software engineering, consulting and industry analysis, with experience in the application of analytics to business processes from fields as diverse as health care to nuclear waste management to cosmetics marketing and many others in between. The recurrent theme in his work is the need for analytics that can be deployed and used by a wide segment of the population. He is a practicing consultant, industry analyst, speaker and author. His articles appear in industry magazines, he is the author of dozens of sponsored white papers for vendors and other organizations and he co-authored the book "Smart (Enough) Systems" with James Taylor.

AMIT RAJARAM

[amitrajaram@hsbc.co.in]
Development Manager, HSBC Group Workflow/BPM Center of Excellence
HSBC Bank, London, United Kingdom.
Amit Rajaram has devoted more than 5 years working with BPM products and applications as a Developer, Architect and Project Manager, with considerable expertise in Pegasystems' PegaRULES SmartBPM Suite. He has led efforts in deploying BPM-based applications for 2 of the Top-5 Global Banks, and has been instrumental in setting up offshore BPM Centers of Excellence. Mr. Rajaram is currently the Manager for International Deployments for the HSBC Group's Payment Investigations Program, a ground breaking programme aimed at unifying the payments investigations business process across 40 countries.

CLAY RICHARDSON

[crichardson@ppc.com]
Practice Leader, Project Performance Corporation.
1760 Old Meadow Road, McLean, VA, USA.
Clay Richardson currently leads Project Performance Corporation's award-winning business process management practice, where he directs process improvement and automation efforts for public and private sector clients, including the U.S. Housing and Urban Development, Government of Bermuda, and U.S. Patent and Trademark Office. Prior to joining Project Performance Corporation, Mr. Richardson served as Director of Professional Services with HandySoft Global Corporation, a pure-play BPM software vendor. Mr. Richardson is a graduate of Boston University's highly regarded Business Process Management Certificate Program and is a regular presenter at BPM industry conferences and events. In addition, he regularly facilitates business process strategy and architecture workshops for public- and private-sector clients.

JEFFREY RICKER

[ricker@jeffreyricker.com]
Principal, Jeffrey Ricker LLC
33 West Shore Dr, Putnam Valley, NY 10579, USA.
Jeffrey Ricker is an experienced technology executive with 15 years of leadership in defense and the private sector. Jeffrey Ricker LLC provides expertise in Eclipse, RCP and OSGi technology to Fortune 500 and start-up clients. Jeffrey was formerly the CEO and founder of Distributed Instruments, a company dedicated to solving the challenges of sensor data fusion. Distributed Instruments was closely involved in the development of Service Oriented Device Architecture (SODA). Jeffrey was the founder, director and executive vice president of XMLSolutions Corporation, the first company dedicated to extensible markup language (XML) technology. He began his career in defense research. As a

technologist, Jeffrey is co-inventor on five patent applications and author of multiple industry technology standards, including Asynchronous Service Access Protocol, Wf-XML and Transducer Markup Language. Jeffrey received his bachelor of science in mechanical engineering from Tulane University. He was an armor officer in the US Army Reserve.

TOMISLAV ROZMAN
[tomi.rozman@gmail.com]
Head of education center, LANCom.
Trzaska cesta 63, Maribor, SI-2000, Slovenia.
Tomislav Rozman, PhD, is currently head of the education center, IT and business analyst at LANCom d.o.o.. Previously, he was a teaching assistant and research engineer at the Faculty of Electrical Engineering and Computer Science, University of Maribor. His work and research interests include software standards, business process and workflow modelling and analysis, complexity and understandability analysis and web application development. He has been involved in several business process reingeneering projects in telecomunications and power distribution sector. He enjoys teaching BPMN to the students and practitioners.

ROBERT SHAPIRO
[robert.shapiro@global360.com]
Senior Vice President, Global360.
Box 1324, Wellfleet, Massachusetts, USA.
Robert Shapiro is a Senior Vice President at Global 360 and remains President of Cape Visions, now a subsidiary of Global 360. As founder and President of Cape Visions he directed the development of Analytics and Simulation software now used by leading Business Process Management vendors. Prior to founding Cape Visions, Mr. Shapiro was a driving force in the creation and promotion of graphical techniques for modeling, analyzing and simulating complex systems. As founder and CEO of Meta Software Corporation, he directed the implementation of a unique suite of graphical modeling and optimization tools for enterprise wide business process improvement. Mr. Shapiro is a participant in the Workflow Management Coalition and chair of the working group on process definition interchange; he plays a critical role in the development of international standards for workflow and business process management.

FEDERICO SILVA
[fsilva@pectra.com]
Marketing Manager,
PECTRA Technology, Inc., USA
2425 West Loop South, Suite 200, Houston, Texas. USA
Federico Silva is Marketing Manager of PECTRA Technology, Inc. He is responsible for the marketing strategy and corporate communications of PECTRA Technology and leads the overall operations dealing with the positioning of all products, services and solutions offered at different markets. Federico carries out marketing-related activities and actions, including corporate communications, internal communications, branding, promotions and advertising. Federico joined PECTRA Technology in April, 2003, to assist and collaborate with US and Canada operations, reporting directly to the Regional Manager. In January 2004, he started to carry out new markets' research and reorganizing the communications contents and channels. In May 2004, he became head of the marketing area. Before joining PECTRA Technology, Federico worked in the media. For over 10 years he was responsible for editing, producing and hosting several TV and radio shows, writing for the press, as well. A graduate from the Cordoba State University (Argentina), Federico has a degree in Communications, specializing in print media and institutional communications. He is 30-years old and is fluent in Spanish, English and Italian.

ROBERTO SILVA
[roberto.silva@sap.com]
Senior Business Consultant, SAP Latin America.
Prol. Paseo de la Reforma 600 Piso 2, Santa Fe 01210, Distrito Federal, Mexico

For more than 15 years Roberto has been involved in business & IT consulting as well as in education, playing many roles and positions in different service firms. He's specialized in BPM, Enterprise Architecture, Change Management and IT Strategic Alignment. Prior to join SAP in January 2008, he worked 2 years in TCDS (a BPM consulting company) as Business Development Director and 5 years as Managing Director of its educational business unit called Impulsare. After more that 10 years working in software development/integration related services, Roberto founded Impulsare in 2002 having BPM as its core discipline. Some of his relevant developments that are the foundations of the current BPM Practice at TCDS are: A BPM Framework for Business Process Life-Cycle Management and BPM Solution Implementation, Business Models (Meta-models for Modeling & Architecture) and Process Patterns, and a Methodology for Process Architecture Mapping. He is an international mentor, speaker, writer, methodologist and certified consultant in software process engineering and BPM. Roberto is a participant in the Workflow Management Coalition. He was also member of the BPMG from 2001 to 2007. Roberto studied applied mathematics at UNAM, and Innovation & Technology Top Management Program at IPADE Business School, both in Mexico City. He has a Diploma in Software Engineering with Microsoft Certification as Solution Developer.

JOEL SO

[joelso@alumni.uwaterloo.ca]
Part-Time Graduate Student, University of Waterloo
200 University Ave. W., Waterloo, Ontario, N2L 3G1, Canada.
Joel is a Master of Mathematics candidate at the David R. Cheriton School of Computer Science, University of Waterloo. He is a member of the Workflow Research & Knowledge (WoRK) Research Group, where his research focuses on autonomous dynamic workflow. In particular, Joel is interested in furthering the theoretical understanding of dynamic workflow, its definition and problem space, its core requirements, and applying this theoretical understanding to extend commercially available workflow platforms to better support dynamic workflow scenarios (such as those commonly found in Healthcare). Professionally, Joel has several years of industry experience working with world-class organizations, including Microsoft Corp. previously, and currently Deloitte Inc.

KEITH SWENSON

[kswenson@wfmc.org]
VP of R&D, Fujitsu Computer Systems.
1250 Arques Ave. , Sunnyvale, CA. 94085 USA
Keith Swenson is Vice President of Research and Development at Fujitsu Computer Systems Corporation for the Interstage family of products. He is known for having been a pioneer in web services, and has helped the development of standards such as WfMC Interface 2, OMG Workflow Interface, SWAP, Wf-XML, AWSP, WSCI, and is currently working on standards such as XPDL and ASAP. He has led efforts to develop software products to support work teams at MS2, Netscape, and Ashton Tate. He is currently the Chairman of the Technical Committee of the Workflow Management Coalition. In 2004 he was awarded the Marvin L. Manheim Award for outstanding contributions in the field of workflow. Mr. Swenson holds both a Master's degree in Computer Science and a Bachelor's degree in Physics from the University of California, San Diego. From 1995 to 1997 he served as Vice Chairman of the ACM Special Interest Group for Group Support Systems (SigGROUP). In 1996, he was elected a Fellow of the Workflow Management Coalition. In 2004 he was awarded the Marvin L. Manheim Award for outstanding contributions in the field of workflow.

JAMES TAYLOR

[james@smartenoughsystems.com]
Principal, Smart (Enough) Systems LLC.
Palo Alto, California, USA.
Prior to co-founding Smart (Enough) Systems, James Taylor was a Vice President at Fair Isaac Corporation where he developed and refined the concept of enterprise decision management or EDM. Widely credited with the invention of the term and the best known

proponent of the approach, Mr Taylor helped create the emerging EDM market and is a passionate advocate of decision management. Mr. Taylor has 20 years experience in all aspects of the design, development, marketing and use of advanced technology including CASE tools, project planning and methodology tools as well as platform development in PeopleSoft's R&D team and consulting with Ernst and Young. He has consistently worked to develop approaches, tools and platforms that others can use to build more effective information systems. He is an experienced speaker and author, with his columns and articles appearing regularly in industry magazines. He co-authored the book "Smart (Enough) Systems with Neil Raden.

Dr. Juan J. Trilles

[juanjo.trilles@auraportal.com]
President, AuraPortal.
Germanias 84, Gandia, Valencia 46702, Spain.
Dr. Juan J. Trilles is Ph.D in Engineering and Science and Master in Business Administration. In 1980 he founded Dimoni Software, which became a very respected Spanish software company. Today, he is President and Chief Software Architect of AuraPortal BPMS, (www.auraportal.com) a company with presence in more than 20 countries in Europe and America that, for the last 6 years has been developing a BPMS with Business Rules, CRM and Document Handling that executes Processes directly from its model without any programming effort. Important customers like PEMEX (Petroleos Mexicanos), one of the 50 largest corporations in the world, as well as Coca Cola, Pepsi Cola, Toyota and other outstanding references use AuraPortal BPMS to manage its processes. Dr. Trilles has authored several papers on innovative ideas (i.e. Domain Cellular Accounting) applied today in enterprise management, which have been published in several countries.

Dr. Andre Trudel

[Andre.Trudel@acadiau.ca]
Professor, Acadia University.
Wolfville, Nova Scotia, B4P 2R6, Canada.
Andre's primary research area is Artificial Intelligence, and more specifically temporal knowledge representation and reasoning. Secondary research interests are measuring the exact size of the Web, and building computer interfaces to interact with dogs. This last research project arose from his interest in field bred English springer spaniels. He has 11 dogs and competes with them at the highest level in field trails across North America.

Romana Vajde Horvat

[romana.vajde@uni-mb.si]
Assistant Professor, Faculty of Electrical Engineering and Computer Science, University of Maribor.
Smetanova ulica 17, 2000 Maribor, Slovenia.
Since 1990 she teaches and works in the field of software process improvement, software quality improvement, project management, IT standardization and computer-mediated communication. For five years she was a manager of the institute and knowledge transfer center "Center of information technology". Romana has a lot of experience with project management and with cooperation between university and industry. She was a director or technical manager for IT development projects, research projects, process improvement projects in Slovenian companies and some international projects. She also cooperated in numerous international workgroups (among others in ISO workgroups for quality management standards development), she is certified as PRINCE 2 Professional and certified trainer for several jobs within EU-Certificates Association. She is mentor to numerous Bachelors of Science and to a three Ph.D. students and she published together with co-authors over 150 publications.

Index